UNDERSTANDING THOMAS JEFFERSON

Also by M. L. Burstein

MONEY
THE COST OF TRUCKING: Econometric Analysis (*with others*)
ECONOMIC THEORY: Equilibrium and Change
RESOURCE ALLOCATION AND ECONOMIC POLICY
   (*editor with Michael Allingham*)
* NEW DIRECTIONS IN ECONOMIC POLICY
* MODERN MONETARY THEORY
* STUDIES IN BANKING THEORY, FINANCIAL HISTORY
   AND VERTICAL CONTROL
OPEN-ECONOMY MONETARY ECONOMICS
THE NEW ART OF CENTRAL BANKING

* *Also published by St. Martin's*

Understanding Thomas Jefferson

Studies in Economics, Law and Philosophy

M. L. Burstein

St. Martin's Press   New York

All rights reserved. For information, write:
Scholarly and Reference Division,
St. Martin's Press, Inc., 175 Fifth Avenue,
New York, N.Y. 10010

First published in the United States of America in 1993

Printed in Great Britain

ISBN 0-312-08693-8

Library of Congress Cataloging-in-Publication Data
Burstein, M. L. (Meyer Louis), 1926–
Understanding Thomas Jefferson : studies in economics, law, and
philosophy / M. L. Burstein.
p. cm.
Includes bibliographical references and index.
ISBN 0-312-08693-8
1. Jefferson, Thomas, 1743–1826—Political and social views.
2. Jefferson, Thomas, 1743–1826—Views on economics. 3. United
States—Economic policy—To 1933. 4. United States—Politics and
government—1775–1783. 5. United States—Politics and
government–1783–1865. I. Title.
E332.2.B87 1993
973.4'6—dc20   93–9790
                                                    CIP

*I have sworn upon the altar of god,
eternal hostility against every form
of tyranny over the mind of man.*

Thomas Jefferson (1800)

For Myrtle
Je me te souviens

Contents

Appendix to Chapter Two
Politics and Banking Theory

Chapter Three
Thomas Jefferson's Constitutional System:
Bad Law; Good Economics

Chapter Four
Thomas Jefferson and American Manufactures:
History, Politics and Economics

Appendix to Chapter Four
The Embargo (Dec. 1807 – Mar. 1809)
A Critical Study

Chapter Five
The Political Economy of Thomas Jefferson

Chapter Six
Thomas Jefferson's Moral Philosophy

Chapter Seven
Thomas Jefferson's Philosophy
The Enlightenment; "Ideology"

Chapter Eight
Thomas Jefferson and the Revolution in France

Annex
Two Studies in Liberty and Virtue

Hohfeld's *Fundamental Legal Conceptions* and Liberty
(A–1)

Frank Knight and the Ethics of Competition
(A–2)

xi

Acknowledgements

My research associate, Craig Penney, make vital contributions as a gofer and fellow student of the theory of liberty; and he set up and supervised indispensable word-processing operations.

Milton Friedman has made valuable comments on some of the book's contents.

The economics department of the University of Virginia (Charlottesville) has been especially supportive. I warily single out John James, Roger Sherman and John Whittaker.

Valuable exchanges with Tyler Cowen led to a number of important revisions.

I continue to be much indebted to T. M. Farmiloe, who may regret suggesting that I be bold.

I was galvanized by Forrest McDonald's work and have been ungrateful: the book may have been provoked by the shattering impact on me of his 1985 book.

Dumas Malone's influence is less salient: my study, since 1950, of his six-volume *Life* of Jefferson bottoms my perception of Jefferson as a person (as father, grandfather, father-in-law, guardian, master of slaves, friend, colleague, etc.). And a fascinating *tête-à-tête* with him more than twenty-five years ago still resonates in my mind.

Bertrand Russell's splendid books untied many knots, as did Frederick Copleston's *History of Philosophy*.

Finally, Thomas Jefferson, a *non-pareil à outrance*, has been happily prominent in my life for three years. But I must leave him. Rolfe Humphries wrote, "This translation is a quick and unscrupulous job. I am not being modest: a modest man would never have started, and a scrupulous one never finished."[1]

---

[1] Rolfe Humphries (1951) *The Aeneid of Virgil: A Verse Translation* (New York: Charles Scribner's Sons), p. xii.

Preface

§1 PROLOGUE

Thomas Jefferson intercepted me on the road to Damascus. He was not at the front of my mind in 1987, when I began to study "liberty and virtue." Frank Knight, Wesley Hohfeld, F. A. Hayek, Elie Halévy, David Hume, Immanuel Kant, Elaine Pagels, J. S. Mill and Bertrand Russell held my attention — and I extracted from their work themes that diffract with those of *Understanding Thomas Jefferson*, viz.,

○ Whig liberty (improperly called "negative" liberty) is incompatible with *freedom*, a problematical idea, except in the mind's inner recesses. Nor does Jefferson always distinguish liberty from freedom.

○ Hohfeld's dualistic theory of jural relations exposes the "bound" properties of liberty (an absence of duty and immunity from coercive excercise of powers), as well as the dark side of freedom, extolled by Rousseau and Nietzche.

○ The correct intension of *individualism* avoids the moral inferno of public-choice theory.

The problem of individualism — and its collisions with Christian liberty, the Good, the classical ethic and Freud's super (or ideal) ego — is fruitfully developed by Bertrand Russell along lines parallel to Tocqueville's. (But see Ch. 5.)

"One of the defects of traditional religion is its individualism, and this defect belongs also to the morality associated with it. Traditionally, the religious life was, as it were, a dialogue between the soul and God. To obey the will of God was virtue; and this was possible for the individual quite regardless of the state of the community. *[See Christian liberty.]*

"During the first three centuries of the Christian era, [Christians] could not alter the ... institutions under which they lived ... In these circumstances it was natural that they should adopt the belief that ... the good life has nothing to do with this world. [But] when Plato wanted to describe the good life, he described a whole community, not an individual; he did so in order to define justice, which is an essentially social conception ... With the loss of Greek freedom comes the rise of Stoicism, which is like Christianity, and unlike Plato, in having an individualist conception of the good life."

On the Good Life. "In the orthodox Christian conception, the good life is the virtuous life, and virtue consists in obedience to the will of God, and the will of God is revealed to each individual through the voice of conscience. The good life involves much besides virtue — intelligence for instance. And conscience is a most fallacious guide, since it consists of vague reminiscences of precepts heard in early youth. [1] ... [Elements of the good life like education, friends, adequate income, good health and interesting work depend] in varying degrees upon the community. ... The good life must be lived in a good society." (Bertrand Russell, 1925, "What I Believe")

o Value-enhancing exchange among autonomous agents is pivotal for both economic efficiency and political liberty.

o The domain of *exchange* transcends economics: a Congress of angels, tuned in on different wave-lengths, would vigorously "log roll": the upshot is deeply probed by the theory of exchange.

o The important distinction of satisfaction (a secondary entity) from desire makes utility theory insignificant for ethics.

o David Hume shows that "the Good," an idea that drives the theory of ethics, cannot be analytically defined. (Also see G. E. Moore, who influenced J. M. Keynes and Bertrand Russell.)

o The economic model of competition does not entail rivalry and harmonizes with many ideas of the Good: the model is ethically neutral, unless non-coercion is to be an end in itself.

▢ The competitive model is one of distributed computing: the information-content at each node is quite slight. Furthermore, paradigms pivoting on maximization of value-weighted sums are the only ones known to be consistent with efficiency of network systems.

▢ That said, objectives promoted by a competitive system may be ethically repugnant — in ways "science" cannot establish.

○ *Self* is a volatile, ephemeral concept; in the upshot, much of contemporary welfare economics crumbles.

○ It follows that the "agents" of economic theory are flickering blobs, whose preferences, if definable, are surely highly volatile ("unstable"). Economics is successful because behaviour of quite large *groups* of consumers is very well defined — see my "Macrofoundations of Microeconomics" (1988).

○ The problem of *harmonization* of interests (Adam Smith's *invisible hand* is an example) is much knottier in moral philosophy than in commodity space — as Smith shows in his *Theory of Moral Sentiments*.

Thomas Jefferson Envelops My Projects

As I worked on "The Political Economy of Alexander Hamilton" (1988), now folded into Ch. 2, Hamilton waned and Jefferson waxed in my thought. Hamilton's pre-Keynesian monetary economics chagrined me; and his "Atlanticist" vision of the New Republic's political-economic destiny left me cold. My image of him dwindled: an *arriviste*, disdainful of the unique country that took him in, preferring England. He and his merchant-followers sought a British aegis; and he hoped to become America's Sir Robert Walpole. Agreed, he was a skilled financier and public administrator who would enhance the Cabinet, before going back to Wall Street.

The same research shows that Jefferson's financial economics, nested in a sound system of "classical" political economy, closely resembles that of an earlier Chicago school: cf. one-hundred-per-cent-reserve banking. And he rejected Hamilton's monetary theories of real economic action.

The scales fell from my eyes. Jefferson, an excellent economist, has been buried by an avalanche of Keynesian rubble; for years, critiques of his economics have been controlled by raw dogmas taught to historians. By 1989 I also saw that the "Bolingbroke-Country Party" interpretation of Jefferson's system, hawked by

Adair and McDonald, is chimerical.

After filling in Jefferson's system of political economy, I turned to his philosophy. Adrienne Koch (1943/1957, p. xi) writes that "Jefferson wanted people to pay attention to the philosophical side of his nature"; and that Gilbert Chinard, after much reflection, withheld the "title" of philosopher from him. (Ibid., p. i) What matters is that Jefferson cannot be understood unless his philosophy is probed.

Reflections on Thomas Jefferson and his Career

After chasing economic, jural and philosophical hares for many months in order to understand what Thomas Jefferson wrote, it is easy to forget that he is perhaps the most consummate politician and party leader in American history — he and his intimate friends, Madison and Monroe, held the Presidency for twenty-four years; and when President, he exercised complete mastery over the Congress. Now put aside this monumental revolutionary's political credentials.

○ I reckon that Jefferson falls short of the highest intellectual eminence, partly because he never shook off the clammy embrace of the British empirical tradition (making Professor Hayek's claim that he lapsed into "Cartesianism" quite bizarre).

□ His intellect is not that profound; nor his creative powers that protean. He does not belong to the immortals *comme* professor of philosophy, although his intellectual accomplishments are unrivalled among great men of action.

○ His action pivoted on ideas: one reason he sought power was to plant the Enlightenment in the New World. He shaped public opinion strategically while adroitly accomodating to it tactically.

○ He does belong to the immortals. His "second American Revolution" guarantees liberty of the mind of man.

What was Thomas Jefferson (TJ) really like? I do not know; nobody does. Perceptions of the historical figure, TJ, are products of interactions between authors and readers: the pertinent substantive is a product of the readers' syntheses of this black-and-white construction; each reader possesses, so to speak, a private TJ. And the reader's "private TJ" is a product of our joint work. Think of a cubist painting: the viewer's transformation of the plane of the canvas into a cube is part of the proper work of art being studied.

The "private TJs" are sourced in a common "data-base" extracted from his biography. I am sure that no other "data-base" supports such an experience.

Perhaps many "private Jeffersons" will be quite drastically altered by studies of this book. But *caveat lector*! The vicarious dialogue between him and me — and you — is selective and makes him more cerebral than he may "really" have been. Still he speaks for himself here — fluently, sometimes torrentially, and with rare intensity.

The book's range is quite wide: Jefferson's is much wider. And the kaleidoscopic procession of materials — going back to antiquity and forward to modern science — is meet: if we are to understand him, we must know where he was going (cf. the limit points he was approaching) as well as where he came from; nor can we escape our own vocabularies and mind-sets when contemplating vestiges of remote events.

§2 WHAT JEFFERSON WAS NOT: AN EXCURSUS INTO AESTHETICS

To understand what Thomas Jefferson is, we must understand what he is not — taking heed of the infinite world of negation.

He was denied a vision of the redemptive power of art: he was vigorously *materialist*. He does not reach the still point of the turning world. [2] The argument flows from diverse sources, including Plato, Dante, Oswald Spengler and Roger Penrose.

Roger Penrose (1989) and Plato's Ideal World. I think Penrose's imagery lacks scientific utility. But he surely penetrates the core of the classical culture — transmitted from antiquity by the Renaissance, which awkwardly infuses it with devotional content. [3] I cannot image a satisfactory aesthetic canon not based on the Platonic parable, which Penrose endows with ontological substance.

Two further comments are in order.

○ Plato's problematical aesthetics are often repressive: some passages of *The Republic* call for virtual socialist-realism.

○ Jefferson's aesthetics seem prosaic. He thought the novel's principal rôle promotion of moral improvement; his favourite novel, Laurence Sterne's *Tristram Shandy*, was one of the few he enjoyed. His canon verges on utilitarianism — see Note 9. Still his mastery of neo-classical/Palladian architecture, and his fine creations in that mode, urge that he heard secret harmonies.

This is how Penrose develops his theme:

"In Plato's view the objects of pure geometry ... were only approximately realized in terms of actual physical things. Mathematically precise objects of pure geometry [inhabit] instead a different world — Plato's ideal world of mathematical concepts. Plato's world consists not of objects, but of 'mathematical things.' This world is accessible to us not in the ordinary physical way, but, instead via the intellect. ... This ideal world was regarded as distinct and more perfect than the material world of our external experiences, but just as real. ... [Thus] the workings of the actual external world can ultimately be understood only in terms of precise mathematics — which means in terms of Plato's ideal world, accessible via the intellect.' " (Ibid., pp. 158–159) [4]

My aesthetical canon is based on an "ideal world," an instrumental myth controlling great art. Since I find Jefferson's earthier canon vapid, a certain distance separates my *Weltanschauung* from his; our rapport is imperfect. And this evokes one of the book's principal points: Jefferson was a man of action — Henry Adams's failure to take this point mars his excellent book.

PLATO *V.* THE LUMIÈRES. Plato's parable of the prisoners in the cave has occupied my mind for fifty years; it seems to me the ultimate rationale for both the life of the mind and art (ironically, denigrated by Plato).

"Picture men dwelling in a sort of subterranean cavern with a long entrance open to the light along its entire width. Conceive them as having their legs and necks fettered from childhood, so that they remain in the same spot, able to look forward only, and prevented by the fetters from turning their heads. Picture further the light from a fire burning higher up and at a distance behind them, and between the fire and the prisoners and above them a road along which a low wall has been built. ... See also, then, men carrying past the wall implements ... some of these bearers speaking and others silent. ... Do you think that these men would have seen anything of themselves or of one another except the shadows cast from the fire on the wall of the cave that fronted them? ... They would suppose that in naming the things that they saw they were naming the passing objects ... In every way such prisoners would deem reality to be nothing less than the shadows. ... This image then, dear Glaucon, we must apply as a whole to all that has been said ... And if you assume that the ascent and contemplation of the things above is the soul's ascension to the intelligible region, you will not miss my surmise. ... My dream as it appears to me is that in the region of the known the last thing to be seen ... is the idea of the good and that when seen it [points] us to the conclusion that this is indeed the cause ... of all that is right and beautiful, giving birth in the visible world to light and the author of light and itself in the intelligible world being the authentic source of truth and reason." (*The Republic*, book vii) [5]

These famous lines adequately support Penrose's interpretation, and my transformation of them: in spite of himself, Plato illustrates the redemptive power of art. [6]

BEAUTY PAST KNOWLEDGE WAS DISPLAYED TO ME, BUT NOT TO TJ. I sympathize with Jefferson's rationalism and admire his battle against superstition. But these qualities bar him from the sacred wood. Plato's parable, in which the Good (transcendental harmonization) becomes known through search, bottoms great imaginative art; but he called Plato's dialogues *ignes fatui*. More happily, the same qualities blocked him off from the "gothic" school, celebrated by Oswald Spengler, which reaches conclusion in W. B. Yeats's brilliant decadence or "perfected rottenness." (?) (For "Beauty past Knowledge ..." see *Il Paradiso*, canto xxx, line 19.)

On Music. [7] I reckon that the boundaries of Jefferson's perception of art are largely drawn by Drs Johnson and Burney:

"For Johnson poetry was, by definition, the 'art of uniting pleasure with truth by calling imagination to the aid of reason.' By 'imagination' he seems to have meant ingenious ornament; by 'truth,' virtue and religion. The pleasure he seeks is that which the men of his generation most assuredly did feel in their literature. He felt it acutely himself." (Archer-Hind, 1925, vol. 1, p. xiv)

Jefferson probably could not have defined his own taste more precisely. Literature was to be utilitarian; it was to display, not discover, truth; imagination was to be caged. Granted, neither Dr Johnson nor Thomas Jefferson was barbaric; but Jeremy Bentham was — he put push-pin on the same aesthetic plane as poetry. And Halévy vividly depicts the ultra-philistine "aesthetic" of Bentham's *éminence grise*, James Mill, and George Grote, published in their organ, *The Westminster Review*:

"The illusions of 'sentimentalism' were to be dissipated at last. The choice must be between poetry and logic. The mistake of the poets was that they did not understand that their sole function was to amuse the public, not to instruct them; if they tried to instruct them, the philosophy they would teach would be a poetic and consequently an illogical and perverse philosophy. *The Westminster Review* created a new kind of literary criticism, and claimed to give contemporary poets lessons in politics and logic." (Halévy, op. cit., p. 405 — cf. *Westminster Review*, no. 1, Jan. 1824, article ii)

His protégé, Charles Burney, adheres to Samuel Johnson's canon. He finds J. S. (and C. P. E.) Bach and W. A. Mozart insufficiently "democratic"; if only the Bachs had found a Salomon! (The musical canons of the emperor Joseph II, the prince archbishop Colloredo and, I reckon, Jefferson hardly differ from Burney's.)

"If Sebastian Bach and his admirable son Emanuel, instead of being musical-directors in commercial cities, had been fortunately employed to compose for the stage and public of great capitals, such as Naples, Paris or London, and for performers of the first class, they would doubtless have simplfied their style more to the level of their judges; the one would have sacrificed all unmeaning art and contrivance and the other would have been less fantastical and *recherché*, and both, by writing in a style more popular and generally intelligible and pleasing, would have extended their fame, and been indisputably the greatest musicians of the present [eighteenth] century." (*History*, vol. 2, p. 955) [8]

Burney admires Mozart's operas ("dramatic music") but finds his other compositions "too capricious and as if he were trying experiments." (*History*, vol. 2, p. 1035) His critiques of his friend Haydn are more profound (and sympathetic). He finds "transcendental expression" proper for sacred or operatic, but not for "pure," music: he doubtless thought the wrenching harmonic turns of Mozart's best laic music capricious and experimental. His comments on Haydn's "The Seven Last Words," clarify my points:

"[His instrumental *Passione*'s] strains are so truly impassioned and full of heart-felt grief and dignified sorrow, that though the movements are all slow, the subjects, keys and effects are so new and so different that a real lover of Music will feel no lassitude, or wish for lighter strains to stimulate attention." (Ibid., p. 959)

This mixed bag catches musical correctness in Jefferson's formative years. See Charles Rosen's *The Classical Style*: Burney's code is explained in "The Popular Style," p. 329ff. [9]

Aesthetics and Thomas Jefferson's Moral Philosophy [10] The way is round about. Oswald Spengler (1918/1928) somehow pens an excellent précis of stoicism with aesthetical overtones.

"The drama of Shakespeare deals openly with the desperate conflict of will and world. Classical man ... was weak in the face of the 'powers.' The κάθαρσις of fear and pity, the relief and recovery of the Apollinian [11] soul in the moment of the περιπέτεια was, according to Aristotle *[See the Poetics]*, the effect deliberately aimed at in the Attic tragedy. As the Greek spectator watched [a character] senselessly maltreated by fortune, without any conceivable possibility of resistance to the Powers, and saw him go under with splendid mien, defiant, heroic, his own Euclidean soul experienced a marvellous uplifting. If life was worthless, at any rate the grand gesture in losing it was not so. The Greek willed nothing and dared nothing, but he found a stirring beauty in enduring." (Spengler, 1918/1928, vol. 1, pp. 203–204)

Spengler then declaims that "all this is masked cowardice." (Ibid., p. 205) What is more, the Apollinian *Weltanschauung* entails "a statical treatment of static genera, and it stands in the sharpest possible contrast to the dynamic fertility of the Faustian with its ceaseless creation of new types and domains of form." (Ibid., p. 205). The Führer's winged chariot whirrs close behind.

TJ REJECTS STOICISM FOR EUDEMONICS. Thomas Jefferson, a quintessential *lumière*, believed in the idea of progress; [12] he too sought to impose "will on the world." [13] He ineluctably preferred a sort of Epicureanism over Stoicism; the bustling mind-set of the Enlightenment is drawn to eudemonics and finds resignation in- congruous.

The excursus into aesthetics supplies insight into Jefferson's moral philosophy — eudemonic, in the school of Aristotle. [14] Bertrand Russell too finds Aristotle's ethical system prosaic and that of the Epicureans sordid (if taken literally). But, late in his life, he made theoretical innovations in his ethical system that took him closer to the twentieth than the seventeenth or eighteenth century.

NOTES

1. See the Freudian super (ideal) ego.

2.   At the still point of the turning world. Neither flesh nor fleshless
      Neither from nor towards; at the still point, there the dance is.
      But neither arrest nor movement. ...
                          ...
      The inner freedom from the practical desire.

The release from action and suffering, release from the inner
And the outer compulsion, yet surrounded
By a grace of sense, a white light still and moving.

T. S. Eliot, Burnt Norton

Ch. 6 reveals the "Stoical" sources of these lines — and Note Six explains that Dante's *Il Paradiso* is probably the source of the "white light" image.

3. Oswald Spengler (1918/1928) grudgingly concedes that great Renaissance art attains the "still point." (This screed's twenty-four printings give hope to all scribblers.)

"And yet, at moments, Renaissance art succeeded in achieving something wonderful ... a feeling for the bliss of perfect nearness, for pure restful and liberating space, bright and tidy and free from the passionate movement of Gothic and Baroque. It is not Classical, but it is a dream of Classical existence, the only dream of the Faustian soul in which it was able to forget itself." (Spengler, 1918/1928, vol. 1, p. 238 — cf. *Form and Actuality*)

4. Revealed religion, perhaps aided by the intellect, does just as well. My friend, John Nelson (the conductor) perceives great music as an imitation of God, so that, for him, Mozart's greatest music achieves a sort of transsubstantiation. See Note Six.

5. See Edith Hamilton and Huntington Cairns, eds, 1961, pp. 575–846 at pp. 747–750. Cf. *The Collected Dialogues of Plato*.

6. My aesthetic canon is "objectivist": the artist seeks an external "truth." It conflicts with much important twentieth-century writing. See Edmund Wilson's *Axel's Castle* (1931). In concluding his excellent book, Wilson writes that,

"The writers *[including Yeats, Valéry, Eliot, Proust, Joyce, Gertrude Stein and Rimbaud]* with whom I have here been concerned ... have tended to overemphasize the importance of the individual, ... they have been preoccupied with introspection sometimes almost to the point of insanity." (Ibid., pp. 297–298)

Objective art need not be realistic; and great art is never realistic. Leonardo did say that art should imitate nature. (See Vasari and, indeed Plato, who bungled the theme.) But, as the editor of *Leonardo da Vinci* (1956) puts it, "it becomes clear that nature is seen as a repository of that religious truth which allows the mind to function and the hand to obey the dictates of artistic creativity." (Ibid., p. 22) Or the laws that govern nature "force the mind of the painter to transform itself into nature's own mind and to become the interpreter between nature and art." (Leonardo, *Treatise*, folio 36)

S. J. Freedberg (1971/1983) makes rather the same point:

"[In Leonardo's work] appearance is reformed into a manifest idea of harmony. ... The image that results is visually distinct from normal expectations, and aesthetically and ethically far superior to them. Yet surpassing reality, it commands us to feel it to be plausible as no image in art was before. A wonderfully subtle knowledge of the look of nature has been subsumed into the harmony of form, and a sense of actual vitality inspires the harmony of mind ... This was the first event ... in the Christian world that resembles ... the classicism of the antique Golden Age." (Ibid., p. 19)

"The *School of Athens* — and the frescoes of the Segnatura room in general — speak of the community of men; they are representations of the greatness man may attain and promote in social concourse. More overtly than in Michelangelo, Raphael's tableaux convey an ethic along with their aesthetic sense, implying identity between beauty and human good." (Ibid., p. 57)

The parable of the prisoners of the cave reprises: the idea of the Good is revealed by study of nature's harmonies, the Platonic music of the spheres. As Knight said, the Classical, or Renaissance, ethic is an aesthetic (see Note 10's *harmonized stasis*). This is where Penrose, following Plato, comes in: there is an ideal, somehow objective, world. I think this construction is bad epistemology, but indispensable for the possibility of redemption through art.

"LIGHT IN LITERATURE"

Bertrand Russell, T. S. Eliot et al. are struck by the radiance of Dante's *Il Paradiso* — along lines anticipated by the passages from *The Republic* quoted in the text. Jefferson would have perhaps been repelled by imagery that was so gothic.

This is what Eliot (1932) wrote about "Dante and Light":

"Nowhere in poetry has experience so remote from ordinary experience been expressed so concretely, by a masterly use of that imagery of *light* which is the form of certain types of mystical experience.

> *Nel suo profondo vide che s'interna*
> *legato con amore in un volume*
> *ciò che per l'universo si squanderna*
> *sustanzia ed accidenti, e lor costume*
> *quasi conflati insieme par tal modo*
> *che ciò ch'io dico è un semplice lume.*

"Within its depths, I saw ingathered, bound by love in one mass, the scattered leaves of the universe, substance and accidents and their relations, as though together fused, so that what I speak of is one simple flame." (Ibid., pp. 199–237 — "Dante," 1929.)

The stringent confines of Thomas Jefferson's ("enlightened") canon exclude full reception of Dante's, as well as Plato's, inspiration.

7. References for *On Music* include the following.
  ○ L. Archer-Hind (1925)
  ○ Charles Burney (1776-1789/1935/1957)
  ○ Alfred Einstein (1945/1962)
  ○ Elie Halévy (1928/1955)
  ○ Charles Rosen (1971)

8. Burney surely mirrors eighteenth-century taste. Alfred Einstein (1945/1962) reports that Baron van Swieten "had never heard a word about [J. S.] Bach" until July 1774, when Frederick the Great (of Prussia) "emphasized the surpassing greatness of Johann Sebastian." (Ibid., p. 150) The Baron put Mozart on to J. S. Bach. The resulting tussle between the *galant* and "learned" styles in Mozart's mind "resulted in a revolution and crisis in his creative activity." (Ibid., p. 151) The consequences perplexed Burney.

Einstein cogently develops Mozart's aesthetic system. He refers to a canon in the second finale of *Così fan tutte*:

"The ordinary listener scarcely notices a passage like this, but for the discerning listener it has a double function: it is a lyric point of repose ... and it allows pure beauty to shine forth as a symbol that everything in this drama is only a pretense; it gives one a sweet and aching feeling of the unreality of the events on the stage." (Ibid., pp. 154–155)

9. Visitors know that Jefferson hung copies of paintings, made to his order, at Monticello. He does not seem greatly interested in painting (Maria Cosway aside); but acquired a good, if conventional, collection.

Merrill Peterson (1960, pp. 399–401) interestingly probes Jefferson's views on painting and music. Did he find art "amusing but unworthy of serious interest"? Perhaps, but, unlike Gilbert Chinard, Peterson cannot reconcile so harsh a judgment with "Monticello."

10. Re "aesthetics and ethics" see "Frank Knight and the Ethics of Competition," infra — and Ch. 6. Cf. Knight (1923/1935).

11. See Spengler, op. cit., vol. 1, p. 183, for a comparison of "Apollinian" and "Faustian" souls — Nietzche is credited for the trope "Apollinian." The Apollinian spirit seeks resolution of dissonance so that a harmonized stasis is created. The Faustian spirit, extolled by Spengler, ceaselessly soars, I should think towards nowhere, unless to a ghastly *Götterdämmerung*. It is supposed to be symbolized by the Gothic cathedral — a problematic image, as Henry Adams's wonderful *Mont Saint Michel and Chartres* (1904/1912/1983) shows.

12. See Chs. 6 and 8 — and ch. 10 of my 1991 book.

13. The futility of trying to explain the theory of human (necessarily wilful) action by evolution is repeatedly explained infra; see especially Ch. 8.

14. Simon Bernstein made a valuable remark to me in this connection.

Chapter One

Introduction

Thomas Jefferson (1743–1826) generated an immense mass of material over a long life, during which he played star rôles on the political stage from 1773 to 1809, when he turned over the Presidency to his intimate friend, James Madison. And the life of the mind — let alone his Promethean mind — concerns Becoming, not Being. It is not easy to understand him: he will not sit still for his portrait. For that matter, he ceaselessly altered the of the Monticello mansion so long as his strength, and money, held out.

Dialogue goes back to the ancients; and will go forward to the twenty-first century. Today, aet. 250, he would — once he shed his Bacon-Locke baggage — quickly become *en courant*; he would resume the presidency of the American Philosophical Society with panache. I hope to explain this, and more. [1]

The heavy weight of his learning, and his scholarly bent, mask his practical flair. What is more:

o He was surpassingly skilful at managing men — he commanded intense, lasting loyalty. And he and his *copains*, Madison and Monroe, occupied the Presidency for twenty-four years.

o The action of a fiery political genius on storied battlefields over more than thirty-five years cannot be assessed like the career of Professor Thomas Jefferson.

o He was an impetuous general, ready to make costly frontal assaults. [2] And he sometimes fought unscrupulously: Ch. 3 compels this conclusion. I try to explain what he said he fought for; and I reflect on what may have been his derelictions. Judge not, that ye be not judged.

1

Was TJ an Egotist? Jefferson's life style at wondrous Monticello was ducal by North American standards — he had the manner of a courteous grandee. What is more, he believed that the dramatic growth and prosperity, under liberty, of the United States was secured by the "second American revolution" of 1800–1801 that put him into the Presidency. The second revolution set up a global beacon: the New Republic would show the way. [3] Liberty, impelled by a sequence of events including the Boston Tea Party, armed American resistance (justified by his Declaration of 1776) and and his triumph over Anglomania and "Walpoleism" in 1801, was irresistible. Transient disappointments in France, and elsewhere, could only delay liberty's global triumph. His tableau of world history is not diffident: he paints himself into the middle of the picture. Was he egotistical? No. Like Washington, [4] he felt a useful tool in a great triumph — a *citoyen* whom Providence appointed to do much to create a state. [5]

TJ comme Social Theorist. I explained in the Preface how I "discovered" that Hamilton's economics pivot on Keynesian-like monetary theories of real economic action; and that the distinctive features of his system project Walpole's onto the New Republic. The Preface also reports my "discovery" that Jefferson was a sound political economist whose policies were firmly rooted in the theories of Adam Smith and, especially, J.-B. Say and Destutt de Tracy. He understood how free-market exchanges enhance value and how political liberty depends on heavy decentralization of economic decision-making. And he was free of Locke's fetishes about property and the labour theory of value. Chapter 4, on the political economy of American manufacturing, both enhances his standing as a political economist and compels reassessment of Alexander Hamilton, who emerges as a first-class financier who looked to the City of London or his ideas and to England as the linch pin of his funding policy. The Preface limns my conclusion that Jefferson's moral philosophy and metaphysics — like most people, he denied he had any metaphysics — are so prescient that he should be introduced to William

James, Dr Freud and Bertrand Russell: indeed his thought projects onto the late twentieth century. Principal topics include utilitarianism, "self," natural economic or social harmony, the idea of the Good and moral sense *cum* Freud's super-ego. By the end of his life, his studies of biology and physiology had led him to the verge of William James's domain (he would not have abided Henry James). And he would have been thrilled by modern physics (he had a good command of mathematics).

Jefferson's rhetoric on *moral sense* resonates in contemporary "human rights" effusions. Would his mature reflections on *utility*, reducing "moral sense" to a replacement set, have eventually led him to jettison it? Very probably not: he never reconciled his heart to his head on "the rights of man."

Jefferson's image in the American mind (see Merrill Peterson, 1960) is hideously distorted. He is widely perceived, especially by his admirers, as a nostalgic pudding-head, obsessed with installing millions of Horatian farmers in the vast American wilderness. (Hamilton is admired as a precursor of modern times who would now shed blinding light in Wall Street if Aaron Burr had not been so beastly.) The book refutes such persiflage from many directions.

A proper assessment of Jefferson's impact on American history pivots on a point that may be obscure. The choice offered by the bitter power struggle, 1793–1801, was to cling to the Atlantic shore, trading under English rules and imitating a system (Walpole's) that was fading away in England or to organize America along radically innovative azimuths [6] intersecting quite different English trajectories — principally Whig liberty and the common law. [7] Nor is that all. It is arguable that the Enlightenment would have been extinguished in America save for Jefferson. [8] *Comme lumière*, he provoked noisy bavardage: he was (not unreasonably) called an athiest, if not an anti-Christ, a bloody Jacobin. Indeed the ghost of Edmund Burke was more prominent than the official Federalist candidates (including the unfortunate President John Adams) in the campaign of 1800, won by Jefferson (and Burr!).

The Alien and Sedition Acts, circa 1798, provoked a crisis leading Jefferson to call his 1800–1801 victory the onset of a second revolution. [9] Dumas Malone (1962) discusses remarks Jefferson made in the heat of battle, in May 1798, that buttress my conjecture that "1800–1801" embedded the Enlightenment (or Chateaubriand's *"l'âge moderne"*) in the American system, cutting off lines of retreat to Walpole and Burke, and aristocratic privilege. The Act let the President deport any alien he thought dangerous. "One of the persons against whom Jefferson thought the law directed against the French philosopher Volney." (Malone, op. cit., p. 386)

"It suffices for a man to be a philosopher, and to believe that human affairs are susceptible of improvement, and to look forward, rather than backward to the Gothic ages, for perfection, to mark him as an anarchist, disorganizer, atheist and enemy of the government." (Jefferson to his son-in-law, Thomas Mann Randolph, 3 May 1798 — quoted by Malone, ibid.)

Malone interestingly glosses this letter. "Volney, erstwhile guest at Monticello, sailed off ahead of time with a boatload of French," including Victor Marie du Pont, whose father *[Jefferson's close friend]*, P. S. du Pont de Nemours, was the subject of a blank warrant, signed by President Adams, lest he come to the United States. And Joseph Priestly seemed likely to be a victim." In fact, Adams *[all hat and no cattle as Grand Inquisitor]* overruled the recommendation of the Secretary of State (Timothy Pickering) that Priestley be deported — indeed he deported nobody. Still "it appeared to [Jefferson] that the law was directed at just the sort of person he most wanted to come to America, men of science and learning." [10]

Ecce homo! This book's diversity mirrors the vast scope of Jefferson's career and his huge *oeuvre*. Large doses of jural theory, philosophy and economics spanning many centuries before and after his time must be supplied.

A *précis* containing thirty selected points, making up a set of hypotheses and conclusions developed in the book, is followed by synopses of Chs. 2–8. The *précis* and the synopses comprise both an exposition and a recapitulation of the body of the book.

§2 PRÉCIS

Ch. 2

1. Jefferson disliked banks of issue; he anticipates the 100-per-cent-reserve-banking school.
2. Alexander Hamilton, a pre-Keynesian, posited monetary theories of real economic action disdained by Jefferson. And he mistakes the true nature of "fluid" capital.
3. *Corruption in a New Republic* (?): Hamilton would bring Sir Robert Walpole's system to America.
4. *The Bolingbroke chimera*: Jefferson was not a partisan of an American country party.

Ch. 3

5. Cf. Thomas Jefferson, David Hume and the Whig myths on English history.
6. Jefferson's theory of the American Constitution put bad law in the service of good economics and perhaps liberty.
7. His Kentucky Resolutions anticipate contemporary ultras, claiming that *any* economic policy is unconstitutional: resulting changes in the jural map surely adversely affect somebody — and so are "takings."
8. The theory of liberty, especially Whig liberty, is explored. (Also see "Hohfeld's *Fundamental Legal Conceptions* and Liberty.")

Ch. 4

9. Cf. Jefferson and Hamilton on American manufacturing. The results will surprise most readers.

10. Jefferson's Embargo (1807–1809), demonstrates Justice Holmes's axiom: "Great cases make bad law."

11. Jefferson, Madison and Gallatin arrived at an industrial policy, twisting the Jeffersonian theory of the Constitution out of shape.

12. The mercantilist, Atlanticist, Hamiltonians faded out of the picture, but ascend to glory in Forrest McDonald's books.

Ch. 5

13. Jefferson's political economy is based on J.-B. Say, Destutt de Tracy and Adam Smith — see, e.g., "Jefferson on Malthus in the New World."

14. He disdains what became Keynesian economics.

15. His policy hinges on promotion of value-enhancing exchange; property is "merely" instrumental.

16. He does not exalt possessive individualism.

17. He anticipates overlapping-generations paradigms (in economic theory) in a quite-radical proposal incorrectly thought to entail repudiation of debt. His bold argument is fatally flawed.

Ch. 6

18. Jefferson's ripened moral philosophy anticipates twentieth-century thought. He reduces the moral sense to a replacement set from which a society draws values along "utilitarian" lines.

19. His *utility* is societal, not possessively individualist. (See "16".)

20. He problematically proclaimed himself an Epicurean. In the (classical) upshot, ethics are an aesthetic.

21. His ripened moral philosophy does not harmonize with any theory of virtue; and is indeed remarkably consistent with Freud's theory of the super-ego (or ideal ego). (Most people think they know what virtue is; but cannot say what it is — see "Frank Knight and the Ethics of Competition.")

Ch. 7

22. Jefferson was a self-described "materialist" (i.e. not a "spiritualist"). He fell into the toils of David Hume's philosophy after all: the idea of *self* cannot be robust for a materialist — what then happens to the idea of *virtue?*

23. Along with his confrères in the Enlightenment, he felt committed to British empiricism. This flawed dogma crippled the *philosophes*; but their adherence to it clears them of charges of "Cartesianism" or "constructionism" that also libel Descartes.

24. The rôle of *evolution,* indelibly associated with Edmund Burke, is (dismissively) discussed. Virtue, whatever it is, is not a residue of survival. "Evolution" is an *ignis fatuus* in the moral domain.

25. Jefferson's adherence to the French *idéologues* led to an inescapable conflict between the moral philosophy he was taught and his mature analytic outlook, a conflict that seems never to have been salient for him. ("Ideology" was more than "a branch of zoology," in Adrienne Koch's phrase, but perhaps not much more.)

Ch. 8

26. Jefferson understood the political-economic and social sources of the French Revolution. And his perceptions conform to Tocqueville's *L'ancien régime,* glossed in Ch. 8.

27. Edmund Burke's *Reflections on the Revolution in France* is polar to Tocqueville's book and is (adversely) critically assessed in Ch. 8. Jefferson and Burke select incompatible dishes from the same Whig menu. Burke fabricated a history of France based on Whig myths (many shared by Jefferson) that do not correctly describe English history either.

28. Tocqueville shows that the eighteenth century *économistes* were indifferent to liberty. Jeremy Bentham also sought to promote "gross national utility" through exercise of authority.

29. The brief appearance of *liberty* in France in 1789 is inexplicable; the obsession with equality after 1789 was fomented by envy and

led to *democratic despotism* — and was engendered by the institutions of the Ancien Régime.

30. The critique of Burke's *Reflections* induced a literature on "evolution" in socio-political affairs. Burke's major premiss is plausible: successful programmes typically draw lessons from experience. But his specific hypothesis that the Ancien Régime required no more than some lubrication and carburetter adjustments for France to achieve "liberty" is absurd. Subsequent writers have transmogrified Burke's premisses into chimerae about "evolution." False analogies have been drawn to ergodic physical processes or natural selection. But ethical outcomes hinge on exercises of *will*: the Good is not a survival property. Put differently, "evolution" is but a muddled revival of the stoical natural-harmony idea; "evolution" implies that it is hubric to defy Nature's will — i.e. to exercise one's own will! These fiendishly-tangled issues dogged Jefferson. He finally found much in common (anachronistically) with twentieth-century philosophers.

§3 SYNOPSES OF CHAPTERS TWO TO EIGHT

Chapter Two

Thomas Jefferson disliked paper money and abhorred bank-issue — but he was not an economic primitive. Indeed he has a fragile claim to have anticipated an earlier Chicago School's one-hundred-percent-reserve-banking proposal. He did not oppose financial intermediation; and is apt to have supported fully-backed bank-paper (virtual warehouse receipts). [11] Thus in his letter to his son-in-law, John Wayles Eppes (24 June 1813, *Writings*, pp. 1280–1286), he proposes that the circulating money stock normally consist of specie and that the national government have a monopoly of paper-issue in time of war. As for banking:

"Let those then among us [12] who have a monied capital and who prefer employing it in loans ... set up banks, and give cash [specie] or national bills for the notes they discount. It is from Great Britain that we copy the idea of giving paper in exchange for discounted bills." (Ibid., p. 1285)

The underlying issues are shrouded in Keynesian fog. Writers like Douglass Adair and Forrest McDonald — awash in Keynesianism — cannot grasp Jefferson's sophisticated system of political economy. Their rationale is his putative nostalgia for feudal order or *rassamblement* of a mythic nation around a patriot king: cf. Henry St. John, Lord Bolingbroke and his exiguous Country Party. Indeed, until recently, respectable economists pilloried Jefferson for, in effect, rejecting the forced-saving idea, monetary theories of real rates of interest and other monetary theories of real economic action. Jefferson's opposition to Hamilton's version of the *"LM"* curve [13] and his allegiance to supply-side economics (see his close ties to J.-B. Say and Destutt de Tracy) were scorned by twentieth-century Keynesian acolytes; and his liaison with French liberals has been bizarrely distorted. He was called him a bloody-handed Jacobin; Professor Hayek labels him a Cartesian constructivist.

Corruption in a New Republic? Alexander Hamilton was obsessed with the system of Sir Robert Walpole, encompassing pervasive corruption in public life. And the profound implications of wide suffrage, soon to develop in Britain and rife in America (where he dwelt uncomfortably) eluded Hamilton — but not Jefferson.

The "corruption" theme spans Hamilton's ties with speculators in Wall Street, and his programme for linking "monied men" to the national government through patronage and inside dope (e.g. on markets in national debt), imitating the Walpolean/Georgian system he admired. So the national government has been linked to the seamy side of Wall Street as far back as 1790. Jefferson properly thought this deplorable: his *riposte* to Hamilton's Walpolian confection was forward looking, not sickly sentimental.

Lord Macaulay, a writer with unrivalled powers of lucidity (and, according to Winston Churchill, also of duplicity), skilfully explains how eighteenth century England's system of corruption was swept away by nineteenth-century reforms; it becomes easy to see why the eighteenth-century English system never belonged in America.

"Between the time when our Parliaments ceased to be controlled by the royal prerogative and the time they began to be ... controlled by public opinion, there was a long interval. After the Restoration ... a member could no longer be called to account for his harrangues or his votes. *[He had to be bought off.]* ... It was natural, it was inevitable, that, in a legislative body emancipated from the constraints of the sixteenth century, and not yet subjected to the restraints of the nineteenth century, in a legislative body which feared neither the King nor the public, there would be corruption.

"The extent to which parliamentary support was bartered for money cannot be with any precision ascertained. But it seems probable that the number of hirelings was greatly exaggerated by vulgar report, and was never large, though often sufficient to turn the scale on important divisions." (Macaulay, 1848–1861/1980, pp. 540–541)

How exaggerated was "vulgar report"? Not much.

"It at length became as notorious as that there was a market for cattle in Smithfield. ... Now and then perhaps a man who had romantic notions of public virtue refused to be himself the paymaster of a corrupt crew, and averted his eyes while his less scrupulous colleagues did what he knew to be indispensable. ... But the instances of this prudery were rare indeed." (Ibid., p. 543)

Macaulay's analysis pivots on the conclusion (that becomes a premiss) that the ascendancy of public opinion, and a broader suffrage, in nineteenth-century Britain, put paid to the "corruption" principle. But Hamilton, circa 1790, was a principal officer in a republic amply satisfying Macaulay's precondition. His bias followed from a shallow, if not simply mistaken, reading of British history. Jefferson, extracting the implications of broad suffrage and public opinion, perfectly anticipated Macaulay.

Lord Bolingbroke. A set of themes centred on Bolingbroke runs parallel to the "corruption" topic. An influential hypothesis, projected by Douglass Adair and hotly clasped by Forrest McDonald, but rejected by influential British historians, holds that Thomas Jefferson was a dreamy, muddled acolyte of a factitious *country party* concocted by Bolingbroke; a pitifully nostalgic Thomas Jefferson is hostile to the progressive schemae of Alexander Hamilton, said to be a precursor of modern thought. The hypothesis is false. Jefferson's financial system — which proved highly viable — is more in line with contemporary monetary theory than Hamilton's — whose influence on historians, and on "monied men" (in his charming locution) derives from unsound monetary theories, projected by Keynes (1936), that have held the field for many years and still control the Wall Street–Washington axis. What is more, Bolingbroke's politics shadowed his inept, clangorous, political adventurism; and never had the substance attributed to it by the Adair-McDonald hypothesis.

Jefferson, like Hugh Trevor-Roper, was intrigued by Whiggish themes in Bolingbroke's political and historical writings, but not by the improper country-party hypothesis. Jefferson's system — for the vast spaces of North America in which virtually universal (white) suffrage was inexorable — is based on classical political economy.

Chapter Three

Thomas Jefferson was prepared to sacrifice jural accuracy, if not intellectual integrity, in order to promote his more-or-less laisserfaire system — and to promote the talisman of Whig liberty, the ark of his tabernacle.

It is not just that American law flows from English sources. During the seventeenth century, England experienced two upheavals that permanently transformed British polity. The revolutions culminating in 1649 and 1688 undermined legitimacy — and provoked theorizing about the nature of political society and about the principles of social-political architecture.

Chapter 3 opens up a field not fully explored until Ch. 8. Why was the dissonance of British and American upheavals (subject to a local difficulty, 1861–1865) resolved so promptly, while French political chords remained unresolved up to 1958? This much is apparent. *Pace* Professor Hayek (in the wake of Edmund Burke), the Anglo-American harmonizations were highly *constructive*; they did not simply evolve; "natural selection" did not take over.

David Hume & Whig Mythology. David Hume is the book's principal philosopher. He solves an intricate puzzle that Thomas Jefferson never could assemble. He signals a practical system of liberty; but his solution requires that Whig icons be smashed. Not only was Jefferson unprepared to perform such a ritual: he pilloried Hume (*qua* Tory historian) much as the Congregation of Amsterdam flayed Spinoza. Ironically, Jefferson, in retirement, came close to Hume's solution — finding his sources in the work of the French *idéologues*; and he skirted utilitarianism, without lapsing into the Benthamite banality (cf. the hedonistic calculus) that J. S. Mill could not escape.

It would be remarkable for the author of the American Declaration of Independence to shed all his seventeenth-century trappings — and put liberty on a "scientific" basis not attained in the 1990s in which "human rights" are revealed values. [14]

What is important is not so much what Hume found as what he escaped from. [15] Christian ontology (Thomism, e.g.) seeks first causes and divine intentions. And its deist variants hardly differ in this respect: systems of natural values allow no more choice than ones pivoting on divine mandates. But humans *choose* their value systems.

Hume's distinction of *ought* from *is* contains the seed of modern moral philosophy. And *ought* inexorably leads to reflection on *self* — a surprisingly evanescent idea. If it is not clear what "I" am, it surely cannot be obvious what "I" ought to do. Hume shows that the right action cannot be deduced from first principles (so Kant tilts at a windmill). Ethics is necessarily an empirical subject; utilitarianism commands a certain respect. [16]

TJ is Barred from Hume's World. Jefferson's temperament never let him dwell in a properly Humean world. He never abandoned the Whig myths, concocted by Sir Edward Coke and trotted out to justify the seventeenthth century upheavals in Britain as retrievals of ancient liberties from usurping Stuart kings. Jefferson adamantly refused to acknowledge the facts of English history, recounted in Hume's *History* and agreed by modern authorities, including Hugh Trevor-Roper:

> "Hume did not believe that sacred 'constitutions' were the guarantee of 'liberty.' To him all constitutions were relative, and effective liberty was the result not of constitutional forms but of social and economic progress and 'sophistication of manners.'... Hume devalued all constitutional' ideas and measured the virtue of government by the extent to which the established forms permitted economic and social progress or 'utility.' ... In his *History*, Hume expressed these ideas with exquisite wit in an irresistable style; and he deployed his wit most mercilessly at the sacred cows of the official Whig faith: at the virtuous Anglo-Saxons, at the mediaeval barons, at the Whig 'patriots' of the seventeenth century." (Trevor-Roper, 1968, p. 11)

Jefferson's fault is magnified in contemporary ideology. The theory of liberty remains undeveloped importantly because leading writers bottom liberty on obscure transactions with divine entities. It is ironic that the inability of so *éclairé* a man as Thomas Jefferson to burn his last bridge to the seventeenth century has so inhibited understanding of liberty, the shibboleth of his fame.

On the American Constitution. The outcome of "1688–1689" in Britain shaped eighteenth-century politics, and political theory, in Britain and America — and deeply affected the French *philosophes*. The Whig triumph established the supremacy of King-in-Parliament, and then of Parliament, elected by universal suffrage as the nineteenth century wore on, making Coke's doctrines irrelevant. The American Constitution of 1787 ingeniously rejiggered the post-1688 British schematization — by contrivance, of course — redistributing powers so that the President and the bicameral Congress exercise functions in parallel, assuring that power-plays are thwarted. And the first ten amendments, the American Bill of Rights, further distance American from British praxis. [17]

In 1789, Jefferson was a Constitutional nationalist. His early critique boiled down to chagrin at the lack of a bill of rights in the 1787 document. (James Madison was then an ardent nationalist; and the confidant of George Washington, a nationalist at least as far back as 1775, when he became Commander of the Continental Army, America's only truly national institution.)

Then, in 1789–1790, Jefferson collided with Alexander Hamilton — daemonically energetic; brilliant in dispatching public business; boundlessly ambitious; especially influential on his senior wartime colleague, General Washington; Anglophiliac; and a dévot of Sir Robert Walpole's system. And in 1798, Jefferson confronted a hysterical reactionary movement, hostile to the Enlightenment, nostalgic over British rule, beholden to a profitable trade with Britain (see Ch. 4), leading to the Alien and Sedition Acts and portending worse to come.

Dumas Malone gingerly hints that Jefferson resorted to "bad law," first in order to block Hamilton's Walpolian system and then to defuse counter-revolutionary threats. [18] Jefferson, and the faithful, double-jointed, Madison, disengenuously twisted the Constitution out of shape in order to limit the sphere of action of the national government. Professor W. W. Crosskey goes further; my great teacher always did. He persuasively argues that Jefferson, and especially Madison, first thought the Constitution (which Madison helped write) a nationalist document; and later reversed their course in order to advance Southern interests.

I accept Malone's conclusions about Jefferson's and Madison's motivations for the Kentucky and Virginia Resolutions, but install an economics-component; and I radically alter Crosskey's gloss in the same way.

The scales fell from my eyes while rereading Crosskey's *Politics and the Constitution* in 1991. He repeatedly chastises Jefferson for seeking to emasculate the national government. [19] His political economy runs in a line from Alexander Hamilton, by way of Theodore Roosevelt, to the activism of Franklin Roosevelt in his heyday. He was vividly familiar with the frustration of Roosevelt's designs by the Supreme Court (the Nine Old Men) that cooked up a stew of "strict construction" and virtual substantive due process. Crosskey believed that bad law blocked good economics.

My study of Jefferson's political economy mandates a drastic reevaluation of his substantive (ex-jural) positions — which I conclude were promoted by "bad law." Chapter Five shows that he was solidly grounded in the "laisser-faire" economics of Adam Smith, J.-B. Say and Destutt de Tracy and in Malthus's "population" studies; and Ch. Two that his monetary economics were anti-Keynesian — while conforming to the theory of an earlier Chicago school. Otherwise perplexing twists and turns of his dubious jural pronouncements promote an enlightened economic doctrine. Bad law served good economics.

Chapter Four

Chapter Four focuses on two well-known, but ill-understood, events — Alexander Hamilton's *Report on Manufactures* (1791) and President Jefferson's Embargo (1807–1809). It clears away obstructions that have long barred understanding of Thomas Jefferson's political economy. The following passage may contain its pith.

The evolution of Jefferson's manufacturing policy occupied no more than seventeen years of federal experience, circa 1790–1807. He never proposed to impede *action* on manufacturing policy. Thus Hamilton's Society for the Encouragement of Useful Manufactures (SEUM) seems little more than a scruffy stock-parking operation which indeed motivated his *Report on Manufactures*. Hamilton had no intention of impeding America's commerce with Britain, the principal source of revenue to finance his funding policy.

The Embargo. The geopolitical reality was stringent. British naval power, ruthlessly deployed in prosecution of a world war "provoked" by the French revolution, made it necessary for the United States either to abandon its overseas commerce or truckle to Britain — something the Federalists were glad to do.

Jefferson and Madison — and Albert Gallatin, the third member of a remarkable triumvirate at the pinnacle of power — failed to square the circle. They played a card that, going back to colonial protests against British mercantile policy, had taken many tricks: peaceable coercion; refusal to deal. [20] Britain was to be subdued by American refusal to supply "essential" raw materials; and to buy finished British products. Trade was to be embargoed. What went wrong? Jefferson and Madison made a studied but incorrect calculation of the underlying elasticities of supply and demand. They did not reckon how high were elasticities of substitution. (See the Appendix to Ch. 4 — Gallatin seems to have loyally enforced a policy he thought badly flawed.)

Industrial Policy. The Federalists centred on the carrying trade; they were anxious to carry British goods, or American goods under British supervision; not to manufacture. The Republicans, desperate to elude British power, bit the bullet: by 1808 Jefferson was fully committed to the encouragement of manufactures and to a concurrent internal-improvements (infrastructural) plan. Hamilton's party (Aaron Burr killed Hamilton in 1804) persisted in its mercantile orientation; and deplored the War of 1812 (*v.* Britain).

Hamilton on Manufactures: Myth & Reality. These are some of the principal points made in Ch. 4's autopsy of Hamilton's *Report.*

o *The Report on Manufactures* is linked to a shadowy scheme, the Society for the Encouragement of Useful Manufactures (SEUM) — perhaps merely a stock-parking operation. Hamilton's fiscal programme, requiring service of a massive national debt, overshadowed exiguous manufacturing prospects.

o Hamilton was anxious to mollify the British (a care leading to virtually treasonable intercourse with British diplomats). The feasible volume of American imports was to be maximized; the last thing he wanted was import-substitution. He sought revenue maximizing, not protective, tariffs.

○ Hamilton's bias was mercantilist. He disdained Adam Smith's invisible hand — which Jefferson clasped.

○ Hamilton's *Report on Manufactures* intensifies the Keynesian thrust of his earlier *Reports* (see Ch. 2); his is a monetary theory of real economic action.

Alexander Hamilton, and the Federalists now fade out of the picture. The narrow confines of their merchant mind-set made them look across the Atlantic, towards Britain and seek to repair, and then thicken, America's ties with Britain, a country many of them idolized. But America's Destiny lay to the West. Jefferson's letters, quoted in Ch. 4, and his Louisiana Purchase and his obsession over the Floridas, show that he looked west: to that extent he foretold America's future. But there is a snag. American expansion cast up the slavery issue: Jefferson, more concerned to finesse than re-resolve American slavery, aptly called the crisis leading to the Missouri Compromise (1820) "an alarm bell in the night." So his "States Rights" tergiversations, culminated by the Kentucky Resolutions, buried a land mine that exploded violently in 1861.

The great chess champion, G. Kasparov, points out that opportunistic players, eschewing combinatorial thinking, are in for nasty surprises. Jefferson and Madison opportunistically deployed "bad law" tactics, starting around 1790. When in power, they largely ignored their wretched dogma — without defusing it. So the Constitution of the United States they tactically distorted for plausible (libertarian) reasons would have been blown to smithereens, save for Abraham Lincoln.

Drew McCoy (1980) on the Political Economy of Manufactures. McCoy belongs to the Adair/McDonald school. He concludes that Jefferson and Madison were nostalgic bunglers, seeking a bucolic other-Eden. (Such writers transmogrify Albert Gallatin into a judicious court eunuch — as does Henry Adams, who wrote an authorized *Life* of Gallatin.) McCoy's argument is easily punctured.

Following Henry Adams, he correctly says that Madison's retaliatory commercial policy, circa 1793–1794, was based on the same foundations as the Embargo. And he correctly calls Congressional rejection of Madison's proposal a victory for Hamilton and his British diplomatic *confrères*. But this triumph was at the expense of American manufactures. It was a victory for Federalist "Anglican" mercantile policy; revenues from import duties were protected by blocking growth of import-substitution.

McCoy makes two corollary errors.

○ While acknowledging that the SEUM came to nothing, he suggests that it was intended to stimulate expansion of American manufacturing. No! The SEUM was a chimera.

○ He describes Jeffersonian manufacturing policy, post 1807, as being much like Chairman Mao's (cf. back yard blast furnaces). His Jefferson (whose letters display his famous practical engineering skill) is a barmy dreamer, crooning verses from the *Georgics*. In particular, he misreads the triumvirate's transient emphasis on light, coarse manufacturing to reflect endemic hostility to sophisticated manufacturing. This canard has been amply refuted. Nor is that all. Hostility to manufacturing, circa 1810, is tantamount to Anglophilia: the triumvirate were not Anglophiles!

Chapter Five

Thomas Jefferson's principal mentors in politcal economy, J.-B. Say and Destutt de Tracy, are anti-physiocratic: their analysis of agriculture, and the rent of land, are perfectly symmetrical with that of any other sector (or factor of production); the classical tripartition of factors of production, decried by Professor Knight, is strictly shunned. (Tracy also categorically rejects labour theories of value.) There are traces of the *Georgics*, but none of the physiocrats, in Jefferson's system.

Tracy made a major breakthrough, endorsed by Jefferson: *exchange* (cf. the gains from trade) is the primary economic engine. *Property* (or private ownership) is only instrumentally pivotal: incentives for value-enhancing exchange are extinguished by inability to retain and/or transfer gains from trade. Jefferson's theory steers clear of Locke's obsession over property. The massive, creaking paraphernalia that clogged seventeenth-century thought, and continued to obstruct analyses by Jefferson's contemporaries, are swept away. Economics escapes from the field generated by Biblical tales of satanic seduction (original sin), the source of the labour theory of value: in the sweat of thy face shalt thou eat bread (*Genesis* 3: 19).

The materials of Ch. 5 can be assessed differently. Most economists attracting media attention supply entrails for Wall Street haruspices. But the *calcul* of finance is radically insufficient for command of the theory of exchange, building towards general economic equilibrium. Thomas Jefferson, projected onto the late twentieth century, would soon qualify as a microeconomic theorist; and would flounder in Wall Street. Alexander Hamilton would sparkle as chief operating officer and media spokesman for a giant Wall Street house, shuttling between Washington and New York with *éclat*. His thought, lying outside the loop of high economic theory, will always attract bustling middlebrows; Jefferson's economics is for highbrows.

SOME TOPICS IN POLITICAL ECONOMY

Mandeville's Fable of the Bees. Keynes's precursors looked benignly at "luxury." Aggregate demand is stimulated by earthquakes, vast conflagrations, etc. — and petty (luxurious) vices. Contrastingly, classical economists may succumb to censorious, sumptuary attitudes. If the secular sufficiency of aggregate demand is assured, expenditures that do not promote capital accumulation or commanding ethical value may look squandered to puritans like John or J. Q. Adams — see Henry Adams's description, in the *Education*, of the Old House in the time of his grandfather. The will of a dyspeptic god is served by sumptuary legislation; and employment is no less full.

Jefferson on Malthus in the New World. President Jefferson, in an interesting letter (1 February 1804) to J.-B. Say, ponders on the implications for Malthus's theory — and, prospectively, for Ricardo's (including its iron law of wages) — of the limitless supply of land in America. At first glance, prospects for economic growth and for viability of a preponderantly-agricultural economy look open-ended. But Jefferson espies a cloud: cf. reciprocal demand — the terms of trade might turn against the immense American farm. Rational choice may be constrained by a stringent trade-off so that moral preference for agriculture may finally entail too high a material cost.

Jefferson did esteem "agricultural" values (cf. the *Georgics*) and the "agricultural man"; but he would never have blocked spontaneous manufacturing-growth. And when geopolitical modalities compelled him to propose to promote manufactures, his commitment to natural harmony made him uneasy: "so invariably do the laws of nature create our duties and interests that when they seem to be at variance, we ought to suspect some fallacy in our reasonings."

Individualism and the Good. If agents' objectives are (simplistically?) well defined, private-ownership market economies, rooted in "the invisible hand of competition" and "distributed computing," are compellingly attractive as schemae promoting maximal creation of economic value. This is as far as Adam Smith the economist takes us — not far enough for Thomas Jefferson, or for Adam Smith the moral philosopher. Economics does not inform us about the Good. But writers like Appleby (1984) and Mayer (1988) think Jefferson an archtypical possessive individualist oblivious to the Good. Chapters 5 and 6 show that they are wrong.

Appleby refers to Tocqueville's discussion (in the *Democracy*) of individualism. Like most others, she equates individualism with a compelling sense of self-interest. But, for Tocqueville, individualism is a fault, with consequences worse than those of selfishness (which, he says, originates in blind instinct). "It throws [the individualist]

back forever upon himself alone and threatens to confine him entirely within the solitude of his own heart." Still, since "individualism proceeds from erroneous judgment," it can be moderated
or eliminated, by reflection, perhaps assisted by education. Chapter
6 shows that Jefferson shares Tocqueville's ethic — but Tocqueville,
no tool of Bolingbroke, exceeds him in bewailing the pernicious
properties of the relation between workers and the esurient "manufacturing aristocracy."

Debt-Maturity Limits. Writers have long been stunned by Jefferson's (1789/1813) proposal that "no generation should be able to
contract debts greater than may be paid during its own existence." [21]
The surprisingly sophisticated mechanics of Jefferson's model (eerily
anticipating the copious "overlapping generations" literature) are
assessed. The analysis leads to a distinction of effects of political
from those of economic malleability along lines established by Wesley Hohfeld's jural theory.

Liberals must avoid a snare. Liberty hinges on immunity from
coercive exercises of power: the liberal economic order hinges on
unimpeded exercises of powers of offer, conferring rights to accept,
that ceaselessly alter the jural map (or matrix). Jefferson was misled
by his inveterate hostility towards mortmain (i.e. the dead hand of
prior restraints like entails). But, as Madison shrewdly pointed out
to him, if this generation cannot contract long-term debt, it may be
unable to attract capital to be used for the benefit of future generations. Maturities of existing paper instruments matter much less
than their malleability. Jefferson's proposal would obstruct trade,
not free it.

Political liberty depends on *un*malleability of the jural matrix of
claims: cf. liberal abhorrence of bills of attainder and ex post facto
laws: any member, x_i, of the broadly-defined class, X, must be jurally fungible with any other member, x_j, if there is to be a rule of
law; and liberty hinges on rules of law, annihilating freedom! Furthermore, political transactions are not accomplished by simple binary exchanges. Nor do price-like signals guide political exchanges;

no invisible hand assures global political optimality, which may not even be definable.

Political "transactions" must be governed by clumsy sets of rules entailing coercion — including majority rule; the monumental evil of Rousseau's General Will flows from ascription of ethical value to polling results — something Jefferson was prone to do. The blocking properties of the 1787 Constitution should not be confused with "economic mortmain." Political liberty requires that political channels be clogged, so that coercion is kept in its cage.

Chapter Six

Thomas Jefferson the Epicurean? Jefferson believed that *Homo sapiens* has an innate *moral sense*; famous letters, dated 1787 and 1814, make this clear. And he probed deeply into the query, "what is the content of the moral sense?" His 1814 answer is startlingly modern: "nature has constituted *utility* to man the standard and best of virtue." Utility in the service of what?

Jefferson's man is a social animal. His utility function cannot be defined on commodity space. Nor is his theory individualist (cf. supra). Adrienne Koch explains how different is his utilitarianism from that of Jeremy Bentham and James Mill.

"His frequent denials of Hobbes's self-interest and sole interest are motivated ... by [faith] in man as a naturally social creature, to whom the actions of peace, good faith and justice are intrinsically as agreeable as ... self-aggrandisement." (Koch, *PTJ*, p. 147)

He proclaimed himself an Epicurean, co-opting Epictatus, who "has given what was good of the Stoics," to the doctrines of the illustrious Epicurus.

The Epicurean ethics seem banal, if not repulsively selfish — but deeper reflection goes some way to moderate this impression. Frank Knight supplies the clue. The ancient ethic is an *aesthetic*. And this is where Epictatus comes in: his ethical principles hinge on the aesthetics of harmonization of human action with nature, with the music of the spheres. Adam Smith's *Theory of Moral Sentiments* puts it well: "man, according to the Stoics, ought to regard himself, not as something separated and detached, but as a citizen of the world, a member of the vast commonwealth of nature." Then "our happiness is perfectly secure, and beyond the reach of fortune."

Ancient (or classical) virtue entails little more than a sort of exalted resignation to nature's caprice (as it may seem); and does not inhere in one's *will*. Jefferson's Stoic-Epicurean mélange does not support a satisfactory theory of virtue, but does anticipate Freud's super-ego, which elides virtue in favour of a sort of prudence. Sigmund Freud turns out to be the best guide to Jefferson's ethical system. Jefferson's mature thought led him into Hume's black hole, in which all ethical systems implode under reductive analysis; it only remains to specify the super-ego.

"The super-ego ... consists of a precipitate of all prohibitions and inhibitions ... impressed on the child by his parents. ... The feeling of conscience depends altogether on the development of the super-ego." (Brill, 1938, pp. 12–13)

"And thus it is that what belongs to the lowest depths in the minds of each of us is changed through this formation of the ideal into what we value as the highest in the human soul." (Ibid., p. 48)

It follows that *utility*, merely characterizing the degree to which unspecified *desires* are satisfied, cannot inform ethical judgment. Anyone confusing utility with the Good follows Hobbes and Bentham into Hume's black hole.

Chapter Seven

Chapter 7 shows how Thomas Jefferson, long-time president of the American Philosophical Society, fell into another of David Hume's toils: Jefferson's ripe "metaphysics" virtually discards the idea of *self*; his analytical philosophy lost contact with his moral philosophy.

Hume's guns tear two gaping holes in the hull of Jefferson's Whiggish boat: neither the theory of the law of the Constitution nor the theory of liberty professed by him survives. Jefferson tacitly submitted to the rigour of Hume's philosophy (*via* an "ideological" route); but never ceased to resist him fiercely on the jural front (see Ch. 3).

Jefferson called himself a "materialist." See Bertrand Russell's capsulization of the philosophy of Democritus: "the soul was com-composed of atoms, and thought was a physical process."

"Mind *v.* matter" looms up. This well-worn dispute is probably otiose for the principles of scientific inquiry: virtual materialism dominates science. But, as John Adams wrote (in a letter to Jefferson), there cannot be a materialist ethics: ethics hinges on moral choice by identifiable minds (or souls). The search for a scientific ethics travels a road to nowhere.

TJ and Empiricism. Jefferson's commitment to British empiricism — linked to Francis Bacon and John Locke, whom he always professed to admire — impeded his progress in the philosophy of science: the rôle of deduction in science is greater than Bacon, or he, supposed. Indeed there is at most an exiguous connection between classic British empiricism and modern science: "we have been seeking ... to define matter so that there must be such a thing if the [mathematical] formulae of physics are true." (Bertrand Russell, 1925b/1985)

The *philosophes* were committed to British empiricism, not to innate ideas, universal deduction or universals. So the philosophical foundations of the French Revolution are not Cartesian. Far from exhibiting "constructivist" bias, the *philosophes* and the *idéologues*, including Jefferson, were sunk in rather raw empiricism. True, they were anxious for improvement, often through reform; and, to their credit, they did not rely on the preposterous idea, uncertainly attributed to Burke, that what came to be called Darwinian natural selection ("evolution") leads to valid "survivor principles" in ethics and politics. Nor were America's Constitutional founders more committed to "evolution," or less "constructivist" than the *philosophes*, who had so little to build on. (See Ch. 8.)

Evolution, Reform & Revolution. Georges Lefebvre (1962) gets it exactly right, along lines followed by Paine, and Jefferson. What was principally important for inveterate enemies of the revolution in France was its abolition of aristocratic privileges:

"[Burke] introduced into history and politics the concept of evolution. ... The book *[Reflections]*, however, attracted contemporaries specifically because of the limits he assigned to society's evolution — class hierarchy to him seemed divinely ordained, and, if he condemned the French Revolution as hellish and destructive of all social order, it was because the revolution meant the downfall of the aristocracy. [Thomas Paine's (1791)] attack on political and social injustice, on kings and lords ... showed the masses what they might learn from the French example."

Jefferson's last letter (24 June 1826) anticipates Tocqueville's conclusion, shared by Lefebvre, that there was no "natural" basis for enlightened reformation of France:

"May [the Declaration] be to the world, what I believe it will be (to some parts sooner, to others later, but finally to all), the signal of arousing man to burst the chains under which monkish ignorance and superstition had persuaded them to bind themselves. ... The general spread of the light of science has already [revealed] the palpable truth, that the mass of mankind has not been born with saddles on their backs, nor a favored few booted and spurred, to ride them legitimately by the grace of God."

Tocqueville on the Enlightenment. Tocqueville readily owns that the leaders of the Enlightenment rather naïvely anticipated substituting for ancient user a legal code and a system of public administration based on reason and "natural laws" (discovered by reason). And he claims that this outlook was unavoidable: the inept Ancien Régime had staggered into a blind alley; a bad government is never more dangerous than when it seeks to reform itself.

The admirable savants supplying the brilliant promise of 1789 lacked the *savoir faire* to accomplish so monumental a task. Their rather pathetic appeals to Jefferson for counsel show how they had got in over their heads.

Attractive analogies run from France circa 1789 to the "USSR" circa 1992. Look at the rubble of the spontaneous collapse of Bolshevik structures; the "CIS" future seems a *carte blanche*. But the Ancien Régime had existed for hundreds of years, nested in a web spun by a thousand years of history. There was no facile resolution of the French crisis; and the Russian reformers of 1992 look even more naïve than their French counterparts two centuries ago. So much for "evolution."

The idea of liberty perished in the turmoil surrounding the crash of the Ancien Régime: "equality" replaced "liberty" as a primary value. And Tocqueville penetratingly assesses corollary points. Voltaire's three-year sojourn in England gave him a taste for comfortable English literary life, relatively uninhibited by censorship; but left him without a clue about the problems of liberal social reconstruction. David Hume looms up once again! Tocqueville's continuing discussion of Voltaire's limitations pertains to the *philosophes* as a group. Reconstruction had to await the arrival of Napoleon Bonaparte.

"Hume's sceptical philosophy, widely ventilated in England, intrigued Voltaire. But the English political system hardly interested him: indeed he had more to say about its vices than its virtues. [Voltaire] envied the English for their literary liberty, not realizing that literary liberty is dependent on political liberty."

TJ & "Ideology." Chapter 7 studies development of such philosophical concepts as *noumenon, idealism,* and *universals.* Jefferson's analytic ("ideological") philosophy is disjoint from his moral philosophy; his "analytics" lose touch with his continuing commitment to liberty as an ethical value; he cannot escape Hume's tentacles.

Adrienne Koch points out that ideology is virtually a branch of zoology: its disjunction from the theory of liberty is inexorable. The ideological theory of *self* — leading to a strictly "materialist" theory of human action — typifies the disjunction.

Destutt de Tracy would substitute "I feel" (*"Je sens"*) for Descartes' "I think" (*"Je pense"* or *"Cogito"*) in "I think, therefore I am" (*"Cogito, ergo sum"; "Je pense, donc j'existe"*). And it is a short step from "I feel" to "There are feelings," the counterpart to Bertrand Russell's "There are thoughts." What is more, feelings are much better suited than thoughts to a materialist description. It boils down to this. Solipsism makes no contribution to science, but is a *sine qua non* for ethical criticism. If, in Bertrand Russell's trope, "I am" is but a biography — if my ideation is described by "there are thoughts" — then I am not to be praised or blamed; "should" is meaningless. "Materialism" allows no more than a pseudo-ethics like Bentham's felicific calculus. Ordinal ranks are assigned to materially-defined outcomes. An impartial observer can measure a subject's responses by following operational instructions — like a polygraph operator or a psychologist probing the algebra of monkey-joy.

Jefferson's (1825) excited reaction to Flourens's experiments, or to the work of Cabanis, carries "materialism" almost into the limit defined by William James. By the end of his life, he found his way to Hume's position; and his moral philosophy finally touched on that of the twentieth century — moral sense came into line with Freud's super-ego. (See Ch. 6.) But, as his last letter shows, he assigned liberty an ethical value that can be explained only by revelation or innate sense.

Chapter Eight

Tocqueville's great book explains why the Revolution could not sustain the momentum of "1789": France could not escape the suction of the Ancien Régime: liberty was soon jettisoned in favour of a chimerical ideal of equality, distorted by ancient antinomies.

Thomas Jefferson, American minister to France, 1784–1789, did not have benefit of hindsight afforded to Tocqueville and was in any case too close to the field of action in 1789 to acquire a magisterial overview. But his on-the-spot perceptions and judgments conform to Tocqueville's. Jefferson — a member of the group of enlightened philosopher-politicians who came close to pulling off a miracle in Paris in 1789 — played his hand well, and gave sage counsel in the cause of Whig liberty.

Sections 1–4 of Chapter 8 are bottomed on Tocqueville's book. Section 5 concerns Jefferson's perceptions of the Revolution — in Paris and from America (to which he returned in 1789 to become Washington's Secretary of State). His analyses of French developments are almost uniformly acute and quite free from Whig hagiography; and his ready acceptance of heavy casualties (cf. the deaths of Louis XVI and the queen and the Terror) displays his adamancy. His biographers neglect his iron will, his latent ruthlessness. See his letter of 23 September 1800 to Dr Benjamin Rush: "I have sworn upon the altar of god, eternal hostility against every form of tyranny over the mind of man."

Now a fox is set among the chickens: Edmund Burke is put into play. I have a low opinion of Burke's historiography and analyses. But his influence was, and is, immense: both Jefferson and Tocqueville find it necessary to answer Burke. Why? Burke's prophetic powers proved so formidable that his "theory" has inevitably exercised more influence than its substance merits.

These are some of Tocqueville's principal points.

o Under the Ancien Régime,

□ French society splintered into self-regarding groups.

□ The nobility became a highly-privileged caste — no longer a cohesive group, selected by "blood" and dedicated to pubic service. "Nobility" became a patent for financial privilege, not a chance for glory.

□ A highly-centralized government levied onerous taxes, from which the nobility — which had become a caste — was exempted. (Jefferson too made this point.)

□ Social homogenization ran parallel to a sense of isolation between groups.

○ As for "economists and the Ancien Régime,"

▫ It was some time before economic reform was linked to political liberty, i.e. before the political ramifactions of the invisible-hand paradigm were understood.

▫ Utilitarianism has collectivist, authoritarian origins. Only the "general good" (*utilité publique*) mattered to the *économistes*. Utilitarianism became transmogrified into a doctrine of natural harmony only much later. (See Elie Halévy's *Philosophical Radicalism*.)

▫ Burke's true *bêtes noires* are the "designing" intellectual parents of Jeremy Bentham.

▫ *En passant*, Adam Smith's economics doubtless has origins in the work of the French *économistes*; but his moral philosophy is more influenced by (his close friend) David Hume than by pre-Benthamite authoritarianism. (See Ch. 6.)

▫ Tocqueville's analysis points up a clash between the system of the *économistes cum* Jeremy Bentham and that of J. S. Mill. For Mill, economic liberty is an instrument that promotes value-enhancing exchange, not an ethical quantity. The *économistes* valued neither political nor economic liberty. They sought to be supernannies, promoting what became Benthamite "gross national utility."

○ After 1789, there was a second (French) revolution, based on an obsession about equality, that stamped out the idea of liberty — cf. democratic despotism.

▫ The brief appearance of liberty in 1789 is mysterious; while the obession about equality follows naturally from the evolution of the Ancien Régime.

▫ Democratic despotism is linked to Rousseau's General Will, an abomination that sometimes seduced Jefferson.

▫ Tocqueville shows how liberty's rejection in favour of equality led to Bonapartism, and was promoted by the *économistes*. Many Frenchmen came to think that to be equal under a master had, after all a certain appeal (*douceur*). The views of the *économistes* of 1750 became far more influential than those of the leaders of 1789. (Jefferson called them "the patriots" of 1789; cf. *nos pères de 1789*).

On the Theory of Liberty. A quite-full discussion of the theory of liberty, comprising a segué between Sections 3 and 4 of Chapter 8, leads to two conclusions, inter alia.

o Neither individualism nor possessiveness is intrinsic to liberty. The liberal ideal pivots on non-coercive cooperation in markets in which exercises of powers enlarge spheres of action open to offerees.

o Liberty and equality are quite disjoint. A government based on a narrow franchise may exempt citizens who are ineligible to vote from duty while protecting them from private exercises of power not requiring their ratification. The unfranchised citizens would have liberty. (Edwardian England is suggestive.)

Edmund Burke & the Revolution in France. Burke urges the French to invent a Whiggish history of France, paying special heed to Montesquieu, so that aristocratic privilege and power would permanently prevail in French polity.

Burke is blind to the facts of "1789," although he uncannily anticipates the Terror. He transmogrifies the Lockian intellectuals of 1789 into bawling Samsons, bringing down the pillars of the Temple of the Ancien Régime. The French should have called in sturdy English mechanics to make needed small repairs.

TOCQUEVILLE ON BURKE'S *REFLECTIONS. Pace* Burke, the French nobility had become a mere caste whose privileges enraged the bourgeoisie.

o The English bourgeoisie readily made common cause with the aristocracy, (say) against the Crown. Nor did they feel heavily taxed.

o In France, plangent material discriminations were made against the bourgeoisie, genealogically identical to many members of the privileged caste.

o Burke did not understand that the administration of the Ancien Régime deprived the French of the ability to help each other: for one thing, the central government (*pouvoir central*) had accumulated almost all the powers that in England were exercised locally.

o *Pace* Burke, the collapse of the hopes of 1789 was not due to the outlook of those who made the "first" revolution. Nor was violence "in the air." Indeed manners had softened and toleration had widened throughout the eighteenth century. But "this revolution, instigated (*préparée*) by the nation's most civilized classes, was taken over by its least civilized ones (*les plus incultes et plus rudes*)." Finally, the liberty cultivated by the "patriots" of 1789 was crushed by democratic despotism. The masses succumbed to envy of the intellectual, as well as the material, refinement of the élite; and thrashed about in escalating episodes of wild play.

I hypothesize that the invasions of France exacerbated the revolution's growing destructiveness — and propelled Bonaparte's rise to power.

o Tocqueville forcefully sums up his brilliant book: the evolution (!) of the Ancien Régime compelled liberty to be the head of a servile body: *"on s'est borné à placer la tête de la liberté sur un corps servile."*

TJ on the Revolution in France. Much of the space of Jefferson's rather misshapen *Autobiography* is devoted to his French mission, 1784–1789. His observations and his experience as a participant in the near-miracle of 1789 greatly influenced his subsequent career. And his perceptions and actions have been grotesquely distorted.

Jefferson's analysis jibes with Tocqueville's.

o The eagerness of the "patriots" of 1789 for his advice suggests that the American and French revolutions have much in common. But most "experts" agree with Raynaud (1989) that "the two revolutions grew out of very different experiences, which led to the formation of two institutional logics at odds on many points." Raynaud confuses circumstantial discrepancies (importantly keyed on the vast American land-reserve) with intellectual ones. Jefferson's correspondence and well-documented recollections sharply contradict Raynaud's hypothesis: thus "a two-penny duty on tea ...

changed the condition of all [the earth's] inhabitants."

  ○ The "monstrous abuses" of the Ancien Régime may not have "ground the French to powder," but Jefferson's litany of entrenched abuses is persuasive. There seems little chance that so wretched a situation would correct itself; a shove was necessary.

  ○ Jefferson doubtless exaggerates both the queen's (Marie-Antoinette's) power and her political malignancy; but Burke's panegyric is absurd. Jefferson remarks on "the rhapsodies of the Rhetor Burke" that "gaudily painted [the queen] with some smartness of fancy, but no sound sense."

  ○ Jefferson abided the liquidation of the king and queen with glacial (if not Lenin-like) calm: so vast an upheaval reckoned to claim a number of prominent victims. Cf. the Terror — which is studied with some care.

The Terror. The bloody excesses of the Terror outraged eighteenth century sensibility: many high-minded friends of liberty turned against the revolution. But President Washington stood fast (circa January 1793). Then Jefferson (soon to retire as Secretary of State), conveying Washington's rebuke to the American diplomat, William Short, for acrimoniously anti-French expressions, turned to wild play: "were there but an Adam and Eve left in every country, and left free, it would be better than it is now." Jefferson's temperament undeniably contained at least a tincture of instability.

What happened during the Terror? Was the horror of the American Anglophiles justified? The Terror was perhaps not so cataclysmic after all. But Anglophone horror may have been unfeigned: the Terror surely shattered the serenity of the old order (just as Burke's premonition of it shattered his). It ran sixteen months, virtually ending with Robespierre's liquidation in July 1794. It claimed approximately 16,600 victims; the twentieth century is innoculated against such "paltry" loss — but human sensibility was far more delicate in the eighteenth century. A corollary conclusion is that Jefferson was much less squeamish than his admirers seem to think.

The Mazzei Letter. In his famous letter (April 1796) to Philip Mazzei, Jefferson — by then leader of the opposition to the second (Federalist) administration of General Washington — shivered political timbers by alleging that the President was a victim of an "Anglican" conspiracy: "men who were Samsons in the field and Solomons in the council, but who have had their heads shorn by the harlot England" have been beguiled by "Anglican" heresies. This was unfair to General Washington. But, by April 1796, Washington was a spent force. Jefferson was looking ahead to the bitter contest for control of the levers of power after March 1797 forward.

NOTES

1. See Albert Jay Nock (1926/1983). I dissent from his interpretations on a number of points.

  ○ He is captivated by Charles A. Beard's pseudo-Marxist economics, although Forrest McDonald et al. have demolished his *Economic Interpretation of the Constitution of the United States.* What is worse, he bases his rather harsh critique of Jefferson's economics on Beard's system.

  ○ He mistakes the manners of the Southern upper class. Jefferson was not aloof within his family or in favoured company; nor was Washington. See Dumas Malone's vivid description of the Monticello scene: noisy grandchildren romping about the cluttered, shabby mansion, etc. Jefferson delighted in all this, reserving only his study-suite sanctum. (The polished magnificence of the "Monticello museum" is misleading.)

  ○ Nock's Jefferson is a character in Chekov's *Cherry Orchard.* He does not explain how Jefferson could have attracted such devotion. Nor does he capture his fire — and ruthlessness.

2. See his letter to William Short (Ch. 8); or his famous tree of liberty, watered by the blood of patriots.

3. Jefferson thought slavery evil and forecast that white America would pay a terrible price for it. But he seems more concerned about the danger of slave insurrection than attracted by opportunities for emancipation. His

bold effort in 1784 to bar slavery in the territories came to naught: why should the aged eagle stretch its wings?

4. That the American Revolution was spared Bonapartism owes more to George Washington than to Thomas Jefferson — or anyone else. Perhaps Washington could have become First Consul, if not king — speculations roundly scouted by the Adamses. See Chateaubriand's *Mémoires*. His report of his interview with President Washington crystallizes early American political manners — and may explain why Thomas Jefferson and John Adams were so queasy about Alexander Hamilton.

Cf. Vicomte François-René de Chateaubriand (1768–1848): *Mémoires d'outre-tombe*, vol. 1, pp. 220–225.

Washington Receives Chateaubriand in Philadelphia (1791). Chateaubriand had always seen Washington as a Cincinnatus. And when he came to present his letter of recommendation to him, he found the simplicity of the ancient Roman.

o The palace of the American President was a small house, indistinguishable from neighbouring ones. He knocked. A young female servant (a slave?) opened the door. After several minutes, the general entered: very tall, a calm mien, more cold than noble.

o During the interview the youthful Chateaubriand said, "it is easier to discover the Northwest Passage than to create a people, as you have done." — "Well, well, young man," he cried and reached out his hand. He invited Chateaubriand to dinner the following day.

o There were six at dinner. The conversation turned to the French Revolution. The general displayed a key to the Bastille he had been sent (now on view at Mount Vernon). So, in Spring 1791, Washington was partial to the revolution. This chagrined the *émigré*: if Washington had seen the conquerors of the Bastille in the gutters of Paris, he would have had less regard for his relic.

Washington and Bonaparte Compared. Washington did not, like Bonaparte, seem to exceed human limits. Nor was Washington among the most talented captains: he defended a remote land with rather few citizen soldiers. But what light would flood forth from this modest man! His battle trophy was the United States of America!

o Bonaparte merely sought fame from his Old World battles.

○ Washington taught a nation how to be free; Bonaparte deprived a nation of its independence.

○ Washington knew *measure*: he did not mistake his being for that of his country.

○ Napoleon, living in the modern age (*l'âge moderne; the Enlightenment*), had outmoded aspirations: diadems, trophies — and his marriage with the apotheosized gothic ornament, the Habsburg princess, Marie-Louise, symptomized a fatal illness.

○ Unlike Napoleon, Washington belonged to the Enlightenment or at least *l'âge moderne*: Washington reflected the needs, the ideas, of his time; he reflected the trends of the day; he wanted what Americans wanted.

Jeremy Bentham Compares Washington with Napoleon. Elie Halévy explains that Bentham's second principle of utilitarianism is that all professions of disinteredness and of purity of intentions are *lies*: "the only reason why Washington did not act in America as Bonaparte did in France ... lies in difference in political conditions." (*Philosophical Radicalism*, p. 405) It is charitable to call this poppycock a symptom of dementia praecox. (The private Bentham seems quite generous: e.g. he supplied James Mill with a house.)

J. S. Mill, in his *Utilitarianism*, tries to escape Bentham's clutches without renouncing his school; his labours produce no more than a *petitio principii* — whatever it is, the Good is utile!

5. I find Dumas Malone's portrait of Jefferson quite plausible — except that Malone pitches down his unshakeable self-confidence.

6. Britain's dithering, after 1945, between a special relationship with the United States and "Europe" eerily imitates the quandary of the American Federalists.

The Louisiana Purchase (1803) implemented Jefferson's system, looking away from the sea.

7. Sir Edward Coke is the most famous figure in the storied linkage of the common law to the Whig interpretation of English history. His (mythical) constructions are studied in Ch. 3. Jefferson never abandoned Coke.

8. Henry Adams mordantly explains that the Jefferson's system is antinomous: free trade *cum* a laisser-faire manufactures-policy could not cope with overwhelming British seapower. *Voilà!*: The Embargo and the tragi-comic War of 1812.

9. Joyce Appleby (1984) asserts that this "second revolution" extolled American greed for wealth, noted by Tocqueville and J. S. Mill. I register a dissent in Ch. 5: Thomas Jefferson was neither Babbitt nor Dodsworth, nor meant to be.

10. Malone's description of Hamilton's position is chilling. And it supports my hypothesis that the Hamiltonians were preponderantly reactionary Anglophone merchants:

"Though Hamilton objected to none of the arbitrary features of the act and believed that the mass of aliens *[Republican supporters]* should be obliged to leave the country, he originally wanted favour to be shown merchants and exceptions made of a few others whose [Federalist] demeanour had been irreproachable *[citing Hamilton's 7 June 1798 letter to his running dog, his enemy's Secretary of State (!), Timothy Pickering]*" (Malone, 1962, p. 386)

11. Adam Smith and Alfred Marshall (in *Money, Credit and Commerce*) interestingly discuss the strange tale of the Bank of Amsterdam.

12. Jefferson's social sense is acute: cf. "those among us" or "we copy the idea." He adopts Aristotle's dictum, "he who is unable to live in society, or has no need for it because he is sufficient for himself, must be either a beast or a god." (*Politics*) The Platonic or Aristotelian state "[serves] the end of man, the leading of the good life or the acquisition of happiness, and [is] *natura prior* ... to the individual and the family." (Copleston, 1946/1962, pp. 92–93) He also writes, "the State must be called a mutual society. The Sophists were therefore wrong in thinking that the state is simply the creature of convention." (Ibid., p. 33) Jefferson is queasily Aristotelian — and an ardent Whig. This pudding of classicism and Whiggery makes him hard to type. His economics are unambiguous. He follows J.-B. Say and Adam Smith: "his" economy is atomistically interactive; the state merely sets a few parameters, affecting the economic process catalytically.

The economic argument can be taken very far without referring to sympathy or moral sentiment. But, like Adam Smith's, Jefferson's complete system fully weighs these factors. The political equivalent to the invisible hand of competition is the theory of Whig liberty, a vexingly difficult subject.

13. I show in Ch. 2 that Hamilton's monetary theory presages Keynes's (1936) "Notes on Mercantilism." Still Hamilton took Ricardo's (and Say's) side in their controversy with Malthus — while Keynes rterospectively sided with Malthus, as did James Madison.

14. The revivalist of "human rights," President Jimmy Carter, was reborn by a divine revelation. I do not know how the editors of the *Wall Street Journal* discovered human rights.

Since indefinable values like "human rights" cannot be inserted into the law without it becoming vague, the human-rights cult undermines liberty.

15. Thomas Hobbes is an important precursor of utilitarianism; and of what became Austinian jural positivism. But he does not escape the pull of social-contract mythology. And, far from creating a rationale for liberty, he is an apostle of Authority.

I think Elie Halévy is correct: Jeremy Bentham belongs to the school of Hobbes. And note that a liberal case has been made for Hobbes. Concentration of authority in the sovereign may be favourable to liberty: dispersed powers may be exercised brutally.

16. The flaw in the utilitarian doctrine — flowing from Benthamite sources, through J. S. Mill's queasy *Utilitarianism*, to the rushing rapids of contemporary economics — is not in its notion that acts' consequences ought to be considered (!), but rather in its tacit rejection of ethical criticism of "desire": "utility" merely "measures" the degree to which desires (lusts?) are satisfied.

"It is not to be expected in a member of a Greek City state that an ethical interest should be completely severed from a political interest, for the Greek was essentially a citizen and he had to lead the good life within the framework of the city." (Copleston, 1946/1962, p. 129)

"According to Socrates that action is right which serves man's true utility, in the sense of promoting his true happiness. ... Of course, we must not suppose that the utilitarian standpoint of Socrates envisages the following of whatever is pleasurable. ... Socrates certainly considered that pleasure is a good, but he thought that true pleasure and lasting happiness attend the moral rather than the immoral man, and that happiness does not consist in having a great abundance of external goods." (Ibid., pp. 130–132)

17. The Constitution partially anticipates Parliamentary supremacy: the President is much weaker than King George. Jefferson remarked early on that American liberty was more at risk from Congress than any other source.

18. Like most revolutionaries, Jefferson was neurasthenically sensitive to counter-revolutionary threats — a fact that has sent Leonard Levey et al. into tizzies.

19. Xanthippe like, Crosskey also resents the warmth of Jefferson's attention to Mr Walker's wife, while deploring his alleged exploitation of Hamilton's hot attention to Mr Reynolds's wife.

20. The Embargo Act became law in late December 1807. The implementation of the embargo, the Louisiana Purchase, the Gallatin-Jefferson proposals in 1807 for a national university, etc. establish a cardinal point of Ch. 3: Jefferson and Madison must have known that their "strict construction" theory of of Constitutional interpretation was preposterous. (Henry Adams said that "no European monarch, except perhaps the Czar," could match Jefferson's 1807 proposals.)

21. Jefferson violates the Ricardo-Barro theorem; and fails to distinguish domestic from external debt. Debt was the bane of his personal life; this doubtless amplified his misdirection.

Chapter Two

Thomas Jefferson and the Political Economy of Alexander Hamilton: The Bank; Assumption; Sir Robert Walpole's System in a New Republic; Lord Bolingbroke

§1 PRELIMINARIES

"If, as Talleyrand said, [1] Hamilton divined Europe, it may be properly added that he also divined the system of *Machtpolitik* under which the European nations operated." (Charles A. Beard, 1934/1966, pp. 48–49)

"Mr Adams observed, 'purge the British constitution of its corruption ... and it would be the most perfect ... ever devised by the wit of man.' Hamilton paused and said, 'purge it of its corruption, and give to its popular branch equality of representation and it would become an impracticable government: as it stands at present, with all its supposed defects, it is the most perfect government which ever existed.' Hamilton was indeed a singular character. Of acute understanding, disinterested and honourable in all private transactions, amiable in society, and duly valuing virtue in private life, yet so betwitched and perverted by the British example, as to be under thorough conviction that corruption was essential to the government of a nation." (Thomas Jefferson, *Writings* [1984, pp. 669–671], from *The Anas*)

As a child, in the West Indies, Hamilton may have thought Europe more agreeable than America's trackless forests, encroaching on its paltry towns. And in his prime he was repelled by America's social and intellectual "incoherence" (see McDonald, 1979) — but not by its avarice, remarked by Tocqueville and J. S. Mill (who coined the trope, "the almighty dollar").

He may have anticipated expatriates like Henry James, Ezra Pound and T. S. Eliot; he was surely misled by his admiration for an England that was to leave him behind and whose situation differed radically from that of the new republic — he was out of touch with the ideas of the British economists who would have so great a day; by 1832, the British system outdistanced him; by 1884, his British model was out of sight.

He did not crave a reputation as an economist! Nor was the *éclat* of his success at the bar important to him. He sought glory; and found it. But his reputation falls short of the pinnacle because his glory lacks *areté*, the quality that makes Washington, Washington. [2] And his thirst for glory may have unbalanced his judgment: he thought Caesar history's greatest figure; Jefferson chose Bacon, Locke and Newton. [3]

The Origins of Hamilton's System. Today Alexander Hamilton would be called Keynesian. And the substance of the financial systems of Thomas Jefferson and Andrew Jackson is classical. And state of the art research into competitive currencies, free banking and homeostatic properties of commodity-money systems, along with strict demarcation between monetary issue and financial intermediation — anticipated by the one-hundred-percent-reserve banking proposals of an earlier Chicago school and by my own (1988) work going *Beyond the Banking Principle* — is congenial to the Jefferson-Jackson system and incompatible with Hamilton's.

Before researching my 1988 study, I thought that Hamilton's financial acuity translates into sound economics and that Jefferson and Jackson were economic primitives. No longer: this chapter, and its appendix, explain why.

Forrest McDonald (1974, p. 48) let the scales fall from my eyes: "Hamilton set out to plant the British system in America, corruption and all." The British System was Walpole's, and Malachy Postlethwayt's *Universal Dictionary*, explaining Walpole's system, was Hamilton's guide. The moment of creation of what became Walpole's system was the formation of the Bank of England in 1694. Walpole's institutions, during his 1721–1742 ministry, included the sinking fund and stock (bond) market interventions by the Bank of England.

"The real purpose ... [of the sinking fund] ... was not to pay the debt but to convince people that it would be paid." (McDonald, 1974, p. 57) And Bank interventions in debt markets were meant to assure the liquidity of debt-holdings, much as aircraft manufacturers might support used-aircraft markets. In a sense, public debt was monetized, so that "Keynesians," then and now, conclude that real costs of capital fell as a result.

Possession of liquid wealth, as well as real property, became a primary source of power in Sir Robert Walpole's time. And corruption was endemic in his system — as was explained in Ch. 1. [4] J. H. Plumb, the premier biographer of Walpole, capsulates his system.

Circa 1717, Britain's public debt impinged on the government's freedom of action. Walpole's response was a Sinking Fund "by which each year certain taxes were used to pay off the debt so that its eventual discharge seemed to be within sight. It had a tonic effect. [People] felt that their money in government loans was secure because it was certain to be repaid." (Plumb, 1950/1963, pp. 56–57) Walpole's successful containment of the South Sea Scheme (Bubble) brought him to mastery in 1721.

Plumb explains that Walpole's sinking fund was just what Hamilton took it to be: a device to make the debt more manageable and buoyant, but not to repay the debt. Indeed Walpole raided the Fund in 1727 and 1733 in order to avert unpopular tax increases. It is easy to vindicate Walpole. But Hamilton's obsession with the British system seems indefensible. Walpole's was a supremely old-world policy, for an insatiable government; surely not a model for a new republic, separated from Europe by the Atlantic, abutting a vast wilderness — a republic's whose baseline expenditures were constitutionally tiny.

§2 THE POLITICAL ECONOMY OF ALEXANDER HAMILTON

(2-1) Conclusions on the Bank and Public Credit Reports

o Hamilton's theories are unsound. Although a great statesman, he was a badly flawed conceptual thinker — high theory bored him.

o Establishment of America's public credit helped attract capital; and the Assumption and Funding proposals in the *Report* are ingenious. But McDonald (1974, p. 91) owns that Assumption was the darling of speculators, jobbers and Treasury toadies. [5]

o Hamilton's bank promoted efficient debt clearance over great distances. But McDonald (1974, p. 61) concedes that there were three banks in the United States, circa 1790, that collectively could have done the job; and the elasticity of supply of banking services in the United States proved to be very high. [6]

o Hamilton properly picks up Adam Smith's "dead stock" analysis: there are economies from substituting paper for metallic substances, as British North American colonies had discovered. But banks, operating under laisser-faire, abhor dead stock; Smith's examples are drawn from "free banking" experience. Nor does "dead stock" have much empirical weight.

o He did not project a modern central bank. He proposed to merge the spheres of Government and Finance: a motley gaggle of planets was to be sucked into his fiery sun, not orbit it. His strategic thinking may have been inspired by Colbert, and surely was by Walpole; but not by Turgot or Adam Smith. He was an *étatiste* financier — not a nascent central banker or a promoter of a laisser-faire economy. He could have installed a sound *dirigisme* for finance of French industry for Napoleon. [7]

o Monetary theories of real rates of interest may be the most dismal Keynesian legacy, and are surely out of place in the theory of a small, open economy. But Hamilton anticipates such theories. Jefferson scorns the utility of enlarging the stock of paper money — in contrast with Franklin, its longtime supporter. [8]

o The money supply of a small, open economy, in a commodity-money régime, is endogenous and, indeed, determined by demand. But Hamilton bases his arguments for the Bank and Assumption (*cum* funding) on a model along Irving Fisher's lines. His closed money-supply model is improper. [9]

o Classical theorists ascribe properties of real economic action to real causes — save for effects of perverse monetary behaviour (see Pigou's "veil of money"); and American eighteenth and nineteenth century experience supports them. Hamilton's activist bias misses the trick taken by Ricardo and other classical writers — mostly after his death in 1804.

o Hamilton did well to promote thick markets in financial paper. But thicker secondary markets undermine the *raison d'être* for banks (see my "Beyond the Banking Principle," 1988). Furthermore, thick financial markets, abetting direct and indirect contacts between savers and borrowers, promote saving and foreign-capital inflow; banks of issue do not, per se, serve these ends. He would have done better to extend his fructuous ideas about markets for public debt to those for private debt, while finessing, if not eliding, banks of issue and their unsound balance sheets. He would have done better to implement Jefferson/Jackson banking doctrine!

(2-2) Analysis of the Bank Report (1791)

On Dead Stock. Hamilton dextrously deploys Adam Smith's argument: see *Bank Report*, pp. 258–262, p. 273 and pp. 306–307. [10] Smith's phrase, "in the room of gold," appears on p. 273.

"The substitution of paper in the room of gold and silver money, replaces a very expensive instrument of commerce with one much less costly, and sometimes equally convenient." (*Wealth of Nations*, book ii, ch. ii, Everyman's Library ed., p. 257)

"When paper is substituted ... the quantity of materials, tools, and maintenance which the whole circulating capital can supply, may be increased by the whole, value of gold and silver which used to be employed." (Ibid., p. 261)

"That part of his capital which a dealer is obligated to keep by him unemployed, and in ready money, for answering occasional demands is so much dead stock, which, so long as it remains in this situation, produces nothing. ... The gold and silver money which circulates in any country ... is, in the same manner as the ready money of the dealer, all dead stock." (Ibid., p. 285)

"If there were two merchants, one in London and the other in Edinburgh, who employ stocks in the same branch of trade, the Edinburgh merchant can ... carry on a much greater trade ... than the London merchant [who] must always keep by him a considerable sum of money ... With the same stock, therefore, [the Edinburgh merchant] can, without imprudence, have at all times in his warehouse a greater quantity of goods than the London merchant." (Ibid., pp. 264–265)

Adam Smith is not quite right. In principle, "London" could operate the same mass of "effective" or "live" capital as "Edinburgh" — and so more capital in all. True, equilibrium would then mandate a higher price in London than in Edinburgh. [11]

DEAD STOCK EX POST. Studies of the Jacksonian "bank wars" imply the potential cost of dead stock to the American economy in the 1790s; Andrew Jackson was prepared to pay a price for a sounder currency.

"As part of his campaign against banks, Jackson supported a proposal to raise the price of gold in the United States in order to attract gold from Europe and to induce the public to use gold instead of bank obligations for their business." (Temin, 1969, p. 78)

What would be the opportunity cost? Stanley Engerman, glossed by Lee and Passell (1979, p. 126), supplies important evidence.

"Using contemporary rates of interest [to estimate] the annual charge for holding precious metal, Engerman finds that the total interest costs of replacing paper money with specie would have averaged 0.46% of GNP in 1825-1834, 0.35% in 1835-1848, 0.43% in 1849-1858."

The opportunity cost of increasing the mass of dead stock was slight.

Money Supply in a Small, Open Economy. Hamilton's interestingly explores money-supply theory in his *Report on the Public Credit*: but he operates a closed-economy money-supply model for the very open American economy in an otherwise penetrating analysis. His idea that reconstituted public debt would become a close money-substitute is ingenious. But, taken in conjunction with a complete, cohesive economic model, the money-substitute idea proves insubstantial.

We now supply a correct analysis, capturing the principal monetary characteristics of the American economy of Hamilton's time. Money supply was endogenous; it tended towards its equilibrium-value through the operation of an autonomous dynamic mechanism, which American experience in the first half of the nineteenth-century suggests operated fluidly and rapidly. And real interest rates are, and surely were, functions of real, not monetary factors — *pace* Hamilton.

The "correct analysis" is supported by later nineteenth-century experience:

"[In 1834] as banks attempted to protect themselves by decreasing their liabilities, credit became harder to obtain. English capital flowed in to fill the void, creating an excess supply of foreign exchange and causing its price to fall. When the price of foreign exchange fell far enough, specie was imported, enabling the banks to strengthen their position by increasing their reserves instead of decreasing their liabilities." (Temin, 1969, p. 67)

The stock of American specie at the outset of 1834 was $51 million; $17 million in specie was imported that year — the stock increased by about one third within a year! Our theory's monetary dynamics are supported. Indeed a more radical proposition becomes plausible: perhaps the Jefferson/Jackson vision of a metallic money was viable after all. See Table (2–2:1).

(2–2:1): Specie Variability

End of Year	Specie ($m)	Specie/Money Stock x 100%
1832	31	5%
1833	41	
1834	51	
1835	65	
1836	73	
1837	98	23%

Source: Temin (1969, Table 3.3, p. 71)

(Money Supply) = net liabilities of the banks plus specie

Obviously, any "shortage" of money in the United States could have easily been corrected by specie inflow. Temin's conclusion that the second Bank's influence on money supply was slight looks attractive. Decentralized market processes worked far better than advocates of a financial colossus modelled on Walpole's system have been willing to concede. There seems to have been no proper reason to create a money interest after all. What is more, Jefferson and Jackson anticipated the divorce of "money" from "credit" so vital for correct monetary economics. (See Jefferson's "Notes on Professor Ebeling's letter" infra.)

Next consider a dynamic analysis of a generic commodity-money standard, together with a theme going at least as far back as Adam Smith and associated with Nassau Senior (1830) — "the purchasing power of money as determined by the cost of obtaining money." Factors such as exploration activity and shifts between monetary and non-monetary gold are explicitly modelled. The formal structure is easily reinterpreted in terms of the crude-oil industry. [12] Indeed a network, or matrix, approach can be developed. See ch. 8 of my 1989 book, developing properties of the distribution of specie across economies in a specialized general equilibrium context through comparative statics *à la* Hicks and Samuelson.

THE CONTROLLING THEORY. Traded and non-traded goods are both cardinally important for *System One*: equilibrium prices of traded goods, and interest rates, are determined by world conditions; but prices of Economy *E*'s non-traded goods are dominated by local market conditions. In the upshot the rate of change of the supply of money (or the specie-stock) of a small, open economy pivots on the "evolution" of the current account of its balance of payments. And excess demand for money in Economy *E* will temporarily depress prices and raise interest rates: excess demand for money triggers specie inflow; and excess supply, specie outflow.[1] Indeed System One is a version of Hume's specie-flow mechanism and belongs to the family of monetary theories of balances of payments.

Subject to some qualification, the system is dynamically stable: the rate of growth of money supply tends to increase, decrease, or stay intact, as it is less than, greater than or equal to the secular money-growth rate.[2]

As for the qualification, the function determining demand for money may have a speculative component, so that falling prices provoke expectations of further falls, stimulating demand for real monetary balances. Then the schematization may be unstable.

System one ignores direct capital-inflow channels in which monetary assets are exchanged for claims to non-monetary ones so that indeed net capital inflow may be nil. (Alexander Hamilton was acutely sensitive to this point.)

---

[1] Some readers will seek a more formal exposition of the text's argument. Thus where π is Economy E's inflation rate and L its money demand,

$$D\pi = f(M/L); \; f(1) = 0; \; f'(M/L) > 0 \qquad (1)$$

[2] Again specializing the analysis to Economy E, the mathematical version of the text's exposition is as follows:

$$DM = \varphi(M); \; \varphi'(M) < 0 \qquad (2)$$

or, where the global rate of money-growth is m^*,

$$m = \psi(m/m^*); \; \psi(1) = m^* \qquad (3)$$

Now consider this passage by Hamilton's protagonist, Forrest McDonald:

"The root cause of the nation's financial mess, Hamilton figures, was that there was simply not enough money in the country to pay for the war no matter how effective the system of taxation. The remedy was to create more money by establishing a national bank."

System Two, centring on real rates of interest and purporting to model a small, open economy like that of the United States in the 1790s, is less attractive than System One. In the eighteenth century, pure real rates of interest substantially obeyed a "law of one price" — and market rates typically included large risk premia. (See my "Colonial Currency," 1988.)

System Two entails a monetary approach to the real rate of interest. And equilibrium monetary growth is determined by a global norm. The disparity of Economy E's real interest rate(s) from the global "natural" rate of interest depends on that of its money growth from the global norm. And the evolution of money-growth depends on the disparity of its interest rates from a global norm. Mathematicians will see that the process hinges on a pair of simultaneous differential equations — see ch. 4 of my 1986 book.[3]

Supplying intuition for System Two, higher interest rates in Economy E induce foreigners to offer monetary for non-monetary assets. In Keynesian paradigms, higher interest rates depress aggregate demand — discouraging imports and stimulating exports — resulting in specie inflow. The schematization mirrors common Keynesian or City reasoning.

If filled in (it will not be), *System Three* portrays how the stock of money, or specie, as well as its growth rate, influences monetary growth (or, better, how the "evolution" of precious metal stocks

---

[3] Call the deviation of E's monetary growth from the global norm, μ; and the global natural (real) rate of interest, r^*.

$$D\mu = F(r \cdot r^*) = h(r); \quad h(0) = 0; \quad F' > 0 \qquad (4)$$

$$Dr = g(\mu); \quad g(0) = 0; \quad g' < 0 \qquad (5)$$

is influenced by their magnitude). Thus the instantaneous growth rate of desired money balances partly depends on excess demand (or supply) of money. If excess demand is not nil, an interest-rate engine kicks in; and monetary growth changes accordingly.

SOME MONETARY HISTORY OF ANCIENT ROME. Edward Gibbon comments on the "adequacy" of the Roman world's supplies of precious metals; and does not mistakenly concentrate on monetized ones. (See ch. 10 of my 1991 book.)

"It was a complaint worthy of the gravity of the senate *[cum Tiberius]* that, in the purchase of female ornaments, the wealth of the state was irrevocably given away *[citing Tacitus, Annal iii, 53; also see Bury infra]* The annual loss [exceeded £800,000]. Such was the style of discontent brooding over the dark prospect of approaching poverty. [Yet the proportion of silver to gold considerably increased from the time of Pliny to that of Constantine. But gold was no more scarce. So] silver was grown more common; that whatever might be the amount of the Indian and Arabian exports, they were far from exhausting the wealth of the Roman world; and that the produce of the mines abundantly supplied the demands of commerce." (*Decline and Fall*, Bury edn., 1909/1974, vol. 1, pp. 60–61)

Professor Bury, supplying copious sources, asserts that "there was certainly *[sic?]* a gradual diminution in the amount of gold and silver in circulation in the second century. Yet ... Gibbon has grasped [the] facts; the spirit of his observation is right."

The amount of gold and silver in circulation was endogenous, responding to demand; while aggregate supplies of precious metals were immense, dwarfing monetary stocks.

Summing up the Roman evidence, non-monetary precious metal stocks much exceeded monetary ones. The quantity of monetary gold and silver appears to have been governed by a convenience yield of non-monetary stocks that may have been exogenous for the money market. Two conclusions follow. (1) Sources of finance included stocks of non-monetary gold and silver. Humps in investment expenditure could be financed from non-monetary stocks. Temporary increases in the monetary circulation were in time refluxed back into non-monetary stocks. (2) The purchasing power of precious metals was steady in ancient Rome. But the real value of the chronically-debased monetary circulation depreciated.

Further Comments Based on Study of the Bank Report. The specie flow mechanism blocked any persistent "shortage" of money — a result pitched up by fluid exchange between immense non-monetary and monetary stocks of precious metals. Fractional-reserve currency is at best irrelevant; nor was there a proper banking purpose that could not be served by decentralized financial enterprise.

○ The Jefferson/Jackson schematization did not entail "free banking": cf. its one-hundred-per-cent-reserve principle. Free banking — supported by Adam Smith and Walter Bagehot — relies on prudential constraints imposed by the market. (See V. Smith, 1936/1990, Goodhart, 1985/1989 and my "Beyond the Banking Principle" [1988].) But both schematizations entail competitive banking markets. Hamilton's giant Walpolian institution was bottomed on an anti-competitive principle.

○ The United States attracted massive capital inflow invariantly against the status (or existence) of the Banks of the United States. Why? Because the Jefferson Administration, and its successors, zealously protected foreign creditors' rights. And the ratio of the stock of American public debt to productive assets or net exports was prudently controlled: the stock of national public debt declined relative to (say) GNP, if not absolutely, throughout the Jefferson-Jackson period (except during the War of 1812). It was the prudential properties Hamilton's system shared with Jefferson's that were important. Jefferson and Gallatin, and their successors, installed prudent procedures; and that was enough. Jefferson's retrospective characterization of the perplex (spilling over into our discussion of Hamilton's *Report on the Public Credit*) seems excellent to me. Jefferson recalls his worries about,

"a corps of interested persons *[viz. traders relying on inside dope]* who should be steadily at the orders of the Treasury. I told [Hamilton] all that was ever really necessary to establish our credit, was an efficient government and an honest one declaring it would sacredly pay our debts, laying taxes for this purpose and applying them to it." (The *Anas, Writings*, pp. 682–683)

○ Keynes deploys a liquidity-preference theory of interest; this is the burden of chs. 13 and 15 of the *General Theory* — and of ch. 23, "Notes on Mercantilism, etc.," especially pp. 333–353, glossed — along with the Keynes-Heckscher debate — in my review, "Homer on Interest Rates" (1967/1988). *Inter alia*, an increase in the nominal quantity of money is to reduce the real rate of interest. Hamilton makes a very similar argument at p. 306 of the *Bank Report*. Indeed, at pp. 302 and 307, he operates an *ISLM*-like system, explaining how a rightward shift of *LM* leads to a lower real rate of interest.

○ Hamilton sophisticatedly analyses monetary velocity, recognizing that an increase in velocity, cet. par., has effects on prices and (nominal?) income like those based on higher money-growth. Velocity effects are deployed in the *Bank Report* (p. 277) in connection with a monetary theory of nominal and real income that does not rely on an interest-rate-effect channel. And he points out that the effective velocity of specie will increase if it is automatically returned to banks who promptly pump it out again. But so Fisherine an approach is improper for a small, open economy.

□ He deploys another argument keyed on monetary velocity at pp. 322–323: funds received for debt-service are quickly restored to circulation by the Bank's lending operations; and repeatedly argues that monetary circulation is stimulated by credit emission (see pp. 309 and 314). (There is an interesting general discussion of financial intermediation at p. 309.) These points are ingeniously developed — but are subordinated to the improper hypothesis that higher velocity is desirable because nominal income will be higher in (Fisherine) consequence. The hypothesis is untenable for an open economy in a fixed-exchange régime. Indeed it is untenable for a closed economy: it entails monetary determination of real action.

○ McDonald (1974) stresses how Hamilton's Bank was to pump up American money supply and support prices of government bonds. [13] (The Bank's notes were to be the principal circulating medium in America. Net currency supply in 1800 was $26.5 million.)

McDonald properly says that "if the Treasury was to peg the market in bonds, it would have to have access to money every day of the year." (McDonald, 1974, p. 61) Alas, the Bank's capital included only $2 million in specie: the exiguous specie available for bond support operations would be quickly exhausted by a bear raid on bonds. [14]

Jefferson and McDonald are *d'accord* on the Bank's *raison d'être*; but they draw very different conclusions from their common starting point. See Jefferson's "Notes on Professor Ebeling's Letter" (*Writings*, pp. 697–702, especially p. 699). According to Jefferson, the Federalists sought the British model; and to form, like the English, "a monied interest, by means of a funding system, not calculated to pay the national debt but to render it perpetual and to make it an engine in the hands of the executive branch of the government which, added to the great patronage it possessed in the disposal of public offices, might enable it to assume by degrees a kingly authority." Stripped of its vivid gloss, this commentary is quite sound: it properly points up the supreme importance of Hamilton's Assumption plan and the debt-management schemae complementary to it: the Bank was to "stabilize" debt markets — a rôle we shall see Hamilton badly misspecified.

o See Jefferson's letter to John Wayles Eppes (his son-in-law), 24 June 1813 (*Writings*, pp. 1280–1286). He proposes that the circulating money stock should normally consist of specie; and that the national government should have a monopoly of issue in time of war. So he anticipates an earlier Chicago school (see one-hundred-per-cent-reserve banking).

"Let those among us who have a monied capital and who prefer employing it in loans ... set up banks, and give cash [specie] or national bills for the notes they discount. It is from Great Britain that we copy the idea of giving paper in exchange for discounted bills." (Ibid., p. 1285)

This seems to me an able exercise in the theory of seigneurage; and, indeed, a rare example of a writer clearly separating "money" from "credit." [15]

o Hammond (1957, p. 118) cogently points out that "it is obvious that in the beginning the politcal prominence of banking in the United States outstripped its economic importance. When there were still only three banks in the country, the subject engaged an inordinate amount of attention."

(2–3) Analysis of the Report on the Public Credit (1790)

"The national debt, if it is not excessive, will be for us a national blessing; it will be a powerful cement of our union." (Hamilton, *Papers*, vol. vi) [16]

The *Report's* (1790) central theme, assumption by the national government of state debt, concerns us only to the (cardinally important) extent that the upshot led the national government to manage a huge, freshly acquired, convertible public debt — pitching up the "Walpole's system" *motif* very high. [17] Two other themes are treated in still greater detail: the notion that the national government's debt would, upon implementation of Hamilton's programme, become a monetary substitute, leading to lower interest rates (see James and Sylla, 1980, pp. 243–272); his *sinking fund*, related to his plan for systematic support of government-bond prices, evokes "Walpole."

Hamilton's mercantilist development of the themes does not survive close scrutiny. What is more, assumption was implemented by Gallatin et al., under Jefferson's strategy at least as effectively as it would have been under Hamilton's jettisoned programme.

Public Debt as a Money Substitute. Monetary effects of funded public debt should be distinguished from those of specie supplied by purchasers of public debt: Hamilton points out that American holdings of foreign assets, as well as specie, increase when British and Dutch bills, and specie, are tendered by foreigners for United States

Government stock (*Papers*: vi, p. 89). This is a typically well-rated tactical point in the service of a mercantilist strategy.

As for "near money," see *Papers*: vi, pp. 70–71. (But government stock was not much deployed as a circulating medium.) According to Hamilton, such a virtual increase in money stock (a subtle point) leads to lower interest rates — a Keynesian conclusion falsified by the data: American interest rates, duly adjusted for risk, seem to have been firmly rooted in the global 4–5 per cent (per annum) range.

Hamilton subtly explores another facet of money substitution, pointing out that a funded public debt supplies liquidity the way bank systems are supposed to do; and the resulting asset is transferable, like bank notes — Beyond the Banking Principle! This prescient reasoning implies that his banking and public-credit programmes are at cross-purposes. [18]

The Sinking Fund. McDonald (1979) supplies a gloss for the sinking fund different from Jefferson's.

"The purpose of the sinking fund was not to retire the debt ... but rather to create the appearance that the debt was being retired [cf. Walpole!]. ... The more important purpose of the sinking fund would be what, in the twentieth century, would be known as 'pegging the market,' ... designed to drive the market price ... to par and maintain it at that level. With the securities stabilized at par, speculation would be ended, public credit would be established, and the public debt would be monetized." (McDonald, 1979, p. 171)

The Bank was to execute this strategy. (See *Papers*: vi, pp. 70, 106–108; and McDonald, 1979, p. 408, n. 10.)

Drop the mercantilist/Hamiltonian/Keynesian idea that pumping up the money supply reduces interest rates and stimulates the real economy. Then the Jefferson/Jackson tactic amply supports public-debt prices: cf. aggressive debt retirement. We shall return to this point.

The sinking fund's *raison d'etre* was specious, if not silly. The Bank's capital was inadequate to mount support operations against sustained pressure. Why should agents take bear positions in markets for quasi-consular debt created by Hamilton's system? They may forecast that the government will fail to service the debt with specie-payments; e.g. they may fret about the government's ability to levy sufficient taxes to finance rising expenditure. A bubble may form.

The intense commitment to debt reduction and hard money of the Jeffersonians and Jackonsians preempted bear attacks on U. S. Government debt, just as Jefferson claimed. The policy of Jefferson, Gallatin and Jackson better accomplished Hamilton's objectives than his glitzy intervention scheme. The Democratic Republicans and the Democrats hit upon a solid price-support programme: they curtailed the supply of U. S. debt, while assuring the debt's service.

Hamilton's debt-management programme engendered the only plausible destabilizing speculation! It could create an atmosphere made fetid by rumour and gossip, if not outright corruption. Most trading might be based on what agents think is inside dope. "Fundamentals" would hardly matter. The upshot might be "a game of Snap, of Old Maid, of Musical Chairs." (Keynes, 1936, pp. 155–156) The market might reach "the third degree where we devote our intelligences to anticipating what average opinion expects the average opinion to be. ..." (Ibid., p. 156) The "natural" system installed by Jefferson and Gallatin blocked speculation against United States debt. [19]

Secondary Debt Markets. Hamilton discusses secondary markets with *panache*: *Papers*: vi, pp. 54 and 62; his notion that a sinking fund promotes thick secondary markets is impressive on the plane of theory and dovetails with my (1988) "Beyond the Banking Principle" theme.

Hamilton reckoned to create a *de facto* non-redeemable asset, made liquid by its thick secondary market. He was within a short step of supplying a rationale for a Jefferson/Jackson financial system; Jefferson and Jackson hit upon a better system and Hamilton a better argument. A conflation would have put the American credit-intermediary system on a sound footing. For the most part, intermediaries would then have been merchant (investment) bankers specialized to rating paper, packaging unit trusts, etc. The clearing and bank-credit systems would have been separated *ab initio*. The clearing medium would have been a composite of specie and conveniently packaged U. S. and other highly rated debt (cf. securitization of mortgage or credit-card debt) — efficiently circulated with the help of banks' technical services. Perhaps the Bank of the United States would have predominated in a competitive environment; perhaps not.

These remarks lead to *land-banks* and like devices, and their relation to innovated clearing. [20] And they encourage the following grand conjecture. Hamilton's system, or the myth of his system, attained intellectual supremacy; and nurtured various Soundness Schools, arguing successfully for a highly centralized, closely regulated financial mechanism, notable for a top-heavy clearing-bank industry and intimate intercourse between the "money power" and the regulatory agencies of government. Thomas Jefferson's apotheosis was accompanied by rejection of his system. (See Merrill Peterson, 1960.)

The Politics of Assumption. Brant (1970) relates that Hamilton asked Madison for his views on debt-reconstruction during 1790; and he had good reason to expect support for Assumption and the Bank from Madison, who carried great weight with Washington at the time. But Madison replied that "foreign debt should be placed on a sound basis" (ibid., p. 241) and that domestic debt should be reduced by public-land sales. Indeed he decried perpetuation of the debt, the practical effect of Hamilton's funding policy.

In 1791 Madison expressed outrage about speculative frenzy in debt markets and insider dealings. And he found "non-discrimination" immoral: he was appalled by failure to distinguish original holders (sometimes war veterans and their relicts) from present holders (sometimes "speculators"). But there was a rub. In 1783, Madison had proposed Assumption and opposed discrimination between holders. He justified his *volte face* this way. Virginia (e.g.), having paid off part of its debt, should not have to pay twice.

Madison proposed to the House of Representatives that the debt be paid in full and that original holders — often misled, if not defrauded, by present holders — be compensated. He may not have been entirely serious; but Brant's gloss is intriguing:

"Madison proposed full payment, while the Hamilton plan impaired contracts by cutting interest and deferring part of the obligations until 1800. The impairment failed to damage national credit *because the funding was undertaken by a government with adequate taxing power.*" (Brant, 1970, p. 245. Brant's emphasis.)

Madison and Jefferson played their cards well. Thomas Jefferson's famous dinner for Alexander Hamilton and James Madison led to a Great Compromise. Assumption was arranged, but credit was allowed for debt paid by the states; and the capital was to be on the Potomac.

THE GREAT COMPROMISE

By August 1791, there was frenzied speculation in public debt stock whose redemption was postponed to 1800. Madison wrote that,

"the stockholders will become the praetorian guard of the government, at once its tool and its tyrant; bribed by its largesses and overawing it by clamours and combinations."

This did not wholly come to pass — perhaps because Walpole's system was so exaggerated by both sides that horror at its mythic shape precluded creation of the real thing.

(2–4) Interpretation of Selected Data — more fully displayed in my Studies *(1988, pp. 131–136)*

(1) Money and Prices

Year	WPI
1787	90
1790	90
1794	108
1795	131
1800	129
1810	131

Source: U. S. Bureau of the Census

The Wars of the French Revolution explain the jump from 1794 to 1795 — one that doubtless stimulated production of foreign-traded goods and boosted incomes of producers and distributors of such goods.

(2) Wholesale price indices (Philadelphia, Benazon) —
industrial goods had a high import content

Year	(1)	(2)	(3)
1790	086.5	089.9	085.4
1794	109.6	120.7	110.7
1795	130.7	141.3	130.4
1800	128.3	138.0	130.5
1810	138.7	147.3	146.2

Source: U. S. Bureau of the Census
(1) = All Commodities
(2) = Imports
(3) = Industrial Goods

(3) Money, Currency & Prices, 1830-1835

Year	(1)	(2)	(3)	(4)
1800	28.0	1.5	26.5	129
1810	58.0	3.0	55.0	131
1820	69.1	2.0	67.1	106
1830	93.1	5.8	87.3	091
1835	154.7	8.9	145.8	100

Source: U. S. Bureau of the Census

(1) = money supply ($m)
(2) = currency in treasury ($m)
(3) = (1) - (2)
(4) = Wholesale Price Index (WPI)

o There was a vast increase in money supply, especially real balances, over the period of observation.

○ The massive money-supply increase was accomplished quite effortlessly: money supply is highly endogenous in the controlling dynamic system. Hamilton's model is virtually irrelevant.

○ Column (4), in conjunction with the other data, shows how exogenous is the price level of a small, open economy.

§3 LORD BOLINGBROKE'S INFLUENCE (?) ON THOMAS JEFFERSON

(3-1) Forrest McDonald on Bolingbroke [21]

Obsessed with showing that Hamilton's machinations display old-world suavity, McDonald seems to extol corruption. In fact Jefferson admired Bolingbroke's purported constitutional theory, not his enmity towards Walpole. Nor did he think the Federalists the natural party of government: Bolingbroke assailed the entrenched Walpole; Jefferson confronted the aberrant upstart Hamilton [22] and his party, anticipating that his Republicans, the natural party of government, would soon come to power. Bolingbroke went in for wild play to try to reverse the course of British history by unseating the ensconsed Walpole.

"The ideology of the English 'country party' ... went back to the writings of Harrington and Sidney, [23] and ultimately to Virgil *[See the Georgics]* if not further back in time. ... It ripened considerably during the controversy surrounding the South Sea Bubble, most influentially in *Cato's Letters*. It reached full fruition in the writings of Bolingbroke in the pages of *The Craftsman*." (McDonald, 1985, p. 78 — see Plumb, infra, on *The Craftsman*.)

"As it related to liberty ... the most striking attribute of the ideology was its belief that there were conspiracies against freedom." (Ibid., p. 78)

Like most consummate revolutionaries, Jefferson feared counter-revolution — Chs. 2 and 3 suggest he was on solid ground. Bolingbroke's exiguous Country Party was never close to obtaining any power; he was spared fears of counter-revolution.

"Then a serpent invaded the garden. To Bolingbroke, the evil started with the Glorious Revolution, which begat two offspring: the Financial Revolution *[cf. the Bank of England, formed to finance the wars against the Sun King, Louis XIV; and the huge permanent public debt, supposedly subject to Walpole's sinking fund]* and the system of government by ministry, rather than the separation of powers that had been embodied in the ancient English constitution." (McDonald, 1976, p. 19) [24]

McDonald succinctly describes what Bolingbroke peddled as his vision:

"When the gentry was supreme, relations based on ownership of land, honest labour in the soil, craftsmanship in the cities, and a system of deference wherein every man was secure in his place [prevailed]; avarice and ambition were reckoned as cardinal vices." (McDonald, 1974, p. 58)

(3–2) Thomas Jefferson (aet. 77) on Lord Bolingbroke

McDonald tries unsuccessfully to forge a link between Jefferson and Bolingbroke based on chimerical nostalgia for the feudal order — so that Jefferson is transmogrified into a precursor of Ezra Pound and T. S. Eliot. The actual, fragile, link, is based on his perception of Bolingbroke as a friend of Whig liberty: he likens Bolingbroke to Thomas Paine! The *Anas* shows how he got misled: Jefferson deplored corruption; Bolingbroke did not. [25]

"And so the assumption was passed, and 20 millions of stock divided among favored states, and thrown in as a pablum to the stock-jobbing herd. ... This mercenary phalanx ... assured [Hamilton] a majority in both houses; so that the whole action of the legislature was now under the direction of the treasury. Still the machine was not complete. The effect of the funding system and of the assumption would be temporary ... and some engine of influence more permanent must be contrived. This engine was the Bank of the United States ... Hamilton was ... for a monarchy bottomed on corruption." (*Writings*, pp. 669–671)

Now the Jefferson/Bolingbroke puzzle is to be solved. See Jefferson's letter of 19 January 1821 to his grandson, Francis Eppes:

"You ask my opinion of Lord Bolingbroke and Thomas Paine [26] ... [Bolingbroke] was called indeed a Tory; but his writings prove him a stronger advocate for liberty than any of his countrymen, the Whigs of the present day. Irritated by his exile, he committed one act unworthy of him, in connecting himself momentarily with a prince rejected by his country. *[A problematical description of the Old Pretender.]* But he redeemed that single act by his establishment of the principles which proved it to be wrong. ... Lord Bolingbroke's is a style of the highest order. The lofty, rhythmical, full-flowing eloquence of Cicero. ... His writings are certainly the finest examples in the English language of the eloquence proper to the Senate [of Rome]. His political tracts are safe reading for the most religionist. His philosophical, for those who are not afraid to trust their reason with discussions of right and wrong. [27] "You have asked my opinion of these persons, and, to you, I have given it freely. But, remember that I am old, that I wish not to give offence to those who would consider a difference of opinion as sufficient ground for unfriendly dispositions."

Why was Jefferson so chary of being thought pro-Bolingbroke? Perhaps because Bolingbroke's reputation was stained by treason against the régime established by the Glorious (Whig) Revolution.

Adrienne Koch (1943/1957, pp. 9ff.) concludes that Jefferson was influenced by Bolingbroke in the following connections:

KOCH ON JEFFERSON-AND-BOLINGBROKE

ethical relativity; the extraordinary proposition that a hypothesis should be abandoned if ever contradicted by experiment; "deism"; uneasy attraction to Bolingbroke's proposal to derive an ethical system from first principles based on reason (cf. self-evident truths) — Ch. 6 shows how he finally escaped from this quixotic (Kantian) temptation. None of these problematical lines of development touches the Adair-McDonald hypothesis.

(3–3) What Was Bolingbroke Really About?

"Bolingbroke, Henry St John, Viscount, 1678–1751. Tory MP from 1701, Secretary for War, 1706–1708, Secretary of State,

1710–1714; opposed Hanoverian succession, fled to France 1715 and was impeached. Returned and pardoned 1723, wrote and intrigued against Walpole." (*Cambridge Historical Encyclopaedia*, p. 342)

Churchill on Bolingbroke. Winston Churchill (1933/1967) is even less flattering. By August 1714, Bolingbroke's career — reaching its zenith with Queen Anne's dismissal of the Duke of Marlborough in 1711 — had crashed:

"The gradations by which Bolingbroke passed from the position of the most powerful and most brilliant Minister to a culprit awaiting his trial succeeded each other with swiftness. His authority had gone. His policy, if he had one, was gone. Indeed, his only hope was to disavow the designs in which he had dabbled." (Ibid., pp. 519–520)

Plumb on Bolingbroke. J. H. Plumb's assessment is less agitated than Winston Churchill's, but, still, Bolingbroke emerges as a flamboyantly trivial adventurer:

"Walpole's monopoly of power presented a target for the opposition. ... [In 1725] Bolingbroke reappeared on the scene. Through his wife he had got at the Duchess of Kendal, possibly bribed her, but certainly he obtained a hearing with George I. For a time it looked as if Bolingbroke might be pardoned absolutely for his Jacobite excesses. [But] Walpole kept him out of Court politics. By 1726 Bolingbroke realized ... that he had no future so long as Walpole remained the king's minister. [So he and William Pulteny] got together and drew up schemes for raising a whirlwind of opposition which was to blow Walpole out of office. One of their chief instruments was to be publication of a lively, trenchant newspaper, *The Craftsman*. No sooner was it launched than George I had apoplexy and died. They became somewhat quiescent until they saw that Walpole was as much in power as ever and then they began in earnest.

"They made politics immensely exciting. ... So popular did ministry-baiting become that theatre managers tumbled over themselves to put on wildly libellous plays ... The satirisation of the Court and the government had never been so relentless ... [Bolingbroke and Pulteney] exploited parliamentary procedure and made life as difficult as possible for Walpole. ... Just as Walpole tried to gain the independents by posing as one of them ... so the opposition tried to win over the country gentlemen by exposing the iniquities of the Court. To public agitation and parliamentary opposition was added Court intrigue. Walpole had enough enemies at Court for the opposition to find channels. ... The opposition to Walpole had a policy, quite a simple one, and they put it squarely to the public. ... [They] asked how a simple Norfolk squire [Walpole] came honestly by such riches. And as for his so-called financial skill ... with his Sinking Fund, Walpole had bamboozled the public into thinking the nation's debts were being reduced; in fact they were steadily increasing. *[So McDonald weaves surface similarities into a rich tapestry.]* As for his taxation policy, that was designed purely to favour the rich. His main skill was in hiding the fact that ultimately his taxation was borne ... by the landowner. *[Were they not rich?]* ... Bolingbroke, to give the opposition greater universality, developed a superficial political theory, based on the idea of a Patriot King who was to rule with the best men drawn from all factions. His books and pamphlets contained the sententious platitudes with which self-justifying politicians like to lard their speeches. *[This patina delighted Jefferson.]* ... No one, certainly not successful opposition, ever thought of putting his ideas into practice. They gave, however, a fine moral note to the opposition's attack." (Plumb, 1956/1966, pp. 79–84) [28]

"True, the king's [George III's] fit of madness in 1765 provoked a flutter of hope and increased the political stature of [the king's] uncle ... for [the Duke of] Cumberland would be regent if the king went entirely off his head. His quick recovery, however, soon extinguished the awakened ambition. Groups out of office, like Pulteney and Bolingbroke before them, had to fall back on other devices. ... And the easiest way of becoming a nuisance was to rouse the public, to bring discredit on the king and his ministers." (Ibid., p. 101)

So the Adair-McDonald hypothesis pivots on an improper characterization of the outlook and policy of Thomas Jefferson; it is rooted in a wholly incorrect perception of the personality and policy of Henry St Jean, Lord Bolingbroke. They were led into a trap by *Jefferson*, who overvalued the work and character of Bolingbroke.

Hallam on Bolingbroke. The arch-Whig Hallam is not deluded by "Country Party" tosh.

"With all the signal faults of [Bolingbroke's] public character, with all the factiousness which dictated much of his writings, and the indefinite declamation or shallow reasoning which they frequently display, they have merits not always sufficiently acknowledged. He seems first to have made the Tories reject their old tenets of exalted prerogative and hereditary right, and scorn the High-Church theories which they had maintained under William and Anne. His *Dissertation on Parties*, and *Letters on the History of England*, are in fact written on Whig principles ... in their general tendency; however a politician who had always some particular end in view may have fallen into several inconsistencies. The same character is due to *The Craftsman*. ... [The pamphlets against Walpole] teemed with exaggerated declamations on the side of liberty ... The supporters ... of the Walpole and Pelham administrations, though professedly Whigs, and tenacious of Revolution principles, made complaints, both in Parliament and in pamphlets, of the democratical spirit, the insubordination to authority, the tendency to Republican sentiments *[Cf. the ghost of Algernon Sidney]* which they alleged to have gained ground among the people." (*Constitutional History of England*, vol. iii) ·

Hallam's *apologia* for Bolingbroke is strikingly like Jefferson's: they discovered classic Whig traits in Bolingbroke's writings. But Hallam says loudly what Jefferson left unsaid (so far as I know): the Country Party ploy is hokum.

NOTES

1. See Jean Orieux (1970) *Talleyrand ou le sphinx incompris* (Paris: Flammarion). His friend's probity amazed Talleyrand. Thus he learned in 1794, at Albany, that Hamilton was to leave the Treasury to build an estate. "Talleyrand n'en crut pas ses oreilles. Un homme qui abandonnait les Finances pour gagner de l'argent." (Ibid., p. 219)

2. Adam Smith interestingly discusses *areté* in his *Theory of Moral Sentiments (TMS)*: part iii, ch. ii, pp. 113ff. Ch. ii is entitled, "On the Love of Praise, and of that of Praise-Worthiness; and of the dread of Blame, and of that of Blame-Worthiness."

"The love of praise-worthiness is by no means derived altogether from the love of praise. ... The most sincere praise can give little pleasure when it cannot be considered as some sort of proof of praise-worthiness. ... Nature, when she formed man for society, endowed him with an original desire to please, and an original aversion to offend his brethren. ... But this desire of the approbation, and this aversion to the disapprobation of his brethren, would not have alone rendered him fit for that society for which he was made. Nature, accordingly has endowed him, not only with a desire to be approved of, but with a desire of being what ought to be approved of." (*TMS*, pp. 114–117).

This is an excellent, if tedious, statement of the eighteenth-century value system of George Washington and the country that idolized him.

3. I explain in Ch. 7 that Jefferson's intellectual development was stunted by his adhesion to the British empirical tradition, i.e. to Bacon and Locke — Sir Isaac Newton is forever at the pinnacle of science.

4. Henry St. Jean's (Lord Bolingbroke's) opposition to Walpole is fully discussed in Ch. 2 — as is the contention of the Adair-McDonald school that Thomas Jefferson was a vicarious member of the "Country Party." Namier's magisterial study of Georgian corruption should be consulted. And see Ch. 1 for Macaulay's (1848–1861/1980) description, complementing Plumb's. Hamilton's attraction to the British system seems the more bizarre.

5. Hamilton is easily vindicated in other respects. Discrimination between holders of what became the national debt was infeasible — and against the national interest. And James Madison extracted a high price for Virginia's assent to Assumption — knowing that the proposal was in the national interest. See McDonald (1974, pp. 69–70); and the text.

6. Jefferson's *Opinion on the Constitutionality of a National Bank* (submitted to President Washington on 15 February 1791 and reprinted in *Writings*, pp. 416–421) interestingly pitches up McDonald's concession and shows that the economics of his opposition to the Bank are quite sound, while his jural argument is baseless:

"It has been urged that a bank will give great facility or convenience in the collection of taxes ... Treasury orders ... and bills of exchange. [But] Treasury orders ... and bills of exchange [by themselves] may prevent the displacement of the main mass of the money collected without the aid of any bank. ... Besides the existing banks will ... enter into arrangements for lending their agency, and the more favourable, as there will be a competition among them for it."

This is a fine example of good economics bottomed by bad law.

A CRITIQUE OF JEFFERSON'S BANK OPINION

*The "points" are Jefferson's. The Critique submitted (*comme Secretary of State to the President on 15 February 1791, follows the plan of Organization of his Opinion. See* Writings, *pp. 416–421.*

POINTS 2–7

Jefferson alleges that the enabling act for the Bank violates common law principles of mortmain, alienage, descents, forfeiture, escheat, distribution, monopoly, etc. This line of argument is inane unless one assumes, *pace* another of Jefferson's theses, that there is a common law of the United States (see Ch. 3). Then, Points 2–7 make sense — but not Jeffersonian sense! They condemn the Bank proposal, but do not prove Congress's incapacity to exercise such bad judgment.

POINT 8

He argues that the Bank Act is unconstitutional; his argument is propelled by the ineffable express-delegation theory, he concocted with Madison and necessarily abandoned by them when President; if anything, Hamilton's Bank opinion understates the absurdity of "express delegation." In particular, Jefferson offers a dubious gloss of the Constitution's commerce clause — contradicting his earlier, sounder, one. (See Ch. 3.)

The commerce clause empowers Congress to regulate commerce with foreign nations, and among the states, and with Indian tribes. Jefferson's Bank opinion defines "regulation" narrowly, so that the national power over commerce would be emasculated. (See *Writings*, p. 418.) The Bank schema, he writes, is not a regulation — so it is unconstitutional per se: he argues that the Bank's *raison d'être* can be found only in the commerce clause: not in the general-welfare clause. What is more, even if the Bank did regulate commerce, it would be unconstitutional: internal commerce would inevitably be affected.

Is this the source of the bizarre "interstate commerce" conception? No! Alexander Hamilton's otherwise exemplary opinion repeatedly writes "between the states" locution. See Ch. 3.

What about the general-welfare provision in the Constitution's Preamble? Jefferson argues that the "general welfare" language must virtually be ignored: otherwise the national government would enjoy a very broad grant of power: Jefferson transforms "general welfare" into an adjectival expression modifying "expressly delegated" (enumerated) powers in a substantively-insignificant way. (See *Writings*, p. 418.) The implausibility of all this is convincing evidence in favour of nationalists like Professor Crosskey — see Ch. 3.

FURTHER COMMENTS

o Jefferson's phrase, "transportation and re-transportation of money between the states and the Treasury," (Ibid., p. 419) makes sense only if "state" means "people belonging to a state." This slip into correct usage undermines much of his argument.

o *Common Law Redux.* (Ibid., p. 420) He repeats that the Bank bill will "break down the most ancient and fundamental laws of the several states." (Cf. mortmain, alienage, etc.) Jefferson must mean common rules of law, comprising a virtual, if not literal, common law of the United States.

· ° It is not surprising that President Washington — who presided over the 1787 convention in Philadelphia — rejected Jefferson's in favour of Hamilton's argument, pivoting on the Preamble and implied powers of the national government.

7. Hamilton's probity may have stupified Talleyrand, but Dumas Malone told me, near the end of a long *tête-à-tête*, he thought Hamilton a "Napoleonic adventurer."

As for "Napoleon and the Bank of France," an institution patterned to some extent on the first Bank of the United States, Felix Markham (1963) reports that, in 1800, the First Consul persuaded "Gaudin, a distinguished treasury official, of the Ancien Régime, to become Minister of Finance. ... Napoleon arrested Ouvard, the leading war contractor, and forced him to disgorge some of his profits. With the proceeds he founded a new private bank, the Bank of France, to assist the government." (Markham, 1963, p. 161). And "Ouvard considered Napoleon's knowledge of economics ... rudimentary. ... Credit was to him an abstract idea, in which he saw merely the dreams of ideologists and the empty notions of economists." (Markham, 1963, p. 162.) Also see Kindleberger (1984, pp. 100ff.).

Liesse (1911, p. 33) — cited by Goodhart (1985) — writes that Napoleon "transformed the Bank of France in reality into a state bank whose capital was furnished by private individuals." The Bank of France remained privately owned into the twentieth century.

The *conte* supplies context for ours: Hamilton's Bank — in its original conception, if not its practice — fits into Walpole's or Napoleon's system, but seems out of place in a new republic.

8. McDonald (1974, p. 54) describes Franklin's brilliant defence of depreciation of the Continental paper currency as the only way open to Congress to impose efficient, fair taxes.

9. McDonald (1974) extols Hamilton's system because it entails an elastic currency. This *raison d'être* is flawed theoretically and empirically. The flawed operating procedures of the Federal Reserve System (1914 et seq.) pivoted on the notion that money supply should satisfy the "needs of trade." But American experience after 1790 — and, indeed, before — showed American money supply to be intrinsically elastic. Hamilton did not grasp open-economy monetary economics.

10. Hamilton's *Report on the Bank (Bank Report)* is reprinted in H. C. Syrett and J. E. Cooke, eds. (1963) *The Papers of Alexander Hamilton*, vol. vii.

Henry Thornton supports the general drift of Adam Smith's dead-stock analysis, † but correctly dissents from Smith's "conservation principle," quoting the following passage from *Wealth of Nations* at p. 95 of *Enquiry*.

"The whole paper money of every kind which can easily circulate in any country, never can exceed the value of gold and silver of which it supplies the place, or which (the commerce being supposed the same) would circulate there, if there were no paper money." (Adam Smith)

Thornton easily crushes the "conservation principle," along lines anticipating "Radcliffe": the proper subject is monetary properties, not "money," so that the definition of money must be open-ended. These are some of Thornton's interesting points.

o What does Adam Smith mean by paper money? In principle, exchequer bills and India bonds are eligible entries — as is book credit (a principal subject of Thornton's book).

"We are led to judge ... by the term 'paper money of every kind' ... that it was his purpose to include bills of exchange; on the other hand, if all bills of exchange of a country are to be added to the bank notes which circulate, it becomes then so manifest, that the whole of the paper must be more than equal to the amount of the money which would circulate if there were no paper, that we feel surprised that the erroneousness of the position did not strike Dr. Smith himself." (*Enquiry*, p. 95)

o Paper's convenience would lead to demand for a larger monetary mass; and the supply of liquid assets (liabilities) is highly elastic — the financial intermediary's supply curve is almost perfectly elastic over the relevant range.

o Thornton links the analysis to bullionism; not surprisingly, this excellent economist is anti-bullionist.

□ He shatters corollary anticipations of monetary theories of balances of payments at p. 103ff., p. 204 and p. 248. ‡

□ At p. 150, he links up the bullionist and in-room-of-gold topics with panache: bad harvests can lead to gold outflow so that consequences of over-issue of paper and trade deficits due to real shocks are observationally indistinguishable. (Further subtleties are developed at p. 155.)

Concluding Comments. I should stress the malleability of the monetary stock even more than Thornton does. An excess of bank paper may be called an excess supply of intermediation, rectifiable by contraction of bank balance sheets: banks sell assets to the public for their paper — the upshot will not not affect prices or the balance of payments.

° See pp. 206ff. of *Enquiry* — comprising a critique of Adam Smith's shaky analysis of effects of "overissue" of bank paper on conjugate gold purchases by the banks (most likely the Bank of England), so that re-fluxed paper can be redeemed. This is the resulting state of play.

□ Overissue of £$X°$ translates into net redemption at rate £$x°$, where $x°$ has the dimension of a flow. If the volume of overissue is sustainable at £$X°$, the banks will issue new notes at the rate £$x°$ for gold. Their gold and note positions will be constant; and the expense of this eccentric modus operandi is measured by transactions costs in the gold market and in their dysfunctionally hyperactive note operation.

Neither Adam Smith nor Henry Thornton obtains the correct solution.

† See *Enquiry.* A long footnote at p. 176 of *Enquiry* supplies an excellent summary of Adam Smith's argument on paper money in room of gold.

‡ I follow similar lines in ch. 9 of my 1989 book.

11. *The Bank of Amsterdam* supplies an interesting case running in parallel to the text. See *Wealth of Nations*, book iv, ch. iii, part i and Marshall (1923).

Adam Smith points out that the Bank of England was not the first bank set up to help a government: cf. the Bank of Amsterdam. And the Bank of France supplies a later example; as does Hamilton's bank — thus government securities were to be accepted at par against debts owed to the U. S. Government.

The Bank of Amsterdam was a very important supplier of bank money — warehouse receipts for specie of well-specified quality; which, indeed, commanded premia over underlying stocks. In time the Bank of Amsterdam undertook to reduce its dead stock: it lent its deposits — an action Marshall piously calls a fraud.

12. I open up new territory in ch. 8 of my 1989 book. Properties of sophisticated financial systems in gold-standard régimes are explored. A deposit rate is introduced, as is a spread between the deposit rate and Thornton's "mercantile rate of profit." Comparative-statics operations are performed: intensities of demand for non-monetary gold are to shift; or liquidity-preference is to shift. (Monetary assets [liabilities] yielded interest under the classical gold standard — see my 1989 and 1991 books.)

13. McDonald (1974) covers the politics of the Bank in ch. 4; and its economics in ch. 3. (There were but three private banks in the United States in 1790.)

14. The capital structure of the second Bank of the United States was even thinner than that of the first:

"Important blocks of stockholders in Philadelphia and Baltimore paid for their stocks by drawing on balances created at the [second] Bank by discounting the Bank's stock as collateral security. [A later report called this] 'an operation of more potency in creating specie than was ever ascribed to the fabled finger of Midas.' " (Chandler, 1959)

15. DISCUSSION OF SOME TOPICS PERTINENT TO THE *BANK* REPORT

HAMILTON ON THE PRINCIPLE OF REFLUX AND A NUMBER OF OTHER MATTERS

See the *Bank Report*, p. 279. Hamilton argues that excess paper will reflux — and as it will if paper is kept on par with gold; so he is a founding member of the Banking School.

As for "other matters," Hamilton's mercantilist mind-set dominates the *Bank Report*, as it surely did his *Report on Manufactures* (see Ch. 4). But he makes an excellent analysis of competitive supplies of money, along lines drawn by Adam Smith, at pp. 318–319.

He displays his mercantilist mind-set at p. 314: foreign purchases of Bank stock induce specie-inflow. But so would sales of any asset to foreigners.

At p. 321, he discusses absorption of part of the basal money stock by government land sales. But, if the land business is "absorbing cash," additional specie can easily be attracted: in a small, open economy, the equilibrium stock of money is determined by demand.

On land prices. Hamilton discusses land prices in the *Report on Public Credit* (*Papers*: vi, p. 72). He associates the post-Revolution decline in land prices with a "shortage of money."(!) But the controlling "pure" cost of capital was determined in world markets, not by domestic money-supply — and money-supply is endogenous in a small, open economy.

McDonald (1974, 1979) interestingly explains how the funding pro-gramme (see [2-3]) could be adverse for land speculators: debt-issues, tenderable for public lands at par, appreciated under the programme: the value of the tender-preference shrunk.

The Washington Administration was endemically sympathetic to land speculation, the national pastime, in which the President was con-summately expert. Hamilton sought to mitigate adverse effects of as-sumption on land speculators by discounting land-prices for those pre-committed to government-debt tenders for public land.

James Madison on the Bank — His Double Jointedness. President Madison supported recharter of the Bank in 1809–1810. And,

"On April 10, 1816, Madison signed a bill creating the second Bank of the United States, requested by him twenty-four years after he denied the power of Congress to create it." (Brant, 1970, p. 254)

Madison justified his *volte face* by claiming that time revealed the Bank's *necessity*. In any case, the triumvirate's practice transformed it operationally: debt-reduction replaced debt-management in high policy — the Bank's operational reform cured its potential defects.

His equivocations do not make him wrong coming and going. Thus the following jeremiad on the flotation of the first Bank's stock is plausible — despite President Washington's praise of the operation:

"Public sale of the national-bank stock built up Madison's dislike of the whole transaction. Shares paid for with depreciated public securities *at face value* were instantly resold at a profit of fifty per cent." (Brant, 1970, p. 254, Brant's emphasis)

(The stock flotation of "Madison's" Bank of the United States, the second Bank, gave rise to the gibe about the fabled finger of Midas.)

Wettereau (1937, 1943) on the Performance of the First Bank. Wettereau (1937, p. 268) explain's Gallatin's Byzantine 1809 *Report* arguing for a modified recharter of the first Bank. The *Report* states that, in 1809, the

Bank's specie holdings were $5m; and its notes and deposits, $8.5m. The facts, known to Gallatin, are that the Bank held $15.31m in specie; and its notes and deposits were $17.32m: Hamilon's Bank came to be managed like the Bank of Amsterdam, before it bit into the fractional-reserve apple. The Jeffersonians transformed the Bank into a staid institution whose policies little resembled the Keynesian innovations contemplated by Hamilton.

American bullion and specie holdings increased substantially as part of the revised programme. Witness Wettereau's table, displaying the Bank's specie positions.

It is easy to support one of Wettereau's conclusions: "the total holdings of specie by the Bank and its branches varied greatly from year to year." Indeed, specie positions and money-supply measures of small, open economies in specie-based régimes are both endogenous and flexible.

The table shatters the principal Hamilton-McDonald hypothesis — that the American money supply was highly inertial. Thus there was acute pressure, in 1804-1805, on the American specie position. "By May 1806," Wettereau reports, "the specie problem was no longer acute, the supply at hand exceeding the Bank's note circulation."

Table [15]: Wettereau's (1937) Data

Source: Wettereau (1937)

Note: State banks held $9.5m in specie in 1811

Date	Bk. Specie $m	Date	Bk. Specie $m
31 Jan. 1792	00.510	11 Nov. 1800	05.672
22 Jun. 1792	00.949	May 1801	04.076
27 Dec. 1793	01.202	26 Nov. 1801	05.247
03 Apr. 1795	00.597	Nov. 1802	08.000
1 Jan. 1796	01.437	Feb. 1809	15.311
04 Jan. 1799	03.075	11 Jan. 1811	05.010

16. See McDonald (1979, p. 72). McDonald indicates that the remark was made between 1784 and 1787.

Malone (1951, p. 29) reports that Hamilton wrote, "a public debt is a public blessing," in the New York *Daily Gazette*, 10 February 1790.

17. In my 1991 book (see chs. 2 and 5), I suggest that assumption of Italian debt by "Brussels" poses knotty problems akin to those confronted by the Washington Administration after Assumption.

18. See Henry Adams (1879/1943) — book iii, "The Treasury, 1801-1813," pp. 267ff. The Jeffersonians disowned Hamilton's public-credit/money-substitute idea, concentrating instead on debt-retirement. Nor was there any proper reason to exploit this ingenious "public-credit/money-substitute" ploy: money supply automatically floated up and down to equilibrium levels.

Jefferson scouted any notion that pumping up the money-mass would lower the real cost of capital. (Indeed the classical theory he adhered to wisely rejects the idea that low interest rates are intrinsically desirable — relying instead on interaction of thrift and productivity in rough general equilibrium.)

Madison and Gallatin valued the Bank's administrative convenience; and Jefferson at least tolerated it for the same reason. Still there is no evidence — despite Henry Adams's "Soundness School" gloss — that state banks were typically imprudent. See the Appendix to Chapter 2.

***

The first Bank's primary contributions were operational. Thus its branch system facilitated distant remittances. See Wettereau (1943) and Wettereau (1937).

19. I discuss the pure theory of cyclical effects of intervention in *The New Art of Central Banking* (1991). See ch. 6.

20. EXTENSION OF THE ANALYSIS TO LAND BANKS AND OTHER ALTERNATIVES TO ORTHODOX MONETARY SYSTEMS

Land Banks Past. The following are among sources on land banks and *Assignats*. Earl J. Hamilton (1968, pp. 78–81; 1969, pp. 123–149), S. E. Harris (1930) and *The Wealth of Nations*. (Adam Smith disdains John Law.)

o Hamilton properly faults land-bank operations up to 1791 in the *Bank Report*.

o Thayer (1953) explains that colonial land banks were flawed: the volume of their potential issue was open-ended.

○ The colonial land banks were to lend out provincial paper money on the security of real property — unimproved lands, farms, houses, etc. The paper was to be backed by land. But, as the system operated, the value of land, measured in paper money, was a function of the volume of paper; depreciation of the paper in terms of land automatically increased the paper value of the currency's "backing"; there was no intrinsic constraint on the volume of issue.

○ A commitment to redeem paper with land would have constrained issue. Nor did the American colonials, or the designers of the *Assignats* schema, entirely miss this point:

"The idea presented itself of using Church lands confiscated in the Revolution as security for the issue of paper money. Notes would be 'assigned' to given land. ... Assignment did not last long." (Kindleberger, 1984, p. 99)

□ Convertibility into land, a non-fungible asset is not feasible. But the land-bank idea is resuscitable, if it is reformed. The quantity of irredeemable paper may be permitted to expand so long as a unit is worth more than x^* acres of land; and must be contracted so long as it is worth less than x^* acres of land. (We tacitly assume that demand for real balances is inelastic at the margin.)

Generalized Land Banks Future. Reformed land banks are not viable; and would not have been in the seventeenth and eighteenth centuries. We simply seek to extract logical properties of systems suggested by historical land banks in order to deepen insight into the principles governing giro systems that will replace bank-based debt-discharge mechanisms. And the following point is central to the innovated version's *raison d'être*. A proper "land bank" does not own land or hold liens against land. A land standard is created, but the authorities do not deal in land.

The specie, or land, value of a unit of paper issue can vary, but emission of inconvertible paper money is securely bounded by the system's operational rules.

The seventeenth and eighteenth century projectors of land banks (swindling aside) clumsily groped towards the dénouement of innovated clearing systems I discuss in my 1986, 1988 and 1991 books. They sought a broader foundation for monetary issue: specifically, they proposed to expand "backing" to encompass "land." In the limit of this line of attack, the idea of monetization becomes so extensive that "money" goes off the board.

All this said, land banks remain a colourful curiosity, not a significant precursor of modern monetary theory.

21. See Forrest McDonald (1985).

22. Jefferson did not go so far as John Adams, who called Hamilton "the bastard brat of a Scotch pedlar," but he surely thought Hamilton an *arriviste*, "ungrateful to the country that received him."

23. See Algernon Sidney (1698/1990) *Discourses Concerning Government* (Indianapolis, Indiana: Liberty Classics; 1990), T. G. West, ed.

West reports that the *Discourses* were written between 1681 and 1683, and that they were primarily "a response to a book by Sir Robert Filmer defending the divine and natural right of kings to absolute rule." (Ibid., p. xvi) See Filmer's *Patriarchia: A Defence of the Natural Power of Kings against the Unnatural Liberty of the People*, published in 1680, but written much earlier.

Garry Wills (1978) writes of Algernon Sidney's (1623–1683) influence on Jefferson. Sidney's work can be mined for many nuggets asserting the natural rights of man; but I see no connection between Sidney — who chose exile rather than recant his acts as an officer of the (Cromwellian) Commonwealth and was executed for Treason against the Stuarts — and Bolingbroke, whose career was ruined by his treasonable transactions with the Stuarts. What is more, far from being nostalgic about patriot kings, Sidney was virtually a republican.

24. McDonald points out that Hamilton readily abided Walpolian corruption, but erroneously implies that corruption is intrinsic to sophisticated finance.

What is more,

○ The British government ceased to be based on distributed powers.

○ Jefferson abhorred Montesquieu's class-based version of "checks and balances."

○ Jefferson's assault on Hume may lend the idea that he favoured Parliamentary supremacy. But he was an American, not an English Whig; and he was an exceptionally strong President.

25. Plumb shows that Bolingbroke's Arcadian theme is frivolous: it was meant merely to titillate sundry country gentlemen — as part of a prolonged, vicious onslaught on Sir Robert Walpole. The fact that Bolingbroke opposed Walpole's system (so attractive to Hamilton) does not equate Jefferson with Bolingbroke.

26. "They were alike in making bitter enemies of the priests and pharisees of their day. Both were honest men, both advocates for human liberty. ... No writer has exceeded Paine in ease and familiarity of style, in perspecuity of expression, happiness of elucidation and in simple and unassuming language. In this he may be compared with Dr Franklin; and indeed his *Common Sense* was, for a while, believed to have been written by Dr Franklin."

27. This tantallizing remark looks back to Greek philosophy while tacitly rejecting Christianity. See Bertrand Russell:

"The close connection between virtue and knowledge is characteristic of Socrates and Plato. To some degree, it exists in all Greek thought, as opposed to that of Christianity. In Christian ethics, a pure heart is the essential, and is at least as likely to be found among the ignorant as among the learned. This difference between Greek and Christian ethics has persisted down to the present day." (*History of Western Philosophy*, p. 109)

Jefferson's remark looks forward to the twentieth century: in his ripe thought the moral sense is a replacement set whose specific content is determined by a sort of utilitarianism, one divorced from possessive individualism. See Ch. 6.

28. See Lord Acton's *Essays in the History of Liberty* (Indianapolis, Indiana: Liberty Classics; 1985), J. Rufus Fears, ed. — a sometimes vapid work. (Cf. John Emerich Edward Dalberg-Acton. The first essay may have been published in 1877.)

○ At p. 221, he describes the dinner given by Jefferson for Hamilton and Adams, recollected by Jefferson in his *Anas*.

○ At p. 224, he refers to proposals to the Philadelphia Convention (1787) by John Jay and Alexander Hamilton to abolish the states. Is it plausible that a Convention calmly receiving such a proposal would have settled on a compact between sovereign states, as Jefferson and Madison said they did? (See Ch. 3.)

Appendix to Chapter Two

Politics and Banking Theory

The appendix keys on Bray Hammond's *Banks and Politics in America — from the Revolution to the Civil War* (1957). After exposition of some economic and jural theory, Thomas Jefferson's financial system is restated — and contrasted with Alexander Hamilton's. Then the régime of "private" banking subsequent to the fall of the Second Bank of the United States is assessed. "Free banking" is supported.

§1 MONEY (CURRENCY) *V.* CREDIT

Some preliminary remarks.

o American confusion between "money" and "credit" goes back at least as far as the colonial-currency debates: it was credit, not currency, that was being sought. And the theory of the Federal Reserve system is rooted in banking-school proposals to tie currency-change to credit-emissions based on "needs of trade."

o Jefferson and Madison did not confuse "money" with "credit." Nor did John Adams.

□ "Thomas Jefferson *[in 1813]* ... attributed complaints about scarcity of money, not to farmers, but to speculators, projectors and commercial gamblers." (Hammond, 1957, p. 34) His argument pivots on a nascent version of the "forced saving" argument that was to come: see my 1991 book, especially ch. 9. "Commercial gamblers" would offer newly acquired (and, indeed, "created") bank notes for real resources, perhaps distorting "natural" channels in which "abstinence" flowed towards creation of productive capital by deficit spending units.

□ Hammond (1957, p. 233) describes Madison's (1815) message to Congress urging a national bank in order to secure a uniform *currency.*

Currency and Credit in the 18th and early 19th Centuries

Bank notes were mere tokens, or counters, in commercial transactions — as are bank deposits now: banks are virtually irrelevant for transfers of real resources. Temin's illustration of a Charleston, S. C. – New York City commercial nexus circa 1836 goes far to make my point.

"Consider the effects of a bill of exchange drawn for a shipment of cotton, drawn, let us say, in Charleston on New York. ... It was discounted by a bank in Charleston [for the bank's notes] and remitted [sent] to New York ... where it was sold or held until it came due. At the time it was sold or came due, the Charleston bank acquired a credit in a New York ... bank. ... A Charleston bank could not continue indefinitely to pile up credits in New York; they would have to be spent. And the way they were spent was to finance purchases in New York for people in Charleston." (Temin, 1969, pp. 33–34)

The Charleston bank requires no capital to do this work. Its notes can be construed as counters signifying magnitudes of clients' claims on New York entities. Once collected, the counters may be burned — along with the bill of exchange; at the end of the transaction, the cotton-shipper has his furniture (or some other New York purchase) and the New York merchant his cotton. There are no financial residues.

Bank-profit has two sources: commission and float. At any time a certain volume of (putatively non-interest-bearing) bank notes will be in circulation; the notes were sold for interest-yielding paper.

Adam Smith on Banking. Adam Smith commands the correct theory. See vol. 1, p. 257ff., of the Everyman's Library edition of *The Wealth of Nations.* He shows how banks obtain seigneurage from "issue"; and the business of banking is to pivot on the supply of currency. [1] (John Adams calls extraction of seigneurage by banks a cheat upon the public.)

Banks, as generic credit intermediaries, lie outside our brief: the Chicago school's one-hundred-per-cent-reserve proposal does not block credit intermediation; what is more banks may simply sell claims on themselves for "old" securities, so that the volume of intermediation has increased without markets for "new" debt being affected.

Alexander Hamilton — a more-sophisticated financier than John Adams — grasps the wrong end of the stick: in 1779–1780 (formulating his first Bank plan) and in 1791, he suggests that real credit flows will be stimulated because of bank-balance-sheet expansion, not merely because of improved circulation. Hamilton mixes up valid theories of currency with chimerical ones of resource accumulation. (Henry Thornton firmly grips the right end of the stick — see his *Enquiry*, p. 120, for one of many excellent passages on the ontology of paper credit.)

Stock-Flow Theory and "Currency v. Credit"

Effects on credit of banks of issue are studied in the *forced savings* literature (see my 1991 book). Both "forced saving" and "seigneurage" concern extraction of resources by paper-issue, purchased by the public more or less voluntarily. [2] During "forced saving," accleration of the money-stock redirects resource-flows; but do Hammond et al. mean to say that acceleration of the stock of Bank liabilities (assets) is a sine qua non for economic progress? (What is more, acquisition of "old" paper expands bank balance sheets as much as new lending.) Indeed, expansion and contraction of the mass of mediation is logically independent of real-resource flows. Currency is the *raison d'être* of a clearing-bank system. [3]

As for Alexander Hamilton:

○ I much doubt if "forced saving" and its "accelerationist" corollary crossed his mind.

o His continuing concern, after persuading the President and Congress that there should be a Bank, was about currency and service of the national debt (in particular the Bank's liaison with markets in national debt).

§2 CORPORATIONS, MONOPOLY AND THE BANKS

Corporation [4]. An incorporated company of traders having (originally) the monopoly and control of their particular trade. ... (OED)

The most powerful discriminant between Hamilton's and the Jefferson-Jackson "school" of banking concerns "public" *v.* "private" banking, not "enterprise" *v.* "agrarianism."

Hammond notes the association of "corporation " with "monopoly" in the eighteenth and early nineteenth century. But he does not follow through: he confuses opposition to the Bank with opposition to banks: true, Jefferson disliked banks of issue (and "bank" came to mean "bank of issue"); but he was also committed to laisser faire (see §4). In particular,

o Hammond knows that the privileges of the Bank of England constrained development of private banking in England; but seems unaware of the strength of English support for *free banking.* (See Véra Smith, 1936/1990, White, 1984 and Bagehot, 1873/1927.)

o He interestingly discusses (ibid., pp. 126–127) efforts to give the first Bank of the United States a monopoly of the nation's banking business. Thus Fisher Ames, writing to Alexander Hamilton on 31 July 1791, hopes that state-chartered banks will be absorbed by the Bank of the United States (BUS).

Adam Smith (WN) on Corporations and Banks

Adam Smith (*WN*, book i, ch. x, part ii) takes for granted that corporations have monopoly power (cf. municipally chartered corporations). And he writes that,

"The great and general utility of the banking trade when prudently managed has been fully explained *[in book ii; cf. infra]*. But a public bank which is to support public credit, and upon particular emergencies to advance to government the whole produce of a tax, to the amount, perhaps of several millions, a year or two before it comes in, requires [more] than can easily be collected into any private copartnery." [4]

The BUS was a public bank, requiring much more capital than any private bank: in a system in which public credit tends to vanish (cf. Jefferson's system) the "great and general utility of banking" can be obtained through private, perhaps "free" banking. [5]

§3 TWO TRADITIONS IN BANKING THEORY AND POLICY

Hammond (1957, p. 3) limns the *yin* and *yang* of banking legislation: the Tunnage Act of 1694 (authorizing incorporation of the Bank of England) contrasts with the Bubble Act of 1720 which "got its real and lasting force from the revulsion following collapse of speculation in South Sea Company stock."

"The Parliamentary Acts of 1694 and 1720 are associated, therefore, with two traditions, which being transplanted to America were for more than a century in growing conflict. The act of 1694 is a monument to faith in the power and beneficence of credit, the act of 1720 is a monument of distrust of it."

Hammond must mean *issue,* not *credit.* And this confusion besets the development of his principal theme, agrarianism *v.* enterprise. (Jefferson is to represent "agrarianism" and Hamilton "enterprise.") These are some variations on the theme.

○ America's agrarians demanded conservative banking; but businessmen (see enterprise) urged liberality: going back to colonial times, "the debtors who owed the most and whose influence was the greatest were business men; and their complaints were ... that borrowing was not easy enough." (Ibid., p. ix)

□ More precisely, "agrarianism" led to more-dispersed banking. In Adam Smith's terms, it promoted "private" over "public" banking. For one thing, both Jefferson and Jackson enjoyed massive urban support: Jefferson is the virtual founder of Tammany Hall.

□ Predominance of quasi-public banking, i.e. a highly regulated banking system displaying intimate ties between high finance and Washington, was more the accidental product of the Civil War than the sort of ineluctable dominion described by Hammond: Hamilton's system was dead until the exigencies of the Civil War generated the war-finance/bond-support nexus that induced a watered-down re-emergence of Walpole's system in America in 1863.

○ "At the same time that British authorities were still governed by the conservative spirit of the Bubble Act, Hamilton and the Federalists pushed the program of enterprise vigorously and creatively forward." (Ibid., p. 8)

□ What enterprise? Why should paper-jobbing be indispensable to enterprise? And Ch. 4 shows that the Federalists looked back across the ocean towards cozy business with Mother England; that the uncertainties of continental development consternated them.

□ How can so good a writer make so egregious an error? He confuses paper-issue with release of real resources; he confuses "money" with "credit."

Hammond (1957) later pitches up his "yin and yang" theme and overplays his hand: we see that his affinity for the Federalists and Nicholas Biddle is based on their pre-Keynesianism; and his contempt for the financial system of Jefferson, Gallatin and Jackson pivots on their laisser-faire principles, verging on those of the new classical macro-economics. And other historians, including Forrest McDonald, are also besotted with "Keynesianism."

"The monetary views of Albert Gallatin and of Andrew Jackson are both obsolete, but Nicholas Biddle's, thanks to the quite independent teaching of Lord Keynes, are alive and orthodox. Biddle sought to make monetary policy flexible and compensatory rather than rigid. [6] He had a vision of national development to which abundant credit was essential. [7] The majority of his country have agreed with him. ... They have shared his bullishness and his energy. They have no use for General Jackson's primitive ideals of a simple agrarian society, except in their nostalgic moods. They have not understood Gallatin's noble aversion for the fierce spirit of enterprise. [8] They have exploited the country's resources with abandon, they have plunged into all the debt they could. [9] ... One cannot help admiring in Nicholas Biddle, as in Alexander Hamilton, the perspicacity and statesmanship to which the complex potentialities of the American economy were so plain and the imagination which formulated the means of realizing them. In the twentieth century, moreover, they may perhaps be admired the more because they were uncontaminated by the doctrine of laisser faire, which to the Jacksonians and their contemporaries seemed to be the last and sufficient word in economic and political wisdom. 'The world is governed too much,' the Jacksonians declared; *'laissez nous faire!'* Accordingly they did all they could ... to undo what Alexander Hamilton and Nicholas Biddle had done to make the state effectively responsible in the economy, and much of the subsequent governmental history in America is concerned with restoring and enlarging federal responsibilities over money which the Jacksonians uprooted." (Hammond, 1957, pp. 541–542)

Hammond disingenuously gives the show away. The proper issue is not "agrarianism" (pastoral nostalgia) *v.* "enterprise." Rather it is *étatisme*/Keynesianism *v.* liberalism. In the narrow frame of banking/currency, the issue boils down to "corporate" *v.* "private" banking, to quasi-monopoly *v.* competition in banking. [10] Nor is that all:

"Alexander Hamilton prepared America for an imperial future of wealth and power, mechanized beyond the handicraft state of his day, and amply provided with credit to that end. Thomas Jefferson represented the yeomanry and designed for America a future of competence

and simplicity, agrarian, and without the enticing subtleties of credit."
(Hammond, 1957, pp. 121–122)

Surely one-hundred-per-cent-reserve banking would not have barred America's emergence as an industrial power. What is more:

o Hammond confuses Jefferson's undoubted preference for a yeoman America, *ceteris paribus*, with willingness to interfere with spontaneous development of American industry, a preposterous suggestion, refuted by the facts displayed in Ch. 4 and contradicting Jefferson's clear commitment to laisser faire.

o Again, Hamilton's system (or "vision") was dead at the outbreak of the American Civil War; and was restored only when the exigencies of war-finance made a watered-down version of his system irresistably attractive.

§4 A SYLLABUS: JEFFERSON ON BANKING AND CURRENCY

o A metallic currency is to be preferred.
□ If there must be a paper currency, it should be nationalized. (See Note 2: Jefferson's *raison d'être* for this dictum is faulty.) A number of comments are called for:

¶ Under free banking, the government's influence over the supply of currency is less than under a nationalized currency — still, under a gold-standard, the quantity of money is endogenous, transients aside.

¶ Jefferson's distaste for laisser faire in currency, like Milton Friedman's, is at odds with his libertarianism.

¶ I suspect that Jefferson would have finally supported a paper currency wholly backed by specie or bullion (as did Ricardo). Such a currency has many practical advantages; and the principles governing its mass are in perfect aligment with the "hard money" ones of Jefferson and Jackson. That said, Jefferson's banking system coheres with the one-hundred-per-cent-reserve banking plan of an earlier Chicago school: the currency would be secure ("hard"); real finance-potential would be unimpaired by making "money" independent of "credit." (Jefferson is quite explicit on all this.)

o Perhaps Gallatin [11] brought Jefferson around on banks of issue: "if there must be banks, let them be Republican."

o Jefferson's banking theory is sometimes inaccurate and incomplete. Still, he sees that banks of issue properly influence currency, not credit (he often wrote about speculators and shadowy schemers obtaining loans of bank notes; and he ridiculed claims that inflation of the money supply was good for trade).

□ Madison too properly distinguishes "credit" from "currency." His message to Congress, in 1815, states that a second BUS was necessary for a sound currency. Visions of Jefferson and Madison, sprawled under leafy trees, reciting Virgil's *Georgics*, yearning for Arcadia, are absurd.

o Ch. 2 shows how slight is the cost of "dead stock"; and a Ricardian bullion standard finesses the awkwardness of hard money.

§5 RETROSPECTIVE AND PROSPECTIVE FEATURES OF PRIVATE AND PUBLIC BANKING

Hamilton's Bank plan circa 1779–1780. Hammond (1957, ch. 2, pp. 40ff.) describes a precocious plan for a "public" bank Alexander Hamilton formulated when still in military service:

"He thought that the scheme stood on a firm footing of public and private faith, that it linked the interest of the state intimately with the interests of rich individuals; and that it afforded, 'by a sort of creative power,' a circulating medium that would be 'a real and efficacious instrument of trade.' The plan also comprehended a foreign loan of two millions sterling and that the bank would be recompensed by the government which was to be its principal borrower and own half its stock."

Reflection erodes the appeal of Hamilton's "public" banking bent; Walpole's system was unsuited to the new republic. [12]

Banking under the Jeffersonians and Jacksonians. American banking grew rapidly after the demise of the BUS in 1811 (see the Jefferson-Say correspondence reported in Ch. 4). Jefferson's contention that the BUS stifled competition in banking, and so its growth, is buttressed. Hammond (1957, pp. 145ff.) awkwardly picks up the pieces:

○ There were 90 American banks by 1811, "when the BUS was let die."

○ There were 250 banks by 1816; and more than 300 by 1820.

○ How could banking have thrived more under its friends than it did under its purported enemies?

□ The clue is this: the Federalists were eager to promote what has become the liaison between Wall Street and Washington (cf. public banking); they opposed or sullenly abided the westward expansion of the United States that fostered rapid growth of private banking.

□ Hammond picks up the clue without overtly abandoning his nostalgic-agrarianism theme; his argument becomes rather incoherent.

"The result was an alignment of the new generation of business men with the genuine agrarians. ... The success of the Republican *[i.e. Jefferson's]* party in retaining the loyalty of the older agrarians while it recruited among the newer entrepreneurial masses was possible, Prof. Beard has explained, because Jefferson's academic views pleased the one group and his practical politics propitiated the other. It was also because equality of opportunity in business and the principle of laisser faire could be advocated with a Jeffersonian vocabulary." (Hammond, 1957, pp. 145–146)

Bray Hammond seems disingenuous. A fairer, less convoluted, conclusion is that the Jeffersonians substantially abandoned their reservations about banks of issue ("if there must be banks, let them be Republican") while fully implementing their commitment to a competitive ("private") banking system, conjugate to their hostility to monopolized ("public") banking.

○ He reluctantly sees the light!

"The Jeffersonian impetus in banking may well have begun in reaction to the Federalist chararacter of the first banks, all of which were conceived and defended as monopolies." (Hammond, 1957, p. 146)

He dissembles: the "Federalist character" of the first Bank of the United States was truly decisive; and this huge corporation had at least quasi-monopoly powers (and privileges).

Over-Issue by Private Banks: Myth and Reality. Albert Gallatin surely thought that private banks "overissued" from 1811 to 1816. His initiative for the second Bank of the United States pivots on this perception, along with his desire to maintain "orderly markets" in the national debt generated in the War of 1812 and facilitate further government borrowing: such exigencies have led to Walpole-like institutions throughout American history.

The fragile data permit two observations:

o The war itself surely accounted for a substantial portion of the expansion of paper issue: monetary discipline disintegrated in the general shambles brought on by this war (mordantly entertainingly described by Henry Adams).

o Restraint exercised by private banks after (say) 1836 bars the conclusion that private banking in nineteenth-century America (under a specie-standard régime) was intrinsically unstable.

Turning to the 1836–1863 interval, Rockoff (1971, pp. 454ff.), following Temin (1969), dismantles the "myth of wildcat banking."

o Profit maximization does not mandate "over-issue" of bank notes (or bank deposits, conjugate to bank lending or "old"-asset purchases). "A profit-maximizing bank would regulate its note-issue so that the marginal returns from any issue of notes were equal to the present value of the costs of issuing the note and administering the increased circulation." (Rockoff, 1972, p. 454)

o Hayek (1976) and Klein (1974, 1975) also point out that the Soundness School are wrong: in private-bank equilibrium, the real value of a bank note does not sink to its negligible marginal cost of production — a monopolist with nil production-cost selects an output-level at which demand is unit-elastic.

91

o Temin (1969) shows that reserves were relatively substantially higher in frontier regions (the alleged habitat of wildcat banking) than in the supposedly more staid East: in 1837 the Northwest's reserve ratio was 0.32; and New England's 0.09.

o I pointed out in 1988 that the note-redemption policy of the BUS was not a central-bank control technique: in equilibrium, pairwise comparisons are symmetrical, regardless of relative bank-sizes. And study of Temin (1969) and Rockoff (1971) buttresses my 1988 analysis. (i) In models of price leadership, the leader, operating relative to a derived-demand curve, sets a price which the other members of the industry, the followers, take. Under the plausible stipulation that, in equilibrium, a unique proportion is borne by BUS liabilities to total banking liabilities, the equilibrium size of the industry comprising the second Bank of the United States et al. is determined by the BUS. (ii) The Bank's target for aggregate bank liabilities can be hit if it properly controls its note-issue: it need only know the value of the "unique proportion."

¶ The derivation is speciously precise: open Economy E's banking industry nests in a complete global model so that its monetary authority cannot control its money supply.

Conclusions. Jefferson's preference for private over public banking is supported by two distinct lines of argument.

o Private, more or less "free," banking was in fact successful, on the whole, from (say) 1836 to 1863. Nor would the paper-thin capitalization of the Banks of the United States have ameliorated the banking panics (accompanied by suspensions of convertibility *comme* safety valves or circuit breakers) that did occur; indeed, in 1930, the well-capitalized Federal Reserve failed monumentally when confronted with an interconvertibility crisis. (Cf. currency *v.* bank money.)

o The Banks of the United States ("public" banks) were globally insignificant. Hamilton and the other Federalists misperceived the controlling economic universe; they operated what became known as a (Irving) Fisherine model of money-supply in a global economy controlled by a specie-flow mechanism; American money-supply was determined by American demand for money in a context like that in which a household "determines" its money stock relative to myriad constraints. (See Girton & Roper, 1978; and my 1986 and 1988 books.)

□ Peter Temin (1969) explains that such events as the intensification of opium use in China (reversing absorption of precious-metal production by Oriental demand) and the Baring Brothers crisis in London caused American monetary volatility — not the actions of Andrew Jackson and Nicholas Biddle. "The antebellum economy was vulnerable to disturbing influences, but it was not a source of them." (Ibid., p. 177)

○ *Au fond*, Jefferson, a good "classical" economist, believed that political liberty hinged on economic decentralization; his banking policy pivots on this point. His reputation was swept away by the now-shipwrecked "Keynesian Revolution," which exalted Hamilton and the Federalists.

NOTES

1. Jefferson's argument takes Adam Smith's slant. (See Hammond, 1957.) He preferred a metallic coinage; and said that, in any case, seigneurage from paper currency should belong to the nation, a faulty argument applying equally well (badly) to any profit obtained in the economy. What counts here is that Jefferson, like Adam Smith, centres on currency, not on provision of real capital by banks (*sic*).

Hammond misconstrues the point and sends the analysis into his "agrarianism *v*. enterprise" domain, so that Jefferson is skewered by naïve Keynesian dogma.

2. I explain in 1988 and 1991 that Henry Thornton's *Enquiry* anticipates the forced-saving literature; and, along with Ricardo (1817), avoids the flaws of Wicksell's analysis. Thornton touches on the topic many times. The tenor of his analysis is put succinctly at p. 232; and the full context (i.e. "the true wealth of nations") is especially salient at p. 274.

3. I prescind from development of a proper money-supply theory. Hugh Rockoff (1971, p. 450) remarks that Temin (1969) et al. build a Fisherine money-supply model for a smallish open economy on a specie standard. Rockoff may not realize how disastrous is the error he has uncovered — see my *Open Economy Monetary Economics* (1989).

Adam Smith deploys a basically correct money-supply theory, subject to Henry Thornton's critique, limned in Ch. 2. He emphasizes how endogenous is money supply in the circumstances described here. And he probes effects of "over-issue."

4. Tax-anticipation certificates comprised much of the paper-issue in eighteenth-century British North America. See B. D. Smith (1985, 1988).

5. Henry Thornton devotes ch. 7, pp. 168ff. of his *Enquiry* to "Country Banks — Their Advantages and Disadvantages." He supplies an able rationale for central banking; indeed his readers are apt to forget that central banking as such was not yet in place.

Putting Hamilton and his bank into perspective, Ch. 2 shows that the BUS was to engross the national banking business, not keep tabs on a growing number of thriving private banks. Thornton's interesting analysis is not *à propos*.

6. Jefferson's banking model, like that of the earlier Chicago School — and Milton Friedman's money-growth rule — is both non-compensatory and rigid. Hamilton's system anticipates Keynes's monetary theory of real action.

The Federal Reserve's flawed money-supply theory goes back to Hamilton's, as was explained in Ch. 2. (Bray Hammond was a Federal Reserve official.)

7. Hammond mirrors the endemic confusion between money and credit which has dogged the Federal Reserve from its inception: it is like original sin. Biddle's Bank, like banks of issue *en général*, was a paper merchant; and banks of issue have, at most, indirect effects on flows of real resources from surplus to deficit spending units: cf. "forced saving."

8. Frank Knight's *Ethics of Competition* has much in common with Gallatin's views, interestingly depicted by Hammond, loc. cit. See "Frank Knight and the Ethics of Competition" infra.

Industry grew dramatically under "Jacksonian" principles; and Andrew Jackson was ardently supported by the urban "masses."

9. Hammond is confused. Expansion of the curency stock is logically unconnected with enlargement of the flow of real credit. This is the *raison d'être* of "one-hundred-per-cent-reserve banking."

Thomas Jefferson's command of this point is displayed in his letter to his son-in-law, quoted in Ch. 2, "let those who wish to commit their capital ... "

10. Adam Smith describes the development of private banking in Glasgow (see Timberlake, 1978 and White, 1984).

"I have heard it asserted that the trade of the city of Glasgow doubled in about fifteen years after the first erection of banks there; and that the trade of Scotland has more than quadrupled since the erection of the two public banks at Edinburgh *[the Bank of Scotland, established by an act of Parliament in 1695; the Royal Bank, by Royal Charter in 1727].* ... If either of them has increased in this proportion, it seems to be an effect too great to be accounted for by the sole operation of this cause. ... That the banks have contributed to this increase cannot be doubted."

o Thornton's *Enquiry* reworks Smith's comments, but retains their purport.

o Hamilton favours "public" banking; Jefferson (perhaps reluctantly), "private" banking. The dramatic expansion of the American economy mandated decentralization of banking: Hamilton's *dirigisme* was feasible only for a smallish American economy.

11. Gallatin induced President Jefferson to accept a New Orleans branch for the BUS.

Andrew Jackson's attacks on banks are tinctured with hypocrisy: Hammond (1957) shows that he enjoyed frequent recourse to them. Jefferson, who loathed Jackson, was intransigent on the point, but hardly hypocritical.

12. See Hammond (1957, p. 229). Circa 1815–1816, Albert Gallatin looked to a second BUS to buoy up the massive government debt incurred in the War of 1812. And the Civil War (1861–1865), generating huge government-debt, gave another, more or less permanent, fillip to the Walpole-Hamilton schemae.

Chapter Three

Thomas Jefferson's Constitutional System: Bad Law; Good Economics

§1 PRELIMINARY REMARKS

Should obscure transactions with divine entities or fictions about barbarian liberty bottom political theory? The political philosophies of Hobbes, Filmer, Locke, et al. seem untenable. And I prefer David Hume's calm "scepticism," leading to his empirical political theory, to Sir Edward Coke's Whiggish myths, enshrined by Lord Macaulay.

Thomas Jefferson found the myths published by Whig historians useful — and may have even believed them. (He found the Ossian saga quite credible.) He conjectured that American liberty is secreted in the interstices of remote British history (but took a pragmatic view of the foundations of nascent French liberty in 1789). British constitutional history is pivotal for his Constitutional system.

Jefferson's theory of the American Constitution seems to me disingenuously unsound. But it supports a sound economic system — in the school of Adam Smith, J.-B. Say and Destutt de Tracy. (Alexander Hamilton's mercantilist system presages the monetary theories of real action projected by Keynes's *General Theory*.)

Jefferson — reacting to American colonial experience under mercantilist regulation and *dirigisme* in France — was more concerned to block "commercial policy" than to support states' rights to impose it; and the United States Government was more apt than the impotent state authorities to concoct *dirigiste* plans. True, the states were prone to impede commerce by obstructing imports from other states, by making their paper legal tender, etc. But the harsh constraints he envisaged for the national government ran parallel to a constitutional view that restrained state governments from impeding value-enhancing trade among private agents.

Jefferson on Some of the Principal Themes of Ch. 3

Section 2 concerns Whig and Tory (Humean) theories of British stitutional history. Jefferson, anticipating some of the most rapturous passages of later Whig historians, supports the Whig view. In an important letter (5 June 1824) to Major John Cartwright — labelled by the editor of *Writings*, "Saxons, Constitutions and a Case of Pious Fraud" — he sets out the fiction he had long lived by, the gist of his quarrel with Hume and Blackstone (who seem to me sounder).

"[The Anglo-Saxons] doubtless had a constitution. ... They have left fragments of their history and laws, from which [such a constitution] may be inferred with considerable certainty. ... And although this constitution was violated and and set at naught by Norman forces, force cannot change right. ... In the pullings and haulings for these antient rights between the nation, and its kings of the races of Plantagenets, Tudors and Stuarts, there was sometimes gain, and sometimes loss, until the final re-conquest of their rights from the Stuarts *[an ultra Whig view of the Glorious Revolution]*. The destitution and expulsion of [the Stuarts] broke the thread of pretended inheritance, extinguished all regal usurpations, and the [British] nation re-entered into all its rights; and although in their bill of rights they specifically reclaimed some only, yet the omission of the others was no renunciation of the right to resume their exercise too. ... The new king received no rights or powers but those ex- pressly granted to him. [1]

"It has ever appeared to me, that the difference between the Whig and the Tory of England, is that the Whig deduces his rights from the Anglo-Saxon source and the Tory from the Norman. And Hume, the great apostle of Toryism, says, in so many words, note AA to ch. 42, that in the reign of the Stuarts, 'it was the people who encroached upon the sovereign, not the sovereign who attempted ... to usurp the people.' And again [quoting Hume] 'the commons established a principle which is noble in itself, and seems specious, but is belied by all history and experience, that the people are the origin of all just power. ... ' And where will this degenerate son of science, this traitor to his fellow men, find the origin of just powers, if not in the majority of the society? Will it be in the minority? Or in an individual of that minority?

"Our Revolution commenced on more favorable ground. ... We had no occasion to search into musty records ... or to investigate the laws and institutions of a semi-barbarous ancestry. We appealed to those of nature, and found them engraved on our hearts." (Ibid., pp. 1490–1491)

This vigorous syllabus is problematical. Hume has no need to derive the *raison d'être* for liberty, but the famed revolutionary, Jefferson, does. The American Declaration of Independence is an *apologia*; and the authors of the seventeenth-century English revolutions nurtured the myths, cherished by Macaulay, Burke et al., in a quest for legitimacy.

Jefferson is ambivalent on Whig hagiography. The British must rummage through musty records to prove their liberty. Americans need only search their (Scottish School) hearts: even Whig lawyers of Jefferson's time had to own that Parliament's jural claims on the American colonists were quite compelling. [2]

There is more. Jefferson's democratic evil genius prevails over his beneficent Whig angel. Defying the Constitution and *The Federalist*, he unleashes the *majority of society* — Rousseau's scourge of liberty (or Democratic Despotism) — against the mild, sensible Hume. [3]

In a letter, dated 12 August 1810, to William Duane (see Ch. 4), labelled "Hume and Montesquieu", Jefferson supplies a more-measured gloss of his position. (See *Writings*, pp. 1227–1231.)

"Everyone knows that judicious matter *[manner?]* and charms of style have rendered Hume's history the manual of every student. ... He first took up the history of the Stuarts, became their apologist, and advocated all their enormities. To support his work, when done, he went back to the Tudors, and so selected and arranged the materials of their history as to present their arbitrary acts only ... and, still writing backwards, he then reverted to the early history, and wrote the Saxon and Norman periods with the same perverted view." (Ibid., p. 1228)

Hume, supported by modern scholarship, merely describes the wide scope of the Crown's prerogative in remote English times.

Section 3 concerns Sir Edward Coke (commonly called Lord Coke), the fountainhead of the theory (or myths) of historic Whig liberty. Jefferson's letter of 17 February 1826 to James Madison ("Take Care of Me when Dead") both extols Coke and laments Blackstone's massive influence on the theory of the Constitution; it is indeed an early exercise in political correctness.

"In the selection of our law professor we must be rigorously attentive to his political principles. You will recollect that, before the revolution, Coke [on] Littleton was the universal elementary book of law students, and a sounder Whig never wrote, nor of profounder learning in the orthodox doctrines of the British constitution, or in what were called English liberties. You remember also that our lawyers were then all Whigs. But when ... the honied Mansfieldism of Blackstone became the student's hornbook, from that moment the profession (the nursery of our Congress) began to slide into Toryism, and nearly all the young brood of lawyers are of that hue. They suppose themselves, indeed, to be Whigs, because they no longer know what Whiggism or republicanism means." (*Writings*, pp. 1512–15, at pp. 1513–14)

Again, the most attractive rationale I can eke out for Jefferson's flawed Constitutional theory is his effort to promote "laisser faire" economics; and his hope, amid the "Terror" of the Alien and Sedition Acts, that the states would be bastions for defence of liberty. Still much of his Constitutional theory became embodied in Supreme Court doctrine.

I reckon that the American Constitution was intended (whatever that means) to establish a truly national government; but the compromises necessary to secure its ratification, and the sea change in American politics, marked by Jefferson's election to the Presidency in 1800–1801, bottled up Constitutional nationalism.

§2 WHIG AND TORY THEORIES OF THE BRITISH CONSTITUTION

Professor Hugh Trevor-Roper seems to me exactly right.

"Sir Edward Coke, the great champion of the English common law, discovered a continuous parliamentary constitution going back to the ancient Britons. More-cautious antiquaries were prepared to settle for the Anglo-Saxons. In the course of the seventeenth century, [Parliamentary] antiquaries built up a historical 'myth' [that] the English monarchy had always been implicitly contractual. Even the rude fact of the Norman Conquest had not interrupted this good old Anglo-Saxon tradition, for William the Conquerer (they said) had accepted and perpetuated the existing constitution ... guaranteed by the Common Law, strengthened by Magna Carta, guarded by Parliament, and those kings who had sought to break the contract [were] deposed. [Witness Edward II in 1327, Richard II in 1399, Charles I in 1649 and James II in 1688.] Of the 'Tudor despotism' of the 16th century, these historical theorists did not find it convenient to speak.

"David Hume ... [advanced] ... a completely new philosophy of history. ... Hume did not believe that sacred 'constitutions' were the guarantee of 'liberty'.... Hume devalued all constitutional ideas." (Hugh Trevor-Roper, 1968/1979, pp. 9–11)

John Morrill (1985) also sees the upshot of the Glorious Revolution of 1688 differently from the Whig historians. For Morrill the principal consequences of "1688" were Parliamentary supremacy and the system of Sir Robert Walpole. [4]

"James II had to secure election of a Parliament which would endorse his actions [including aggressive use of his prerogative to enhance the position of Catholics, removal of three-quarters of all JPs and remodelling of borough charters]. ... The birth of a male Catholic heir in June 1688 ... and the trial of seven bishops led major figures across the political spectrum to invite William of Orange *[married to Mary Stuart]* to England to protect the Protestant religion and ancient liberties. ... In the event, the king had a form of nervous breakdown and fled the country without a fight." (Ibid., p. 204)

WHAT HAPPENED IN THE REIGN OF WILLIAM AND MARY?

"In order to protect England from Louis XIV, who sought to restore James by force of arms, William *[ruling alone after Queen Mary's death]* had to maintain a standing army and a large bureaucracy, and he built up a body of 'place men' in the Commons to ease government measures through the House. ... Two developments of the reign were of lasting significance. One was cabinet government, a small group of ministers drawn from within Parliament, who enjoyed the support of the Houses and could guarantee parliamentary support for government business. *[The American Constitution of 1787/1789 was meant to set up a more balanced régime.]* The other was creation of a National Debt, that vast capital sum raised to wage war with Louis XIV. This debt was never to be repaid. Already by 1701, annual sessions of Parliament were required to raise the necessary taxation to meet interest payments. At long last, faced by the threat of foreign invasion to impose popery and arbitrary government, Englishmen submitted themselves to universal rational and substantial taxation. The bureaucracies of war and finance which had eluded the Stuarts were created to keep them out, and they gave the Hanoverians the means to conquer and defend a world empire." (Ibid, pp. 204–205)

Macaulay and Hallam on Whig Myths

Macaulay argues (loc. cit., p. 11) that, if the Plantagenets had been able to unify their French and English dominions, England's identity would have disappeared. And Macaulay thought linguistic subsubordination the worst disaster of all (!): "the noble language of Milton and Burke would have remained a rustic dialect." (See the Everyman ed., vol. 1) Thank God for the follies and vices of the seventh Plantagenet sovereign, King John (!). With his death in 1216, one year after Magna Carta,

"commences the history of the English nation. ... [It is during the 13th century] that we must seek for the origin of our freedom, our prosperity and our glory. Then it was that ... our fathers became emphatically islanders. ... Then it was that the common law rose to the dignity of a science." (*History of England*: 1: pp. 12–13)

Macaulay then expounds on the Whig syllabus — see pp. 21–24, ibid. He buttresses his contentions with the authority of Henry Hallam, who sinks his claws into Hume's *History*:

"The government of England was a monarchy bounded by law, far unlike the actual state of the principal kingdoms on the continent. ... Hume has laid hold of a passage in Raleigh's *History of the World [supporting the idea that Britain's kings were absolute; but Hallam heatedly insists that Raleigh exercised no valid authority — op. cit., p. 278]* The arbitrary acts of our Tudor princes were trifling in comparison with the despotism of François I and Henri II. ... No permanent law had ever been attempted in England, nor any internal tax imposed, without consent of the people's representatives. ... Henry VII, the most rapacious, and Henry VIII, the most despotic, of English monarchs, did not presume to violate this acknowledged right." (Hallam, op. cit., pp. 277- 278)

o Hume surely does not deny that liberty flourished in Britain: he merely contends that enlightenment matters more for liberty (and other values) than the distribution of power between Parliament and the Crown.

o To the end of his days, Hume insisted that Whig dogma misspecified the British Constitution. "I was so little inclined to yield to [the Whigs'] senseless clamour, that in above a hundred alterations, which further study, reading, or reflection engaged me to make in the reigns of the two first Stuarts, I have made all of them invariably to the Tory side. It is ridiculous to consider the English constitution before that period as a regular plan of liberty." [5] And he is supported by modern scholarship.

o Hallam's admissions that there were was no more than occasional parliamentary resistance to Henry VII and that Parliament stood prorogued more than seven years during the reign of Henry VIII seems to support Hume.

o Hallam's assertion that "no permanent law had ever been attempted in England" without the consent of the Commons is deceptive. The Crown often ruled by decree. Such episodes were called temporary; but Parliament was often out of session for years.

What is more, he acknowledges that ad hoc taxes were often imposed.

Hallam roundly asserts, as does Macaulay, that the Stuarts sought to overthrow Britain's constitution. Hume disagrees.

Hume's History (vol. v) on James I and Charles I

JAMES I

o There is going to be a head-on clash with the Whigs. At pp. 87–88, Hume refers to unprecedented interference by Commons in foreign affairs.

o James I argued that "the privileges of parliament [are] precarious." Hume sides with Parliament: "in fact no age can be shown when the English government was altogether an unmixed monarchy." (Ibid., pp. 94–95)

o At pp. 128–129, Hume tepidly defends the Stuarts along an azimuth anticipating the conclusions of Morrill (1985). The Stuart kings were compelled to guard their prerogative, and to seek to expand it, by their inability to obtain a secure, ample revenue:

"By the changes which have since been introduced, the liberty and independence of individuals has been rendered much more full, entire and secure. ... And it seems a necessary, though perhaps a melancholy, truth that, in every government, the magistrate must either possess a large revenue and a military force, or enjoy some discretionary powers, in order to execute the laws, and support his own authority." (Ibid., pp. 128–129)

o Hume explains why the Whig historians tend to finesse the Tudor era:

"The liberty of the press was incompatible with [Tudor] maxims, and ... was therefore quite unknown in that age. Besides employing the two terrible courts of star-chamber and high commission, whose powers were unlimited, Queen Elizabeth exerted her authority by restraints upon the press. She passed a decree in her court of star-chamber, that is by her own will and pleasure, forbidding any book to be printed in any place but in London, Oxford and Cambridge." (Ibid., p. 130)

CHARLES I

○ As in France about 150 years later, instability was generated by chronic inability of the Crown's revenues to feed its insatiable appetite for funds: "the nation was very little accustomed at that time to the burthen of taxes, and had never opened their purses in any degree for supporting their sovereign. [Even Queen Elizabeth could not] extort from [Commons] the necessary supplies." (Ibid., p. 159)

○ "Liberty" did not include freedom of conscience. Toleration of the Romish religion was anathema to the Commons. (Ibid., p. 165)

○ The Commons "resolved to seize the opportunity which the king's necessities offered them of reducing [the prerogative's] compass. ... They boldly embraced the side of freedom, and resolved to grant no supplies to their necessitous prince, without extorting concessions in favour of civil liberty." (Ibid., p. 160)

○ Until the seventeenth century, "the history of England had never ... afforded one instance where any great movement of revolution had proceded from the lower house." (Ibid., p. 170)

○ In 1626, shortly after the accession of Charles I, [6] the Commons went onto the offensive — in connection with grants of supply made at the beginning of a king's reign. "[Commons remonstrated] against levying of tonnage and poundage without consent of Parliament." (Ibid., p. 173) But these levies, together with taxes on merchandise devised by James I, would have deprived the king of almost half his revenue. He would have been reduced "to total subjection and dependence."

○ Hume supplies a litany of royal violations of the "rights and liberties" of the commons: "forced loans ... taxes without consent of Parliament, arbitrary imprisonments, the billeting of soldiers, martial law." (Ibid., p. 192) These grievances were to be redressed: English history was to be rewritten.

"[The commons] aimed only at securing [powers or privileges] which had been transmitted [to] them from their ancestors: [they] summoned up the ancient constitution, not any infringement of royal prerogative or acquisition of new liberties."[7]

Hume was an honest writer, not a foe of liberty. His rejection of revealed religion made him reviled by many who were chagrined at his *History's* repudiation of other myths; Jefferson loathed him for different reasons.

○ The king's men argued that the Stuart régime had become far more liberal than the lamented Tudor one. The star chamber and the court of the high commission had been abolished. The prerogative had shrunk and triennial parliaments had been ordained (v: 454). But the Parliamentary commissioners did not want a settlement. Their appetites grew upon what they fed on. (v: 456, a point not completed even at p. 524)

○ Hume's summing up of "the tragic death of Charles" displays his benevolent scepticism.

"[Are] the people, in any case, entitled to judge and to punish their sovereign? ... Government is instituted, in order to restrain the fury and injustice of the people; [8] and being always founded on opinion, not on force, it is dangerous to weaken, by these speculations, the reverence, which the multitude owe to authority. ... But between resisting a prince and dethroning him, there is a wide interval; and the abuses of power, which can warrant the latter violence, are greater and more enormous, than those which will justify the former. [9] ... Charles himself [finally] inferred that it is dangerous for princes, even from the appearance of necessity, to assume more authority, than the laws have allowed them. [10] But it must be confessed, that these events furnish us with another instruction, no less natural, and no less useful, concerning the madness of the people, the furies of fanaticism, and the danger of mercenary armies." (Ibid., pp. 544–546)

At their best, Jefferson and Madison took Hume's point about the madness of crowds. But Jefferson never quite repressed Rousseau-like proclivities; he did not always bottle up his Promethean temperament.

§3 SIR EDWARD COKE: A FOUNTAINHEAD OF WHIG DOGMA [11]

○ The mystique of the common law burgeoned under the Tudor monarchs — whose rule was quite absolute. And "the parts of the common law relating to the powers of the crown were particularly obscure." Furthermore, appeals, based on the common law, against the crown almost always failed. (Holdsworth, 1924, vol. 5, p. 435)

○ But, in late Tudor times, a parliamentary opposition began to emerge. Leading members of the opposition sought out obscure precedents that justified constraints on exercises of royal power. Coke, *comme* Whig, emerged in this connection: "the most offensive of attorney generals had been transformed into the most admired and venerated of judges." (Ibid., pp. 435–436)

○ Coke ingeniously inflated ancient precedents into Whig principles. He carried all before him. (Ibid., pp. 471–472)

○ He conjured up out of thin air antique Parliaments subscribing to the common law. Indeed he "discovered" that "the common law owed little or nothing to the Conqueror or his successors." (Ibid., p. 475)

○ He inspired the seventeenth-century Whigs. But, "we now see that the public law of the seventeenth century was very obscure; and that, though the victory of constitutional principles was undoubtedly beneficial to the state, the legal principles upon which the leaders of the constitutional opposition relied were often very dubious." (Ibid., pp. 475–476)

A young lion, Thomas Hobbes, appears — Holdsworth explains that Coke was temperamentally a Tudor statesman.

"[Hobbes] approached English constitutional law and [political liberty] from a new and critical standpoint. ... Coke's [jural] and political theories were essentially mediaeval, and therefore wholly illogical from the standpoint of the new doctrine of sovereignty. ... Hobbes attacked Coke's legal theories with those weapons which Austin has made familiar to modern lawyers, [12] and the subject matter of some of the rules laid down by him, with those arguments based on reason and utility which Bentham was later to urge with so great an effect. There is a very modern ring to his criticisms. Law, he says ... is but the command of the sovereign which, though it may be iniquitous, cannot be unjust. Neither case law nor custom is truly law. Law is no product, as Coke would have it, of artificial reason: [13] it should be so clear to ... ordinary reason ... that a layman should be able to give as good an opinion [on its meaning] as a lawyer. The absurd rules which Coke either explains or defends should be altered; and the useless distinctions which he invents should be declared to be baseless. Hobbes's criticisms were approved by Sir James Stephen." (Ibid., pp. 480–481)

"Hobbes and Stephen saw part of their truth, but not the whole. ... Bacon suggested a much more conservative reform *[than codification]*." (Ibid., pp. 485–487)

Jural Inertia and Liberty. Jefferson, committed to Coke, and doting on common-law forms, was a jural conservative. And codifiers are apt to be more concerned with "logical coherence" than with liberty; régimes of liberty seem incoherent to radicals, including the younger, if not the ripe, Jeremy Bentham. (See Elie Halévy's *The Rise of Philosophical Radicalism.*) But jural inertia and incoherence — as it seems to radicals — are indispensable concomitants of liberty. [14] Holdsworth's conclusion, that it would have been disastrous for England to have adopted a Napoleonic code *à la* Hobbes and Bentham, seems warranted. Coke's mediaevalism blocked needed reform. But reform's victory could have been Pyrrhic: Hobbesian rationalization was, as Hobbes readily owned, congenial to tyranny.

"The statute book badly needed a revision in Elizabeth's reign, but no revision was undertaken until the nineteenth century. ... If English law had been restated in the seventeenth century along the lines advocated by Bacon ... the Admiralty, the Star Chamber and the ecclesiastical courts would have all put forward their claims; and these rivals of the common law would have gained a permanently larger share of jurisdiction. ... If the common law had lost its supremacy, would Parliament have gained the victory? And if it had gained the victory without the help of a common law which claimed to be the supreme law of the state, would our constitutional law be what it is today? This may be doubted ... In the seventeenth century the Parliament handsomely repaid this debt by helping Coke and his fellow lawyers to maintain the mediaeval conception of the supremacy of the common law, and to apply it to the government of a modern state. ... If their influence upon some parts of our modern law has not been wholly satisfactory, let us remember that they saved Englishmen from a criminal procedure which allowed use of torture." (Ibid., pp. 491–493)

§4 JEFFERSON ON THE AMERICAN CONSTITUTION

A syllabus of selected themes on the interpretation of the American Constitution is set out; and Jefferson's positions are glossed relative to the "bad law/good economics" conjecture. But the Kentucky Resolutions (1798) cannot be squeezed into so parsimonious a format. True, they exhibit bad law; but their context is strictly political — liberty seemed threatened by the President in Congress (analogously to King in Parliament). Jefferson thrashed about, to defend liberty against the assault of the high federalists; he hit upon nullification. This was neither the first nor the last time that he displayed a capricious penchant for wild play.

American Constitutional Themes; Corollary Cases

THE THEMES

1. Implied Powers
2. Common law of the United States (?)
3. The Commerce Clause
4. Ex post facto clauses, etc. (See especially *Calder v. Bull* [1798])
5. Judicial Review — of Congressional and Presidential action
6. Judicial Review — of state action

(1) Implied Powers

(See Ch. 2: especially Jefferson's Opinion on the Constitutionality of the Bank of the United States.)

The Constitution's enumerations are not meant to limit the spheres of action of the departments, or branches of the American national government. The strict-construction idea, projected by Jefferson and Madison during the Bank debate, was little more than an *ignis fatuus*. I think Professor W. W. Crosskey proves this point. And, indeed, Jefferson, before he perceived the scope of Hamilton's Walpolian system, seems to have favoured general legislative powers for Congress as early as 1775 and as late as 1787.

"[In 1787] Jefferson, in a letter to James Madison, had denounced as a 'sophism' and 'gratis dictum' the view then being urged by some of the less truthful advocates of the Constitution that Congress ... would be limited to 'the powers especially enumerated' therein. ... Jefferson ... did not, at that time, oppose ... a scheme for general legislative power for Congress. For, after some initial floundering around when he first began to think about the subject in the previous summer, Jefferson had written to George Wythe ... that, in his opinion, the several states ought to be left with power only in [whatever concerned themselves alone].

"As a member of the Second Continental Congress, in 1775, Jefferson had been, according to his own explicit statement, one of the enthusiastic supporters of the plan for an American 'General Congress' [proposed by Benjamin Franklin]." (W. W. Crosskey, 1953, vol. 1, pp. 211–212)

Why were there enumerations? [15]

"A considerable proportion of Congresss's enumerated powers ... previously belonged to the old Congress under the Articles of Confederation ... [The necessity of doing this arose from] the fact that the old Congress's powers were not merely legislative, but partly executive and judicial; and from the fact that the Federal Convention desired to divide the powers of the old Congress between the President, the Judiciary, and the new Congress, under the Constitution." (Ibid., pp. 410–412)

So all the powers exercised by the old Congress were enumerated for clarity's sake.

Now turn to Constitutional enumeration of powers that the British Crown exercised and which the Convention wished to confine to the new Congress. Crosskey, at pp. 415ff., bases himself on Blackstone, who exercised great sway in America.

"In the light then of all the foregoing facts, it is clear that ... it was desire to establish a threefold division of power within the government, and desire to cut down or control 'the executive power,' which dictated the enumerations and specifications the Convention made." (Ibid., p. 418)

An Example. The founders decided to vest in the President the English king's veto power, subject to important limitations: an "enumeration" was mandated.

There were subtractions too, especially in the commercial field: patents were to come under legislative power (administered by the President). Since that changed British practice — described in Blackstone's *Commentaries* — another "enumeration" was mandated.

Crosskey's contention that the Constitution's enumerations (and other details he cites) show that the powers Congress "was not to have, as against the states, played a very small part" in the "enumerations." (Ibid., p. 425)

This is how Crosskey ends his excellent ch. xv (vol. 1, pp. 409–467):

"It has been demonstrated clearly, as to all these specifically enumerated powers that their 'special and careful enumeration,' to use James Madison's words, was not according to the ideas of 1787, 'nugatory' and 'purposeless,' and certainly it was not 'improper' or misleading, even though Congress was, at the same time, given general legislative power. [Enumeration] of these powers was inescapable, given the notions of 'executive power' under the prior law, and the thing the Federal Convention had determined to do." (Ibid., p. 467)

The law evolved in a way that infuriatingly perplexes the laity: the Jefferson-Madison "strict construction" rubric was preserved; and the substance of American Constitutional law came to jibe with

Crosskey's interpretation. Was the upshot bad law and bad economics?

The Tenth Amendment to the 1787 Constitution. This amendment, reserving to the states powers not expressly delegated to the national government, gives colour, if not credence, to the Jefferson-Madison Constitutional theory; and must be explained away by constitutional nationalists like Professor Crosskey.

Crosskey's treatment of "reserving" is masterly. But he barely copes with "expressly." A "nationalist" is pretty much reduced to saying that, since an express-delegation interpretation makes the national government both impuissant and incoherent, classic rules of construction bar it. [16]

"Reserve" is a technical legal term that had, for a long time, commonly indicated "the creation of a new interest, never previously existing as such, in respect of a thing conveyed. The most common example, with which most eighteenth-century Americans were probably familiar, was the conveyance of a piece of land, whilst creating (reserving) at the same time, a right of way, never previously existing as such over it." (Ibid., vol. 1, p. 701) He concludes that,

"The use of the word 'reserved' implied, first of all, that the whole thing — 'sovereignty' — out of which the 'reserved powers' of the states were 'created,' i.e. 'reserved' — had, at the same time been conveyed to the nation. ... That the foregoing was all fully intended by the draftsmen and proposers of the Tenth Amendment — i.e. by the First Congress — is further confirmed by the presence in the amendment of the words, 'or to the people.' The reason for the inclusion of these four words has long been something of a puzzle; but it is not a puzzle if 'reserved' is used in its technical sense." (Ibid., p. 705)

Thus reservations run only in favour of grantors, here the people of the United States (so that "states" must mean "the people of X, the people of Y, etc."): " 'the States respectively' and 'the people' in the Tenth Amendment do not therefore signify different persons; they signify the same persons." (Ibid., p. 705)

Jefferson's Presidency illustrates the disingenuousness of the "express-delegation." He was imprisoned by his rhetoric: he toyed with a Constitutional amendment to validate the Louisiana Purchase — but myriad other Presidential actions would then require Constitutional amendment. (His embargo wholly contradicts his putative Constitutional theory — see the Appendix to Ch. 4.)

Taking a different tack, attribute a proper (privately-held) Constitutional theory to Jefferson. *Comme* laisser-faire economist, he very plausibly recoiled from its implications — including legitimacy of activist economic policy (now jurally dominant as a result of tortuous twisting of the enshrined "Jeffersonian" Constitutional theory!). Enter, Alexander Hamilton! Jefferson thought Hamilton an ambitious, very talented "Anglican" adventurer who had the ear of President Washington; and Hamilton did propose to install Walpole's corrupt system in America. Jefferson made a jural *volte face*. And he would have written better Kentucky Resolutions if the threat to liberty posed by the Alien and Sedition Acts had been less sinister. He did not always scruple.

(2) Common Law of the United States?

Jefferson emphatically, and repeatedly, denied that there was a common law of the United States. [17] Crosskey, after setting the stage, vividly describes the heat generated by the issue.

"There was nothing at all to alter the earlier American view of the common law as a single complex body of traditionary law that the entire country had in common. ... [Long before 1787] there was a vast body of customary law in use in the American states that was common to England and all America." (Ibid., vol. 1, p. 607)

As for the issue's high political charge,

"Randolph fell out with Washington and the Federalist party in 1795. [18] Thereafter he sought favor with the 'States Rights' group that Jefferson, [and] Madison organized. But though Jefferson had [held] the same view in his recent past ... Randolph ... was taxed with this view and asked, apparently, what his view was now." (Ibid, p. 630)

Why was the "U. S. common law" issue so highly charged? The Federalist-packed national courts would outrank the state benches; and, in time, America would experience the sort of uniformity established in Britain, so that the state courts (dominated by Republicans) would be thoroughly subordinated to the higher national courts across the judicial board. And Congress's inherent power to amend a common law of the United States would establish "the complete generality" of Congress's power.

The proper issue concerns restraint of the national government, not aggrandisement of the power of the wretched state governments. Of course, the "wretchedness" of the state governments appealed to proponents of laisser faire.

There is more. The judiciary act of 1801 (enacted by the Federalists just before Jefferson become President) supplies evidence, despite its suspect timing, that the Constitution is compatible with a national common law. Perhaps naïvely, Crosskey opines that the Jeffersonians opposed the act because it implied a "national legislative power of equal scope." (Ibid., vol. 2, p. 763)

Swift v. Tyson belongs to a set of cases putting a Jeffersonian patina on the law of the Constitution — much to Crosskey's chagrin: hence *Politics and the Constitution.* His cup of gall runs over: the decision in *Swift v. Tyson* was written by Justice Joseph Story, whom he revered. [19]

"It was contended, however, in *Swift v. Tyson*, that certain later New York decisions had established a local state rule to the contrary, which the U. S. Circuit Court in New York was bound to follow in preference to the two existing Supreme Court precedents." (Ibid, vol. 2, pp. 856–857)

Crosskey is convinced that Justice Story "must have been well aware of the historical inaccuracy of what he said." (Ibid., p. 860) Why did he so travestize? He feared that a correct decision would precipitate a political firestorm blowing away Constitutional correctness. Keynes (1936, p. 183), quoting Ibsen, supplies a *motif.* "The wild duck has dived down as deep as she can get — and bitten fast hold of the weed and tangle and all the rubbish that is down there, and it would need an extraordinarily clever dog to dive after and fish her up again." [20]

Why TJ Opposed a National Common Law. The common law of England did not, and does not, brake the action of Parliament in the economic sphere and offered scant protection for "civil rights" in the eighteenth and early nineteenth centuries. So a common law of the United States, interpreted by Jefferson's enemies on the federal bench, would shield massive Hamiltonian economic interventions. And the Federalists, who had passed the detested Alien and Sedition Acts, became still more "monocrat" and "Anglomanic" out of power; they even posed a puny counter-revolutionary threat at the Hartford Convention (1814–1815). "Bad law" looked prudent, before becoming habitual, after Jefferson's time.

(3) The Commerce Clause

Jefferson's interpretation of the commerce clause looks silly — but, bizarrely, Alexander Hamilton can be cited in its favour. The principal ingredient of the stew is "interstate commerce," a wretched locution, not in the Constitution, whose meaning has long been twisted out of recognition of what it may have originally meant.

The commerce clause, properly read, confers vast latent commercial powers on the national government; liberal economists are still aghast at the potential for *dirigisme* embedded in the national commerce power — restored by macabre twists of the Jeffersonian "interstate" doctrine enshrined in Constitutional orthodoxy.

Crosskey seems correct: "commerce among the states" must refer to business (commercial) dealings among people resident in the various states: otherwise the clause makes no sense. Yet Hamilton's Bank opinion (1791) repeatedly refers to commerce *between* the states. And John Marshall's opinion in *Gibbons v. Ogden* (1824) is a mixed bag for Crosskey — and me! Marshall's opinion (for the Court) holds that the United States are not a single nation in *in re* all commercial regulations — only for those of commerce concerning more states than one. Crosskey correctly says that this entails much more than interstate commerce *pur et simple*; but the brunt of the decision is against him — indeed, like Jefferson, he rails against Marshall's excessive *obiter dicta*. (See Ibid., pp. 252–259) The commerce power was finally construed *à la* Crosskey; and the national government became more bloated and intrusive than anyone imagined possible: "bad law" postponed the dénoument. [21]

(4) Ex Post Facto Clauses, etc.

Narrow construction of the national government's power to regulate commerce doubtless appeals to liberals — who also seek to curtail the ability of state governments to impede commerce, thus clogging exchange. Jefferson's professed constitutional system impaled him on the horns of a dilemma; there was a price to be paid for bad law.

As early as 1798, in *Calder v. Bull*, the Supreme Court construed ex post facto narrowly, confining its purport to criminal statutes, although Jefferson, in his private correspondence, took a broader view, so that a law impairing a patent would be an ex post facto law. Indeed "ex post facto" seems to have been broadly construed: thus legislation making paper money legal tender was typically considered ex post facto legislation.

The *Dartmouth College* case (1819), extending a number of "Georgia" cases, got things back on track. In the upshot, the states were amply restrained from impairing exchange; just as the national government was transiently impeded from much exceeding a laisser faire brief. (The Supreme Court's *Dartmouth College* ruling held that a charter from a state was a contract which could not be impaired by future legislation unless the right had been *reserved* — so that Crosskey's insightful analysis of "reservation" is further supported — see Haines, 1959, p. 311.)

The *Dartmouth College* case was extended by *Fletcher v. Peck* (1810) and *D. C. v. Woodward* (1819). Haines (1959) describes the dénouement from a Jeffersonian slant that may still predominate:

"The cases of *Fletcher v. Peck* and *D. C. v. Woodward* [began] an extensive series of restrictions upon state legislation made possible through the fact that many laws may be attacked [as infringements] of property rights — [which were thus substantially] placed entirely beyond the control of state legislatures. The decision aligned on the side of nationalism the economic interests of corporate organizations." (Ibid., pp. 313–314)

Put aside the paucity of "corporate organizations," let alone big business (!), in 1810; Haines's outlook is tainted by prairie radicalism or populism. John Marshall is flat-footedly on the side of free economic exchange: Jeffersonians, like Haines, run the risk of breaking the liberal china if they fail to distinguish constraint on national-government intrusion into commerce from constraint on state government obstruction of commerce; both constraints are mandated by Jefferson's dogma.

Concern about intrusion by the national government into commerce, taken into the limit, would castrate the commerce power. See "Substantive Due Process." It is preposterous, I should say, to argue that the American Constitution, properly construed, virtually bars economic legislation because it inevitably changes the jural map. (Cf. ex post facto laws: "compensation" is infeasible in the wake of complex legislation: to require it is virtually to bar economic legislation.)

"The whole doctrine of 'substantive due process' is without justification in the actual words of the document, as against either Congress or the states. ... The paradox remains that a good deal of what the Court has done in the name of 'substantive due process' against the states is not unconstitutional." [*I.e. the ex-post-facto, contracts and full-faith-and-credit clauses of the original Constitution suffice to strike down legislation struck down under cover of substantive due process.*]

"The situation is different against Congress. This is true, not only because there is, in the Constitution, no 'equal protection' guaranty applying to Congress. ... It is true likewise because, more generally, there is, against Congress, no general right in the Supreme Court of judicial review." (Ibid., vol. 2, p. 1155)

(5) Judicial Review of Congressional and Presidential Action

"Judicial review" is coloured by the supremacy of Parliament in Britain after 1688. So Jefferson's hostility to judicial review of Congressional and Presidential action — and so to Marshall's dictum in *Marbury v. Madison* (1803) — has solid jural foundations. But Jefferson went farther: he opposed intrusion of the national judiciary power into the sphere of state action.

Crosskey shares Jefferson's position on judicial review of acts of Congress (!):

"That there was, when the American Revolution occurred, no judicial right, under English law, to review the validity of acts of Parliament is a complete certainty. *[Blackstone is surely right; and Coke's conjectures wrong.]*

"If, then, the men in the Federal Convention held the same view of what constituted America's standing law, upon the subject of judicial power, which, we have seen they did on the subject of executive power, they must have concluded, in the light of the foregoing indubitable fact of English law, that the right of judicial review would not be possessed by the United States Supreme Court, as to acts of Congress, unless that right was in some clear way provided." (Ibid., vol. 2, p. 941)

In fact, the Supreme Court did not strike down an act of Congress until 1857, when Roger Taney handed down the celebrated *Dred Scott* decision. (The *dictum* of *McCulloch v. Maryland* [1819] confirmed judicial review of acts of Congress.)

Coke and Jefferson on Judicial Review. Now consider Coke's theory of judicial review — especially interesting because Jefferson is pitted against his paladin; and another of James Madison's serpentine trails.

Coke's theory of judicial supremacy is patently absurd; but intriguing perplexes are posed by its (mostly rhetorical) implementation in America. Thus John Marshall, supposedly more committed to Blackstone, implemented Coke's doctrine; while Thomas Jefferson, Coke's professed acolyte, scorned judicial review of Congressional, or Presidential, action.

Although Coke's primary target was the Crown, Parliament —
feeble until Stuart times — also came under his fire. Was Jefferson
a better Whig than Coke? Or was it that Jefferson had Hobson's
choice, circa 1798–1805? The Federalist-dominated judiciary was a
most inadequate Republican instrument! Nor should too much be
made of judicial review: it was practically a dead letter until Taney's
egregious proposition (in *Dred Scott*, 1857), that the Missouri Compromise was unconstitutional, put the torch to American politics. [22]

Finally, Jefferson's position on judicial review is less sharp than
Crosskey's. He argued that *no* department was supreme in determining constitutionality; his doctrine permits courts to refuse to
issue enforcing process; just as it supports Andrew Jackson's *démarche*, "John Marshall has made his decision; now let him enforce
it."

Serpentine Trails on Judicial Review. Crosskey is always in top
form when he has James Madison in his sights.

"One factor impugning Madison's reliability as a witness on judicial
review ... is that in the course of his long political career, he shifted his
position ... several times. Thus, in the early part of 1788, after Hamilton
had avowed what amounted to the 'tripartite' view in no. xxxiii of *The
Federalist*, Madison hinted obscurely, and without supporting reasons, in
No. xxxix, that the Supreme Court had been intended, under the Constitution, as the supreme and authoritative interpreter of Congress's
powers. ... It is not surprising that we find Madison writing, in the fall
of the same year, ... in a different tenor." (Ibid., vol. 2, p. 1009)

Haines (1959), a supporter of judicial review, and much more
friendly to Madison than Crosskey, buttresses Crosskey's contention. Viz.,

o Elliot's *Debates* suggest Madison argued (in 1787) for Parliamentary supremacy: Congress is supreme in the field of national
government; and Madison said that the Supreme Court is to decide
whether state laws conform to the "supreme law" *à la* the Preamble. (See Haines, 1959, pp. 234–235.) Of course, Madison's 1787
construction jibes perfectly with Crosskey's.

○ By 1829, Madison denied the "supremacy" of the Supreme Court over the states on federal Constitutional questions. (Ibid,. p. 238) This seems nonsense.

○ By 1834, Madison seemed to favour judicial review! (Ibid., pp. 239–240)

Alexander Hamilton made but two ineffectual appearances — which seemed "royalist" to many — at the Philadelphia Convention, in 1787. But, as *Publius*, along with James Madison and John Jay, he did much to secure the Constitution's ratification — *The Federalist* papers were written for the hotly-contested New York ratification poll.

Perhaps ratification of the Constitution was a Pyrrhic victory for nationalists: verbal concessions made to secure ratification set in train the decay of the nationalist features the 1787 authors meant to install. Even Hamilton wavered on the commerce clause and on judicial review. Crosskey's title is well chosen: *Politics and the Constitution*. This is what Crosskey writes about his paladin, Hamilton, on judicial review.

"Hamilton's first position [in *The Federalist*] was ... that Congress was the constitutional judge of its own constitutional powers. Thus in No. xxxiii of *The Federalist*, Hamilton declared quite openly that 'the national government, like every other, must judge, in the first instance of the proper exercise of its powers, and its constituents in the last.' As the Supreme Court has no constituents, it is evident that Hamilton must have been speaking of Congress and the President." (Ibid, vo!. 2, pp. 1026–1027)

That is not all. "Hamilton, in a later number of *The Federalist*, declared, in effect, that the Supreme Court had the right of judicial review against Congress." (Ibid., p. 1027) See no. lxxviii of *The Federalist*. Crosskey's attempt to play down the dénouement seems insipid.

(6) Judicial Review — of State Action

Crosskey argues that decay of the proper rule began in the case of *Cohens v. Virginia* (1821) — see Crosskey, op. cit., vol. 1, p. 815; and its doom was sealed in *Green v. Neal's Lessee* (1832). Haines (1959) sees the line of cases beginning with Story's opinion for the Court in *Martin v. Hunter's Lessee* (1813) in a less lurid light. Where Crosskey emphasizes limitations on review of state legislation and judicial decisions relative to state laws, Haines plays up the fact that *Martin v. Hunter's Lessee* and, later, *Cohens v. Virginia* vindicate review by the Supreme Court of state action relative to the Constitution of the United States, assuring uniform interpretation.

Jefferson's support of "states' rights," perhaps in order to block Federalist derogations of political and economic liberty, compelled his party to deny power to the Supreme Court to liquidate state clogs on commerce (value-enhancing exchange) and to accept sometimes-chaotic irregularity in American law, leading *inter alia*, to forum shopping, all in derogation of the 1787 mandate. [23]

Jefferson's Kentucky Resolutions [24]

These are the principal features of the Kentucky Resolutions, surreptitiously supplied to the Kentucky legislature, *via* John Breckenridge, by Vice President Thomas Jefferson in 1798.

○ *Resolution One.* The system established by the Constitution is essentially a league of sovereign states — a compact between states, so that the Constitution's Preamble ("We the people of the United States ... ") is empty rhetoric. Each state is able to determine that acts of the United States Government are null and void.

□ Resolution One is mischievously preposterous. Jefferson's anxiety to hide his authorship — not revealed until 1814 and not widely noted until 1821 (see Malone, 1962, p. 400) — is understandable.

○ *Resolution Two.* Its major premiss is that "reservation" in the tenth Amendment supports the express-delegation hypothesis — *pace* Crosskey. So there is no common law of the United States. And Federal crimes are confined to those enumerated in the

Constitution; criminal statutes exceeding such bounds — see the Alien and Sedition Acts — are null and void.

▫ *Swift v. Tyson* (1842) later confirmed Jefferson's major premiss, to the chagrin of Professor Crosskey. But nationalist substance was restored via generous interpretation of implied powers. Resolution Two can be gingerly supported as a desperate *ad hoc* expedient in the cause of liberty.

○ *Resolution Three*, glossed by Malone (1962), argues, *pace* Crosskey, that the Bill of Rights does not run against the states: the last bastions of American liberty are to be immune to the process of the Federalist bench. And the Alien and Sedition Acts are said to vioviolate the Bill of Rights (running against the national government) — and are therefore null and void.

▫ Jefferson's fragile claim that the original Bill of Rights does not run against the states unless expressly so stated became deeply embedded in American constitutional law: not even the post-Civil-War fourteenth Amendment could dislodge it for a long time.

○ *Resolution Four* concerns "alien friends." Jefferson relies on the express-delegation hypothesis to void the Aliens Act. Why? Probably because he takes for granted that due process refers only to criminal procedure and to personal liberty. (Cf. infra.)

○ *Resolution Five*. The Constitution (concerned about slave traffic) bars Congressional interference with migration to the United States until 1808. So the Aliens Act is void.

▫ Jefferson is on shaky ground: the "1808" clause implies that Congress is free in general to legislate on immigration, an unenumerated power.

○ *Resolution Six*, concerning the unutilized power conferred on President Adams to evict aliens, is also argued narrowly, unlike Resolution Eight.

○ *Resolution Seven* would merely be asinine if it had not become enshrined in the controlling law of the American Constitution. It asserts that the general welfare and "necessary and proper" clauses do not mean what they say: only expressly delegated powers are relevant. [25] He suggests that a new Constitution be written "at a time of greater tranquillity," but not now; he seems to be writing a new Constitution in 1798! [26]

□ The economic thrust of the jurally absurd argument of Resolution Seven is sound. For many years after 1801, *dirigisme* was suppressed in favour of something like laisser faire; Walpole's system was consigned to the dust bag of history; the influence of Hamilton's mercantilist mind-set faded away; and Hamilton's programme of close liaison between (what was to be) Washington and Wall Street went off stream until the Civil War.

○ *Resolution Eight.* Jefferson catches the scent of glorious battles *déjà.* "Every state has a natural right ... to nullify. ... " But the great revolutionary stifles his penchant for wild play — and merely calls for palaver by Kentucky with other states on the crisis, for the nonce. And the lengthy passage, completing the eighth resolution, backs down from undiluted nullification (without abandoning it in principle) in favour of improbable joint nullifying action.

○ *Resolution Nine* need not detain us.

How are we to explain this extraordinary transaction of the Vice President of the United States? Justice Holmes may hold the key: "great cases make bad law." (True, Jefferson was committed to bad law before 1798.)

The case was surely a great one. The Alien and Sedition Acts, shocking in themselves, reflected a rising "monocrat," "Anglican" counter-revolutionary hysteria that could plausibly be extrapolated into full-blown counter-revolution. And Jefferson was hoist on his own petard: under the Constitutional system he projected, the courts probably could not restrain Congress *cum* the President; nor did the Federalist bench want to. (His Constitutional theory squares with Crosskey's nationalist one on this point.) His fears for liberty may have forced him into wild play. Dumas Malone (1962, p. 394) writes that "in seeking a weapon against [the Alien and Sedition Acts] he turned to state arsenals." True, but the nullification card had no tactical value; it was at most a rhetorical device.

Dumas Malone puts a brighter gloss than Professor Crosskey on Jefferson's self-serving jural theorizing, while largely supporting Crosskey's substantive conclusions. Such a consensus must be taken seriously.

"[Jefferson's] earliest critical comments on the Constitution of 1787 related, not to the reduction in the powers of the states, but to the lack of safeguards for individuals. ... He always held that the powers of the general government were and should be defined and limited, but the degree of liberalism or literalism with which he interpreted the constitutional instrument cannot be separated from the particular circumstances in which he found himself. The indubitable fact is that where he appeared [in his *Bank* opinion] to be a strict constructionist it was in opposition to Hamilton's system. ... The Constitutional arguments that he advocated throughout [the 1790s] were conditioned by his fear of potential tyranny, and time was to show that he took a less rigid position when that fear was relaxed *[when he was in power]*; but his chief concern at all times was not to aggrandize state power for its own sake, but to safeguard the freedom of individuals." (Malone, 1962, pp. 395–396)

I think Malone's summary excellent: Jefferson's — and Madison's and Hamilton's — essays in the law of the American Constitution lack jural gravity. Hamilton's instance is especially interesting.

o It shows how the ratification struggle provoked indirection and sophistry, generating a smoke screen that has never lifted.

o The American Constitution has been coated with political sludge from 1787–1788 on; that is Professor Crosskey's point.

o Dumas Malone (1962, p. 397, n. 6) cites an interesting article by Douglass Adair (1944, pp. 100–101). "Adair says one of the reasons why Hamilton declined to have the authorship of individual numbers of the [*Federalist*] papers made known was that he did not want to reveal his responsibility for these sayings. Neither did Madison want to reveal his early advocacy of liberal construction." What did Hamilton say? See *Federalist* papers numbers 26 and 28. In number 28, he forecasts that, if liberty is threatened by the national authority, the state legislatures will contrive counter-measures "for the protection of their common liberty." Alexander

Hamilton anticipates Thomas Jefferson's Kentucky Resolutions! In number 26, he writes that the state legislatures will be, if necessary, the arm of discontent.

Concluding Observations and Reflections

Dumas Malone (1962, p. 397ff.) points out that, in March 1789, Jefferson anticipated that the judiciary would support a Bill of Rights against Congressional intrusion; he did not fear the national judiciary in 1789; and Madison publicly made this point still more saliently. Malone's continuing discussion buttresses the hypothesis that Jefferson and Madison interpreted the national judiciary power opportunistically, if not irresponsibly. He stops just short of my assessment of Jefferson's Kentucky Resolution adventure, viz. a neurasthenic reaction to sinister, often counter-revolutionary, behaviour of high Federalists — to a siege by crabbed enemies of the Enlightenment. [27] The upshot was the worst possible law. Nor is this our last glimpse of Thomas Jefferson as Hotspur.

§5 ADDENDUM TO CHAPTER THREE: SOME OF THE PRINCIPAL
SUPREME COURT DECISIONS ASSESSED IN CHAPTER THREE

Marbury v. Madison (1803). The dictum of *Marbury v. Madison* asserts that the Court has the power of reviewing the Constitutionality of Congressional enactments.

Fletcher v. Peck et al. (1810).[1] The *Fletcher, Martin, Cohens, Brown* and *Green* cases establish the Court's power of review of state legislation, e.g. taxation of the Bank of the United States by Maryland. State taxation of federal entities is unconstitutional. If *Marbury v. Madison* is more than *obiter dictum*, Dred Scott is the second asser-

---

[1] The other cases are *Martin v. Hunter's Lessee* (1813), *Cohens v. Virginia* (1821), *Brown v. Maryland* (1827), *Green v. Neal's Lessee* (1832) and *Dred Scott* (1857).

tion by the Court of its power to review Congressional action.

Gibbons v. Ogden (1824). This decision limits the national commerce power; but the scope it allows is wider than "interstate commerce." "Interstate" came to be defined very broadly.

McCulloch v. Maryland (1819). *McCulloch* is famous for its discovery of implied powers of the national government: the Bank is Constitutional.

Calder v. Bull (1798) and *D. C. v. Woodward* (1819). *Calder v. Bull* confines the ex-post-facto clause to criminal cases; but *Dartmouth College* denies power to states to impair contracts.

Swift v. Tyson (1842) asserts that there is no common law of the United States. Since the decision was written by Joseph Story, the *dénouement* chagrins nationalists.

Chisholm v. Georgia (1797). *Chisholm* led to the Eleventh Amendment to the Constitution. One distinguishes a state government's liability to suit, or writs of mandamus by the Supreme Court, from a Supreme Court power of judicial review.

1. These remarks on express delegation and/or implied powers display a disingenuous slipperiness that infects Jefferson's various interpretations of the Constitution of the United States — e.g. in his 1791 opinion on the constitutionality of the Bank of the United States and in the egregious Kentucky Resolutions. He wants to restrain the Crown's prerogative: express delegation! And he wants to keep open rights and privileges vis-à-vis the Crown: implied rights and privileges! Furthermore, he evades the purport of Parliamentary supremacy, secured by the (1688) revolution.

It is inconceivable that the author of these lines, admittedly aet. 81, could have ever believed that the Powers of the United States Congress were confined to those described by certain clauses the Jeffersonians (including the supremely elusive James Madison) claimed comprised a set of express delegations.

2. The Declaration castigates King George III not long after Americans had petitioned the king virtually to disown the reformed constitution of 1688–1689 in order to buttress American privileges against Parliament.

3. Garry Wills (1978, pp. 367–368) refers to Jefferson's singular commitment to "expatriation," followed by new social contracts at the founding of the American colonies; i.e. embryonic American independence. And Wills problematically deploys this tenuous theory to link Jefferson with the Scottish Enlightenment. Jefferson was too good a lawyer to rely on a *raison d'être* for the American revolution based on continuity of British constitutional law in the new world. (I reckon that no such case can be made.) So he turned to antique myths.

4. Alexander Hamilton was enamoured of the Glorious Revolution's accumulation point; and Thomas Jefferson with its mythic apology. It becomes attractive, but perhaps simplistic, to attribute Hamilton's "nationalist" interpretation of the American Constitution to his purpose to imitate Walpole's system (including its public corruption); and Jefferson's restrictive interpretation to his commitment to mythic Whiggism.

5. David Hume, "My Own Life," reprinted in the six-volume Liberty Classics edition of Hume's *The History of England*, vol. 1, p. xxxi.

6. The Cambridge *Historical Encylopaedia* pithily reports that Charles I (1600–1649) "encountered reluctance of Parliament to grant money for his expensive foreign policy in time of economic depression. [He] ruled without Parliament 1629–1640 but used unpopular financial expedients. [He was] forced to call 'Short' and 'Long' Parliaments by [the expense of] Bishops' Wars, 1640. ... [The] Civil War began [in] 1642." (Ibid., p. 345)

See C. V. Wedgwood's celebrated three volume work, *The Great Rebellion* (1955–1964/1991):

° vol. 1, *The King's Peace, 1637–1641* (1955/1991), cited as [1–000]

° vol. 2, *The King's War, 1641–1647* (1958/1991),

° vol. 3, *A Coffin for King Charles: The Trial and Execution of Charles I* (1964/1991), cited as [3–000].

Wedgwood substantially supports Hume and Trevor-Roper, while making more salient than they do how the king's rigid mind-set and political incompetence led to instability, successfully exploited by his Parliamentary enemies: cf. the emergence of Parliamentary supremacy.

The story's principal theme is the Crown's financial unviability. Its provocative second subject is the king's jural pronouncements, provoking political instability.

THE KING'S JURAL THEORY PROVOKES A CRISIS THAT DESTROYS HIM

Robert Berkeley, a king's man, capsulates the royal jural theory. "Freedom rested on law, and the law was in its ultimate essence the expression of the king's benevolent will." [1–196] The king's rhetoric was alarming; and his financial vulnerability blocked him from coping with ensuing turbulence.

Perhaps the most distinctive implementation of the king's jural theory concerns the ecclesiastical Court of High Commission, whose *raison d'être* was to inquire into abuses. "Common lawyers" were aroused by the Commission's attempts to enlarge its jurisdiction. "The old mediaeval conflict between spiritual and secular justice was thus revived. ... The pretensions of the High Commission Court created an alliance between the common lawyers and the Puritans." [1–101]

Au fin the king's largely rhetorical pronouncements catalysed the triumphant Whig dogma. See the indictment read to the king at his trial, 20 January 1647.

"[King Charles] had been trusted with a limited power to govern by and according to the laws of the land, and not otherwise. ... [He had, however, conceived] a wicked design to erect and uphold in himself an unlimited and tyrannical power to rule according to his Will, and to overthrow the Rights and Liberties of the People." [3-148]

Parliament had no intention of rescuing the king from the financial distress that levered their power against him. Wedgwood succinctly develops this crucial point at [1-153, 162] The Ship Money is pivotal. "The revival of the Elizabethan impost was calmly received." But then "the king tried the critical experiment of extending the tax to the inland counties." [1-166ff.] The "experiment" put the torch to British politics. For one thing, the judiciary, after hearing baroque arguments, found the tax unconstitutional. [1-192ff., 205] The appetite of the Whig lawyers grew upon what it fed on.

"What they wanted was ... the transference of effective power from the King's hands into that of the High Court of Parliament. ... They believed themselves to be preserving the ancient balance of the constitution *[sic ?]* but the plain truth was that ... the ordinary life of the country [depended] on them, and hardly at all upon the crown. The entire machine ... could run without the king; but it could not run without the gentry." [1-367]

King Charles was doubly enveloped: his financial collapse made him the tool of the forces his jural and theological pronouncements had alarmed. The Long Parliament ruthlessly solved the equation. "[It] attacked the roots of sovereignty. This was not done by pompous statements of political theory; it was done ... by fastening systematically in turn upon every vital place." [1-382/4 at 383]

7. Hume does not rigorously deploy jural concepts like right, power or privilege. See Hohfeldian categories studied in "Hohfeld's *Fundamental Legal Conceptions* and Liberty" infra.

8. Hobbes makes this point with special force. And he conflates it with a case for absolute monarchial power. In the upshot freedom and liberty are antithetical. See James Madison's *Federalist Number 10* for a fine development of the point.

Hume seems to me soundly liberal. Thus he is sensitive to the horrors of democratic despotism. It is not surprising that, after a quite lengthy friendship, Rousseau turned fiercely against Hume, congenitally immune to his poisons.

9. Hume displays true Tory sentiment, sliding towards ground later occupied by Burke. Here the positions of Hamilton and Hume may converge: friends of liberty are repelled by prospects of unimpeded action of the Demos.

Jefferson's confrontation of this perplex moves along an azimuth that has thrilled people ever since. He asserts that the paraphernalia of fealty to high-born chevaliers can, and should, be discarded, surely in the New Republic; the source of his quarrel with Montesquieu's system becomes transparent. But he entraps himself in a crucial contradiction: by all means, discard the myths of aristocratical ineluctability; but why retain those of Whig history? Perhaps his queasiness about illegitimacy (echoing that of earlier English revolutionaries) explains this. Both he and the Tories take shelter under mythic constructions: he relies on an imaginary history, leavened with smatterings of revelation of the rights of man — revelations that have Scottish professorial, not divine, inspiration; Hume cannot shake off the magnetic appeal of feudally inspired hugger-mugger, requiring fealty to descendants of fierce bygone warriors.

10. What laws? Hume seems to abandon his more-or-less positivist position — turning instead to some sort of revealed law.

11. W. S. Holdsworth, an exemplary scholar and writer, is my primary source for the text's assessment of Coke, a principal figure for Jefferson and the America of his time. See Holdsworth (1924).

12. See "jural positivism," expounded with panache by Edward Levi in his *Introduction to Legal Reasoning*.

13. "Ancient user" seems to me preferable to the clumsy locution, "artificial reason."

14. I discuss a counterpart problem in my 1991 book. Natural economic systems may behave better than controlled ones; indeed "control" may impose a forced oscillation on the system's natural vibration that causes it to resonate.

All that said, it is a short step from praise of "inertia and incoherence" to promotion of myths and rituals of obescience, if not massive grants of power, to mediocre descendants of defunct warriors.

15. James Madison is said by Crosskey to have assiduously propagated a myth of expressly delegated powers. Still, in *Federalist* paper xli (1788), he asks, rhetorically, "for what purpose could the enumeration of particular [Congressional] powers be inserted, if these and all others were meant to be included in the preceding general power?" And Madison's last official act as President was to veto a bonus bill because the powers to enact such a bill were not expressly given — the supremely elusive Madison showed considerable consistency for twenty-six years. Crosskey replies, in effect, that "it is all a fraud." His more-sober rationale for enumerations, glossed in the text, makes his point more satisfactorily.

Crosskey quixotically seeks certainty of jural interpretation — he falls prey to the novice's illusion that there is a Platonic form, *the* law; and that the jural forms are penetrated by knowledge. In his way, Crosskey supports strict construction *à la* Edwin Meese — a fatally flawed doctrine.

16. Crosskey's treatment of "expressly" seems to me thin and contrived.

"The men in Congress were not willing to exclude what we now understand by 'implied' powers and among these, it must be remembered, were the powers 'implied' by the statement of the Government's 'objects' in the Preamble. In addition to this, the votes meant that the men in Congress were completely unwilling to institute a constructionary rule requiring that every doubt and ambiguity ... should be resolved in favor of 'retained' sovereign powers in the several states. For the sense of expressly ... in which the word meant 'clearly' or 'unambiguously,' would have had this effect: it would have compelled a systematic abandonment of the rule, which the Preamble requires, that all doubts and ambiguities that the Constitution may contain shall be resolved in favor of the full and effective attainment cf the 'objects' which the Preamble states." (*Politics and the Constitution*, vol. 1, p. 684)

His gloss of "expressly" is necessary for coherence; but his assertion that there is conclusive corroborative evidence from Congressional sessions, etc., does not wash.

Another Serpentine Trail? Crosskey argues that James Madison understood that the Tenth Amendment made no change in the 1787 Constitution:

"Years later, long after he had changed his mind as to the desirability of general powers in the [national] government, Madison ... cautioned that [the Constitution's words were unguarded] against the construction then being urged: 'that they were a grant of general substantive legislative power to Congress.' [The letter to his political colleague, Martin Van Buren,] establishes that James Madison in 1826 saw nothing in the Tenth Amendment in any way impugning the existence of general legislative authority in Congress; and it would seem, therefore, that he must, in 1789, have drafted the Tenth Amendment so as to leave such power existent." (Ibid., p. 689)

This line of argument is quite fruitful: it is easy to show that Madison was a nationalist in 1789; and he gave no sign that he wrote the Tenth Amendment in order to undo what he, and the other Convention nationalists, had constructed in 1787. Crosskey's indirect evidence *in re* Jefferson, mostly already glossed in the text, is similarly promising:

"It has already been mentioned [in ch. 7] that Jefferson advocated a general welfare power for Congress in 1787, as indeed he had also done in 1775. ... When he read the Constitution in Paris, in 1787, his conclusion was that Congress was not limited to its enumerated powers; and in the spring of 1788, he opposed any amendment of the Constitution which would have so limited Congress's authority." (Ibid., vol. 2, p. 764, n; also see vol. 1, pp. 211–213)

A More-Subtle Analysis of Enumeration. Crosskey concludes that confusion over "enumeration" is linked to that over "common law" and that the Tenth Amendment is misread in this connection.

"The view of Madison, at least, that the Tenth Amendment was not intended to make any change from the original Constitution, was not unknown, and this [Madison's view] seemed to corroborate the view ... that the enumeration of Congressional powers, contained in Article I had actually been made to secure the powers there enumerated, as against the states. ... If the enumeration of Congressional powers could not be understood ... the Common Defense and General Welfare Clause simply had to have some other meaning than what it seemed to say." (Ibid., vol. 2, pp. 1165–1166)

The Constitution is silent about a common law of the United States. Crosskey's contention that the rules of Constitutional construction extract a common law of the United States moves along the general lines of his excellent "enumeration" analysis.

17. Dumas Malone (1962, p. 403) writes that Jefferson, in 1798, "completely repudiated the doctrine that the federal courts already had common-law jurisdiction over seditious libel. *[The context concerns the Sedition Act; some said that the actions were common-law crimes, so that the Act was irrelevant.]* He regarded the doctrine that the common law was in force in the federal courts without specific legislative action as 'an audacious, barefaced and sweeping pretension.' "

Jefferson could well have been aghast at the notion that seditious libel was intrinsic to American law. But that does not justify his theory: Congress can correct common-law abuses; as did King-in-Parliament for many centuries.

18. Flexner shows that Randolph was "set up" by Federalist colleagues. Crosskey camouflages the facts, which speak ill of his Federalists and of the stability of the ageing President's judgment.

19. My first publication (1949) concerned *Swift v. Tyson cum Erie v. Tompkins.*

20. The context is Keynes's attack on the classical theory of interest.

21. In 1786, Jefferson may well have accepted Crosskey's inclusive definition of commerce, one giving the commerce clause a very long reach, buttressing the "bad law, good economics" theme. Go back to John Dickinson's pre-revolutionary *Letters from a Farmer.* Writing about the *Letters* after the war, Jefferson interpreted Dickinson's concession of Parliamentary "authority to regulate trade" — or, as Jefferson put it, "to regulate commerce," in precisely "Crosskey's" sense.

22. The *Dred Scott* case could have been decided much more narrowly. So "judicial review" is but *obiter dictum* in Taney's *Dred Scott* decision too.

23.Consider further *Chisholm v. Georgia* (1793) and its aftermath, the Eleventh Amendment to the Constitution. The Supreme Court held in *Chisholm v. Georgia* that states (like Georgia) are subject to the process of the Court. But underlying jural issues were obscured by political smoke from the beginning. In order to secure ratification of the 1787 Constitution such nationalists as Madison (!), Hamilton and Marshall said that states were not subject to such process. So *Chisholm* led to the Eleventh Amendment: "The judicial power of the United States [does not] extend to any suit in law or equity versus a state by citizens of another state or citizens or subjects of a foreign state." The Eleventh Amendment has a short reach. It does little more than block suits against states in national courts. It does not affect judicial review by the national courts of state acts within the compass permitted by the *Cohens*, *Green* and *Martin* cases.

24. See Jefferson's *Writings*, pp. 449–456, supplying his October 1798 draft.

25. See Adrienne Koch (1950/1964). She supports the Constitutional theory of Jefferson and Madison.

Jefferson's cramped construction of "general welfare" is evident in his *Bank* opinion and in his letter of 9 September 1792 to President Washington on Hamilton's Report on Manufactures. He thinly veils his real concern (confirming Malone's conjecture, reported in the text). "The object of [Hamilton's] plans taken together is to draw all the powers of government into the hands of the general legislature, to establish means of corrupting a sufficient corps under the command of the Secretary of the Treasury for the purpose of subverting step by step the principles of the Constitution, which he has so often declared to be a thing of nothing which must be changed." (*Writings*, pp. 992–1001 at p. 995)

It is hard to believe that Jefferson's characterization of Hamilton's disdain for the Constitution is spun out of thin air: if Washington had not heard the same thing, Jefferson's credibility would vanish. And there are many authoritative references to Hamilton's withdrawn, disdainful manner during his sparse appearances at Philadelphia in summer 1787. Washington, the President of the 1787 Convention, was well able to judge the soundness of Jefferson's remark that "you will see ... that my objection to the Constitution was that it wanted a bill of rights. ... Colonel Hamilton's was that it wanted a king and a house of lords." (Ibid., p. 996)

26. The "necessary and proper" clause includes the phrase "make all laws ... necessary and proper for carrying into execution the powers vested by the Constitution in the government of the United States."

27. Malone (1962, pp. 406ff.) comments that "as introduced and adopted, the Kentucky Resolutions of 1798 did not contain the term 'nullification'." Nor, so far as Malone knew, was Jefferson's use of the word "nullification" in 1798 known to the South Carolinian incendiaries in 1832.

In 1832, Senator John C. Calhoun (a Yale graduate) urged the South to nullify a national tariff bill. President Andrew Jackson, while making it emphatically clear that he would not countenance secession (he said he would come to South Carolina and hang Calhoun et al. if they went too far), accepted a compromise bill in 1833. So the Constitutional conflagration was postponed.

Chapter Four

Thomas Jefferson
and American Manufactures:
History, Politics
and Economics

§1 THE EMBARGO (1807–1809) AND INDUSTRIAL POLICY

Henry Adams's (1889–1890/1986) history of the embargo shows that the United States had Hobson's choice: America had either to abandon its lucrative overseas commerce or to truckle to British naval power, something the Federalists were glad to do. Jefferson and Madison, along with Gallatin, [1] sought to square this circle: they chose peaceable coercion — thus the embargo. The strategy failed: once again a great case made bad law.

The Appendix to Chapter 4 explains that the embargo's underlying strategic conception, nested in a convoluted economic-geopolitical perplex, was not absurd. Still Jefferson et al. erred. Why? Like other unpolished economists, they underestimated controlling elasticities of supply and demand; they underestimated British powers of resistance.

Section 1 probes the embargo's origins and its consequences for American "industrial policy": Jefferson finally resolved to deal decisively with the vexing consequences of economic dependency on Britain.

There follow two "extenuating comments" on Jefferson's and Madison's errors in economic theory — and a quotation from Jefferson's 1808 message to the Congress on industrial policy.

○ Henry Adams remarks that Jefferson and Madison were deceived by the success of non-intercourse/refusal-to-deal strategies,

137

going back to colonial resistance to British power.

o The embargo's pressures led to palpable unrest in Britain.

o Once he saw the implications of dependency on Britain, Jefferson jettisoned laisser faire, which Ch. 5 shows he esteemed. He, not Hamilton, activated the "infant industries" theory:

"The suspension of our foreign commerce, produced by the injustice of the belligerent powers ... are subjects of just concern. The situation into which we have thus been forced has impelled us to apply a portion of our industry and capital to internal manufactures and improvements. The extent of this conversion is daily increasing, and little doubt remains that the establishments formed and forming will — under the auspices of cheaper materials and subsistence, the freedom of labor from taxation with us, and protecting duties and prohibitions — become permanent." (8th annual message [1808] to Congress, *Writings*, pp. 543–548)

Henry Adams on the Embargo's Antecedents

"Perceval [2] called for a measure which should shut out colonial produce from France and Spain altogether, unless it came from England and had paid a duty at a British customs house to enhance its price." (Ibid. pp. 982–983)

"[Perceval] took the ground that England might do what she would with American commerce because America ... had not already forced Napoleon to recall a decree from the application of which the United States notoriously had till six weeks before been exempted." (Ibid., p. 986)

"The true object of Perceval's orders was ... to protect British trade from competition. Perceval did not wish to famish France but to feed her. [3] His object was commercial, not political; his policy aimed at checking American commerce in order to stimulate English commerce.

"The general intention of [the Orders], however confused, was simple. After Nov. 11, 1807, any American vessel carrying any cargo was liable to capture if it sailed for any port in Europe from which the British flag was excluded. In other words, American commerce was made English.

"Such outrages could be perpetrated idly upon a helpless people. Even in England ... few people believed that peace could be longer preserved." (Ibid., pp. 997–999)

America would be crushed by Britain in a naval war. (After some early successes, American naval resistance on the high seas in the War of 1812 was snuffed out by the Royal Navy.) And non-intercourse with Britain proved infeasible: Britain could not be successfully coerced by trade wars waged in the tradition of successful colonial protests. Nor could America build a navy able to cope with the British fleet that so stringently constrained American policy options. [4]

"The evil had reached a point where some corrective must be found, but four years of submission had broken the national spirit. [5] ... [The people] hoped to escape the necessity of fighting under any circumstances whatever, anxiously looking for some expedient or compromise which could reconcile a policy of resistance with a policy of peace. This expedient [non-intercourse] Jefferson and Madison had for fifteen years been ready to offer them. [6]

"The fascination which [Jefferson's policy of peaceable coercion] exercised over his mind was quite as much due to his temperament as to logic; for if reason told him that Europe could be starved into concession, temperament added another motive still more alluring. If Europe persisted in her conduct, America would still be safe. ... The idea of ceasing intercourse with obnoxious nations reflected his own personality in the mirror of statesmanship." (Ibid., pp. 1021–1022)

I read Jefferson's mind differently from Henry Adams. I think he made a studied, if incorrect, calculation of the underlying elasticities. (See the Appendix to Ch. 4 for a much fuller discussion.) Henry Adams venomously describes his hope to play Britain off against France in the Florida negotiations (in which Spain was a pathetic party); and he had earlier contemplated an alliance with Britain if France's grip on New Orleans could not be relaxed; and he may underestimate Jefferson's cold disdain for the British governing class — doubtless tinctured by the rude treatment he and John Adams received from King George III at the Court of St. James.

What may have been Henry Adams's perverse pleasure in portraying Jefferson as a distracted, sentimental, rather comic, dreamer has been picked up by historians as a measure of his greatness as a pacifist philosopher-king. Theodore Roosevelt adds his own twist to his friend's: TR thought him deceitful and duplicitous, if not unmanly — and Jefferson's intellectualism clashed with TR's "pragmatism." Incomprehension of the life of the mind has transformed Jefferson's image into that of a professor of philosophy who, with his close friends, Madison and Monroe, inadvertantly climbed to the top of the greasy pole for twenty-four years. (See Merrill Peterson, 1960.)

Jefferson Arrives at an Industrial Policy

Henry Adams shows, in ch.xvi, p. 1175ff., how Jefferson arrived at an industrial policy *cum* internal improvements. [7]

"This avowal [of support for manufactures, and even protection] did much to increase the ill-will of New England, where Jefferson's hostility to foreign commerce as a New England interest was believed to be inveterate and deadly." (Ibid., p. 1176)

The Federalist position was bottomed on concern for the carrying trade, and frankly embraced dependency on Britain; the Federalists wanted to carry goods under British protection, not manufacture them: see Hamilton's conversations — bordering on treason — with the British diplomats Hammond and Beckwith. Jefferson rejected such timorousness: see his eighth annual message to Congress — in which he lurched into a call for internal improvements. Henry Adams supplies a wicked gloss:

"The whole meaning of this paragraph was explained by other documents. March 2, 1807, the Senate *[which adopted very little the President did not suggest to them]* adopted a Resolution calling upon the President for a plan of internal improvements. April 4, 1808, Gallatin made an elaborate report. ... A national university was intended to crown a scheme whose scale no European monarch, except perhaps the Czar, could match. Jefferson cherished it as his legacy to the nation." (Ibid., p. 1177)

§2 JEFFERSON AND HAMILTON ON MANUFACTURES

The Evolution of Jefferson's Policy on Manufactures

I examine Jefferson's "manufacturing policy" along three azi-muths. The first is broadly political. The second concerns his rap-port with such French economists as J.-B. Say and Destutt de Tracy; he shuns physiocratic error. The third azimuth concerns how these materials play into the proclamation of the embargo and how the embargo-experience, together with the War of 1812, fed back into his political economy during his long retirement.

Jefferson's policy evolved over no more than seventeen years (say) 1790–1807. He never sought to impede any action on manufacturing policy. Thus Hamilton's Society for the Encouragement of Useful Manufactures (SEUM) seems little more than a bond-parking opera-tion, impelling his *Report on Manufactures*; he had no intention of impeding American commerce with Britain, the principal source of revenue to finance his funding programme. (See Ch. 2.)

His rejection of possessively-individualist ("greed is good") utilitarianism has fostered misunderstanding of his "manufacturing policy"; many libertarian writers are naïvely uncomfortable with what they call the "civic humanism" of his ethical theory. (See Chs. 5 & 6.)

His reply to Query xix (*Notes on the State of Virginia*, 1781/ 1787/1986) is strong stuff, whether interpreted as a statement about comparative advantage or about the merits of agriculture as a way of life. It evokes myths of the Roman Republic that so influenced the American founders — cf. Republican Virtue.

"Those who labour in the earth are the chosen people of God, if ever he had a chosen people, whose breasts he has made his peculiar deposit for substantial and genuine virtue. ... Corruption of morals in the mass of cultivators is a phaenomenon of which no age or nation has furnished an example. ... The mobs of great cities add just so much to the support of pure government, as sores do to the strength of the human body." (*Notes on Virginia, Writings*, pp. 290–291)

He is not demurring to a programme supporting manufacturing; there was none until he shaped one up. And eighteenth-century London and Paris have more in common with Lagos or Mexico City today than Düsseldorf — London and Paris *déjà* were not sites for humming mills. Moreover "the mobs of great cities" is evoked, in part, by ancient Rome: he was a student of Virgil (and of poetry *en général* — see his fine "Thoughts on English Prosody," communicated to Chastellux in 1786, *Writings*, pp. 594–622).

"The lines, standing on the very first page of Virgil's published work, have a prophetic ring. The poet, like his rustic speaker, will discover Rome; and will find that Rome is something very different from the innocent joys and sorrows of country life. The imperial city, with its fabulous wealth and power, can at will reward or destroy. That will be a central problem for the *Aeneid*." (*Oxford Dictionary of the Classical World*, p. 618)

Or consider *The Georgics*: "Book 2 closes with an emotional passage extolling the life of the farmer ('O all too happy, if they knew their luck!'), contrasting rustic innocence with the vicious luxury of the city, and extolling the life of the poet who (like Virgil) knows the rustic gods." (Ibid., p. 624)

A Cooler Analysis of Manufacturing Policy. In 1785, in a letter (from Paris) to John Jay, Jefferson analyses "agriculture *v.* manufacturing" more coolly, displaying a grasp of "Malthus," the Ricardian theory of rent and of elasticities of reciprocal demand curves. Jay, in his letter of 14 June 1785, asked him "whether it would be useful to carry all our own production or none?"

"We have now lands enough to employ an infinite number of people in their cultivation. Cultivators of the earth are the most valuable citizens *[in civic, not physiocratic, terms].* ... As long therefore as they can find employment in this line, I would not convert them into mariners, artisans or anything else. But our citizens will find employment in this line till their numbers, and of course their productions, become too great for the demand both internal and foreign. This is not the case as yet, and probably will not be for a considerable time. As soon as it is, the surplus of hands must be turned into something else. I should then perhaps wish to turn them to the seas in preference to manufactures. ... However, we are not free to decide this question on principle of theory only." (*Writings*, pp. 318–319) [8]

The chronicle resumes in 1813, after the sea change in Jefferson's praxis signalled by the eighth annual Presidential message (1808). Mr John Mellish informed Jefferson of the progress of manufacturing in the west. Jefferson replies that he has set up cloth manufacturing at his farms.

"A great blessing for us will grow. I have not formerly been an advocate for great manufactories. I doubted whether not labor, employed in agriculture, and aided by the spontaneous energies of the earth, would not procure us more than we could make ourselves of other necessaries. *[Cf. Ricardian comparative advantage!]* But other considerations entering into the question have settled my doubts." (*Writings*, pp. 1267–1268)

There is much more, embellished by these lines from a letter to William Short (25 November 1814).

"Farewell all hopes of extinguishing public debt!. ... Our enemy has indeed the consolation of Satan in removing our first parents from Paradise: from a peaceable agricultural nation, he makes us a military and manufacturing one." (Ibid., p. 1357) [9]

Alexander Hamilton on Manufactures: Myth and Reality

o Neither his *Report on Manufactures* (1791/1966) nor any cabinet business entails any significant programme. What mattered to him was federal-debt service, bottomed on customs revenue, hinging on overseas commerce and which would be impaired by import-substitution: imports, not exports, were taxed.

o The *Report* is linked to a shadowy scheme, the Society for the Encouragement of Useful Manufactures (SEUM), purporting to promote industrial planning, but more plausibly a bond-parking operation run on Hamilton's behalf by the Wall Street speculator, William Duer.

HAMILTON'S REPORT ON MANUFACTURES (5 DECEMBER 1791)

The Syrett–Cooke (1966) Introduction (Pp. 1–15)

In their Introduction, Syrett and Cooke, Hamilton's hapless protagonists, remorselessly expose the faults of his analysis; but fidelity to their paladin bars acknowledgement that the SEUM was a subterfuge.

Syrett and Cooke write that "in the *Report on Manufactures*, Hamilton reiterates his view of the public debt as an acquisition of artificial capital available for the promotion of manufactures." (Ibid., p. 3) This is nonsense. The paper similitude of wealth, the certificates of public debt, cannot create real wealth; the comment feeds suspicion that the *Report* is a front for a bond-price-support operation. They continue:

"The *Report on Manufactures* cannot be divorced from Hamilton's view of public credit and banking, but an equally close relation exists between this report and his attitude on foreign policy. ... He did not attempt to [twist] the [British] lion's tail." (Ibid., p. 3)

A disingenuous remark! Hamilton's secret conversations with British diplomats found him working hand-in-glove with them, perhaps because of intense concern for his funding policy. And they say that the published report deletes Hamilton's outspoken praise of mercantilism in earlier drafts.

Jefferson was a political economist of the school of Say and Tracy: his manufactures policy hinged on principles of comparative advantage, modified by the geopolitical consequences of British naval power. Whatever was Hamilton's interest in manufacturing was subordinated to his financial policy.

Syrett and Cooke (at p. 8) report the *Report's* rejection of Adam Smith's invisible hand, pivotal for Say, Destutt de Tracy and Jefferson, who wrote that,

"So invariably do the laws of nature create our duties and interests, that when they seem to be at variance, we ought to suspect some fallacy in our reasonings." (*Writings*, p. 1143 — letter, 1 Feb. 1804, to J.-B. Say)

The liberal, Jefferson, never sought to suppress manufacturing; for some years he was against *promoting* manufactures through a "forcing" policy.

The Report on Manufactures (Papers: x: pp. 230–340)

Some preliminaries are to be cleared away.

o The *Report* was a response to a request from President Washington (a persistent supporter of American manufacturing) to study possibilities for military autarky for the United States — a limited brief, implying that manufactures were on the periphery of the Administration's policy — for which public debt was central; and to one from Congress.

o Hamilton supplies, at p. 237, a competent anti-physiocratic argument, based on Adam Smith's; Tracy was still more emphatic.

o He writes, at p. 262, that, in a "system of perfect liberty," the United States would not properly promote manufactures. But, under constraints *en vigueur*, the United States should promote them. What is the principal constraint? Incursive British sea power. The argument seems to unfold like Jefferson's. Unless the United States produces much of its manufactures directly, instead of indirectly (i.e. trading for such goods), it will become Britain's tool. But he is quick to write, at p. 264, that "remarks of this kind are not made in the spirit of complaint." Why not? He is thoroughly "Anglican"; and his funding system hinges on customs revenue.

Hamilton Spurns the Invisible Hand. The *Report's* core begins at p. 266 (*Papers*: x):

"Experience teaches us that men are often so much governed by what they are accustomed to see and practise that the simplest and most obvious improvements in the [most] ordinary occupations are adopted with hesitation, reluctance and by slow gradations. The spontaneous transition to new pursuits, in a community long habituated to different ones, may be expected to be attended with proportionately greater difficulty.

... To produce the desirable changes, as early as may be expedient may therefore require the incitement and patronage of the government." (*Papers*: x: pp. 266–267)

This interesting passage is at odds with the one in *The Wealth of Nations* in which the immortal invisible hand appears and industrial policy is deplored. [10] Jefferson shares Smith's position; nor does his political economy owe anything to neurotically reactionary country parties.

In fact, Hamilton did not, in Smith's phrase, have folly and presumption enough to fancy himself fit to exercise authority over American capital flows: he only proposed the shadowy SEUM.

A Segué to the SEUM Affair. [11] "Public Funds answer the purpose of Capital, from the estimation on which they are usually held by Monied men; and consequently from the Ease and dispatch with which they can be turned into money." (*Papers*: x, p. 277)

o The language about "monied men" is chilling. And surely public funds cannot literally be converted into real capital. [12]

o There is more. Hamilton's continuing discussion leads, anachronistically, to a hyper-Keynesian dénouement. Public "funds" substitute for money; and, if the supply of money, or virtual money, is pumped up, real capital is automatically generated — Hamilton's earlier *Reports* can be read this way. (See Ch. 2.)

AH's Monetary Theory of Real Investment; His Anglomania. After refuting Adam Smith's rather asinine argument that funding destroys real capital, Hamilton returns to his main track at p. 281, supplying a supremely monetary theory of real investment, while displaying anglomania. The contrast with the Say-Tracy-Jefferson theory, and with good contemporary theory, is stark:

"The force of monied capital which has been displayed in Great Britain and the height to which every species of industry has grown up under it, defy a solution from the quantity of coin which that kingdom has ever possessed. Accordingly it has been coeval with its funding system. ... Among ourselves appearances thus far favour the same conclusion. *[This assertion denies liberal political economy. Hamilton seems to be saying that the evolution of real output is an increasing function of the money stock and/or its growth rate.]* In the question under discussion, it is important to distinguish between an absolute increase of capital, or an accession in real wealth, and an artificial increase of capital, as an engine of business, or as an instrument of industry and Commerce. In the first sense, a funded debt has no pretensions of being deemed an increase of Capital; in the last, it has pretensions which are not easy to be controverted. Of a similar nature is bank credit and in an inferior degree, every species of private credit." (Ibid., p. 281)

The second paragraph verges upon a correct analysis: the institutional utility of liquid capital is indeed great. (Thus monetary exchange is fructive; but increases in the nominal money stock do not enhance such fructiveness.) Then it mutates into a paean to an increase in broadly-defined money-supply; it transforms into a monetary theory of real interest rates, if not real output. [13]

A Hype for the SEUM? After enumerating manufacturing activities *en vigeur* (p. 283ff.), Hamilton extols the superiority of a mixed over a purely agricultural economy. How is the United States Government supposed to overcome inertia? The SEUM turns up; it seems Hamilton's only project. Indeed his text, at the bottom of p. 290, strongly supports Nelson's (1987) conjecture that the *Report* is ancillary to Hamilton's financial policy — that its principal purpose is to hype the SEUM.

The remainder of the *Report* is a mixed bag.

○ Hamilton again flirts with mercantilism, and is hostile to the ideas of Adam Smith (and Say, Tracy and Jefferson), at p. 290: "But the uniform appearance of an abundance of specie, as the concomitant of a flourishing state of manufacture(s) and of the reverse, where they do not prevail, afford a strong presumption of their favourable operation upon the wealth of a country." (Ibid., pp. 290–291)

○ At pp. 309–310, the Bank of the United States is properly extolled for promoting manufactures by facilitating remittances. But

Jefferson's (1790) argument that a competitive banking system would do a better job is bolstered by subsequent data.

o The *Report* closes with a long list of products meriting protection or other encouragement. (I defer bounties to the last.) Hamilton's budgets never sought to fund these concepts: public-debt service was bottomed on customs revenues; import-substitution undermined Hamilton's principal programme.

o Hamilton shrewdly points out that there was prejudice against bounties as giveaways of public funds (*Papers*: x: p. 301). And he makes the excellent point that bounties (unlike protective tariffs) do not cause scarcity: competitive supplies of foreign products are unaffected. (Marshall and Pigou later picked up this point, problematically.)

□ So far as I know, Jefferson wrote nothing interesting on the economics of bounties. His opposition to them, when he was Secretary of State, was on purported Constitutional grounds. (See the *Anas, Writings*, p. 677.) In the same conversation with President Washington, he claimed that Hamilton's "paper system" drained capital from manufacturing and other enterprises. This is bad economics, but friendly to manufacturing.

NELSON (1987) ON THE REPORT ON MANUFACTURES, ETC.

Nelson's grand strategy is revealed at p. xiv. It pivots on the commitment of the triumvirate (Jefferson, Madison and Gallatin) to a market system; and against government intervention. He appraises the *Report on Manufactures* at p. 48:

"Examined within its historical context, the *Report on Manufactures* loses much of the superhistorical aura accorded to it in retrospective analyses. ... [It] served a specific end: advancing the SEUM. [Alexander Hamilton did not conceive] of it as a grand plan for an industrial America ... He hoped only to convince investors of SEUM's viability and possibly induce some congressional legislation amenable to its prosperity." (Ibid. p. 48)

Nelson overstates his case: the *Report* was requested by Congress and the President (who James Flexner shows had a small axe to grind).

The SEUM. Nelson begins an acute analysis of the SEUM project at p. 38 — it does look like a stock-parking job.

"Ninety per cent of the SEUM stock would be subscribed in six per cent government stock and the remainder in six per cent deferred stock. A foreign loan at 5.5 per cent would then be obtained using the government and bank stock for collateral and interest payments."

SEUM's true capital was to be the foreign loan; and government stock was to be tidily parked. True, the one-half million absorbed by SEUM's capitalization would be quite slight relative to the $80 million national debt. But $0.5 million could bulk large in daily transactions.

"Hamilton believed that 'the operation must favour the holders of the public debt and Bank stock by creating a new object for them; and taking large sums out of the market. [14] With this in mind, he wrote to William Duer, future chairman of the Society [and a notorious speculator], 'the more I considered the thing the more I feel persuaded that it will equally promote the interest of the Adventurers & of the public and will have an excellent effect on the Debt.' " (Ibid., p. 38)

At p. 39, Nelson reports that the market for government stock was buoyed by fresh (flow) demand for SEUM subscriptions. But the matter is less transparent than he may realize. Only $0.5m in stock was parked; once sold to foreigners, it would return to general circulation; and subsequent selling offers would exert transient downward pressure on prices. Everything about this affair seems half-baked.

The long-overdue *Report on Manufactures* appeared three weeks after the birth of the SEUM. There was no follow-up: Hamilton never proposed to increase duties to protective levels. (Cf. pp. 46–47)

Hamilton's Foreign Trade and Manufactures Policies. Nelson makes a compelling case that Hamilton's policy was *au fond* at least as "Anglican" as Jefferson claimed. More charitably, he was wholly committed to his funding policy; and that required a cozy, if not subordinated, relationship with England.

The pieces of the puzzle were in place in late 1793:

"After the British Orders in Council of 1793 translated into wholesale seizures of American ships bound for France, a crisis developed which revealed the incompatibility of [Hamilton's] programme with defiance of England. ... [The thrust of James Madison's plan to coerce Britain into rescinding the Orders] was the interdiction of English manufactures and the development of domestic industries." (Ibid., p. 59)

Hamilton saw that his programme (let alone his political ideal) was incompatible with defiance of England. He told the British Minister, Mr Beckwith, that Britain's Orders were just; and he delivered on a complementary assurance to him: during 1794, American policy came into compliance with the Orders. (By then Jefferson had demitted as Secretary of State; Congressman James Madison led the Republicans in Philadelphia.)

Madison's Policy of Retaliation, 1794: A Precursor of the Embargo. Nelson, like Henry Adams, points out that the embargo-idea is a thread running through Madison's outlook back to the revolution itself. Madison proposed an embargo in 1794 in retaliation against the Orders in Council of 1793. Of course, the conjugate to such an embargo is stimulus to domestic manufacturing.

Nelson problematically remarks that, "just as unrestricted neutral trade would make America a de facto ally of France, so a repression of it would coerce America into a de facto alliance with Britain." (Ibid., p. 59) And the Republicans supported unrestricted neutral trade. But,

o The government of Louis XVI made American independence possible — at enormous expense, contributing to the crisis that boiled over in 1789; a treaty of mutual support was in effect in 1793–1794. The United States and France were *de jure* allies. True, the British fleet vitiated the practical value of the relationship.

○ Unrestricted neutral trade was probably mandated by international law — but the bulk of unrestricted trade would have been with Britain, not France. Nor does Nelson catch the mercantilist mind-set of the British and French.

▫ Napoleon's Continental System later mirrored perfectly the French economic-war strategy: England was to be prevented from exporting, not importing. And recall Henry Adams's remark: "Perceval did not wish to famish France but to feed her." (France could feed herself!)

Three fragments refine Nelson's thesis.

○ In 1791, Hamilton proposed excises on *domestic* manufactures. Nelson suggests (p. 56) that Hamilton did not wish to incur the wrath of merchants importing British goods.

○ Hamilton wanted revenue, not protection, from tariffs; and a Laffer-like curve mandated that tariffs be moderate. (p. 53)

○ Writing as "Americanus," Hamilton showed his true hand: retaliation against Britain would dry up revenues from commercial duties; the funding programme would be upset. (p. 60)

At pp. 60–61, Nelson essays a dense argument about the ways in which Hamilton's programme was geared to British trade: the revenues of the American government were geared to imports, not exports.

"By 1794, Britain accounted for less than one-half of total American trade; a year later it was under one-quarter. Nevertheless, British imports still [supplied] two-thirds of the revenue." (Nelson, 1987, p. 60)

Holders of much of the stock of the U. S. government traded with Britain. Pressures against them (e.g. those generated by Madison's retaliation policy of 1794 or 1807–1809 Embargo) would cause much stock to be thrown onto the market. Who would comprise the potential pool of buyers? The *sellers* of stock! Ergo, the New England merchants fanatically supported Hamilton.

Nelson's Errs on a Small Point. Echoing Jefferson's flawed plaint against the Bank, Nelson writes (p. 85) that "most venture capital, which might have been invested in manufactures, was absorbed by the ... sponge of stock and land speculation." [15] There is a seller for each buyer. Sellers will seek to deploy their proceeds. Shuffles of matrices of claims are often confused with processes that absorb real resources. (See Nelson's useful "Note on Commercial Discrimination," pp. 173–175.)

"POLICY AND PRINCIPLES IN THE AGE OF JEFFERSON"

Mayer (1988) endorses Nelson's (1987) policy-analysis, but not his "inadequately sophisticated treatment of the ideology of Jeffersonian Republicanism."

"In practice [his] fiscal programme dictated Hamilton's foreign policy. *[Also his "Anglomania"]* Funding an accumulating national debt through tariff revenues meant acquiescence in foreign, chiefly British, restrictions on American trade. To impose protective tariffs and discriminatory tonnage duties against Britain — as Madison and Jefferson proposed in 1793-1794 — would be disastrous for Hamilton's programme because that programme depended on British imports for revenue and on American merchants engaged in the British trade for political support. ... "

"In contrast, Jefferson's foreign policy was twofold: commercial discrimination to free foreign markets from restrictions on American trade and development of domestic industry to attain independence from closed markets." (Mayer, 1988, p. 10)

Mayer's second paragraph is flawed: Jefferson did not grasp his foreign policy's implications for manufactures until 1807.

At p. 11, Mayer quotes from Nelson (1987, p. 165):

"[Hamilton's nationalism] extended only to formation of a central government; otherwise he sought commercial alliance with Britain, which effectively precluded economic independence. Hamilton's policies would have maintained an agrarian America, under the control of a merchant faction, while the policy proposals of Jefferson, Madison and Gallatin in the early 1790s would have advanced economic independence through expanded foreign markets and some degree of industrialization."

Mayer correctly extracts the principal implications of the various positions while overlooking two key points: Jefferson and Madison knew their 1793–1794 recommendations were politically futile.; Jefferson's policy did not become coherent until 1807.

MCCOY (1980) ON AMERICAN MANUFACTURES

McCoy belongs to the Adair-McDonald school. Thus he writes (p. 133) that Alexander Hamilton understood the practical need for inequality; and that Thomas Jefferson and James Madison nostalgically sought to restore ancient (Roman) republican virtue — but these "aristocratic" owners of large estates and many slaves were not utopian socialists. The perplex is promptly resolved: he esteems Hamilton's vision of the United States as a great state founded on corruption. He transmutes Jefferson's abhorrence of corruption and fear that "monocrats" would contrive a vicarious imitation of the European class system into nostalgic frippery.

McCoy properly finds the 1793–1794 trade crisis seminally important. Subsequent to the British Orders in Council of 1793, Madison — in charge of the republican forces in Philadelphia, advocated retaliatory commercial legislation.

"Madison's overriding aim was to remove the British manacles on American commerce, and his vehicle was always retaliatory commercial legislation in the form of discrimination." (McCoy, 1980, p. 138)

Jefferson and Madison surely underestimated values of controlling elasticities (see this chapter's appendix): Madison asserted in the first session of the first Congress that, since "the produce of this country is more necessary to the rest of the world than that of other countries to America, we possess natural advantages which no other nation does." (Ibid., p. 140)

The Jay Treaty, affected by Hamilton's improper dealings with British diplomats on the back channel, climaxed the episode:

"The upshot of the 1794 crisis was a stunning defeat of the Madisonian system. Discrimination *[i.e. the Madisonian system]* was never implemented, and the famous treaty that resulted from John Jay's mission to London consummated Hamilton's triumph *[sic]*, for that treaty explicitly bound the United States to a renunciation of discrimination for at least ten years." (Ibid., p. 164)

Hamilton's "triumph" was not one for American manufactures: it effectively blocked serious American manufacturing for ten years; Madison tacitly endorsed official support for manufacturing on a larger scale than Hamilton ever contemplated.

"But though the Hamiltonian system was victorious for the moment, its triumph was not without setbacks and ironies. By 1795 the SEUM was defunct. The colossal failure of this project thwarted Hamilton's desire *[sic?]* to introduce this type of large-scale manufacturing into America. ... The European demand for American produce and raw materials, instead of diminishing, as Hamilton had predicted, mushroomed to unprecedented heights after the outbreak of the wars of the French revolution in early 1792." (Ibid., p. 164)

We have seen that Jefferson favoured laisser faire for manufactures up to 1807; stimulus to manufacturing was incidental to his proposals, in 1793–1794, to retaliate against Britain. [16]   Until 1807, he was interested in what was to happen to manufactures, not in action programmes. But McCoy puts a different spin on the Federalist system:

"Appropriately, the emphasis in the Federalist system gradually shifted from developing manufactures *[sic]* to reaping the profits of a burgeoning foreign commerce. ... The capital, primarily in the form of government securities from the funded debt, could just as easily be channeled into commerce as industry. Thus the short-lived but heated discussion about manufactures in the early 1790s had no major immediate policy implications." (Ibid, pp. 164–165)

But paper parked with the SEUM was not productive capital, granting that Europeans soon made immense direct American investments.

Jefferson and Gallatin on Manufacturing — The Real McCoy? Appraising Jefferson's views on coarse and refined manufacturing, Amercans' inexperience and their still-rudimentary technique mandated concentration on coarse manufactures — in greater demand than refined ones. Jefferson's letters owe much more to Sir Richard Arkwright than to Virgil's *Georgics*. (See his letter to J.-B. Say, Ch. 5.) McCoy writes:

"Despite Jefferson's emphasis on traditional household industry, it is important to recognize he never abandoned his long-standing interest in adapting new advances in machinery to American manufacturing."

So far we have Arkwright. But McCoy claims that a Maoiste Jefferson was committed to the equivalent of backyard steel furnaces. (See pp. 231–232.) And he trumpets the nostalgia theme again. It is easy to reverse his spin.

McCoy's Albert Gallatin differs from Mayer's — but he supports the hypothesis that the scrupulous Gallatin shared his colleagues' policies, while believing that the scope of the Constitution's grant of powers to the national government was larger than they owned.

"In a *Report on Manufacturers* (April 1810) ... Gallatin acknowledged with pleasure that both forms [*i.e. household manufacturing and manufacturing by 'establishments on a substantial scale'*] were making rapid progress in the United States; he was particularly impressed by the recent extraordinary increase in household manufactures." (Ibid., p. 231)

He claims that Gallatin extolled a crofter-like scheme in New York state. No! He was simply reporting what was going on. In fact he was a manufacturer; and was surely not duped by Bolingbroke. Gallatin a utopian dreamer?; was he nostalgic about anything?

§3 AMERICAN NEUTRALITY AND PROSPERITY; GROWTH OF
AMERICAN MANUFACTURES IN THE NINETEENTH CENTURY

American Neutrality and Prosperity. The data confirm the plausible hypothesis that agriculture is the key to puzzles about American economic growth over the 1790–1840 interval. See David (1966).

"Tench Coxe, in 1787, reckoned that nine out of ten persons were engaged in agriculture. ... The shift away from farming which seemingly accompanied the blossoming of maritime commercial activity after 1792 did not proceed thereafter without interruption. ... Of the 20 percentage point contraction in the agricultural sector's share of the American labour force recorded between 1800 and 1840, fully four-fifths took place in the years following 1820." (Ibid., pp. 166–167)

Douglass North (1966) offers a conflicting hypothesis: the apparent surge in American prosperity, 1793–1807, was due to the stimulus to American exports supplied by the wars of the French revolution; and the collapse of these prospects, punctuated by Jefferson's embargo, led to a lengthy period of stagnation.

North's hypothesis has not survived cliometric inspection. Indeed it seems intrinsically improper:

○ The fluctuations of the preponderantly-agricultural economy should have responded mostly to changes in the terms-of-trade.

○ The export-led-growth theme is simplistically Keynesian; "classical," "supply-side" economics casts more light on the American economy of the time.

○ The poor quality of the data compel impressionistic evaluation of patches of data: more-formal statistical analysis is apt to be dominated by errors of measurement. What is more, farmers supplied their own needs to a large extent — leading to still more econometric havoc. [17]

Adams's (1980, p. 713) characterization of his study seems well rated.

"This paper argues that, aside from substantial increases in the re-export sector, domestic trade exhibited little deviation from the long-run ante-bellum [pre 1861-1865] trend. The benefits that did result from neutrality were highly concentrated and must be balanced against the direct and indirect costs of wartime commerce." [18]

Subsequent Growth of American Manufacturing. There follow some scattered observations on subsequent development (especially technological development) of American manufactures.

o It reflects the shock, and aftershocks, of the embargo, together with effects of the canal system, and then the railroads, a much-superior energy equation, a rapid increase in the size of the home market, etc.

□ The "energy equation" concerns the ratio borne by the quantity of kinetic energy required to create a unit of output to its potential energy.

o The Cambridge *Historical Encylopaedia* comments, at p. 272, on coke, very important in the energy equation.

"Smelting by coke, eliminating the sulphur content of raw coal, [was] perfected by A. Darby in 1709. But there was a need for a stronger blast in iron production: coke was inhibited. Then Watt's steam engine was applied to blast furnaces from the mid–1770s, so that by 1790 coke was efficient in iron production." (See Cort's puddling process as well, discussed by Lee & Passell, 1979, p. 94.)

o Lee & Passell (ibid., p. 83ff.) make a number of interesting points about this period.

□ There were important innovations in cotton spinning, including "Slater's mill," as well as Lowell's innovations (1814).

□ Cf. the steam engine. "High pressure engines opened the possibility of enormous efficiency improvements." (Ibid., pp. 95–96)

□ Cf. "water *v.* steam." (Ibid., pp. 96–97)

§4 SOME GRAPHICS, DERIVED FROM NELSON (1987, PP. 177–186)

Comments on Nelson's Graphs

GRAPH THREE (IMPORTS & CUSTOMS RECEIPTS, 1791–1800). The importance of trade with Britain for the customs revenues is evident. The relative importance of this trade declined on the 1791–1800 interval; but American overseas trade, for whatever destination, was under the eye of the British fleet.

GRAPH FOUR (U. S. TRADE IN MILLIONS OF DOLLARS, 1790–1800) reinforces this point: see especially the dramatic increase in total American foreign trade.

GRAPH FIVE (MAJOR DESTINATIONS OF U. S. EXPORTS AS A PERCENTAGE OF TOTAL EXPORTS, 1790–1800). The relative importance of exports to the British empire substantially declined from 1790 to 1794; so that exports to the British and French empires were roughly the same in 1794. By 1798, American exports to Britain were relatively as important as in 1792; while exports to France shrivelled up. The Orders in Council achieved their purpose.

GRAPH ELEVEN (U. S. EXPORTS TO THE BRITISH EMPIRE AS A PERCENTAGE OF TOTAL U. S. EXPORTS) buttresses this line of development: in long-run equilibrium, Britain was to be prominent, but not predominant, in American foreign trade. And, since the post-1800 data were generated by the Jefferson-Madison-Gallatin-Jackson policy, targeting extinction of the national debt, trade and funding policies became disjoint. (Peter Temin, 1969, picks up the story with panache.)

GRAPH FOURTEEN: U. S. EXPORTS AND REEXPORTS TO LATIN AMERICA The data are generated by some very special circumstances; but they yield a glimpse of America's "manifest destiny."

American expansion re-arranged the pieces on the high-politics board: territorial issues, encompassing slavery, inter alia, replaced those studied in this book — and led to the Missouri Compromise of 1820, followed by the Mexican War, 1846–1848, and vast territorial annexations, triggering bitter controversies, not resolved by the Compromise of 1850, that were exacerbated by "Bloody Kansas" and the Dred Scott decision (1857). The ghastly dénouement was the Civil War, 1861–1865.

Alexander Hamilton's world-view seems dwarfish; Thomas Jefferson's focuses on boundless American lands that could "employ an infinite number of people in their cultivation" — conjugate to an undeniably imperialistic vision of the New Republic — proved supremely relevant. [19] (Subsequent acquisitiveness described by Tocqueville in the *Democracy*, and deplored by the last surviving signer, Charles Carroll, would have pained the Sage of Monticello. See Reeves, 1982.)

Some of Nelson's Graphs Reworked

Graphs 1, 4, 7 and 10 are based on Nelson (1987, appendix C, "Graphs," pp. 177–186).

Figure One, "Aggregate Federal (National) Debt, 1791–1814," is based on Nelson's graphs 1 and 10.

Figure Two, "U. S. Trade in Millions of Dollars, 1790–1800," is an "eyeballed" version of Nelson's graph 4.

Figure Three, "Wholesale Price Indices, 1789–1800," is an "eyeballed" version of Nelson's graph 7.

FIGURE ONE

Aggregate National Debt
1791-1814

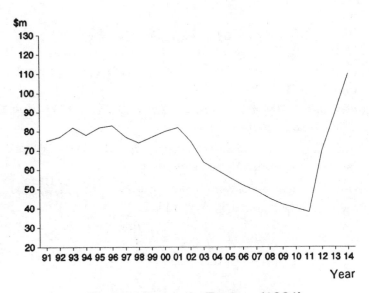

Events: Peace in Europe (1801)
Louisiana Purchase (1803);
Gallatin's Reports (1808, 1810);
War of 1812

FIGURE TWO

U. S. Trade in Millions of Dollars:
1790-1800

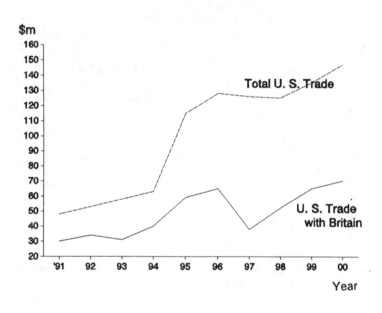

FIGURE THREE

Wholesale Price Indices
1789-1800

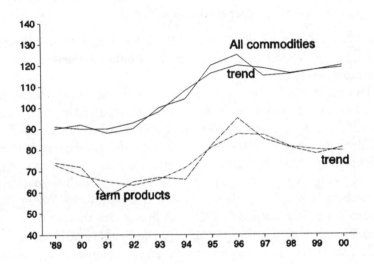

Appendix to Chapter Four

The Embargo (December 1807–March 1809): A Critical Study

§1 PRELIMINARIES

Synopses of a number of important interpretations of the embargo follow a narration. Then elementary cliometrics are deployed to estimate the economic impact of the embargo on the United States and Britain. The sparse comments made at the beginning of Chapter 4 are greatly deepened and widened.

A Narration. Like the French Terror (see Ch. 8), the embargo had unhappy effects that were, on the whole, less severe than is commonly believed.

The Embargo Act was passed on 18 December 1807 and signed into law on 22 December 1807 by President Jefferson, who "suggested" it to his pliant Congress; it was repealed in March 1809, at the dreary end of his Presidency. Initially, the embargo was more defensive than coercive: American ships and seamen (many in danger of being "impressed" by the British) were recalled to safety. Something will turn up: John Quincy Adams told his father that Jefferson's policy up to end-1807 was little more than that. Nor is it surprising that nothing turned up: the British and French had little reason to make concessions to undo a temporary embargo. Inevitably a companion theme was thrust up: peaceable coercion, an American ploy going back to colonial times.

Economic coercion has been misunderstood: the supply and demand sides are not distinguished. It is easy to see that closure of American markets to British goods would exert little pressure on Britain: Henry Adams points out, from his pre-Keynesian slant, that the American market was not vast enough for its closure to give America geopolitical leverage; and there are myriad ways — aside from the "Spanish bonanza" he describes — in which trade patterns can be rearranged. As for "input dependence," a brief (prospective) analysis, based on the American Civil War — cf. the blockade of the Confederacy — shows how substantial are elasticities of substitution.

Cliometric work suggests that, although the embargo reduced aggregate American income by no more than five per cent, local consequences were acute: cf. widespread bankruptcy, desolated seaports, etc. (Still Madison easily won the Presidential election of 1808.)

The political-economic analysis is influenced by a conjecture provoked by Henry Adams's *History*. "Local" victims in the British Empire were politically impotent and disregarded by the political élites; but members of American élites were prominent among "local victims" — e.g. New England shipowners and traders. The conjecture obviously enhances British chances in an economic war of attrition.

Complementary Features of the Embargo Affair. British policy was to engross commerce and so displace, or subordinate, American shipping interests. And,

o The New England mercantile and shipping interests, and the "High Federalists" who represented them, were glad to subordinate themselves to England, whose ruling class they idolized.

o At first Americans massively supported the embargo. But support flowed away: foreigners seemed indifferent; various American interests were increasingly damaged. Sen. Armstrong, Minister to France, reported on the former, and Gov. Sullivan of Massachusetts on the latter.

o Readers of Ch. 3 will be startled at the reach of legislative and, especially, Presidential power in formulating and enforcing the embargo — making mock of the theory of the law of the Constitution that Jefferson and Madison may have held.

§2 CRITICAL SYNOPSES

Selected works of three authors — Henry Adams (1889/1890/ 1986), Dumas Malone (1974) and Forrest McDonald (1976) — are critically compared relative to six topics.

(1) Jefferson's Motivation
- □ *A French Tool?*
- □ *A Utopian Dreamer?*
- □ *The Embargo as an Interim Defensive Measure?*
- □ *Peaceable Coercion*

(2) British and French Motivations: Engrossment of Commerce

(3) Aggrandisement of Congressional and, especially Executive power; reversal of the Jefferson-Madison jural theory

(4) Surge and Ebbing Away of Support for the Embargo

(5) Economic Effects on the United States

(6) Economic Effects on Britain and the British Empire

(1) Jefferson's Motivation, etc.

HENRY ADAMS (1889/1890/1986)

○ (See ibid., p. 1086.) Henry Adams emphatically refutes the notion that Jefferson sought to succour Napoleon (whom he abhorred). But the embargo was bound to affect England more than France, a point taken by Napoleon: "the Embargo seemed to him, as to Jefferson, an act of hostility which answered the immediate needs of France." (p. 1142) And American commercial ties with England were very strong: "the United States had become an appendage to England. The Americans consumed little but English manufactures, allowed British ships to blockade New York and Chesapeake Bay ... [and] suffered their commerce with France and Spain to be plundered without resistance." (p. 1142)

○ Still he portrays Jefferson as a woozy phantast who imposed an embargo in a fit of righteousness. But his grandfather, John Quincy Adams, supported the embargo and lost his Senate seat.

"Under less-serious circumstances, in 1794, Congress had imposed an embargo for thirty days. ... By common consent, an embargo was the proper measure to be taken in the face of an expected attack on commerce. ... An embargo for thirty or sixty days, or even for three months, might be required before reaching some decision as to peace or war."

This is the line Gallatin took (see pp. 1043–1044); and similar language is prominent in the President's draft message, quoted by Adams at p. 1043. He refers, at p. 1068, to the initially non-coercive conception of the Embargo: as late as June 1808, the American Minister in London, William Pinkney, "received instructions, dated April 30 [1808], authorizing him to offer a withdrawal of the embargo on condition that England should withdraw the Orders in Council." (p. 1156) Since long-run exceed short-run elasticities, Jefferson's reasoning was cogent, up to a point: if the embargo were to bite, it would have to be soon. But his continuing strategy was fatally flawed: the embargo's efficiency reckoned to diminish over time. [20]

o Events made the embargo-strategy coercive: the Sullivan and Armstrong letters, infra, make sense only in a "coercive" setting.

o The conflict escalated. "Each government tried to overthrow the other." (Henry Adams, op. cit., p. 1154) Slanders against him by the New England Federalists, led by Timothy Pickering, [21] buttressed British policy: the British public thought Jefferson isolated. And then the Spanish card was played. "At this unexpected good fortune, England went well-nigh mad." Cf. the fall of King Joseph (Bonaparte), re-opening the Spanish market to England.

o Britain reacted intensely to the embargo.

"So ill balanced had the British people become in the excitement of their wars and industries that not only Cobbett but even a man so intelligent as William Spence undertook to prove that foreign commerce was not a source of wealth to England, but that her prosperity and power were derived from her own resources, and would survive the annihilation of her foreign trade. James Mill replied at great length *[Commerce Defended, 1808]* to the eccentricities of Spence and Cobbett, which the commonsense of England would in ordinary times have noted with a laugh." (Ibid., p. 1156)

DUMAS MALONE (1974)

o Malone (1974, p. 483) quotes Jefferson's private letter of 6 January 1808 to John Taylor of Caroline: "the embargo ... saves us the necessity of making [the capture of our ships and men] the cause of immediate war. This gives time .... "

o Malone (1974, pp. 474–475) points out that the Patriot party had successfully deployed non-intercourse in colonial times. And his discussion of Madison's 1793 proposal follows Henry Adams's, save for Adams's acerbic gloss. And he shows that England was not Jefferson's sole target.

o Malone amplifies Henry Adams's description of his grandfather's reaction to Timothy Pickering's abuse of the President: "he was amazed that his colleague made no reference to the most important cause of the measure, the British Order in Council of 11 November 1807, and was alarmed that a Senator of the United States should have wholly accepted the contentions of another government while labelling those of his own as mere pretense." (Malone, 1974, pp. 571–572)

FORREST MCDONALD (1976)

o McDonald (1974, pp. 139–159) — see Ch. 7, "Shipwreck" — revels in the "Utopian dreamer" theme; and opines that Madison is the principal author of the embargo; while Gallatin, who knows better, reluctantly goes along. Malone (1974, p. 591) reports that Gallatin supported the embargo.

o McDonald (1974, pp. 143-144), somewhat against the grain of his *obiter dictum*, agrees that, at its outset, the embargo was an interim, more-or-less-passive, measure; and quotes Jefferson to this effect.

(2) British and French Motivations

"Napoleon's argument was more respectable than that of Spencer Perceval and George Canning. [He] could say with truth that the injury he did to America was wholly consequential on the injury he meant to inflict on England. He had no hidden plan of suppressing American commerce in order to develop the commerce of France." (Adams, op. cit. p., 1043)

The harsh measures imposed by the King's proclamation of 17 October 1807 belonged to a programme, already laid out, for imposing dependency on the United States.

(3) Jefferson and Madison Change Course

o There were escalating accretions to Presidential power, flowing from legislation that Jefferson and Madison would surely have earlier called unconstitutional. (See Frankel's analysis infra, as well as Ch. 3.)

▫ Escalation was inevitable: "the Act signed on 22 December 1807 was powerless to prevent evasions in the seaports and left untouched the trade with Canada and Florida. A supplementary act was necessary." (Adams, op. cit., p. 1065)

▫ And further supplements were passed. Adams reports, at p. 1099, open defiance on the Canadian border. (See the discussion of Frankel, 1982, infra.)

(4) Surge and Ebbing Away of Support for the Embargo

o At first the embargo enjoyed solid support; and the President had an iron grip on Congress. But support waned as important interest groups were damaged. (Cf. infra.)

▫ See the 21 July 1808 letter to Jefferson from the friendly governor of Massachusets, James Sullivan. Sullivan had seen Sen. J. Q. Adams fall to the Essex Junto; was he next? "[The embargo has lost support since people] do not perceive any of the effects from it the nation expected; they do not perceive foreign powers influenced by it." (Quoted by Adams, loc cit., p. 1104)

▫ See the 30 August 1808 letter to Sec'y Madison from Sen. John Armstrong, Minister to Paris: the embargo is not felt in France and is forgotten in England.

(5) Economic Effects on the United States

○ Aggregate effects on American Ecfare were not severe. But severe "local" effects were politically important: American losers were politically influential.

▫ While the export business of grain growers in the middle states was crushed, effects on farmers were mitigated by their virtual self-sufficiency (think of a heavily "diagonal" input-output matrix); and Pennsylvanian manufacturing was stimulated.

▫ If anything, effects on southern planters were more severe than those on New England merchants and shippers. But differences in commercial ethics reversed the situation's political thrust: Southern debtors simply stopped payments; Yankee creditors did not countenance default — and the prospect of insolvency, familiar for Southern planters, mortified Yankees. [22]

▫ A number of lags buffered the political impact of the embargo; Henry Adams convincingly describes the political breakdown in America: ibid., pp. 1122–1123. (Frankel's, 1982, statistics are fatally insensitive to these lags.)

"During the first few months, while ships continued to arrive from abroad and old stores were consumed at home, the full pressure of the embargo was not felt; but as the summer of 1808 passed, the outcry became violent." (Ibid., p. 1122)

▫ Debts could not be paid: punctilious New England was horrified. (Henry Adams may exaggerate, not for the first time. Cf. infra.)

(6) Economic Effects on Britain and the British Empire

The British defences were indeed formidable: e.g. British losers to the Embargo were not as politically influential as American ones: the British Government did not come under politically-inexorable pressure. But the embargo did put pressure on Britain. Henry Adams claims that the Prime Minister, Perceval, feared paralysis of major British industries. He said to the Cabinet that, "it must be admitted that it is extremely desirable that America should relax her embargo." (Adams, ibid., p. 1149) And he came up with a scheme to strengthen the position of his New England Federalist friends: Britain would guarantee the safety of any ship on a voyage to and from a British port. (The Adamses are much less generous than Forrest McDonald to the Federalists.)

Adams sets out along a "Keynesian" line, loosely based on mercantilist and Mandevillean sources: he is concerned with loss of vents for surplus, not sources of supply. "The total value of British exports to America was said to be $50m; but the Americans regularly re-exported to the West Indies merchandise to the value of $10m or $15m. [23] The embargo threw this part of trade back into British hands." (Ibid., p. 1152) He arrives at a provisional figure of $35m.

Refining his estimate, he adroitly takes a Keynesian trick: "Napoleon's decrees must in any case have greatly reduced the purchasing power of America." After some quite subtle adjustments to his naïve model, [24] he concludes that $45m per annum is an upper bound for the loss of British profits (relative to a stipulated 20 per cent profit rate). So his macro-statistics find the embargo politically indecisive. This conclusion is bolstered in a number of interesting ways.

○ The $35m (lost exports) figure is small relative to an "annual expenditure" figure of $350m. ("Annual expenditure" may be a GNP-like statistic.)

○ British exports are reckoned at $200m in 1807 (of which $35m were net exports to the United States). "According to the returns, the exports of 1808 exceeded those of 1807 by about two million." This important statistic strongly supports the hypothesis that Jefferson and Madison (and Gallatin?) seriously underestimated elasticities of substitution. [25]

Adams does not make the following points — further supporting his hypothesis:

o The British input-output matrix reckoned to be more "diagonal" in 1807 than it was late in the nineteenth, let alone the twentieth, century.

o Jefferson and Madison doubtless centred on pressure against Britain based on American refusal to sell, not buy. Jefferson was a classical, not a "Keynesian," economist: Henry Adams has the wrong end of the stick.

□ Jefferson and Madison (and Gallatin?) moved along the proper ("supply side") azimuth; but they overestimated their leverage — they underestimated governing elasticities.

□ The following illustration, from "1860–1866," shows how Jefferson and Madison went wrong. (See Lee & Passell, 1979, p. 242, based on Ellison, 1968, and Wright, 1974.)

¶ In 1860 Britain imported 3.357m bales of cotton, including 2.581m from the United States. ˌ

¶ From 1862 to 1865, Britain imported 2.122m bales; only 0.216m from the United States.

¶ In 1866 British imports recovered to 3.638m bales; 1.163m being imported from the United States. The American market-share was but 31%, *v.* 77% in 1860 — and it never reached 77% again. (The American share rose to 73% in 1878–1879, rising from 60% in 1876-1877.)

Longer-run elasticities of substitution can be very high: in 1861 et seq., Britain successfully coped with much greater dislocation than Jefferson's embargo could have imposed on her — granting that British cotton stocks were exceptionally high at the outset of the Civil War.

§3 SOME CRUDE CLIOMETRICS

Adams on the Embargo's Consequences for the United States

o Ironically, the "Boston Federalists" seem to have substantially underestimated the aggregate (American) welfare loss imposed by the embargo:

"The Boston Federalists estimated the net American loss of income *[Adams doubtless means profits]* ... could not be less than ten per cent for interest and profit on the whole export of the country — or $10.8m on a total export value of $108m." (Ibid., p. 1116)

o Henry Adams then slashes this estimate, attributed to Josiah Quincy (in Congress on 28 November 1808). I am quite sure he is mistaken — but his supporting argument is gripping:

"This estimate was extravagent even if the embargo had been wholly responsible for cutting off American trade; it represented in fact the loss resulting to America from Napoleon's decrees, the British orders and the embargo taken together." (Ibid, p. 1116)

o But he confuses effects of the embargo on government revenue (very sensitive to imports) with social-welfare loss.

My Coarse Estimate of the Embargo's Burden on the U. S.

o The American population in 1810 was 7.2 million, of whom 1.3m were non-white. These 1.3m persons were chattels! It seems meet to stipulate a population of six million.

o Turning to per capita income, first access data supplied by David (1967). American physical output is estimated at 64.4 in 1800, 61.9 in 1810 and 67.6 in 1820 — 1840 = 100. (The decline in output from 1800 to 1810 is in line with the five per cent "Ecfare" loss that will emerge: 2.3/67.6 = 0.034; and 1810- exceeded 1800-population.)

□ Relying on data supplied by Fogel and Engerman (1974/1989, p. 248), calculate per capita income in 1840 in 1860 dollars — $96. (A Warren-Pearson price index, supplied by North, 1961/1966, yields an 1840 price deflator of 102.5 [1860 = 100].) Real 1810 income reckons to be sixty 1840 dollars: American wholesale prices in 1810 exceeded 1840 levels by more than 30 per cent — cf. *Historical Statistics of the U. S.*, Series E 52. An estimate of nominal per capita income of $100 in 1810 — or national income of $600m — is plausible.

o $30m seems an upper bound to losses of gains from trade occasioned by the embargo — i.e. an upper bound to welfare loss of 5 per cent. (Effects of stock depletion may not be accounted for.) And

□ Since long-run exceed short-run elasticities, the net welfare loss probably peaked in 1808 — relative to a counter-factual stipulation sustaining the embargo for some years.

□ If the embargo's depressing effects persisted into 1810, the proper (1807) denominator is the larger — so that the estimate of the embargo's cost is the smaller.

o The aggregated analysis does not pick up the embargo's politically disruptive effects.

§4 JEFFREY FRANKEL (1982) ON THE EMBARGO

Frankel supplies an abstract of his interesting article. [26]

"[The embargo's lack of success] has generally been attributed, first, to a lack of effective enforcement, and second, to an inability to inflict greater economic damage on Great Britain ·than was suffered by the United States." (Frankel, 1982, p. 291)

Stop!

o The embargo was a geopolitical ploy. Success required that Britain (and, to a lesser extent, France) bend to the American will. They did not do so. And, if continuing pressure would have similarly failed to break their resistance, the embargo's failure would be the worse. Frankel's relative-damage criterion is fatally flawed:

Jefferson's objective was to bring about a change in British policy, not to make the British suffer more than the Americans. He brushes against this point at p. 392, but makes nothing of it.

○ Frankel does not realize that, at the outset, the embargo was defensive, not coercive.

He continues:

"This paper challenges both explanations. It is argued, first, that the embargo did effectively reduce both countries to autarky. *[Sic]* [And] that ... the relative price in Britain of agricultural products that had previously been imported rose by more than the relative price in the United States of manufactured goods that had previously been imported." (Ibid., p. 291)

There are two gaping holes:

□ The United States may have been reduced to autarky; Britain was surely not — Henry Adams reports that aggregate British foreign trade *increased* in 1808. Frankel comes 'round at p. 308, but defines away the substance by limiting "autarky" to a trivial two-country model.

□ His criterion is irrelevant for the controlling geopolitical problem.

○ Nor does he perform multivariate analysis: partial effects gradients cannot be filtered out of his model: he offers little more than *post hoc, ergo propter hoc.*

A Critique of Frankel

1. *Enforcement (including control of smuggling).* These are some of Frankel's pivotal points.

○ The official statistics show that American intercourse with the world dropped dramatically, but what about smuggling?

○ He ingeniously deploys British data, noting that the British would be apt to overstate smuggling. The upshot suggests that the embargo was successfully enforced: British imports from America declined by 73.18%; and British exports to America by 56.17%.

(Ibid., p. 295) The export statistic is affected by the "indirectness" of many British exports to America.

□ Nor does it seem that there was significant indirect smuggling: figures for British trade with countries other than America do not pick up indirect smuggling. (Ibid., p. 295)

□ What about direct smuggling? (pp. 297ff.)

¶ "... The American authorities made little effort to enforce the Embargo in the first quarter [of 1808], or whatever effort they made was offset by early sailings of ships anxious to clear port. ... " (Ibid., p. 298)

¶ And the proportion of British imports from America carried in British ships seems to have fallen.

○ Frankel is well aware that his cliometric approach clashes with "anecdotal" evidence of rife defiance of the embargo on the Canadian frontier: Henry Adams and L. M. Sears (1927/1966) supply ample testimony. Of course, Frankel properly seeks to filter such evidence through his "indirect smuggling."

COMMENTS ON "1". Frankel makes the student of history uneasy.

○ By all accounts, the triumvirate (Jefferson, Madison and Gallatin) were intensely worried about smuggling, especially across the Canadian border: the President seems almost hysterical.

□ Henry Adams wonderfully describes the "enforcement ambience," in a way that brings out the complementary collapse of Jefferson's jural theory.

¶ "The principle was thus settled that the Constitution, under the power to regulate commerce, conferred upon Congress the power to suspend foreign commerce forever; ... to subject all industry to governmental control; ... and finally, to vest in the President discretionary power to execute or to suspend the system, in whole or in part." (Henry Adams, ibid., p. 1111)

¶ See letters from Gallatin to Jefferson, dated 19 July 1808 and 11 August 1808, cited by Adams at pp. 1107-1108, ibid. Gallatin wrote on 11 August that "[I conclude] that Congress must either invest the Executive with arbitrary powers ... or give up [the embargo] altogether." Adams reports that Jefferson's reply "showed no sign of offence ... 'Congress must legalize all means which may be necessary to obtain its end.' "

▫ Ch. 3 shows how desperate Jefferson must have been to reach such extremes. Frankel's work is disturbingly dissonant with the narrative or "anecdotal" evidence.

2. *"The Relative Effects of the Embargo on the U. S. and Britain."* (Frankel, 1982, pp. 301–308)

○ Frankel concludes that British adaptation to the embargo was less successful than the American one; he relies on "macro" evidence.

▫ He points uneasily to deterioration in the British trade balance during a world war ruthlessly fought by the iron-willed British ruling classes against the daemonid genius of Napoleon, perceived as a mortal threat to the "sceptered isle."

¶ Particular attention is paid to the cotton industry (not as important as it became later).

▫ "The embargo pulled Britain farther away from its free-trade consumption bundle than the United States. ... The evidence points toward greater economic suffering [in] Britain than in the United States."

COMMENTS ON "2". Frankel's analysis is fatally flawed. It has been explained that his prosaic criterion borders on irrelevance for the governing geopolitical forces. But his criteria are badly based even relative to his theory's flawed foundation.

▫ He neither focusses on relative welfare loss nor translates his materials into a form tenable for a welfare analysis. What if Economy B, much larger than A, suffers measurable consequences substantially larger than those experienced by A? The relative effect on B may be much smaller. (See America's edge in negotiations with Canada.)

○ He reports, at p. 296, that "cotton imports from all places other than the United States remained remarkably steady ... in the three years ending Jan. 5, 1807, 1808 and 1809." Indeed, longer-run are larger than short-run elasticities. But there is a twist.

□ So long as the embargo was perceived as temporary, it would not be attractive to develop alternative cotton-sources, surely not if long-run marginal costs of production exceed the previous price-norm for cotton.

○ He shows that American shipping earnings were about 40% of the aggregate of commodity exports. Of course, shipping interests led the charge against the embargo.

NOTES

1. Henry Adams is quick to belittle Jefferson and Madison; but he puffs wind into the sails of the third member of the triumvirate, Albert Gallatin. All measures of Presidents Jefferson and Madison he approves of are ascribed to Gallatin's influence.

2. Spencer Perceval, an ancestor of Joan Robinson, is the only British prime minister to have been assassinated.

3. This illustrates the continuing sway of mercantilist dogma. See Ch. 2: Hamilton's mercantilist bent becomes more striking still in Ch. 4.

4. Henry Adams contests this conclusion: Jefferson aborted President John Adams's naval construction programme, in favour of a rather inane gun boat programme. But even if a proper naval construction programme had been feasible, the public would have been unwilling to pay for it.

5. "Submission" following Jefferson's victory over Henry Adams's great-grandfather, John Adams, in the election of 1800 (?).

6. Nelson (1987, p. 70) refers to Jefferson's letter of 17 April 1791 to James Monroe.

"Our Treasury [*Alexander Hamilton*] still thinks that these new encroachments of Great Britain on our carrying trade must be met by passive obedience and non-resistance lest any misunderstanding with them should affect our credit or the prices of our public paper."

Nelson suggests that Jefferson and Madison hatched the embargo idea as early as 1793 (buttressing Henry Adams's argument): "We have a right to judge what market best suits us and [the British] have none to forbid [it]." (Thomas Jefferson) "Lacking the military power to compel concessions from European empires, Madison had proposed in the first Congress that America employ selective trade and tariff barriers to induce these concessions." (Nelson, 1987, p. 70) And Jefferson wrote that "nations may be brought to do justice by appeals to their interests as well as by appeals to arms."

These ideas are not woolly-headed tosh. Naval resistance to Britain was hopeless: the only potentially feasible sanctions were economic; and the Federalists proposed submission to Britain.

Nelson refers to Jefferson's "Report on Commerce to the House" (16 December 1793). He was prepared to offer national subsidies to manufacturers; and urged massive state subsidies as well. (See Nelson, 1987, p. 73.) This point is crucial for the text.

7. These policies harshly conflict with Jefferson's putative theory of the law of the American Constitution, analysed in Ch. 3: implementation of the theory would geld the national government. Presidents Jefferson and Madison were compelled to jettison their jural theory.

8. Jefferson then reflects on the vulnerability of sea-going commerce to alien (surely British) naval power. His somewhat muddled discussion shows the problem to be as intractable *in posse* as it became *in esse*.

"This reasoning leads to the necessity of some naval force. ... If a war with England should take place, it seems to me that the first thing necessary would be a resolution to abandon the carrying trade because we cannot protect it. Foreign nations must in that case be invited to bring us what we want, etc." (Ibid., p. 819)

9. Letters to P. S. du Pont de Nemours (28 June 1809), General Thadeusz Kościuszko (28 June 1812) and Benjamin Austin (9 January 1816) strongly reinforce the text's theme.

"The interruption of our commerce with England, produced by our embargo and non-intercourse law, and the general indignation excited by her barefaced attempts to make us accessories and tributaries to her usurpations on the high seas, have generated in this country an universal spirit for manufacturing for ourselves, and of reducing to a minimum the number of articles for which we are dependent on her. ... No temporary suspension of injuries on her part, or agreements founded on that, will now prevent our continuing in what we have begun. The spirit of manufactures has taken deep root among us and its foundations are laid in too great expense to be abandoned." (*Writings*, 28 June 1809, p. 1208)

"Our manufactures are now very nearly on a footing with those of England. She has not a single improvement which we do not possess and many of them better adapted by ourselves to our ordinary use. ... Nothing is more certain than that, come peace when it will, we shall never again go to England for a shilling where have gone for a dollar's worth. Instead of applying to her manufactures there, they must starve or come here to be employed." (28 June 1813 — war having been declared on 18 June — *Writings*, p. 1264)

"You tell me I am quoted by those *[the Federalists]* who wish to continue our dependence on England for manufactures . There was a time when I might have been so quoted. ... Under [peaceful prospects *circa* 1786] the question seemed legitimate, whether with such an immensity of unimproved land, courting the hand of husbandry, the industry of manufacture [would be optimal]. ... He therefore who is now [in 1816] against domestic manufacture, must be for reducing us either to dependence on that foreign nation, or to be clothed in skins, and to live in dens and caverns. ... Experience has taught me that manufactures are now as necessary to our independence as to our comfort. ... [The Federalists are using my] former opinion only as a stalking horse to cover their disloyal propensities to keep us in eternal vassalage to a foreign and unfriendly people." (9 January 1816, *Writings*, p. 1369ff., at pp. 1370–1372)

On 9 January 1816, Jefferson contemplates prospects for exporting manufactures.

"Will our surplus labor be then most beneficially employed in the culture of the earth or in the fabrications of art? We have time yet for consideration ... and the maxim to be applied will depend on the political circumstances which shall then exist; for in so complicated a subject as political economy, no one axiom can be laid down as wise and expedient for all times and circumstances." (*Writings*, p. 1372)

10. This is the passage under discussion.

"As every individual, therefore, endeavours as much as he can to employ his capital in the support of domestic industry, and so to direct that industry that its produce may be of greatest value; every individual necessarily labours to render the annual revenue of the society as great as he can. He generally, indeed, neither intends to promote the public interest, nor knows how much he is promoting it. By preferring the support of domestic to that of foreign industry, he intends only his own security; and by directing that industry [so] that its produce may be of greatest value, he intends only his own gain, and is ... led by an invisible hand to promote an end which was no part of his intention. ... What is the species of domestic industry which his capital can employ, and of which the produce is likely to be of the greatest value, every individual, it is evident, can, in his local situation judge much better than any statesman or lawgiver can do for him. The statesman should attempt to direct private people in what manner they ought to employ their capitals would not only load himself with a most unnecessary attention, but assume an authority which could safely be trusted, not only to no single person, but to no council or senate whatever, and which would and which would nowhere be so dangerous as in the hands of a man who had folly and presumption enough to fancy himself fit to exercise it." (Adam Smith, *Wealth of Nations*, 1776, Everyman's Library ed., i: pp. 400–401)

11. At p. 267, Hamilton evokes the authority of Jacques Necker (1732–1804) — the father of Mme de Staël, *née* Germaine Necker (1766–1817) — as well as that of Steuart. See Marcel Gauchet (1988/1989, p. 287ff.):

"Necker's whole analysis is in fact designed to demonstrate that the goal toward which he was working, and which determined his conduct, was attainable: 'one should have today in France the government of England perfected, if the king, the nobility and the Third Estate had each desired it at a certain moment, and had been able to will it all together at one time.' The great word was spoken: the Constitution of England. This was the model that should have been adopted, at least as a point of departure, not in order to follow it servilely but in order to bring to it 'all the amendments made advisable by reason and experience.' In the English Constitution the fundamental political problem was if not fully resolved then at least provided with a relatively satisfactory solution: the marriage of efficiency with liberty." (Ibid, p. 290)

Necker and Burke are *d'accord* on the reason for the downward turning point of the French Revolution (after 1789 — see Ch. 8): the French had "a credulous confidence in figures traced by theory and a thoughtless contempt for realities etched by experience." Hamilton was Necker's deft pupil. And Talleyrand (1754–1838) admired his close friend.

12. Foreigners may prefer public funds to direct holdings of real capital; bonds may be sold to foreigners — and the proceeds may be spent on imports. But Hamilton has just shown (at p. 276 ibid.) how easy it is for America to attract foreign investment.

13. Forrest McDonald swallows Hamilton's monetary theory of real action without heeding the sophistication of much of Hamilton's surrounding text.

14. It is hard to make out to whom this is said. And the trick is picked up in 1863. The National Banking Act made government stock an interest-bearing, reserve-eligible asset, an *IBEL* in British parlance (the *liability* being the government's however). The market for Union debt was to be buoyed up.

15. Similarly-incorrect remarks were made about absorption of capital by stock-market speculation circa 1929.

16. On 21 March 1801, Jefferson wrote George Logan (1753–1821), famous for provoking the Logan Act, that the Republic had "the means of peaceable coercion. Our commerce is so valuable to [the nations of Europe] they will be glad to purchase it when the only price we ask is to do us justice." (Cited by McCoy, 1980, p. 209) This was not to be so.

Jefferson and Madison did not err in the way the Adair-McDonald school say they did; but they made errors in economic theory that are still common.

　○ Jefferson feared that Hamilton's financial policy would suck real capital into the government-stock markets — and away from industry. This solecism refutes chimerae that he sought a fantastical Arcadia.

o Matthews (1984, p. 111ff.) reports that Madison supported Malthus in his controversy with Ricardo (*cum* Say) reported by Keynes; and that Hamilton took what would later be an anti-Ricardian stance — he denied that machinery could cause unemployment.

17. Adams (1980, p. 716) buttresses the text's conclusion:

"Of course, not all changes in the terms-of-trade index were related to America's neutral status. As an example, American grain prices abroad skyrocketed in the 1790s, significantly improving the terms-of-trade index. This increase, however, was a result of poor harvests in Britain and on the Continent, not neutrality. In fact, [physical] American exports of both wheat and flour were lower on average from 1796 to 1799 than between 1790 and 1795."

The input-output matrix of the American economy (say) from 1790 to 1820 was highly diagonal: e.g. the agricultural sector was virtually self-sufficient.

18. Adams clarifies the last sentence of the text's abstract at p. 722: "In short, a portion of the increased earnings that accrued to American consumers who paid higher prices for imported goods and at the cost, at least initially, of a reduction in the volume of American goods sold abroad." Cf. the decline in the physical volume of exports.

19. R. W. Tucker & D. C. Hendrickson (1990) tell a different story.

20. The text prescinds from stocks (inventories). Stock depletion may delay an embargo's, or a blockade's, impact. Indeed the full effect of the Union blockade of Southern ports during the Civil War was deferred for some months because of heavy British cotton stocks at the outset of the war.

21. "[Pickering's] hatred for Jefferson resembled the hatred of Cotton Mather for a witch." (Henry Adams, op. cit., p. 1231) See a letter from Pickering to his nephew (4 February 1809) in which he dwells on his certainty that Jefferson and Bonaparte are bosom friends.

22. Henry Adams writes as follows.

"The growers of wheat and live stock in the Middle States were [severely affected]. Their wheat, reduced in value from two dollars to seventy-five cents a bushel, became practically unsalable. *[But consumers gain: economists must treat this report gingerly.]* They were reduced to the necessity of living on the produce of their farms; [nor was] the task [of living off one's farm] ... as difficult as in later times. And the cities still furnished local markets not to be despised. The manufacturers of Pennsylvania could not but feel the stimulus of the new demand; so violent a system of protection was never applied to them before or since. Probably for that reason the embargo was not so unpopular in Pennsylvania as elsewhere. ...

"The true burden of the embargo fell on the Southern States, [especially] Virginia. ... With astonishing rapidity Virginia succumbed to ruin, while continuing to support the system that was draining her strength." (Op. cit., pp. 1120–1121)

He surely exaggerates: the restoration of Virginia's strength was displayed in the Civil War; the southern input-output matrix was also quite diagonal; and Adams reminds us elsewhere of the South's safety valve — debt-service suspension.

23. See Douglass North (1961/1966). He reckons total American exports in 1807 at $107m, falling to $24m in the trough of the embargo; and re-exports were $60m, falling to $19m in the embargo's trough. And imports fell from $148m to $52m. (Ibid., p. 24ff.)

He writes plausibly (at p. 55) about commercial and maritime distress that strongly resonated politically. But aggregate effects were not as great as North suggests.

24. Henry Adams is no mean cliometrician; and he is a quite-good political economist. But his intense interest in physics (especially "entropy") is misguided. See his "A Dynamic Theory of History" (1904) and "A Law of Acceleration" (1904), in E. & J. N. Samuels, eds.(1983), pp. 1153–1175. And in 1909 he wrote "The Rule of Phase Applied to History," referring to the work of the great Josiah Willard Gibbs. (See Samuels & Samuels, 1983, p. 1214.) There is more. His *Letter to American Teachers of History* proposes a theory of history based on the second law of thermodynamics and the principle of entropy! That so consummate a

master of political history should have been so deluded by pseudo-science probably reflects general excitement about the new physics.

Perhaps the most remarkable of his excursions into pseudo-science centres on *The Virgin and The Dynamo* — stimulated by his visit to Coutances in Normandy, soon after one to the St. Louis Exposition in 1904. (See *The Education of Henry Adams*, pp. 1146–1152.) Indeed this theme occupied his mind at least as far back as 1900. The Samuelses report (at p. 1214 ibid.) that he was especially impressed by the Hall of Dynamos at the Paris Exposition of 1900. This provoked a poem, "Prayer to the Virgin of Chartres," including a "Prayer to the Dynamo," published in Mabel La Farge (1920) *Letters to a Niece*.

Karl Popper's *The Poverty of Historicism* (1957) and *The Logic of Scientific Discovery* (1959) famously refute mechanistic theories of history — as do a number of works by Professor Hayek.

25. Adams's narration shows that the incidence of the embargo's burden in Britain was politically comfortable for the British Government.

"Doubtless the embargo caused suffering. The West Indian negroes and the artists of Staffordshire *[cf. the china factories]*, Lancashire *[cf. textile production]* and Yorkshire *[wool works?]* were reduced to the verge of famine, but the ship-owners rejoiced and country gentlemen and farmers were enriched.

"The population of England was about 10m. Perhaps 2m were engaged in manufactures. The embargo, by raising the price of grain, affected them all, but it bore directly on about one tenth of them. Poor relief was £4.268m in 1803 and 1804; £5.923m in 1811; and in 1813, 1814, and 1815, when the restrictive system had produced its full effect *[the war intensified the embargo]*, the poor-rates averaged £6.130m. The increase was probably due to the disturbance of trade and was accompanied by a state of society bordering on chronic disorder. *[Would that 'chronic disorder' were documented.]*†

"Probably at least 5,000 families of working-men were reduced to pauperism by the embargo and the decrees of Napoleon; but these sufferers who possessed not a vote among them and had been in no way party to the acts of either government, were the only real friends whom Jefferson could hope to find among the people of England and his embargo ground them in *[to?]* dust in order to fatten the squires *[grain growers]* and ship-owners who had devised the Orders in Council. If the English laborers rioted they were shot; if the West Indian slaves could not be fed, they died. The embargo served only to lower the wages and moral standard of the laboring classes throughout the British empire, and to prove their helplessness." (Henry Adams, *History*, 1889/1986, vol. 1, pp. 1153–1154)

†An editor suggests the following books by J. L. and Barbara Hammond on this point: *The Town Labourer, 1760–1832* (1917); *The Skilled Labourer, 1760–1832* (1919); *The Village Labourer, 1760–1832* (1911). Also E. P. Thompson (1963) *The Making of the English Working Class.*

26. The embargo was "against the world," not merely Britain; and Jefferson loathed Bonaparte. He sought neutrality. True: it mostly affected trade with Britain, America's most important trading partner by far.

Chapter Five

The Political Economy
of Thomas Jefferson

Thomas Jefferson was virtually the protégé of two eminent anti-physiocratic French writers, J.-B. Say and Destutt de Tracy, whose *Political Economy* extols exchange and makes property, so sacred to Locke, an instrument. (Jefferson supervised its American translation and publication.)

Jefferson's feelings about agriculture owe something to Arcadian myths, going far back into antiquity, and rather more to common-sense observation. But his multifaceted analysis of agriculture is quite sophisticated and owes nothing to economic superstition; it is sensitized to what became reciprocal-demand theory and to later editions of Malthus's *Population*. His first annual (Presidential) message to the Congress (8 December 1801) mirrors his economics:

"Agriculture, manufactures, commerce and navigation, the four pillars of our prosperity, are the most thriving when left most free to individual enterprise. Protection from casual embarrassments, however, may sometimes be seasonably interposed." (*Writings*, p. 507)

§1 THOMAS JEFFERSON AND J.-B. SAY

Jefferson's intimate ties to "intellectuals" o'er the world, and his scholarly bent, are incomprehensible to students of the modern Presidency. [1] The peer-exchanges, let alone the solitary lucubrations, of the astute party leader who maintained such supple relations with Congress were on a different plane from that on which he met most political associates.

Some anecdotal material pitches up these points. Destutt de Tracy dedicates his *Commentaire sur l'esprit des lois de Montesquieu* to Jefferson: "je l'avais écrit pour M. Jefferson, l'homme des deux mondes que je respecte le plus." Or consider Jefferson's intimate exchanges with J.-B. Say, who always sent copies of his new works to him. Upon receiving a copy of the *Traité de l'économie politique* in 1804, the President apologized for the fact that "my occupations permit me only to ask questions. They deny me the time, if I had the information, to answer questions." When, in 1814, he received a later version of the *Traité*, he reported that he liked the new version even better than its predecessor, which he had thought the best available. [2] He was a serious student of political economy, not a neo-feudal poetaster — *pace* Forrest McDonald et al.

Say's Traité: *Sundry Subjects.* Say's *Traité* is an excellent book; and I found the *Cours complet d'économie politique*, etc. (1843/1968) quite remarkable. The following interesting points, extracted from the Prinsep translation of the *Traité* (1834/1964), were doubtless taken by Jefferson. [3]

o Say eschews physiocracy. "A nation, or a class of a nation, engaged in manufacturing or commercial industry, is not a whit more or less in the pay of another than one employed in agriculture. The value created by one branch is of the same nature as that created by others." (Say, 1834/1964, p. 69)

o At p. 123 he subtly analyses consumer durables, as did Adam Smith.

o Say and Ricardo properly reject monetary theories of real rates of interest.

"The quantity of specie or money in the market might increase tenfold without multiplying the quantity of disposable or circulating capital. Wherefore, it is a great abuse of words to talk of the interest of money; and probably this erroneous expression has led to the false impression that the abundance or scarcity of money regulates the rate of interest." (Say, 1834/1964, p. 353)

It is not an abuse of words to talk of the interest of money, deeply probed by Ricardo. But Say is right in calling it an abuse to confound interest for loans of money with real yields, determined by Fisherine forces of thrift and productivity. And Jefferson's support of Say's theory of interest — explained in Ch. 2 — bottoms the most important of his "technical" disputes with Hamilton, whose monetary theory of real rates of interest still attract the stock jobbers who so admire him.

Say and Tracy on Luxury. At p. 357ff. Say (1834/1964), like Destutt de Tracy (cf. infra), is surprisingly hostile towards luxury. The analysis traverses a number of interesting azimuths, including its contradiction of Mandeville, whom Keynes so admires; it brings us to the edge of the Say's Law business, consummately dispatched by the young J. S. Mill in his *Unsettled Questions in Political Economy.* (Mill picks up Say's depiction of "Versailles" as a drain on France, not a source of fiscal stimulus.)

In his discussion of *la luxe*, Say reveals a weakly-egalitarian sense that need not detain us (nor did it the Master of Monticello) — other than to note that such disdain naturally flows from Greco-Roman classicism; the Summum Bonum is not bottomed on material profusion.

Tracy (1828, pp. 193ff.) too rails against luxury — see Head (1985, p. 143). Like Say, he does not subscribe to (pre-Keynesian) Mandevillean odes in praise of extravagance *qua* stimulus to aggregate demand. Their macro-theory yields an implication Marx could not escape from: if we prescind from their consumption, capitalists are trustees for the unborn and for sources of subsequent consumption of living workers. (Marx's capitalists do not consume: "accumulate, accumulate, that is Moses and the prophets.") But a purely-economic analysis is insufficient. John Adams supported sumptuary legislation; and Jefferson sometimes expressed distaste for (others') consumption of luxuries. The myth of the sternly virtuous (and, in some sense, devout) Roman republic was vivid for the American founders. And the Enlightenment disdained the aristocratic talisman — evolving from barbarous destruction of the Roman empire — of a free-spending warrior class that despised trade and which, in Jefferson's telling phrase, saddled up its vassals in pursuit of glory and grandeur. [4]

Keynes, Adam Smith et al. on Mandeville. Keynes (1936, pp. 358-362) extols *The Fable of the Bees* (1714/1924), along with such precursors of Mandeville as Laffenas (1598), Petty (1662), Fortrey, von Schrötter, Barbon (1690) and Cary (1695), while again defending Malthus against Ricardo and praising soldiers in the brave army of heretics like Mummery, Hobson and Major Douglas at pp. 362–371.

At p. 371, Keynes awards oak-leaf clusters to "Mandeville, Malthus, Gesell and Hobson, who, following their intuitions, have preferred to see the truth obscurely and imperfectly rather than to maintain error, reached indeed with clearness and consistency and by easy logic; but on hypotheses inappropriate to the facts." I support Say, Ricardo, both Mills, and Thomas Jefferson, on "Say's Law" in my *Open Economy Monetary Economics* (1989).

Adam Smith comments on Mandeville in *The Theory of Moral Sentiments*: "Dr Mandeville considers whatever is done from a sense of propriety, from a regard to what is commendable and praiseworthy, as being done from ... vanity." (*TMS*, p. 308) The position Smith ascribes to Mandeville would be abhorrent to Jefferson, who surely thought people imperfectly benevolent. (See Ch. 6.)

Mandeville attracts support from Keynesians and from adherants of possessively individualist egotism. Whigs find him abhorrent from the standpoints of both economics and moral philosophy; Keynes disapprovingly quotes Leslie Stephen to this effect. Consider this compromise. *Vices are virtues.* Cf. possibilities for conflating selfish actions into economic harmonies. *Vices are vices.* That the ith agent's cupidity may promote the jth agent's avarice is immaterial for ethical criticism, let alone Pauline-Kantian virtue.

FURTHER COMMENTS BY ADAM SMITH (TMS) ON MANDEVILLE

"It is the great fallacy of Dr Mandeville's book to represent every passion as wholly vicious. ... But how destructive so ever [Mandeville's] system may appear, it could never have imposed on so great a number of persons, nor have occasioned so general an alarm among those who are the friends of better principles, had it not in some respects bordered on the truth." (*TMS*, pp. 312–313)

Adam Smith is tantalizingly inconclusive. If Mandeville really thought passions vicious, he takes on the coloration of an early church father, enmeshed in the divine curse embodied in original sin; but I am quite sure that Mandeville was serenely amoral. (See Pagels, 1988.)

§2 THOMAS JEFFERSON AND A.-L.-C. DESTUTT DE TRACY

Jefferson and Tracy (1754–1836) make contact at two loosely related points:
  ○ Tracy's economics explain Jefferson's views on exchange (*cum* property), money-and-interest and agriculture in the national economy.
  ○ Brian Head (1985) shows that Tracy divorces the "separation of powers" (see Montesquieu) from the Crown/hereditary nobility/Commons paradigm that Jefferson found so horrid.

Economics: Sundry Points. I studied the 1817 translation (supervised by Jefferson) of Tracy's *Traité de la volonté* (1815), republished in 1823 as *Traité d'économie politique* — a charmingly ramshackle edition. Several arguments run parallel to Say's — one, on luxury, has already been studied. (There are also important parallels to Locke's notions of sense-perception-and-self at pp. 43–44.)
  ○ "Once again, agricultural industry is a branch of our manufacturing industry, which has no specific character which separates it from all the others." (Tracy, 1815/1817, p. 23)
  ○ "Since we rent horses, coaches, furniture, houses, lands, in a word whatever is useful and has a value, we may rent money also. ... This rent of money is what is called interest. It is as legitimate as any other rent." (Ibid., p. 95) J.-B. Say slips up on this point.

o Head shows that Tracy denies the labour theory of value and has a wider view of productive labour than Adam Smith (pp. 131 -132). And Tracy complains that Smith and Say do not rigorously elide all traces of physiocratic thought. What is more:

"The entrepreneur holds a special status in the political economy of Say and Tracy. *[Richard Cantillon should be cited as a seminal forerunner.]* Among French writers, the distinction between the passive owner of capital (receiving interest on his investment) and the entrepreneur (receiving profit on his enterprise) was more carefully developed than among the British writers." (Head, 1985, p. 141)

Economics: Property and Exchange. Head (1985) cogently points out that Tracy's economics pivot on exchange and on coordination of productive efforts by management teams, in a book dedicated to Jefferson, who supervised its translation.

"The great effects of civilized society are entirely a product of the 'reciprocity of services and multiplicity of exchanges.' Relations of exchange, says Tracy, have these remarkable effects. In the first place, social or collective labour is far more productive than acting independently." (Head, 1985, pp. 86–87)

JEFFERSON AND HUTCHESON (1694–1746) ON PROPERTY AND EXCHANGE. For all his praise of Locke, Jefferson's economics — and Hutcheson's and Tracy's — pivot on exchange, not property, so important for Locke. [5] ("Pursuit of Happiness" replaces "Property" in the Declaration.) Still property and exchange are complementary: there is no incentive to seek good trades without rights of possession and free alienation; property rights are not less important for being instrumental. Hutcheson, who exercised great influence on Jefferson circa 1776, saw things just this way.

"[For Hutcheson] the right of exchange is the basic one, not the right of retention. He sees the clearest need for title to goods arising from man's social interdependence, on the necessary division of labour and exchange of its product." (Wills, 1978, p. 231)

This is what Hutcheson said:

"The common interest of all constantly requires an intercourse of offices and joint labours of many. ... There must therefore be a continual course of contracts among men, both for the transferring of property of [in] real rights and the constituting claims to certain services, and to certain quantities or values, to be paid in consideration of these services — which are personal rights." (4:163–164 — cf. 5:288–289)

Hume too grounds the right of property in man's need for social intercourse, symbolized by the division of labour.

"By society alone that he is able to supply his defects. ... By the partition of employments our ability increases, and by mutual succour we are less exposed to fortune and accidents." (Quoted by Wills, 1978, p. 232)

Wills makes the excellent point that economic cooperation matters most for Adam Smith. The private-ownership market-economy is a schematization of coordination, based on dispersed computing, in which each agent has very little information. Nor can much of this information be digitally encoded: much knowledge is not quantifiable and may be inchoate. If agents' objectives can be well defined, private-ownership market economies are compellingly attractive.

This is as far as Adam Smith, the economist, goes. Not far enough for Thomas Jefferson, or for Adam Smith, the moral philosopher. Economics cannot reveal the Good, which G. E. Moore [6] says cannot be defined. (See A–2.)

Politics; Montesquieu Refuted. Head (1985) explains that, for Tracy, men are imperfectly benevolent and conflicts between egoistic impulses and civilized benevolence are not spontaneously soluble. There is a rôle for government. Thomas Jefferson agreed.

Head (1985, p. 168) explains how Tracy (1828) sharply distinguishes the American from the British system — much in favour of the American one. (See Ch. 3 supra.) Tracy deplores the Crown's influence and hereditary nobility.

"This notion of changing and cross-cutting loyalties, taken up by Tocqueville into modern political sociology, is one of Tracy's arguments against a class analysis of modern society. People exercise several economic rôles, which draw them in different directions." (Ibid., p. 153)

Jefferson's letter of 20 January 1811 to Tracy marks his concurrence.

"I had with the world deemed Montesquieu's work of much merit, but saw in it ... so much of paradox, of false principle and misapplied fact, as to render its value equivocal on the whole." (*Writings*, pp. 1241–1242)

And he acted:

"I have another enterprise to propose to some good printer. *[He finally found a bad one.]* I have in my possession a MS work in French, confided to me by a friend whose name alone would give it celebrity were it permitted to be mentioned. ... It is a commentary and Review of Montesquieu's *Spirit of Laws*. I translate and enclose the commentary on Montesquieu's eleventh book." (*Writings*, pp. 1229–1230)

(Napoleon came to abhor Tracy's philosophy, and predictably quashed its publication. ... Jefferson had not carefully read all the uneven book.)

FURTHER CRITIQUE OF MONTESQUIEU'S DOCTRINE. Montesquieu's doctrine does not even remotely describe the British system of (say) 1705: Burke's assessment of the revolution in France is the more asinine — see Ch. 8. Jefferson and Tracy misspent their energies fretting over Montesquieu: by (say) 1730 the supremacy of a committee of Parliament (Cabinet government) was imminent; and Sir Robert Walpole was *primus inter pares*. Macaulay elegantly develops the point:

"From that time the House of Commons has been really the paramount power in the state. It has, in truth, appointed and removed ministers, declared war, and concluded peace. ... Three or four times, indeed, the sovereign has been able to break the force of an opposition by dissolving the Parliament. But ... if the people should be of the same mind with their representatives, he would clearly have no course left but to yield, to abdicate or to fight." (From Macaulay's commentary on the work of Sir James Mackintosh, printed in the abridged version of Macaulay's *History*, 1968/1979)

Montesquieu's construction has enjoyed such *éclat* that people have been blinded to what happened in Britain. (See Ch. 3.)

Macaulay singles out Parliament's virtual assumption of the powers to declare war and conclude peace. In the old constitution these powers pertained to the Crown's prerogative — illustrating Crosskey's point: each of the enumerations of the American Constitution has special purport; the national government is not limited by the enumerations. (Manin, 1989, p. 728ff. at p. 731, points out that Montesquieu is concerned with creative tension brought about by co-assignment of rôles, not separation of powers. The American Constitution pivots on a principal feature of Montesquieu's system.)

§3 FURTHER TOPICS IN POLITICAL ECONOMY

Jefferson on Malthus in the New World. President Jefferson, wrote to J.-B. Say on 1 February 1804 thanking him for a copy of his *Traité*:

"[I have been] engaged in giving the leisure moments I rarely find to the perusal of Malthus's work on population, a world of sound logic, in which some of the opinions of Adam Smith, as well as of the economists *[i.e. the physiocrats and other eighteenth century French writers]* are ably examined. I was pleased, on turning to some chapters where you treat the same questions, to find his opinion corroborated by yours. ...

"The differences of circumstances between this and the old countries of Europe furnish differences of fact whereon to reason in questions of political economy, and will consequently produce sometimes a difference in result. There, for instance, the quantity of food is fixed, or increasing in a slow and only arithmetical ratio. ... Our food may increase geometrically with our laborers. ... Again, there the best distribution of labor is supposed to be that which places the manufacturing hands alongside the agricultural. ... Would it be best here? ... Or would it be better that all our laborers should be employed in agriculture? In this case, a double or treble creation of food would be produced, and its surplus would go to nourish the now perishing births of Europe, who in turn would manufacture and send us in exchange our clothes and other comforts. ... In solving this question too, we should allow its just weight to the moral and physical preference of the agricultural, over the manufacturing man." (*Writings*, pp. 1143–1144)

Jefferson finally, reluctantly, arrived at promotion of manufactures. He would never have blocked their natural growth: in his 1 February 1804 letter to Say he writes that, "so invariably do the laws of nature create our duties and interests, that when they seem to be at variance, we ought to suspect some fallacy in our reasonings."

Some Economic Analysis of Law. Thomas Jefferson had much to do with the great land ordinance of 1784. (See Hughes, 1987, p. 89.) He successfully sought to dispose of vast tracts of government land; in the upshot lands were held in fee simple, and there was direct inheritance and free alienation, while primogeniture and entails were barred.

Jefferson, a member of Congress in 1784, sailed for Europe from Boston on 5 July 1784, not to return to America until 25 November 1789. Dumas Malone (1948, pp. 412–414) comments on the fate of his report in the Continental Congress.

o The report urged that the new territories "remain forever" a part of the United States.

o Slavery would be abolished in the territories, south and north of the Ohio, after 1800; the destructive issues of the 1850s would have been squelched.

▫ Congress rejected the abolitionist clause.

Individualism. Joyce Appleby (1984) makes a number of good points, not including her treatment of individualism: "at the beginning of the seventeenth century, 'individual' was first applied to human beings to denote a single person, as opposed to society or the family, and not until Tocqueville's *Democracy in America* do we get the word 'individualism.' " (Appleby, 1984, p. 15, citing the 1840 Reeve translation of the *Democracy*, iii: 203) But,

○ Surely Christianity concerns salvation of the individual soul; and the Old Testament describes personal "transactions" with God. True, the contrast between "Christian individualism" and "the individualism we know," and which Appleby seems to love, is quite stark: individuals are saved, or condemned to perdition, and their fates are determined by their voluntary acts; but they inhere to a seamless web spanning man and God. Individualism, in Tocqueville's pejorative sense, is incompatible with Christian thought, *pace* Bertrand Russell (see the Preface).

Was Thomas Jefferson a Precursor of George F. Babbitt? This is Appleby's interpretation of the republican view of economic progress.

○ The economy was perceived as a natural system with law-like regularities, *pace* Alexander Hamilton who considered self-reguated commerce a "wild speculative paradox." (Appleby, 1984, pp. 87–88)

□ Smith's invisible hand was extolled.

○ Comfort, not thrift and frugality, was sought; luxuries were sought and necessities only grudgingly acquired. (Ibid., pp. 90–92)

She pushes ahead, towards an inevitable "radical" utilitarian conclusion.

"At the most general level, the republican expectation of a sustained prosperity based on an ever-expanding global exchange of goods undercut the federalist rationale for energetic government." (Appleby, 1984, p. 92)

"The modern concept of self-interest gave to all men the capacity for rational decisions directed to personal ends ... Jeffersonian republicans seized upon the liberating potential in this new conception of human nature and invested self-interest with moral value. ... Limiting the scope of government ... limited the [ability] of special interests to interfere with that natural society created by human wants and the uniting ... of our affections." (Ibid., p. 97)

"Even when the republicans seemed to be talking about the traditional concept of civic virtue, the alchemy of material improvement produced gold from the mercury of self-interest." (Ibid., p. 96)

So Thomas Jefferson sought to establish the dominion of sheer possessive individualism under cover of Epicureanism; and James Mill is the founder of American ideology. These remarkable propositions are *wrong*.

TOCQUEVILLE ON INDIVIDUALISM. Tocqueville's *Democracy* explains why American rhetoric has misled Appleby — see *Democracy*, vol. ii, book ii, ch. ii, "Of Individualism in Democratic Countries." For him, individualism is a *fault* bred by democracy — but Americans are not peculiarly individualistic.

"Individualism is a mature and calm feeling, which disposes each member of the community to sever himself from the mass of his fellows. ... Selfishness originates in blind instinct; individualism proceeds from erroneous judgment; ... it originates as much in deficiencies of mind as in perversity of heart."

"As social conditions became more equal, the number ... who have acquired ... sufficient education and fortune to satisfy their own wants increased. ... They are apt to imagine that their whole destiny is in their own hands. Thus not only does democracy make every man forget his ancestors. ... It throws him back forever upon himself alone and threatens to confine him entirely within the solitude of his own heart." (Ibid., p. 99)

But the Americans "have combated by free institutions the tendency of equality to keep men asunder." (*Democracy*, ch. iv, pp. 102–105)

o The localization of American political life "leads ... citizens to value the affection of their neighbours."

o And opulent citizens do not want to seem to stand aloof from the people, who, in America, are their neighhbours.

Tocqueville does more to sap Appleby's thesis. [7]

"The Americans ... are fond of explaining almost all [their] actions by the principle of self-interest. ... They show with complacency how an enlightened regard for themselves constantly prompts them to assist one another. ... I think they frequently fail to do themselves justice. ... The

Americans seldom admit they yield to emotions of this kind." (Ibid., p. 130)

Appleby conflates Americans' choice for more-limited government (vis-à-vis the Europeans [8]) and their reluctance to own up to altruistic motivation into a putative reign of philosophically radical terror. [9] But Ch. 6 will display the abyss separating Thomas Jefferson and James Mill. Nor could Tocqueville and other astute observers see what she says was there.

Tocqueville Extends his Analysis. He remarks on the consummate mediocrity of American politicians — see Henry Adams's description of President Jefferson's pliant Congresses for a charmingly acerbic development of this point. In democracies, business-talent is esteemed and unfolds vigorously; but is reined in by "the slight esteem" for productive industry in an aristocracy. (*Democracy*: ii, 165)

o Ch. xx of book two (*Democracy*), "How an Aristocracy may be Created by Manufacture," explains Jefferson's unease. Nor is Tocqueville a member of a country party or a nostalgic *dévot* of Bolingbroke.

"The territorial aristocracy of former ages was either bound by law or ... usage to come to the relief of its serving-men and to relieve their distresses. But the manufacturing aristocracy of our age first impoverishes and then debases [them] ... I am of the opinion ... that the manufacturing aristocracy which is growing up under our eyes is one of the harshest that ever existed." (Ibid., p. 171)

On Debt-Maturity Limits: An Intriguingly Flawed Analysis. In letters to James Madison (1789/1790) and his son-in-law, John Wayles Eppes (14 June 1813), Jefferson contributes to the economic analysis of law and public choice. [10]

"I set out on this ground which I suppose to be self evident, 'that the earth belongs in usufruct to the living,' that the dead have neither powers nor rights over it." (*Writings*, pp. 959–964, at p. 959 — written on 6 Sept. 1789 and sent on 6 Jan. 1790)

"Suppose a whole generation of men to be born on the same day *[see overlapping generations]* to attain mature age on the same day, and to die

199

on the same day, leaving a succeeding generation in the moment of attaining their mature age together.

"No generation should be able to contract debts greater than may be paid during its own existence." (Ibid., p. 960) [11]

"At 21 years of age, they may bind themselves and their lands for 34 years; at 22 for 33; ... at 54 for one year only. [12]   What is true of a generation all arriving to self-government on the same day ... is true of those on a constant course of decay and renewal [13] with this only difference ... generations changing daily ... have one constant term beginning at the date of their contract, and ending when a majority of those of full age at that date shall be dead. Then 19 years is the term beyond which neither the representatives of a nation, nor even the whole nation itself assembles, can validly extend a debt. ... We seem not to have perceived that, by the law of nature, one generation is to another as one independent nation to another. ... Every constitution then, and every law, naturally expires at the end of 19 years. ... It may be said that the succeeding generation exercising in fact the power of repeal, this leaves them free." (Ibid., pp. 960–963)

Jefferson proposes to expand the bridgehead just established. He anticipates the "dynamic subset" of Hohfeld's paradigm of jural relations (see A–1): he loathed mortmain — property's rôle is instrumental, albeit important.

"This principle that the earth belongs to the living and not to the dead is of very extensive application. ... It enters into the resolution of the questions Whether the nation may change the descent of lands holden in tail? Whether they may change the appropriation of lands given antiently to the church ... to perpetual monopolies in commerce? ... In all these cases the legislature of the day could authorize ... such establishments for their own time; but no longer; and the present holders ... are in the case of *bona fide* purchasers of what the seller had no right to convey." (Ibid., pp. 963–964)

Madison replied incisively (on 4 February 1790). "He pointed out to him that debts may be incurred for the benefit of the unborn no less than for the living, and that obligations could be rightly inherited along with benefits." (Malone, 1951, p. 291) [14] And he posed another telling objection. Much of Jefferson's argument hinges on majority rule. But the thrust of Madison's famous *Federalist Number 10* is to block oppression of minorities by majorities; such *blocage* is conjugate to liberty.

Unlike Madison, Jefferson was prone to accept majority rule uncritically; he exposits Whig liberty imperfectly. Was he a radical (?); or a good Whig, prone towards radicalism (?).

Reflections on the Overlapping-Generations Issues Raised by Jefferson's (1789/1813) Conjectures. Two lines of development flow from this fructive material: one concerns public debt; the other, a "dynamic Hohfeldian analysis." But first consider a comment vitiating both Jefferson's and contemporary overlapping-generations theory. An unwarranted sense of discreteness is induced by a mathematically improper discrete-time format. In continuous time, it is impossible to discern distinct "generations."

o The first "line of development," studied by Gunter (1990), concerns net worths of successive generations. Madison's critique lies here: we may be able to increase our descendants' net worths by selling equities to foreigners, so that they hold claims against our economy in perpetuity. [15]

o The second concerns uncoerced malleability of matrices of claims. Economic efficiency mandates its maximization: that is what the Coase theorem is about. Thus entails are undesirable: clogs on alienation reduce malleability of the matrix of claims.

A right in fee simple is a perpetuity and entirely consistent with maximized malleability. If, at date *t*, all debt is in perpetuity, and malleable, no economic harm is done: consols are transmutable into sight liabilities. Say that Blackacre is owned by *A* in fee simple, and subject to a covenant requiring that it be confined to petunia cultivation; and that Greenacre is entailed by primogeniture, and otherwise unclogged. Blackacre is freely alienable; Greenacre is not. Blackacre's uses are unmalleable; the clog on Greenacre is benign.

Political v. Economic Malleability. The analysis leads to a distinction between effects of political and economic malleability. As much advantage flows from substantial unmalleability of the political subset of the jural matrix of rights, duties, privileges, powers, liabilities (exposures) and immunities as from near-perfect malleability of the economic subset. Political transformations are not accomplished by simple binary exchanges. Nor do price signals guide political exchange. And political "transactions" must be governed by clumsy sets of rules entailing coercion. Think of majority rule, often carelessly extolled by Jefferson. Whig liberty mandates quite-heavy insulation from majority opinion: majority rule is at best a preferred modality for exercise of intrinsically-undesirable coercion. But the monumental evil spawned by Rousseau's General Will ascribes ethical value to polling results. [16] Inability of majorities to coerce minorities blocks tyranny, not the freedom of the will; nor do aggregations have wills. (Nor should the blocking effects of the Constitution, contrived by the American founders to promote liberty, be confused with "economic mortmain.")

NOTES

1. Dumas Malone writes amusingly of the President's rotating dinners for members of Congress. The exquisite wines, delicate viandes, baked Alaska, etc., titillated the Solons, eager to be asked back.

2. In a letter to John Norvell, 14 June 1807, President Jefferson wrote, "if your views ... go ... to the subjects of money and commerce, Smith's *Wealth of Nations* is the best book to read, unless Say's *Political Economy* is to be had, which treats the same subject on the same principles, but in a shorter compass and more lucid manner." (*Writings*, pp. 1176–1177)

In the same letter, he comments on works on British history. "The elegant one of Hume seems intended to disguise and discredit the good principles of government. [In Baxter, Ludlow's *Memoirs*, Mrs M'Cauley's and Belknap's histories] a sufficient view will be presented of the free principles of the English constitution."

Not only did Jefferson recommend books to friends. He reformed their cuisines and wine-cellars, as well as their gardens. He designed their houses, supplying bricks and nails for their construction; and served as interior decorator, choosing (copies of) paintings, etc. He supervised purchases of musical instruments; and expertly played the music in rooms he may have designed.

3. Jefferson's letter to J.-B. Say (2 March 1815) shows how close were their ties; and it demonstrates the excellence of Jefferson's economics in a number of directions, including American manufactures. See Say's *Cours* (1834), "Mélanges et Correspondance," pp. 596–600.

The Peace of January 1815 (followed by the Battle of New Orleans) elates him. He reports that Americans have become manufacturers to an amazing extent, thanks to the political suicide of the English. "We shall surely not revert to a régime of foreign influence, and you should consider this fact if you should decide to live among us."

The last clause signals a serio-comic episode. Say's son seems to have visited Monticello shortly before March 1815; and to have broached the possibility that Say would emigrate to America in order to go into the cotton business (!). "Your spinning mill should not be too big." Jefferson suggests that the mill be parlayed with a large farm. Cotton thread is in strong demand; and cloth is still more demanded. But he concludes nevertheless that, at Say's age, especially in view of his comfortable life style, it would be better that his children, not J.-B., come over. (p. 599)

Say has asked about American land prices. Jefferson's reply displays his consummate command of factual detail, as well as his acute sense of system and order. And it diverts onto banking. It is hard to measure land values in gold: the circulating medium is bank notes, whose gold-value fluctuates. American banking capital has grown from $1 million (1 bank) to $29.112m (324 banks) in 1803. In 1815 there are probably 100 banks with $100m in capital, authorized to issue $300m in notes for a population of 8.5 million. (Ibid., p. 598) Jefferson's image never persists: the kaleidoscope whirrs on and on.

4. Balzac depicts the embourgeoisiement of nineteenth-century society, leading to a materialistic saturnalia anticipated by Tocqueville in his *Democracy*.

5. Bertrand Russell writes that:

"[Locke's] immense influence in eighteenth-century France was primarily due to Voltaire [see his *Lettres philosophiques*]. The *philosophes* and the moderate reformers followed him; the extreme revolutionaries followed Rousseau. His French followers, rightly or wrongly, believed in an intimate connection between his theory of knowledge and his policies." (*HWP*, p. 585 — see chs. xiii–xv)

Mona Ozouf chillingly describes Voltaire's version of Whig (Lockean) liberty. Rousseau's spectre looms up:

"[Voltaire] began by identifying liberty with will. Somewhat later, his reading of Locke persuaded him that the idea of free will is an absurdity ... and that all liberty is contained in the power to execute. ... His speculative uncertainties did little to modify his deep sense of liberty as the human capacity to free one's self from tradition, to define a new order and give a life. The idea of negative liberty ... was always accompanied in Voltaire's mind by a positive image of man's ability to break the bonds of slavery, servitude and perpetual vows." (Mona Ozouf, 1988/1989, p. 869ff. at p. 873).

Zarathustra matters more than Coke for this version of whig liberty. Tocqueville is a much sounder French authority.

The Influence Exercised By Locke's Philosophy. Wills (1978, p. 169ff.) seems correct: Locke held great sway as an epistemologist. And his coarse epistemology suited Jefferson, Tracy and other "ideologists." (His conjugate proposition is that Locke's political theory was not exceptionally influential. Locke's reputation was based on his *Essay on Understanding*.)

"Locke was, for men of Jefferson's period, the Newton of the mind — the man who revealed the workings of knowledge, the proper mode of education and the reasonableness of belief. ... When Jefferson refers to Locke's politics, he links him ... invariably with [Algernon] Sidney ... Locke was seen *[as per John Dunne, 1969]* as a typical anti-absolutist of the Whig tradition, without very specific reference to his originality. Locke was the Newton of the mind, not the state." (Ibid, p. 171)

Jefferson's theory of property rights was not impeded by Locke's bad one. He grasped the importance of exchange.

6. Bertrand Russell — who, like J. M. Keynes, was once mesmerized by G. E. Moore — points out that "Aristotle agrees — mainly, though not wholly — with those who think that the first business of ethics is to define the good, and that virtue is to be defined as action tending to produce the good." (*HWP*, p. 190)

7. Tocqueville comes back to "individualism" in *L'ancien régime et la Révolution*.

"Our fathers lacked the word individualism: in their time group-consciousness was universal: each person was perceived as a group member. And French society consisted of thousands of self-centred groups — leading the way to the proper individualism we recognize." (Ibid., p. 176)

This passage supports Appleby as an etymologist; but her substantive point remains wrong. The best case I can make out for Tocqueville is that he wrote about political or sociological consciousness; not about ethics or eschatology. He goes on to show how multiplying distinctions between people who had become much alike made such distinctions the more odious *aux hommes déclassés*: this outcome follows from a sense of class-membership, not from "pure" individualism. (See Ch. 8.)

8. Tocqueville's *L'ancien régime et la Révolution* claims that a salient fault of the highly-centralized administration of the old monarchy was its stimulus of a sort of individualism.

Jefferson wrote to Madison, on 28 August 1789, that "there is no country where the mania for over-governing has taken deeper root than in France, or has been a source of greater mischief." (See Tocqueville, *Democracy*, vol. ii, p. 373.)

9. She has supporters like Vernier (1987) and Mayer (1988).

10. Professor Peterson labels the June 1813 letter, "Debt, Taxes, Banks and Paper." See *Writings*, pp. 1280–1286. It somewhat elaborates on the 1789 letter to Madison; and also discusses banks of issue. (See Ch. 2.)

11. The proper context concerns *external* debt. See ch. 8 of my 1986 book and ch. 5 of my 1991 book.

12. See the "bills of mortality." Twenty-one-year-olds could expect to live for 34 more years. Subtle calculations, based on data developed by M. de Buffon, underlay Jefferson's work. See especially the nineteen-year maximum maturity infra.

13. I comment on Marshall's gloss of his representative firm and Pigou's description of the stationary state in my 1988 book.

14. Dumas Malone recommends Adrienne Koch (1950), especially ch. 4.
Alexander Hamilton's famous phrase, "a public debt is a public blessing," appears in a piece he wrote for the New York *Daily Gazette*, 10 February 1790. (See Malone, 1951, p. 291.)
Madison (4 February 1790) nicely develops the theory of an internal-debt nexus. (So did President Franklin Roosevelt — his trenchant phrase, "we owe it to ourselves," was highly controversial though.) See ch. 8 of my 1986 book: modern theorists study the Ricardo-Barro theorem on the invariance (?) of real action to the mode of finance of public expenditure, etc.

15. Gunter (1990, pp. 13–14) shows that the practical importance of Jefferson's schematization has faded: modern "bills of mortality" call for a 48-year, not a 19-year, maximum term.

16. Madison points out Jefferson's suspect majoritarian criterion is tainted by Rousseau's General Will. (He does not refer to Rousseau.)
Bertrand Russell, the godson of J. S. Mill, pithily extracts the implications of Rousseau's philosophy in lines written during the war.

"[Rousseau] is ... the inventor of the political philosophy of pseudo-democratic dictatorships as opposed to traditional absolute monarchies. Ever since his time, those who considered themselves reformers have been divided into two groups, those who followed him and those who followed Locke. Sometimes they cooperated, and many individuals saw no incompatibility. But gradually the incompatibility has become increasingly evident. At the present time, Hitler is an outcome of Rousseau; Roosevelt and Churchill, of Locke." (*HWP*, p. 660)

Russell's continuing discussion of Rousseau's ideas should give pause to "majoritarians," but does not drive me into the "unanimous consent" camp of Professors Buchanan and Tullock.

"[Rousseau's Social Contract] consists 'in the total alienation of each associate, together with all his rights, to the whole community.' ... The alienation is to be without reserve ... This implies a complete abrogation of liberty and a complete rejection of the doctrine of the rights of man. ... The sovereign is the sole judge of what is useful or useless in the community. ... Only a very feeble obstacle is ... opposed to collective tyranny." (*HWP*, p. 670)

Karl Popper's readers will recall *holism*: "the people" is a clumsy locution that, whatever it may mean, does not mean a jural entity: "the people" cannot be just or unjust, correct or incorrect, etc.

Chapter Six

Thomas Jefferson's Moral Philosophy

§1 THOMAS JEFFERSON ON UTILITARIANISM, EPICUREANISM,
CIVIC HUMANISM AND POSSESSIVE INDIVIDUALISM

Thomas Jefferson surely believed that *Homo sapiens* has an innate moral sense.

"He who made us would have been a pitiful bungler if he made the rules of our moral conduct a matter of science. For one man of science, there are thousands who are not. ... Man was destined for society. His morality was therefore to be formed to this object. He was endowed with a sense of right and wrong merely relative to this. ... The moral sense, or conscience, is as much a part of man as his leg or arm. ... This sense is submitted indeed in some degree to the guidance of reason; but it is a small stock which is required for this, even a less one than what we call common sense. State a moral case to a ploughman and a professor. The former will decide it as well, & often better, than the latter, because he has not been led astray by artificial rules." (From a letter to Peter Carr, more or less his ward, from Paris, 10 August 1787, *Writings*, pp. 900 ff., pp. 901–902)

His letter (from Poplar Forest) to Thomas Law, 13 June 1814, supplies a much fuller statement of his ethical theory.

"The Το χ μ λ ο ν of others is founded in a different faculty from that of taste, which is not even a branch of morality. [1] We have indeed an innate sense of what we call beautiful *[?]* ... [but] the domain of criticism or taste is a faculty entirely distinct from the moral one. Self-interest, or rather self love, or egoism, has been more plausibly substituted as the basis of morality. But I consider our relations with others as constituting the boundaries of morality. With ourselves we stand on grounds of identity, not of relation. ... To ourselves, in strict language, we can owe no duties, obligation requiring also two parties. Self-love, therefore, is no part of morality. Indeed it is exactly its counterpart. It is the sole antagonist of virtue, leading us constantly by our propensities to self gratification in violation of our moral duties to others. [2] Accordingly, it is against this enemy that are erected the batteries of moralists and religionists, as the only obstacle to the practice of morality. Take from man his selfish propensities and he can have nothing to seduce him from the practice of virtue, or subdue those properties by education, instruction or restraint and virtue remains without a competitor. *[Jefferson next considers the pleasure of doing good acts.]* This indeed is true. But it is one step short of the ultimate question. [3] Because nature has implanted in our breasts a love of others, a sense of duty to them, a moral instinct, in short, which prompts us irresistibly to feel and succor their distresses. ... The Creator would indeed have been a bungling artist, had he intended man for a social animal, without planting in him social dispositions. [4] It is true they are not planted in every man, because there is no rule without exceptions. ... Some have argued against existence of a moral sense, by saying that if nature had given us such a sense, impelling us to virtuous actions, and warning us against those which are vicious, then nature would also have designated, by some particular earmarks, the two sets of actions which are, in themselves, the one virtuous and the other vicious. Whereas, we find that the same actions are deemed virtuous in one country and vicious in another. The answer is that nature has constituted *utility* to man the standard and best of virtue. Men living in different countries, under different circumstances, different habits and regimens, may have different utilities; the same act, therefore, may be useful, and so virtuous, in one country which is injurious, and vicious, in another differently circumstanced. I sincerely then believe with you in the general existence of a moral instinct. I think it is the brightest gem with which the human character is studded, and the want of it is more degrading than the most hideous of bodily deformities." (*Writings*, p. 1335ff., at pp. 1336-1338 — Jefferson's emphasis)

The principal quandary is "what is the moral sense about?," not "is there a moral sense?" An ethic based on a crucified god would doubtless repel Jefferson as much as Fr Copleston says it would Aristotle; [5] for him, ethics should be based on acts' consequences, not on the actor's good will. He does not accept what Knight calls the Pauline ethic, systematized by Kant; his idea of virtue is classical, not Pauline (or Kantian). The key words are "utility" and "happiness"; but the controlling argument lies outside of Benthamism and the *Westminster Review*.

Utility in the service of what? What consequences are ethically significant? Pleasure? The regress is remorseless: Bertrand Russell, Frank Knight et al. point out that pleasure is at most a measure of fulfillment of desire or want(s). Like all "ethicists," Jefferson finally ponders on the Summum Bonum in ways untenable for the *Westminster* Review. Following Aristotle, he calls man a social animal: his utility function can no more be defined on commodity space (which he sampled generously) than can Knight's (see "Frank Knight and the Ethics of Competition"); his ethical theory is not individualistic.

Summarizing the purport of Jefferson's thesis, moral sense reduces to a replacement set, V, of ethical values. Man, a social animal, is sensitized to social interaction. A society draws vector v^* from V, relative to its circumstances. The replacement set V is intrinsic to *Homo sapiens*; the drawing v^*, selected from V, may be determined quite deliberately. And coercion is ineluctable, as it is in building Freudian super-egos; even ethical values commanding very wide consensus will mandate actions that may be repulsive to a fair number of people (perhaps comprising a smallish minority). Finally, Adrienne Koch makes crystal clear how Jefferson's utilitarianism differed from Jeremy Bentham's and James Mill's:

"[Jefferson's] frequent denials of Hobbes's self-interest as sole interest are motivated, just as for Grotius, by the firm faith in man as a naturally social creature, to whom the actions of peace, good faith and justice are intrinsically as agreeable as any move for direct self-aggrandisement." (Koch, *PTJ*, p. 147)

I too am an Epicurean

"I consider the genuine (but not the imputed) doctrines of Epicurus as containing everything rational in moral philosophy which Greece and Rome have left us. Epictetus, indeed, has given us what was good of the

Stoics; all beyond, of their dogmas, being hypocrisy and grimace." [6] (Letter to William Short, 31 October 1819, *Writings*, p. 1430)

Jefferson's "Syllabus of the Doctrines of Epicurus" (1819: *Writings*, p. 1433) seems to me very accurate:

> "Happiness is the aim of life.
> Virtue the foundation of happiness
> Utility the test of virtue *[!]*
> Pleasure active and in-do-lent
> · In-do-lence is the absence of pain, the true felicity
> Active, consists in agreeable motion; it is not happiness,
>   but the means to produce it
> The Summum Bonum is not to be pained in body, nor
>   troubled in mind
> ... To procure tranquility of mind, we must avoid desire
>   and fear, the two principal diseases of the mind
>   *[surely a Stoical notion]*
> Man is a free agent
> Virtue consists in 1. Prudence 2. Temperance
>   3. Fortitude 4. Justice
> To which are opposed 1. Folly 2. Desire 3. Fear
>   4. Deceit."

Fr Copleston closes up this line of discussion. Like Bertrand Russell, he asks, "is not Epicureanism selfish?"

"In spite of the fact that the ethic of the Epicureans is fundamentally selfish, or ego-centric, in that it is based on the individual's pleasure ... [they] thought it really pleasanter to do a kindness than to receive one." (Ibid., p. 153)

Furthermore, Epicurus, like Aristotle, put much store in friendship; Matthews (1984, p. 92) even says that such friendship must be so complete that one loves one's friends to the same degree as oneself. [7]

Continuing Copleston's syllabus of the doctrines of Epicurus,

"Like the Cyrenaics, Epicurus made pleasure the end of life. ... Epicurus meant not the pleasure of the moment, individual sensations, but the pleasure which endures throughout a lifetime, and secondly, ... pleasure for Epicurus consisted rather in the absence of pain than in positive satisfaction *[a point made in Jefferson's syllabus]*. This pleasure is to be found pre-eminently in the serenity of the soul." (Ibid., 1946/1962, p. 151)

Copleston emphasizes (at pp. 152–153) how important was intellectual pleasure for the Epicureans; and that the Epicurean ethic leads to "a moderate asceticism, self control and independence." A certain tranquillity of the soul is conjugate to a virtuous state. If he is correct in saying that the Epicureans valued virtue for its power to yield pleasure, Epicurean virtue is not an end in itself; it is not Good in G. E. Moore's sense.

I find Epicureanism incoherent, and uninspiring. Its more satisfactory features slide towards Stoicism, as Adam Smith makes clear. (Cf. infra.)

Plato and Aristotle on Virtue and Pleasure. In the *Nicomachean Ethics*, Aristotle refers to Plato's *Eudoxus* (book ten, ch. II). "The life of pleasure [Plato] argues is more desirable with intelligence than without it. Now if pleasure plus something else is better than pleasure by itself, pleasure cannot be the supreme good." What is more, it is only the good man's pleasures that are truly human. Aristotle is not a utilitarian in the philosophically radical intension of the word.

Now turn to Edith Hamilton's introduction to Plato's *Meno* (Ibid., p. 153):

" 'Can virtue be taught?,' asks Meno. Socrates replies that he certainly cannot do it for he does not know what virtue is. ... The last part of the dialogue is taken up with Socrates' demonstration and Meno's reluctant agreement that virtue ... is not knowledge which can be used and taught."

But Copleston (op. cit., p. 245) writes that, "to the idea that virtue is knowledge and that virtue is teachable, Plato seems to have clung, as also to the idea that no one does evil knowingly and willingly." My inexpert conjecture is that the *Meno* is unrepresentative of Plato's view on the teachability of virtue.[1]

Jefferson and Plato on "Can Virtue be Taught?" Jefferson's theory leads to Freud's super-ego (ideal ego): attitudinal structures that promote utility are to be induced: Jefferson's virtue is a quality valued for its objective, or positive, consequences. People are to be conditioned to believe that these, somehow optimal, structures are virtuous: in this way v^* is drawn from V — his moral sense is an empty box. Plato seeks knowledge of timeless forms that is surely not relative to local conditions. (See *HP*, 1:I, ch. 22, "Moral Theory of Plato," pp. 242ff.)

"Plato's ethic is eudamonistic in the sense that it is directed towards the attainment of man's highest good in the possession of which true happiness consists. ... The good life must include all knowledge of the truer type, the exact knowledge of timeless objects. But the man who was acquainted only with the exact and perfect curves of geometry, and had no knowledge ... of rough approximations to them [in] daily life would not even know how to find his way home. ... A man need not turn his back completely on this mortal life and the material world in order to lead the truly good life, but he must recognize that his world ... is but a poor copy of the ideal." [8] (Ibid., pp. 242–243)

Knowledge may reveal the secret of the blend; the secret is knowledge of proportion: we reach the verge of the theory of (musical) harmony; Knight's conjecture that the ancient ethic is an aesthetic seems fulfilled.

---

[1] Plato's *Symposium* far surpasses his other critique of friendship, the inconclusive *Lysis*, in which Socrates is made to say, "the poets ... put forward no slight claims for those who happen to be friends, but tell us that it is God Himself who makes them friends." In the *Symposium*, virtue is indistinguishable from beauty; and "all earthly beauty is but a shadow of true Beauty, to which the soul aspires by Eros." (*HP*, vol. 1:i, p. 164) But "this vision of the very soul of beauty" (Diotama) is attained dialectically, not by revelation. So the *Symposium* tacitly supports the hypothesis that virtue is a sort of knowledge — and can be taught.

"Happiness must be attained by the pursuit of virtue, [i.e.] as like to God as is possible for man to become." (Copleston, 1946/1962, p. 244)

It is easy to see why Plato appealed so much to the Patristic Church; and to comprehend salvation by works (akin to the secular ideal of achieving happiness by pursuing virtue).

§2 MORE CONTEXT FOR JEFFERSON'S MORAL PHILOSOPHY: DAVID HUME, ADAM SMITH AND SIGMUND FREUD

David Hume on Morals. Adam Smith's *Theory of Moral Sentiments* relies on David Hume's work. Hume argues that reason alone cannot reveal what is right and wrong; and that an instinct of sympathy or benevolence is important in forming moral and [political] attitudes — see Ayer (1980). Two corollary observations follow.

o Both Ayer (1980) and Lindsay (1911) — see his introduction to the *Treatise on Human Nature* — emphasize how narrowly Hume defines *reason*: "reason is the discovery of truth and falsehood." Kant's categories lead to the same result.

o Lindsay (1911, p. xv) limns Hume's version of a point made so plangently by Freud (cf. infra):

"[Hume's political theory] bases society on the 'selfishness and confined generosity of men.' In society we extend and strengthen the limited sympathy with which we are originally endowed." [9]

We are a short step from super-ego formation *à la* Freud. But first ponder on Ayer's development of the theme, "Humean Virtue, a Quality of Action, not Motivation:

"To anyone who has studied Kant, who notoriously held that an action is moral only when it is done from a sense of duty, it may come as a shock to find Hume saying that an action must proceed from some motive other than a sense of its morality if it is to be morally good. Hume does not deny that men can and do act out of a sense of duty. What he denies is that this in itself confers any merit on an action. [A miser may] force himself to perform acts of generosity. In time his initial reluctance to perform them may or may not be overcome. It is not, however, necessary that it be overcome for his actions to become morally good. Their goodness depends on their conforming to an habitual practice of generosity [and that is all]. ... It is the consequences that call the tune; and motives are brought to the fore only because they can be counted upon regularly to produce beneficient actions. To have a sense of duty as one's primary motive for behaving well is rather to be deprecated, since this suggests that one is deficient in natural benevolence. In fact the opposition between Hume and Kant ... goes deeper, since Kant's ground for tying morality to the sense of duty was that an action could have moral worth only if it was performed freely." (Ayer, 1980, pp. 87-88)

Thomas Jefferson surely sided with his *bête noire* David Hume. For him, virtue is a property of action; he too values acts for their consequences.

Two Christian Theories of Virtue. Jansenists put another twist on "natural benevolence." A *Jansenist* is a Roman Catholic, likely to be French, who holds with Cornelius Jansen [d. 1638] that the natural human will is perverse and is, in any case, unable to work for the good: freedom of the will cannot lead to good: one's sense of virtue deceives one — virtue is a chimera. See François Mauriac's *La Pharisienne (A Woman of the Pharisees)* or Graham Greene's *The Heart of the Matter.*

Early Christian virtue can hardly be keyed to consequences of action in a world about to come to an end. It must instead centre on states of mind qualifying souls to enter Paradise — or avoid perdition. Bertrand Russell and Frank Knight, *inter alios*, make this point.

Adam Smith's Theory of Moral Sentiments. Raphael and Macfie (1976/1982) say that "Stoic philosophy is the primary influence on Smith's ethical thought." (Ibid. p. 5) But they also write, at p. 12, that Adam Smith takes for granted that moral rules are inductive generalizations and that moral concepts must arise from feeling. We are left with a tough nut to crack:

"Smith's ethical doctrines are in fact a combination of Stoic and Christian virtues — or, in philosophical terms, a combination of Stoicism and Hutcheson. Hutcheson resolved all virtue into benevolence, a philosophical version of the Christian ethic of love." (Ibid., p. 6)

I should not call Hutcheson's doctrine Christian. Thus Bertrand Russell, no Christian, writes that his longing for love governed his life (*Autobiography*, p. 9). *[Did he long to love?]* And "love and knowledge, so far as they were possible, led upward toward the heavens. But always pity brought me back to earth." (Ibid., p. 9) [10] What is more, Raphael and Macfie's own characterization of Hutcheson's doctrine supports the view that it is not Christian.

"Moral action is motivated by the disinterested feeling of benevolence, and moral judgment expresses the disinterested feeling of approval that Hutcheson called the 'moral sense.' Since benevolence aims at producing happiness or preventing unhappiness ... the morally-best action is that which 'procures the greatest happiness for the greatest numbers.'... The approval of virtue is like the appreciation of beauty, a feeling aroused in a spectator." (Ibid., p. 12)

At pp. 12–13 they distinguish Hume's position from Hutcheson's. "[Hume] distinguished natural from artificial virtue *[i.e. benevolence from justice]*. ... [He] retained the view that all virtue is connected with beneficial effects. ... Although Hume distinguishes justice from benevolence, he connects both with utility." I should say that the sense of justice is a product of super-ego formation; see Dr Skinner, as well as Dr Freud, on how the super-ego is formed; indeed see Thomas Jefferson, who, late in his life, saw that the specific contents of the moral sense depend on circumstances, including training and instruction (entailing rewards and punishments *à la* Skinner).

What did the Stoics say? "According to Zeno, the founder of the Stoical doctrine, every animal [is] by nature recommended to its own care, and [is] endowed with the principle of self-love." (*TMS*, p. 272) How are Stoical principles different from Aristotelian ones?

"As all the events in this world are conducted by the providence of ... God, we might be assured that [all is for the best]." (Ibid., p. 274) I find this passage unsatisfactory. Stoical ethics entail transcendent aesthetic properties of harmonization that permeate western art; and are miraculously, if awkwardly, fused with Faith in Renaissance art.

ADAM SMITH VERSUS INDIVIDUALISM

"Man, according to the Stoics, ought to regard himself, not as something separated and detached, but as a citizen of the world, a member of a vast commonwealth of nature. ... We should view ourselves, not in the light in which our own selfish passions are apt to place us, but in the light in which any other citizen of the world would view us." (*TMS*, pp. 140–141) [11]

This passage illuminates the *impartial observer*; and the eighteenth century's notion of *areté*. It is consistent with Thomas Jefferson's ethical canon and, especially, George Washington's.

SMITH MEETS FREUD, BUT NOT ST PAUL AND KANT

The following material seems to conform to Thomas Jefferson's ripe philosophy, while mirroring Adam Smith's position (note the Humean source for Smith's *justice*):

"There is, however, another virtue, of which the observance is not left to the freedom of our own wills, which may be exhorted by force, and of which the violation exposes to resentment, and consequently to punishment. This virtue is justice." (*TMS*, p. 79)

Reflecting on Adam Smith's discussion of duty (*TMS*, pp. 109-178) it is hard to conceive of people being born with senses of duty; but easy to believe that *Homo sapiens* is uniquely endowed with a potential to feel a sense of duty. Up to a point, Drs Freud and Skinner (and Dr John Watson, who so intrigued Bertrand Russell) can be consulted on the case. Up to a point, Lord Copper: Drs Skinner and Watson seem blind even to potential moral sense: they repudiate the idea of *self*. (See Ch. 7.)

FURTHER MATERIALS FROM THE CONSPECTUS OF VIRTUES IN TMS

"Wherein does virtue consist? [Does virtue consist of benevolence] as Dr Hutcheson imagines; or in acting suitably to the different relations we stand in; or in the wise and prudent pursuit of our own real and solid happiness?" (*TMS*, pp. 265–266)

There are three accounts of the nature of virtue. (See *TMS*, vii.ii, pp. 266ff.)

o One is *propriety*. Cf. "the proper government and direction of all our faculties." Aristotle seems to me the prime exponent of such prudential virtue; but Adam Smith chooses Plato, whose ethic seems so aesthetical. "In the system of Plato (*Republic*, book iv) the soul is considered as something like a little state or Republic, composed of three different faculties or orders." And Adam Smith continues, "justice ... took place ... when each passion performed its proper duty. ... In this consisted that complete virtue, that perfect propriety of conduct, which Plato, after some of the ancient Pythagoreans, denominated Justice." (*TMS*, p. 269) This seems to depict classical ethics very well indeed.

o *Prudence.* "According to others virtue consists in the judicious pursuit of our own private interest and happiness, or in the proper government and direction of those selfish affections which aim solely at this end. [Then] virtue consists in prudence."

o *Benevolence.* "Another set of authors make virtue consist in those affections only which aim at the happiness of others, not in those which aim at our own. According to them, therefore, disinterested benevolence is the only motive which can stamp upon any action the character of virtue." [12]

"According to Epicurus, [13] bodily pleasure and pain are the sole ultimate objects of natural desire and aversion." (*TMS*, p. 295)

How banal! How dispiriting! How could Jefferson avow so dismal a dogma?

Like J. S. Mill's, Adam Smith's better angel compels him to beat a retreat from such squalor. "All the pleasures and pains of the mind, though ultimately derived from those of the body, were vastly greater than their originals." (*TMS*, p. 295) Humane utilitarians share a common fate: civilized definitions of pleasure lie outside the domain of the vocabulary of "utility."

Adam Smith discusses utility in *TMS*, vii, iii, "Systems which make Virtue consist in Benevolence." "That system which places virtue in utility, [14] coincides with that which makes it consist in propriety." (*TMS*, pp. 305–306) Utility cannot bear the weight of this argument: utility merely reflects desire(s). A proper discussion of virtue centres on properties of desire(s), not on the extent to which courses of action satisfy *given* desires. "Utility" may be as otiose in moral philosophy as it is in economic theory.

As for virtue, "according to Aristotle, [it] consists in the habit of mediocrity, according to right reason. [For] Aristotle, virtue [does] not so much consist in those moderate and right affections, as in the habit of this moderation. In order to understand this, it may be observed that virtue may be considered either as the quality of an action or as the quality of a person *[Cf. Pauline/Kantian virtue]*." (*TMS*, pp. 270–271) The editors gag at virtue as mediocrity, suggesting instead that "virtue is a disposition (or state of character) concerned with choice, consisting of a mean that is determined by reason." This will not do: they transmute Aristotle into Immanuel Kant. Nor is Smith's moral sense "Pauline." And his links to the Stoics are exiguous.

His prolix elaboration, at p. 321 of *TMS*, of the idea that qualities of good and evil "belong to the objects of [the moral] faculties, not to the faculties themselves," reduces to "Jefferson's ripe result." Moral sense is a replacement set from which samples of judgments are drawn; there is a (an inborn?) proclivity to make moral discriminations. The quality of such discrimination is another matter; and the discriminations are surely not innate.

We are prepared to move on to "Freud"; and perhaps also to "evolutionary" doctrine — there may be survivor tests for codes of ethics too; are we on a collision course with Immanuel Kant? He *deduces* ethical codes from the Categorical Imperative — surely an idle exercise for David Hume, Adam Smith, Thomas Jefferson et al. But ours is not a dire choice between Kant and Benthamite utilitarianism (welfare economics?). See Ayer (1980, pp. 83–84).

"Hume is not a forerunner of utilitarians like Bentham and Mill. ... He associates the conventional virtue of justice with regard to the public interest, but he by no means takes it to be a general feature of the objects of our moral approbation that they promote anything of the order of the greatest happiness of the greatest number."

The Super-Ego and the Theory of Morals. Turn now to Dr Freud and his expositor, A. A. Brill. [15] (In "my" super-ego, "parent" is loosely defined.)

"According to Freud's formulation, the child brings into the world an unorganized chaotic mentality called the *id*, the sole aim of which is the gratification of all needs. ... *[Id-action is instinctual]* As the child grows older, that part of the id which comes into contact with the environment through the sense learns to know the inexorable reality of the outer world and becomes modified into what Freud calls the ego. This ego, possessing awareness of the environment, henceforth strives to curb the lawless id-tendencies whenever they attempt to assert themselves incompatibly. ... Just as the ego is a modified portion of the id as a result of contact with the outer world, the *super-ego* is a modified part of the ego, formed through experiences absorbed from the parents, especially from the father. The super-ego is the highest mental evolution attainable by man, and consists of a precipitate of all prohibitions and inhibitions, all the rules of conduct which are impressed on the child by his parents and by parent-substitutes. The feeling of conscience depends altogether on the development of the super-ego." (Brill, 1938, pp. 12–13)

SIGMUND FREUD: THE EGO AND THE ID

"The ego has the task of bringing the influence of the external world to bear upon the id and its tendencies, and endeavours to substitute the reality principle for the pleasure-principle which reigns supreme in the id. In the ego, perception plays the part which in the id devolves upon instinct. The ego represents what we call reason and sanity, in contrast to the id which contains the passions." (Ibid., pp. 29–30)

The *super-ego* (or *ideal ego*) introduces *ought* into the equation, but is quite remote from Pauline-Kantian virtue. "It also comprises the prohibition, 'you must not be such and such.' ... " (p. 44) And "conflicts between the ego and the ideal will ... ultimately reflect the contrast between what is real and what is mental, between the external world and the internal world." (p. 48) The epistemological foundation for this remark is exceptionally fragile; Freudian theory depends on the existence of a real or "true" external world.

Freud verges onto the ethical theory running from the ancients, through Hume, Smith and Jefferson, et al., to the present day; he gropes toward an aesthetic, possessive, individualism does not control Freud's ethical theory.

"Owing to the way in which it is formed, the ego-ideal has a great many points of contact with the phylogenetic endowment of each individual — his archaic heritage. And thus it is that what belongs to the lowest depths in the minds of each one of us is changed, through this formation of the ideal into what we value as the highest in the human soul." (Ibid., p. 48)

1. Classical virtue, surely Epicurean virtue, is plausibly an aesthetic. And Jefferson declares himself an Epicurean.

2. See Amartya Sen (1987), esp. ch. 1, "Economic Behaviour and Moral Sentiments," pp. 1–28, including "Self Interest and Rational Behaviour" (pp. 15–21) and "Adam Smith and Self Interest" (pp. 22–28).

Sen's remark at p. 20 should guide public-choice theory: "the mixture of selfish and selfless behaviour is one of the important characteristics of group loyalty." And, anticipating our subsequent discussion of Adam Smith's *Theory of Moral Sentiments*, Sen continues:

"The notion of 'self command' which Smith took from the Stoics is not in any sense identical with 'self interest' or what Smith called 'self love.'

"Indeed, the Stoic roots of Smith's understanding of 'moral sentiments' also makes it clear why both sympathy and self-discipline played an important part in Smith's conception of good behaviour. As Smith himself puts it, 'man, according to the Stoics, ought to regard himself, not as something separated and detached, but as a citizen of the world, a member of a vast commonwealth of nature.' *[Bentham's utilitarianism can be derived from the Epicureans, but not from the Stoics.]*

"The fact that Smith noted that mutually advantageous trades are very common does not indicate at all that he thought self-love alone, or indeed prudence broadly constructed, could be adequate for a good society. Indeed, he maintained precisely the opposite. He did not rest economic salvation on some unique motivation." (Sen, 1987, pp. 22–24)

3. Excellent! See Bertrand Russell's and Frank Knight's distinction of pleasure from underlying desire: pleasure merely measures satisfaction of desire. The point is further developed in the text infra.

4. Jefferson plunges far ahead of Adam Smith's impartial observer. And the "pitiful bungler" of 1787 is a "bungling artist" in 1814.

5. See Jefferson's rather acerbic letter to William Short, 4 August 1820, "Jesus and the Jews." "No writer, antient or modern, has bewildered the world with more *ignes fatui* than Plato." He is utilitarian in religion too.

"That sect [the Jews] had presented for the object of their worship a being of terrific character, vindictive, capricious and unjust. Jesus taking for his type the best qualities of the human head and heart *[an echo of the famous dialogue for the benefit of Maria Cosway]* ... and adding to them power, ascribed all of these to the Supreme Being, and formed him really worthy of their adoration. ... Moses had bound the Jews to many idle ceremonies, mummeries and observances, of no effect towards producing the social utilities which constitute the essence of virtue." (*Writings*, pp. 1435ff., at p. 1437)

Comparing Moses with Jesus, Jefferson writes that:

"Jesus had to walk on the perilous confines of reason and religion; and a step to the right or left might place him within the grip of the priests of the superstition, a blood-thirsty race *[I take it the priests are the blood-thirsty race]* as cruel and remorseless as the being whom they represented as the family God of Abraham, of Isaac and of Jacob, and the local God of Israel." (*Writings*, p. 1437)

6. See Copleston (1946/1962). This is how he depicts the doctrine of Epictetus (much admired by Marcus Aurelius):

"The essence of good and evil lies in an attitude of the will and this will lies within a man's power, for 'the will may conquer itself, but nothing else may conquer it.' That which is necessary for man is, therefore, to will virtue and to will victory over sin." (Ibid., p. 176)

This doctrine seems to me closer to Christian liberty than Classical resignation.

7. Russell makes the same point about Jeremy Bentham that Copleston does about the Epicureans: the man was much "wetter" than the writer.

The text's essay in ethical criticism is little informed by economic theory. "More pleasurable" merely means "more preferred." Critical moral philosophy concerns the sources of "pleasure," or, better, preference: cf. characteristics of desires. Economists exit at this point: economic theory does not inform critical (or Kant's practical) judgment.

Matthews (1984) points out that Jefferson's sense of obligation to engage in public life differed from Epicurus's: Jefferson enjoyed performing this duty.

St Paul and Kant come close to denying that pleasurable actions can be virtuous; Jefferson is steadfastedly "classical" in deeming acts virtuous, or vicious, according to their consequences, but it is unclear what sorts of consequences he means.

8. Recall Penrose's (1989) interesting comments on formal aspects of the text above; and see the Preface.

"Plato's world consists ... of 'mathematical things.' This world is accessible to us not in the ordinary physical way but, instead, via the intellect." (Ibid., p. 158)

"I imagine that whenever the mind perceives a mathematical idea, it makes contact with Plato's world of mathematical concepts. ... The mental images that each one has, when making this Platonic contact, might be rather different in each case, but communication is possible because each is directly in contact with the same external existing Platonic world." (Ibid., p. 428)

Immanuel Kant pondered deeply on this.

9. Lindsay (1911, p. xv) — see his editorial introduction to vol. 2 of Hume's *Treatise of Human Nature*.

10. The conclusion of Russell's *Autobiography*, pp. 727-728, is especially poignant.

"I set out with a more or less religious belief in a Platonic eternal world, in which mathematics shone with a beauty like that of the last Cantos of the *Paradiso*. I came to the conclusion that the eternal world is trivial, and that mathematics is only the art of saying the same thing in different words [*pace Penrose*] ... I have lived in the pursuit of a vision, both personal and social. Personal: to care for what is beautiful, for what is gentle. ... Social: to see in imagination the society that is to be created where individuals grow freely, and where hate and greed and envy die."

11. There is more. "The wise and virtuous man is at all times willing that his own private interest be sacrificed to the public interest. ..." This, and the surrounding discussion, seem to me vapid. What is the public interest? Nor is this material "Stoical." The Stoics' music of the spheres is hardly equivalent to public interest. All that said, Adam Smith could hardly be less individualist.

12. Adam Smith comes back to the Stoics in a passage which may seem a paean to Stoical values, but the upshot falls far short of the joy in the practice of virtue so vibrantly conveyed to Dante's readers, if they reach *Paradiso*. And it reduces Stoical "harmonization" to banality, although the last sentence reaches higher ground:

"Human life the Stoics appear to have considered a game of great skill; in which, however, there is a mixture of chance. In such games the stake is commonly a trifle, and the whole pleasure of the game arises from playing well, from playing fairly, and playing skilfully. *[One doubts that he ever gambled seriously.]* Losing is no great matter. The good player has enjoyed the *process*. For the bad player, the situation is very different. ... If we place our happiness in winning the stake, we place it in what depends on causes beyond our power. [If we are Stoical] our happiness is perfectly secure and beyond the reach of fortune." (*TMS*, pp. 278–279)

13. He cites Cicero. Refocussing his argument, the Stoics are linked with Plato, so that virtue is an aesthetic sense of symmetry. And the Epicureans base virtue on utility (as Jefferson saw too).

The ethic of the public-choice literature is a sort of Epicureanism.

14. The editors comment, n. 7, p. 305, that "the following sentence shows that Smith has Hume in mind."

15. See Brill's Introduction (1938, pp. 3–32). At pp. 11–12, he characterizes a case of female hysteria in terms of "the conflict between her primitive self and her ethical self, between what Freud now [1938] calls the Id and the Ego."

Chapter Seven

Thomas Jefferson's Philosophy: The Enlightenment; Ideology

§1 PHILOSOPHICAL PRELIMINARIES

Like most people, Thomas Jefferson disdained metaphysics; and like all serious thinkers, could not elude ultimate existential quandaries. He called himself a *materialist*. What does that mean?

"Democritus [in the fifth century B.C.] was a thoroughgoing materialist; for him ... the soul was composed of atoms, and thought was a physical process ... There were only atoms governed by mechanical laws." (Bertrand Russell, *History of Western Philosophy*, p. 89)

"[Hobbes] proclaims, at the very beginning [of *The Leviathan*], his thoroughgoing materialism. Life, he says, is nothing but a motion of the limbs." (Ibid., p. 533)

"Descartes allowed three substances, God and mind and matter; Spinoza admitted God alone." (Ibid., p. 565)

Bertrand Russell then sets out what may be called the ontological credo of modern science. The credo lacks ethical content: moral and analytic philosophy are disjoint — as David Hume showed.

"It remains to be asked whether any meaning can be attached to the words 'mind' and 'matter.' Everyone knows that 'mind' is what an idealist thinks there is nothing else but, and 'matter' is what a materialist thinks the same about. ... My own definition of 'matter' [is] what satisfies the equations of physics. There may be nothing satisfying these equations; in that case either physics, or the concept 'matter,' is a mistake. If we reject 'substance,' matter will have to be a logical construction. ... As for 'mind,' when substance has been rejected, a mind must be some group or structure of events. ... It will be seen that, according to the

227

above definitions, a mind and a piece of matter are, each of them, a group of events." (*HWP*, p. 633) [1]

"Mind *v*. matter" is otiose for science.

Like David Hume, Bertrand Russell, et al., when pondering on liberty and virtue, Jefferson travelled along the road built by non-materialists like St Augustine, St Thomas Aquinas, Martin Luther and Spinoza. Ethical discourse is, at the least, transmitted by non-material existents, comprising a sort of aether. For "utilitarians" like Jefferson, it does not matter whether this aether is an instrumental fiction or a vision of God. (John Adams makes a like point in a letter to Jefferson [1816], trenchantly remarking that the idea of liberty is empty if "spirit [is] a word without meaning.")

The Emergence of Modern Science. Bertrand Russell nominates Galileo, along with Copernicus, Kepler and Newton, as the founders of modern science. (Copernicus and Kepler play the rôle Jefferson assigns Bacon.) Galileo and, especially, Newton projected physics onto its mathematical quasi-deductive (or quasi-inductive) path.

Descartes and Leibniz are problematical figures in the history of science. Their mathematical eminence is not in question; nor is the predominance of mathematics in physics. But their attempts to infer all material particulars from universal mathematical constructions clash with the quasi-empirical paradigms that finally emerged. [2]

The work of Bacon and Locke — extolled by Jefferson — is surveyed in Section 2. At most they helped more-subtle thinkers get science onto the right track. True, their onslaught against prejudice transformed the battlefield's topography. But the marvellous physics that has emerged makes little contact with the sensations and sense-data of Locke and Hume: mathematical modelling of the sort devised by Descartes, Leibniz and Newton drives science.

The Enlightenment. The *philosophes* of the Enlightenment thought they owed much more to Locke than to Descartes — interpretations of the revolution in France based on Burke are the more suspect. The complex, consisting of "Jefferson and the Enlightenment," the French revolution and "Radicalism," has been viewed through Burke's lurid spectacles: the French revolution — the subject of Ch. 8 — has been distorted by a hyper-Whig theory of the Glorious Revolution (1688), conflated with a Montesquieu-like theory of British government that lost touch with reality before 1832 *cum* a simplistic, fatally flawed reading of the Ancien Régime: Tocqueville's great book (*L'ancien régime et la Révolution*) has been neglected in favour of Burke's *Reflections* — and Thomas Jefferson has been undervalued.

The Idéologues. (See §4) In principle, the *idéologues* (the ideologists), including Jefferson, were committed to crude Lockean empirics. But they developed a sort of "bio-physics," attaining higher ground: see especially the work of Cabanais and Flourens, reaching the threshold of William James's (1904) denial of *self*. Jefferson understood the difficulties posed by the empty intersection of analytical philosophy in the empirical tradition and moral philosophy: the author of the Declaration did not become a pure materialist.

§2 FRANCIS BACON, JOHN LOCKE & SOME HISTORY OF SCIENCE

Francis Bacon. Thomas Jefferson esteemed Francis Bacon (1561-1626); and Bacon's towering reputation as a jurist and jural theorist was glossed in Ch. 3. [3] But Ch. 7 accords him scant space (let alone praise!): empiricism is untenable for science.

Bacon sought to perfect induction. "Laws," i.e. generalizations from elaborately catalogued observations, are to be tested against tirelessly accumulated further observations. Bertrand Russell politely skewers him:

"Bacon's inductive method is faulty through insufficient emphasis on hypothesis. ... The part played by deduction in science is greater than Bacon [or *Thomas Jefferson*] supposed. Often, when a hypothesis has to be tested, there is a long deductive journey from the hypothesis to some consequence that can be tested by observation. Usually the deduction is mathematical, and in this respect Bacon underestimated the impor-tance of mathematics in scientific investigation." (*HWP*, p. 529)

Professor Hayek (1952/1979, pp. 22–23) is less polite. He calls Bacon "the demagogue of science" — citing M. R. Cohen (1926).

Jefferson was surely duped by Bacon's faulty analysis. Thus in answering Query VI, in his *Notes on Virginia*, he writes, "a patient pursuit of facts, and [accurate] combination and comparison of them, is the drudgery to which man is subjected by his Maker, if he wishes to attain some knowledge." (Adrienne Koch points out, at p. 97 of *PTJ*, that Jefferson was a better scientist than his credo allowed.)

Nor does Bacon lack support:

○ He staunchly fought science's bane, scholasticsm.

○ It is vital to sort out data, make meticulous records, etc.: experimental and theoretical physics work in harmony (but "theo-retical" and "applied" economics hardly touch one another). And the hypotheses of theoretical physics are suggested by induction.

John Locke. Bertrand Russell calls Locke a mediocre analyst with an excellent cause who appeared at just the right time. Still he sug-gests that Locke has a claim to be called the founder of empiri-cism. (*HWP*, p. 589) Corollary comments follow.

○ Fr Copleston claims that St Thomas Aquinas anticipated em-piricism in the thirteenth century.

○ The distinctive dogmas of British Empricism and French Ide-ology are impediments to the progress of science.

○ Locke exercised vast influence on the Enlightenment and French Ideology. His influence on Voltaire is well known; [4] and "according to d'Alembert, the French Encylopaedist, Locke created metaphysics in much the same way that Newton created physics. By metaphysics ... d'Alembert meant the theory of know-ledge as conceived by Locke." (Copleston: 5: i, p. 151)

○ Copleston (*HP*: 5: i) explains how Locke combated a number of ideas that blocked the advance of science.

□ *innate ideas* (held by Descartes)

□ *universal deduction* (Descartes' disastrous obsession)

□ *universals* (not obviously adverse to the advance of science) [5]

Copleston sums up pithily:

"Locke's general principles, that all our ideas are grounded in experience and depend on it, was basic in 'classical' British empiricism. And in view of the fact that rationalist philosophers, such as Descartes and Leibniz believed in virtually innate ideas, we can speak of it as the empiricist principle."

Some History of Science. Karl Popper (1959) points out that physics is at most quasi-inductive. "Theories of some level of universality are proposed and deductively tested." (See Ferris, ed., 1991, p. 796.) Popper's remark suits my contention that "classic" British empiricism had little to with the amazing science that arose from Newton's mathematical method. Corollary remarks augment this cryptic assertion. The literature teems with two errors about the interface of the history of science and the intellectual manifold including the Enlightenment, the revolution in France and the thought of *idéologues* like Thomas Jefferson.

○ One is quite general. Too much distance is placed between Leibniz and (especially) Descartes and modern science, which is concerned about empirical verification in a very special sense, having little to do with the empiricism of Jefferson's *Notes on Virginia.*

○ The other error concerns a horrid distortion of the facts. It is said that eighteenth- and nineteenth-century French thought, spanning an interval including the *philosophes* and Henri Poincaré, and ending near the birth of Louis de Broglie (1892), was antithetical to the science so exiguously linked to the British empiricists Jefferson thought so important.

COHEN & NAGEL ON SCIENTIFIC METHOD. "[A] deductive elaboration of an hypothesis must follow its formulation." (Cohen & Nagel, 1934, p. 204)

"Modern science is often contrasted with the science of antiquity [or with that of Leibniz and Descartes] as being 'inductive,' while the latter was 'deductive.' ... Part of this characterization ... is certainly wrong. The essence of deduction is not the derivation of particular conclusions from universal propositions, but the derivation of conclusions which are necessarily involved in the premisses." (Ibid., p. 273)

(Induction cannot be expected to uncover all the instances. Scientific should not be confused with mathematical induction.)

BERTRAND RUSSELL ON SCIENTIFIC METHOD. "The space-time of physics has not a very close relation to the space and time of the world of one person's experience." (Bertrand Russell, 1929, p. 131) [6] This remark highlights the virtual irrelevance of "classic" British empiricism for modern science. Physics surely does not study Humean sensations. Russell's discussion of his table (in *The Problems of Philosophy*) develops the point:

"If we looked at [the table] through a microscope, we should see roughnesses and hills and valleys. ... Thus, again, confidence in our senses with which we began deserts us. ... It becomes evident that the real table, if there is one, is not the same as what we immediately experience. ... [It] must be an inference." (*Problems*, pp. 10–11)

At p. 12 of *Problems*, Russell points out that George Berkeley (1685–1753) took a different, but related, path. Berkeley is the first to bring "prominently forward the reasons for regarding the immediate objects of our senses as not existing independently of us."

"Realism" seems, at the least, instrumentally necessary to science (and I should think sanity). Russell writes: "we have been seeking ... to define matter so that there must be such a thing, if the formulae of physics are true." (1925b/1985, p. 147).

The school of John Locke has little or nothing to do with modern science.

§3 ON THE ENLIGHTENMENT: WHAT IT IS; AND WHAT IT IS NOT

I argue, in Ch. 8, that the history of France, and the history of ideas, would be more transparent *sans* Edmund Burke. And Burke's influence has grotesquely warped perception of the American Feder-al period as well as of the revolution in France.

We seek to put the Enlightenment, and René Descartes, into cor-rect perspective. The upshot clashes sharply with the Burke-Hayek interpretation of the philosophy of the revolution in France; just as Ch. 8 leads to a still more violent collision with Burkean inter-pretations of that revolution, requiring (perhaps radical) revision of American history as well. Fr Copleston insightfully ponders on the Enlightenment:

"We have to remember that what we are witnessing is the growth and extension of the scientific outlook. The eighteenth century French phi-losophers believed strongly in progress, that is, in the extension of the scientific outlook from physics to psychology, morality and man's social life. [7] [*Les philosophes*] were considerably influenced by English thought, especially by Locke and Newton. [8] ... They were in agree-ment with the former's empiricism. The exercise of reason in philosophy did not mean for them the construction of great systems deduced from innate ideas of self-evident principles *[pace Descartes?]*. ... This is not to say that they had no concern at all with synthesis ... but they were convinced *[chimerically]* that the right ... approach is to go to the phenomena them-selves and by observation to learn their laws and causes. ... [See] the interest of the eighteenth century philosophers in doing for human psych-ical and social life what Newton had done for the physical universe. [9] And [they were] inspired by the empiricism of Locke rather than by ... speculative systems." (Copleston, 1960/1964, pp. 15–17)

The Enlightenment & Religion, etc. The most prominent targets of the *lumières* were Church-dogma and the clergy. It is easy to ex-aggerate the extent to which the *philosophes (lumières)* believed in the "perfectability of man": the eschatological outlook of the Church, pivoting on Final Judgment *cum* eternal life (or torment) after earthly death, is diametrically opposed to any system keyed on secular welfare. The choice was substantially between reason and faith. The *philosophes* reckoned they were combating strongly entrenched superstition; their goals for the foreseeable future were far more modest than *creation* of (say) a clockwork economy; to the contrary, they were committed to laisser faire.

Copleston predictably approaches "the Enlightenment and religion, etc." from an angle different from mine. See his interesting analysis of the connections between the *philosophes* and religion and utilitarianism — *cum* the linked topic, variability of moral convictions. (See Ch. 6.)

"[The attitude of the *philosophes*] towards religion was clearly of cultural significance and importance. For it   RELIGION
expresses a marked change from the outlook of the mediaeval culture, and it represents a different cultural stage.
... If they tended to reject revealed religion and sometimes all religion, this was partly due to their conviction that religion ... is an enemy of intellectual progress and of the unimpeded and clear use of reason." (Copleston, 1960/1964, p. 15)

Thomas Jefferson successfully sideslipped charges of atheism and impiety (perhaps more rife in America now than then). Like Renan, he extolled the man Jesus, whose shining moral teachings, he said, were transmogrified into mumbo jumbo by St Paul et al.

For all its banality, and other faults, utilitarianism expresses the undoubted truth that, to   UTILITARIANISM
some extent (if not altogether), actions should be valued relative to their consequences.

"Voltaire [agreed] with Locke about the absence of any innate moral principles. But we are so fashioned by God that in the course of time we come to see the necessity of justice. True, Voltaire drew attention to the variability of moral convictions. Thus in the *Treatise on Metaphysics*, he remarks [as does Jefferson] that what in one region is called virtue is called vice in another, and that moral rules are as variable as languages and fashions. At the same time there are natural laws with respect to which human beings in all parts of the world must agree." (Ibid., p. 36)

Interpolation: the Renaissance and Whig Mysticism; Edmund Burke and the Emperor Julian the Apostate. The Renaissance looked back, past mediaevalism, to the classical Greeks and Romans; it awkwardly infused classical principles into devotional art, illustrated by the *oeuvres* of Leonardo, Michelango and Raphael.

The plastic retrospection of the Renaissance is as successful as myths of socially-contracting (noble?) savages are chimerical. Burke supplies an ingenious variant of the fabulous paradigms of Hobbes, Locke, Rousseau et al.: cf. "evolutionary" trial and error, i.e. survivor tests of social and jural structures — prescinding from human will.

Burke seems less perspicacious then the emperor Julian (the Apostate). The myths, making up the state-religion Julian promoted, were but a device for infusing Romans with a shared sense of their glorious history; and a cult based on a crucified god was bound to unsettle the classical mind. Burke would have had the French invent a past that could be invoked to promote British civic myths in Gaul in the interest of a failed system, bottomed on superstition and dysfunctional privilege. (See Ch. 8.)

René Decartes and the Enlightenment. Russell and Copleston lucidly explain Descartes' monumental importance, as well as a problematical element in his philosophy that is easily twisted out of shape.

"[The line of development leading to *cogito, ergo sum*] is the kernel of his theory of knowledge, and contains what is important in his philosophy. ... 'I think, therefore I am,' makes mind more certain than matter and my mind (for me) more certain than the minds of others. [10] [So] in all philosophy derived from Descartes, a tendency to subjectivism, and to regarding matter as something only knowable, if at all, by inference. ... These two tendencies exist both in Continental idealism and in British empiricism — in the former triumphantly, in the latter regretfully." (Bertrand Russell, *HWP*, p. 548)

"[Descartes] did not say that Scholastic logic is worthless, but in his view 'it serves better for explaining to others those things which one knows ... than in learning what is new.' [As for a new logic, leading to unknown truths of physics] Descartes did not in fact deny the rôle of experiment. The problem facing Descartes ... was to reconcile his actual procedure with his ideal picture of a universal science and of a universal quasi-mathematical method. But he never gave any satisfactory solution to this problem." (Copleston, *HP*, vol. iv, 1960/1963, pp. 82–83)

The problematical element of Descartes' philosophy did not infect *les philosophes*, sunk in British-inspired empiricism. The Enlightenment was not Cartesian.

Descartes, Burke, Lefebvre & Hayek: the Genesis of a Blunder. Hayek (1960) is wont to make French thinkers look like Cartesian simpletons; and to accept even the most lurid of Burke's passages on the revolution in France. Nor does he spare Thomas Jefferson, who he says became a convert to Cartesianism, much as healthy Anglo-Saxons have long been said to surrender their British virtue in Paris's beguiling dens.

Hayek deplores French proclivities for "system building," unfavourably compared with "evolution"; and that is where Edmund Burke comes in. [11]   Georges Lefebvre (1962) credits him with putting *evolution* into play in social thought. [12]   (See Ch. 8.)

"[In November 1790] Burke had brought out his celebrated *Reflections*, which became and has remained the gospel *[sic?]* of counter-revolution. ... He introduced into history and politics the concept of evolution. ... The book, however, found favour among contemporaries specifically because of the limits he assigned to society's evolution: class heirarchy to him seemed divinely ordained, and if he condemned the French revolution as hellish and destructive of all social order, it was because the revolution meant downfall of the aristocracy. Better than any of his contemporaries, he perceived the most essential and enduring aspect of the revolution in France *[the toppling of aristocracy]*. [Thomas Paine's] attacks on political and social injustice, on kings and lords, spoke directly to the people, and his *Rights of Man* (1791) ... showed the masses what they might learn from the French example." (Lefebvre, 1962, pp. 189–190)

Recall Jefferson's last letter (24 June 1826), declining an invitation to visit Washington on the Fourth of July, the day he and John

Adams were to die. The Declaration was a signal to all to burst the chains of monkish ignorance and superstition; and to insist on self-government: "all eyes are opened, or opening, to the rights of man." The light of science has "laid open the palpable truth" that aristocratic privilege is a usurpation. Burke himself was prepared to make war on the French Republic in order to restore the old order. And science is a human creation, not a mutation of faunae. Spontaneous "natural" reformation was at least as infeasible in France as it had been in America. Any change had to be contrived against powerful, intransigent resistance; "evolution" is codswallop.

Coda to §3: Tocqueville on the Enlightenment; Newton, Kant, Morality and Religion (See Ch. 6)

Tocqueville on the Enlightenment. Tocqueville's précis shows how easy it is to misperceive Enlightenment thought:

"Discarding details in order to arrive at basal ideas, one easily sees that the various *philosophes* shared a common general idea: all thought it valuable to substitute simple, basic rules, intrinsic to the natural law, for prevailing clotted customs and traditions. This is the predominant idea in eighteenth-century philosophy." (Op. cit., pp. 230–231)

Tocqueville (Ibid, p. 231) shows that this outlook was unavoidable; and not just in France.

"It is not by chance that the eighteenth-century *philosophes* developed ideas opposite to those bottoming the society of their times. The spectacle of abusive, ridiculous privileges weighed more heavily on them as their rationale dimmed: "natural equality" came to dominate the *philosophes*. In seeing seemingly indestructible irregular and bizarre institutions, products of another age, which did not accomodate the new requirements, which had lost any value they once had, the *philosophes* readily became hostile towards the old ways and found it appealing to plan to rebuild society on new plans infused by the light of reason."

Looking ahead to Ch. 8 (especially the decay of the brilliant promise of "1789"), the inexperienced savants did dote on abstraction; but in no case would they have had the opportunity, ample in England circa 1688, to bring about gradual reform. (Ibid., p. 233)

"I have long studied history; and I dare say that there has never been a revolution that had, at its outset, so many patriotic, disinterested, large-minded leaders. Their principal fault, and their principal virtue, mirrored that nation's: youthful inexperience (in politics); generosity of spirit." (Ibid., p. 252)

What with the reversal of the laws on religion, the amplitude of change was immense; so much change was probably indigestable.

The revealing heading of ch. iii, book iii, "comment les français ont voulu des réformes avant de vouloir des libertés" ("how the French preferred reform to liberty"), is central for his book; and his comments on Voltaire are especially interesting.

"Of all the ideas and all the sentiments leading to the Revolution, the taste for political liberty appeared last and disappeared first.

"Voltaire's three-year stay in England let him see liberty, but not to love it. He greatly admired English philosophical scepticism (Hume's for example), but English public law hardly affected him; he was more influenced by English vices than English virtues. Above all, he envied the English their "literary" liberty, but cared little about their political liberty — as if the first could survive for long without the second." (Ibid., p. 254)

Tocqueville's imprecision is explained by the intractability of the theory of liberty. James Madison may have made the first breakthrough: he shows, in *The Federalist*, that for *A* to have liberty (i.e. to be able to claim immunity and absence of duty over a wide jural ambit), *B* must not be free to impinge upon *A*: freedom is antithetical to, not synonymous with, liberty! (See Wesley Hohfeld's formal analysis, glossed and criticized infra.)

Newton, Kant, Morality and Religion. Copleston completes his absorbing chapter, "Kant (5): Morality and Religion," ch. 14 of vol. 6 of his *History of Philosophy*, with a compelling discussion of the Supreme Good. I should conclude that neither pure reason nor a hedonistic calculus, let alone social evolution, can bottom "the moral law." Immanuel Kant thought differently:

"The Kantian philosophy of religion is clearly a feature of his attempt to reconcile the world of Newtonian physics, the world of empirical reality governed by causal laws which exclude freedom, with the world of freedom. The theoretical reason, of itself, can tell us only that it sees no impossibility in the concept of freedom and in the idea of supra-empirical noumenal reality. [13] The concept of moral law, through its inseparable connection with the idea of freedom [14] gives us a practical assurance of the existence of such a reality. ... But, so far as we can see, it is God alone who is capable of achieving the ultimate harmonization of the two realms. If so, therefore, the 'interest' of practical reason should prevail and if the moral law demands, at least by implication, this ultimate harmonization, we are justified in making an act of faith in God, even if reason in its theoretical function is incapable of demonstrating that God exists.

"The mind seeks to find some connection between the two orders or realms. It may not, indeed, be able to find an objective connection in the sense that it can prove theoretically the existence of noumental reality. ... But it seeks at least a subjective connection in the sense of a justification ... of the transition from the way of thinking which is in accordance with the principles of Nature to the way of thinking which is in accordance with the principles of freedom." (Copleston, *HP*, 6: ii, pp. 139–140)

§4 THOMAS JEFFERSON AND IDEOLOGY

What is Ideology?

John Adams expostulated: "Three volumes of ideology! Pray explain to me this Neological title? What does it mean? ... The science of Lunacy?" (Letter to Thomas Jefferson, 16 December 1816, quoted by Koch, *PTJ*, p. 54) Copleston supplies an answer: "Ideology is the study of the origin of ideas. And its main concern is with human faculties."[15] (*HP*: 9:i, p. 38)

Ideology is easily sucked into zoology: and the *idéologues* were hostile to metaphysics: thus Destutt de Tracy's lecture at the *Institut National* (reported by Adrienne Koch) flogs metaphysics. David Hume did not need to rouse awake awaken Tracy from metaphysical slumber.

"When the Germans say that the *idéologues* are disciples of Condillac, they forget that Condillac was not dogmatic, that he did not create a system, that he shunned the cosmological and theological matters that for the Germans constitute metaphysics." (Destutt de Tracy)

The *idéologues* were less shallow than they tried to seem: e.g. they probed deeply into the idea of self along lines owing more to Descartes than to Locke. And they obtained a number of seminal results, anticipating William James and echoing Hume; Jefferson's commitment to this fructive line of development climaxed shortly before his eighty-second birthday, leading to a fascinating letter to John Adams aet. 90: see Koch, *PTJ*, p. 86. (Hayek, 1952/1979, accurately describes the *idéologues*. He seems later [1960] to have overlooked Jefferson's relation to Tracy et al.)

Ideology and Self: Thomas Jefferson Meets William James

"[Descartes] avait dit: Je pense, donc j'existe; il aurait du dire plus exactement; Je sens, donc j'existe; il aurait ou dire simplement; j'ai froid, j'ai chaud, j'ai faim, j'ai soif ... donc j'existe." (Destutt de Tracy, *Eléments*, iii, p. 164)

Tracy's line of argument is tenable for physical science (or certain branches of psychology), but barren for moral philosophy; Jefferson was compelled, even if unwittingly, to partition off his "materialist" theory of human action from his moral philosophy.

The argument concerns self. "Self" is otiose for science; and central to theories of ethics. Consider this paradigm. Mental function may be described electronically (updating the zoological imagery of the *idéologues*). Think of a model of computer memory. [16] The matrix of charges is arranged in a certain way; mental events are, in principle, explained by transitions of the matrix. It suffices in science to describe all mental states the way we necessarily describe those of others. To this extent Cabanis and William James are plausible. [17]

In science, digitally encodable biographies suffice (in principle) to "define" people. But, if we ask, "should *A* have done that?," we confront a difficulty that David Hume lucidly explains — and resolves by partitioning off his moral philosophy from his metaphysics. I should say that modern moral philosophy begins, and may end, with the following lines.

"In every system of morality which I have hitherto met with, I have always remarked that the author proceeds for some time in the ordinary way of reasoning, and establishes the being of a God, or makes observations concerning human affairs; when of a sudden I am surprised to find, that instead of the usual copulations of propositions, *is*, and *is not*, I meet with no proposition that is not connected with an *ought* or an *ought not*. ... [I] am persuaded that ... the distinction of virtue [from] vice is not founded merely on the relations of objects, nor is perceived by reason." (David Hume, *A Treatise of Human Nature*, Book iii, "Of Morals," Part i, "Of Virtue and Vice in General," Section i, "Moral Distinctions not Derived from Reason")

Flourens, Jefferson, James, Russell, Locke and Copleston

Adrienne Koch sets the table.

"The experimental work of Flourens in the psychology *[physiology?]* of the brain excited Jefferson profoundly. [Jefferson wrote to John Adams on 8 January 1825 that] 'Flourens proves that ... the cerebrum is the thinking organ; and that life and health may continue, and the animal be entirely without thought, if deprived of that organ. I wish to see what the spiritualists will say to this.'

"These passages are of singular interest. They show that Jefferson's real concern with materialism is caused by his devotion to the hypothesis of special faculties, and the progress of reliable knowledge about human events." (*PTJ*, pp. 98–99)

Adrienne Koch goes too far: one can have reliable knowledge of some human events; one cannot have reliable knowledge of the spiritual manifold. [18]

FR COPLESTON ON SELF. While glossing some interesting passages by Locke, Copleston reaches the heart of our matter.

"In organic things ... we are accustomed to speak of the organisms as being the same organic body, even though obvious changes in the same matter have taken place. ... The case of animals is similar. The continued identity of an animal is in some ways similar to that of a machine. *[I am fond of saying 'I today am not I tomorrow.']* For we speak of a machine *[perhaps an airplane]* as being the same, even if parts of it have been repaired or renewed, because of the continued organization of the parts with a view to the attainment of a certain end or purpose." (Copleston, *HP*, 5: i ["Hobbes to Paley"], pp. 109–110)

Copleston predictably sends the analysis into a teleological domain. But he soon puts his cards face down again. He asks, at p. 11, ibid., what does personal identity consist of? And, echoing Locke, replies "consciousness" — a short distance from "je sens, donc j'existe."

WILLIAM JAMES AND BERTRAND RUSSELL ON SELF. At p. 550 of *HWP*, Bertrand Russell, ceaselessly orbiting around *self* over his long career, writes that "the word 'I' is really illegitimate, [Descartes] ought to state his ultimate premiss in the form, 'there are thoughts.' " He credits William James for this proposition, which startled the world. (William James sometimes objected to Russell's translations, which I prefer to the originals.) And Jefferson's excitement, aet. 82, over the Cabanis-Flourens analysis takes him very close to James, who denies, in "Does 'Consciousness' Exist?," that the subject/object relation is fundamental — finessing "mind *v.* matter."

○ In science, "there are thoughts" can indeed replace "I think"; for scientific purposes, a person is, in Russell's phrase, a mere biography; Russell's "private worlds" have no place in science. (See Bertrand Russell, 1929.)

○ "Subject/object" or "mind/matter" must be retained in (say) the Pauline ethical tradition, encompassing Judeo-Christianity: virtue pivots on personal responsibility and so on "Christian liberty": one cannot be virtuous if one is not free to choose the wrong action. Such is the irreducible content of moral philosophy — cf. "ethical atomism," a counterpart to Russell's "logical atomism." Virtue pivots on self.

○ Copleston (1966/1967) penetratingly discusses Bertrand Russell's oscillating views of self.

"There was a time ... when [he] thought that the phenomenology of consciousness or awareness implies that the I-subject is uneliminable. Later on, however, he depicted the self as a logical construction out of events, thus developing the phenomenalism of Hume. But it [is] clear that when sentences beginning with the pronoun 'I' have been translated into sentences in which only 'events' are mentioned and the word 'I' does not appear, an essential feature of the original sentence has been omitted." (*HP*: 8: ii, ch. 21, "Bertrand Russell [3]," pp. 251–252)

Sentences with "I" subjects are otiose in science; and ones without "I," or "he/she," subjects are otiose in ethics.

NOTES

1. See Russell's excellent *The Problems of Philosophy*. Physics does not study Humean (or Lockean) sensations. Russell peels off layer after layer of "sensation" before reaching the core of quantum "reality." Cf. his parable of his table, discussed in the text of Ch. 7.

2. Anglophone commentators, besotted by Burke, have libelled René Descartes. A byproduct has been monstrous distortion of Jefferson's ties to French thought and of the French revolution.

3. Bertrand Russell trenchantly describes Francis Bacon's spot of trouble with the Crown.

"In 1618, he became Lord Chancellor. But after he had held this great position for only two years, he was prosecuted for accepting bribes from litigants. He admitted the truth of the accusation, pleading only that presents never influenced his decision. ... The sentence was only very partially executed. ... But he was compelled to abandon public life, and so to spend the remainder of his days ... writing important books. ... After five years spent in retirement, he died of a chill caught while experimenting on refrigeration by stuffing a chicken full of snow." (*HWP*, pp. 526–527)

4. See Voltaire (1734/1964), pp. 81–88, "Sur M. Locke." *Lettres philosophiques* buttresses Garry Wills's contention that Locke's epistemology, not his political theory, deeply influenced the Enlightenment. (See Ch. 5, n. 5.)

"Sur M. Locke" makes Burke's strictures on the *lumières* all the more preposterous: Voltaire extols Newton's system, finding it much superior to the Cartesian one. (See his *Eléments de la philosophie de Newton*, 1737.) And his praise of Locke's scepticism has a modern ring:

"Locke simply said to the scholastics: 'At least admit that you are as ignorant as I am; neither of us can grasp how a material organism acquires ideas. You cannot perceive matter or spirit; so how can you be sure of various points?' " (Ibid., p. 86)

5. The problem of Universals goes back at least as far as the Platonic Forms. See Plato's doctrine of Ideas.

Aristotle is thought to have criticized the Forms quite devastatingly. (See Copleston, *HP*, 1: ii, pp. 36–44 and this note.) But the notion has a certain tenacity — Roger Penrose finds it irresistible.

Bertrand Russell discusses Universals in chs. ix and x of *The Problems of Philosophy*. Indeed he frequently reverts to the subject in his vast organum. (Also see *HWP*.) "The true ground ... is ... linguistic; it is derived from syntax." (*Problems*, p. 177) This remark rounds out an earlier one:

"What is signified by a proper name is a 'substance,' while what is signified by an adjective or class-name, such as 'human' or 'man,' is called a 'Universal.' A substance is a 'this,' but a Universal is a 'such' — it indicates the sort of thing, not the actual particular thing." (*Problems*, p. 176)

Russell comes back to Universals in *An Inquiry into Meaning and Truth* (1940).

"If I make a number of true statements concerning a given shade of colour C, they all have different verifiers. These all have a common part, 'C.' ... The question involved is the old question of 'Universals.' ... A 'Universal' may be defined as 'the meaning (if any) of a relation word.' " (*Inquiry*, pp. 342–343)

See Russell's Propositional Functions — e.g. in *Inquiry*, p. 260. The values x, drawn from the replacement set X, for which the statement, "x has the property C," is true, comprise a universal.

Aristotle and Universals. Aristotle posits Forms meant not to be universals. But Zeller's *Aristotle*, cited by Russell (*HWP*, p. 179), demonstrates that Aristotle has not, *pace* most opinion, corrected Plato after all:

"The 'Forms' had for [Aristotle], as the 'Ideas' had for Plato, a metaphysical existence of their own, as conditioning all individual things. And keenly as he followed the growth of Ideas out of experience, it is none the less true that these Ideas, especially at the point where they are farthest removed from experience and immediate perception, are metamorphosed in the end from a logical product of human thought into an immediate presentment of a super-sensible world, and the object, in that sense, of an intellectual intuition." (Zeller, *Aristotle*, vol. i, p. 204, cited in *HWP*, p. 179)

6. See Bertrand Russell (1929) — especially Lecture iv, "The World of Physics and the World of Sense," pp. 130–137.

7. The seeds of "social engineering," lauded by Popper, are thus planted. But it was shown in Chs. 4 and 5 that Jefferson, a liberal, wanted none of it.

8. We have seen that Newton's and Locke's scientific outlooks clash and that it is Newton's influence that counts.

9. The impression that the *philosophes* are "constructivist" owes to their conflict with the clergy, sunk in revealed religion and an eschatology devaluing the importance of life on this earth. Compared with the clergy, most people look like "social engineers." What is more, able researchers have quite recently viewed society mechanistically.

"Mathematical economics before [John] von Neumann [1903–1957] tried to achieve success by imitating the technique of classical mathematical physics. ... The procedure relied on a not completely reliable analogy between economics and mechanics. The secret of the success of the von Neumann approach was the abandonment of the mechanical analogy and its replacement by ... games of strategy and ... the ideas of combinatories and convexity." (P. R. Halmos in Ferris, ed., 1991, pp. 614–628, at p. 626)

Interestingly, the original title of "A. d'Abro's" (1951) *The Rise of the New Physics* was *Decline of Mechanism* (1939). *Nota bene*: the *mechanisms* of classical physics are replaced by quantum *mechanics*.

Recent important work in economic theory, based on property-rights-assignment characteristics, is surely non-mechanistic. There is growing recognition that Halmos's point is very sound.

10. The intensity of one's sense of self, together with the obscurity of one's sense of others' selves, is salient in moral philosophy and almost irrelevant for science.

11. The American political system is one of the most "constructed," or contrived, in all history. Nor were the American founders "Cartesian."

12. See Georges Lefebvre (1962), vol. 1 of a two vol. translation by Eliza-beth Moss Evanson. His *La Révolution française*, vol. xiii of the series "Peuples et Civilisations," published by Presses Universitaires de France.

Vol. 1 of the translation encompasses the first three parts of *La Rév-olution*. *LRF* was first published by Lefebvre in collaboration with Ray-mond Guyot and Phillipe Sagnac in 1930. Lefebvre himself brought out the translated version in 1951. E. M. Evanson translated the 1957 edition of the work first published in 1951.

13. See the OED: "Noumenon (... introduced by Kant in contrast to phenomenon). In the philosophy of Kant, an object of purely intellectual intuition, devoid of all phenomenal attributes." Then the *OED* quotes from Caird (1877), *Philos. Kant,* ii, xiii, p. 498. "In a negative sense, a noumenon would be an object not given in sensuous perception; in a positive sense, a noumenon would be an object given in a non-sensuous, i.e. an intellectual perception." (Compact Ed., *OED*, i, p. 1949)

Bertrand Russell and Fr Copleston treat the noumenon less straight-forwardly than Caird does.

"Kant does not at most times question that our sensations have causes [i.e. components], which he calls 'things in themselves' or 'noumena.' What appears to us in perception, which he calls a 'phenomenon,' consists of two parts: that due to the object, which he calls 'sensation,' and that due to our subjective apparatus, which he says causes the manifold to be ordered in certain relations. This latter part he calls the *form* of the phenomenon. This part is not itself sensation. ... It is always the same; ... and it is *a priori* in the sense that it is not dependent upon experience." (*HWP*, p. 685)

See Copleston, *HP*, vol. 6, part ii (*Kant*), see pp. 61–66. At p. 63, Copleston, citing Kant, argues that the positive sense of noumenon ought to be neglected. And Kant himself offers this "negative" definition of noumenon: "a thing in so far as it is not the object of our sensuous intuition." It is easy to see why Caird writes as he does; and hard to see how he can be wrong. The following passage from the *Critique of Pure Reason* becomes especially important:

"If, by the term noumenon, we understand a thing so far as it is not an object of our sensuous intuition, thus making abstraction of our mode of intuiting it, this is a noumenon in the negative sense of the word. But if we understand by it an object of a non-sensuous intuition, ... an intellectual intuition ... the very possibility of which we have no notion — and this is a noumenon in the positive sense." Immanuel Kant (1787/1934, pp. 186–187)

I am baffled by Copleston's attempt to square this circle: "[Kant's] remark about abstracting from our mode of intuiting the noumenon must not be taken to imply that, according to Kant, we intuit, or can intuit, in a non-sensuous manner." (Op. cit., p. 63) But I agree that the "positive" sense of noumenon ought to be neglected: it makes no sense! The "negative" sense of noumenon is another matter: it is central for understanding the crucial subject/object relationship, indispensable to the idea of conscience, among many other things.

An uneasy analogy runs to "moral-philosophy space." Super-ego (ideal-ego) formations comprise a subjective apparatus organizing the purely sensual ("sensational") material of id-action.

14. I cannot take the right action unless I am free to take the wrong one. This is the *sine qua non* for Pauline-Kantian virtue, entailing Christian Liberty.

15. The literature mandates reference to Auguste Comte: I think his work is vapid and his reputation unmerited; I have no idea what "positive knowledge" means; and "sense impression" does not inform modern science. Agreed, positivism and ideology follow Locke. But science would not suffer if work in Locke's mode were to vanish. Copleston appraises Comte and Positivism more generously in *HP*: 9: i, p. 93ff.

See Adrienne Koch, *PTJ*, p. 66. "We may place ideology in its traditional setting by calling the roll of Bacon, Condillac and Locke." (Jefferson would call this roll.) The *Encyclopaedia* enshrined Bacon's views on scientific method; and Tracy calls Locke a forerunner of ideology, which Koch suggests is truly founded by Condillac. Koch's cogent précis of ideology puts it in a brighter light than I do.

"The broad structure of this argument is that of Condillac's sensationalist version of Lockean epistemology. Tracy agreed with Condillac on these basic points: (1) that all ideas are derived from sensations; (2) that any pure sensation is only a modification of our own being, containing neither a perception of relationship nor any interpretative judgment; and (3) that only the sensation of resistance can inform about references to things outside ourselves." (Ibid., p. 74)

Koch correctly reports that ideology is virtually a branch of zoology: the *idéologues* more accurately described gorilla than human life. This brings us to the verge of William James's work, reached by Thomas Jefferson.

16. Roger Penrose (1989/1990) — chs. 9 and 10 — argues that Turing machines do not really think. I simply point out that a "materialist" description of mental and judgmental processes suffices for physics, positive economics, etc.

17. See Adrienne Koch (1943/1957), ch. 9, "Cabanis and the Issue of Materialism." She describes Jefferson's admiration for Cabanis at p. 114ff. In 1803, President Jefferson wrote to Cabanis, seeking to explain thought as a "faculty of our material organization."

18. Koch comments on the philosophy of Dugald Stewart — whom Jefferson admired, and consulted with on selection of professors for the new University of Virginia. And the following passage further undermines Professor Hayek's description of Jefferson's thought:

"In fact, Stewart's *Elements of the Philosophy of the Human Mind* has something in common with both the philosophy of the *Encylopaedia* and Ideology. All three philosophies are primarily 'anti-metaphysical' (a favourite term of the *idéologues*), which seems to mean primarily anti-Descartes, mediaeval rationalism, 'spiritualism.' In Stewart's case, it meant in addition anti-Hume and anti-Kant." (Koch, *PTJ*, p. 49)

She remarks, at p. 50, that Stewart, the encyclopaedists and the *idéologues* all claim "the same historical progenitor, [Francis] Bacon," condemning themselves to banality I should say.

Stewart's hostility towards Hume doubtless appealed to Jefferson.

Chapter Eight

Thomas Jefferson and
the Revolution in France

§1 PRELIMINARIES

Chapter Eight exorcises the Burkean demon while establishing Tocqueville's authority: Tocqueville shows how the feeble flicker of whig liberty in France was snuffed out by the evolution of the Ancien Régime.

Section 2 ("*L'ancien régime et la Révolution*") shows how evolutionary forces blocked all possibilities for spontaneous generation of a liberal order. The upheaval, but not its chaotic, bloody sequel, was ordained. The reasons why events took so baffling a path leads to Section 3 (The Revolution in France and Democratic Despotism).

Section 3 is a segué to Section 4 ("Burke") which refutes influential canards against Jefferson and the Revolution itself; Sections 3 and 4 rely heavily on Tocqueville's authority.

Section 5 portrays Jefferson's thought and action in the French Revolution. He participated in the liberal triumphs, up to October 1789; his advice was sought by liberal ("Patriot") leaders. He urged moderation, cautioning against the specious appeal of measures calculated to shape, or design, whole societies. Preposterous claims that he was a "Cartesian Jacobin" have distorted American, as well as French, history.

François Furet on Tocqueville's Ancien Régime

François Furet's (1989b) article on Tocqueville puts Chapter Eight into clear perspective.

251

"Tocqueville examines the misinterpretation of one of his greatest predecessors, Burke. In speaking of the Ancien Régime, the Whig M.P. *[whom Jefferson called the Rhetor]* had lectured the French that they could have avoided the illusion of the democratic *tabula rasa* by improving the constitution of their monarchy or even by borrowing from English common law." (Furet, 1989b, p. 1023)

But the Ancien Régime's "traditions" subverted evolutionary possibilities. Subversion? Furet lucidly depicts Tocqueville's argument.

"[Cf.] the subversion of the old society by the monarchial state. What was *ancien* about the Ancien Régime ... was precisely the society that existed prior to the growth of the centralized state, a society he called indiscriminately 'feudal' or 'aristocratic' to indicate ... hierarchical dependency." (Ibid., p. 1024)

Furet then develops Tocqueville's principal corollary points:
o French society splintered into self-regarding groups, losing social cohesiveness.
o "The nobility lost both its principle, blood, and its function, public service." (Ibid., p. 1026) It became instead a highly privileged, geneologically diverse caste.
o So the idea of natural equality appealed to the enraged bourgeoisie, including many economists. Cut loose from their moorings, the intellectuals readily fell into a revolutionary, surely a radicalized, orbit.
o The philosophy of the Enlightenment helped subordinate liberty (a much more complex notion than Furet realizes) to equality. [1] So France became vulnerable to Rousseau's execrable General Will — a progenitor of collective welfare constructions and even worse things. Furet lurks in the neighbourhood of my point when he writes that "the idea of reform could be embodied just as well in the despotism of one man as in the sovereignty of the people, the latter being merely a matter of substituting the nation as a unitary body for the king." (Ibid., pp. 1028–1029)

o *The Second Revolution.* After October 1789, politics were driven by a fever for equality (accompanied by class hatred). Aspirations for Whig liberty gave way to a mania for equality (but it cannot be clear what "equality" means), almost inevitably tyranically engineered from the centre. Furet's continuing discussion is especially important.

"In fact the degeneration from liberty to equality in 1789 can be explained in Tocqueville's system of interpretation more easily than the divine surprise of 1789. The first phenomenon illustrates a general truth developed at length in the second part of *Démocratie en Amérique*, that the passion for equality is more accessible and in any case more universal than the passion for liberty. [2] ... Equality, encouraged by centralization and the movement of ideas, was the dominant passion of the French under the Ancien Régime; and this same source, broadened and strengthened even further, fed the French revolution and revealed in it the same indifference to liberty as under the Ancien Régime.

"Therefore, it is the sharp break that occurred in 1789 that becomes difficult to understand. ... Just as there is in Tocqueville a philosophical mystery of liberty, there is also in his vision of French history an enigma surrounding liberty's brief appearance." [3] (Ibid., pp. 1031–1032)

§2 THE ANCIEN RÉGIME

Thomas Jefferson (Minister to France), in a letter to James Madison, dated 28 October 1785, (*Writings*, p. 840) describes the massive concentration of property ownership in France, together with widespread rural poverty, made more salient by the vast amount of good land reserved for royal and aristocratic hunting. And, reacting against the regressive tax-system, he proposed more-progressive taxation for France. (He describes the pathetic gratitude of a peasant for his small gift; but Arthur Young's beneficiaries were ungracious.) In another letter, cited by Tocqueville, he reflects on the Ancien Régime's penchant to over-govern.

Tocqueville (1856/1967) on the Ancien Régime

From the time of Charles VI (called the Mad or the Well Beloved, 1368–1422), [4] the crown imposed heavy taxes from which the nobility were exempt: the régime's flaws set in early on — heavy taxation of the third estate and exemption of the nobility from taxation, followed by sales of titles (conferring tax exemptions), led to invidious class feelings. (Ibid, p. 180.)

The Ancien Régime was highly centralized, but faint pulses of "localism" were discernable. This motif runs parallel to the Whig interpretation of English history, espying primitive liberty (see Ch. 3); and links up with Tocqueville's earlier visit to America.

"I recall my surprise, when I first studied the records of a parish of the Ancien Régime, at finding points in common with the political organization of rural America that I had thought unique to the new world. In both, general assemblies of inhabitants, sitting in one body, elected their magistrates and managed their principal affairs. The two societies, whose fates were so different, had the same birth. ... The rural parish of the middle ages became the New England township; and in France it became what we have seen." (Ibid, pp. 117–118)

At p. 122, ibid., he finds another feeble pulse of liberty. There was no other European country where ordinary courts depended less on the government; but there was hardly another country where there was more recourse to special courts — the English Star Chamber was a "special court."

Social Fission. At p. 159 of his book, Tocqueville explains how a certain homogenization among the French accompanied group alienation, i.e. a sense of isolation between groups. The material status of the fourteenth-century bourgeois was surely inferior to that of the eighteenth-century one. But, in the fourteenth century, the group to which he belonged was incontestably eligible to participate in government.

Finally, the nobility became a caste.

"As the nobility steadily lost its right to command, their exclusive prerogatives as first servants of the master (the king) steadily grew. The more the nobility ceased to be an aristocracy, the more it appeared to be a caste." (Ibid., p. 165)

Nobility became a patent for financial-privilege, not an opportunity for command, let alone glory.

The Economists and the Ancien Régime. It was some time before economic reform was associated with political liberty: Benthamism, rooted in authoritarianism, evolved into a liberal creed only tortuously. And Thomas Jefferson, a student of J.-B. Say and Destutt de Tracy, was one of the first to make the connection between economic laisser faire and political liberty. He, and his party, saw that economic decentralization is a necessary condition for political decentralization. Tocqueville's extended commentary along these lines merits close attention. (See ibid., pp. 254–256)

○ Towards the middle of the eighteenth century, there appeared a number of writers specializing in problems of public administration — viz. *les économistes*, including the physiocrats.

○ The economists deplored virtually all the institutions of the Ancien Régime. They displayed a revolutionary egalitarian sentiment: not only did they resist privilege, but they were obsessed with equality.

○ Anything not consistent with their designs was to be discarded. Contracts did not move them; and they paid no heed to individual rights — which were to be subordinated to "public utility" (*utilité publique*).

○ For all this, the economists' manners were gentle; they were honest, able magistrates and officials despite the authoritarian spirit of their work.

Tocqueville reveals the true origins of Benthamite utilitarianism, and contemporary economism. See Elie Halévy's admirable *Philosophical Radicalism*. He demonstrates — *pace* Professor Lionel Robbins — the authoritarian origins of Benthamism; and how utilitarianism, under the influence of its (English) economist adherants, became transmogrified into a doctrine of natural harmony — partially renouncing its debt to Rousseau.

(Adam Smith's economics are influenced by the French economists, including the physiocrats. But it is insufficiently remarked that Adam Smith's moral philosophy is more influenced by his friend, David Hume, than by the virtual authoritarianism of the économistes — leading to Benthamism).

Tocqueville writes that,

"The economists simply scorned the past: no institution, however ancient, however embedded in our history, was exempt from their overriding concern for symmetry." (Op. cit., p. 256)

Burke's true *bêtes noires* are the monstrous parents of Jeremy Bentham! Are the Terror, Robespierre, etc. byproducts of economists' theories?

○ The economists anticipated the Revolution's social and administrative reforms before liberty came to the front of their minds.

○ They supported free exchange and *laisser faire ou laisser passer* in commerce and industry; but they were indifferent towards political liberty.

○ Most economists disliked deliberative assemblies at provincial or local level; and they opposed historic counterweights to central power — intrinsic to liberal societies. Thus Quesnay said that political systems based on counter-forces are fatally flawed. The economists considered such systems quite chimerical. (Ibid., p. 256)

□ These remarks explain a clash with J. S. Mill, who cherished political liberty. (Economic liberty was for him but an instrument promoting value-enhancing exchange.) *Les économistes* did not value liberty at all: they proposed to be super-nannies; they wished to "build structures" promoting Benthamite "gross national utility." Nor did Turgot, whom Hamilton admired, value political liberty.

"Turgot, like the economists, said that the primary political modality was proper public instruction, supplied by the state." (Ibid., p. 257)

The following passage succinctly describes what Benthamism is really about.

"According to the economists, the state should not so much dictate to the nation as make its spirit conform to their model. Bodeau, perfectly capsulating the theories of the economists, said that the state makes what it wants of men." (Ibid., p. 257)

§3 THE REVOLUTION IN FRANCE AND DEMOCRATIC DESPOTISM

Section 3 mostly concerns how things went wrong — leading to Section 4, on Burke. Its *Leitmotif* is democratic despotism, the lurid successor to 1789's "miraculous season." But the onus of the Revolution's sordid excesses cannot properly be put on Descartes — or on the Enlightenment's rejection of myths about liberty flourishing in elden forests.

By 1793, the Revolution careened into democratic despotism. [5] In both democratic despotism and its more attractive sister, social democracy, privileges (absences of duty) are exchanged for rights (entitlements).

Tocqueville on Democratic Despotism

○ The middle ages had no idea of the form of tyranny called democratic despotism.

○ Virtual sovereignty, mistakenly perceived to be legitimately vested in a people composed of putatively entirely-equal individuals, is more tyrannical than a prototype heirarchical régime based on class distinction; the mass of people, as such, are unable to direct a proper government.

○ The worst of all outcomes is for the mass to appoint a nominee (e.g. Bonaparte) to act in the name of the people without consulting them. Such an agent is in fact a master. (Ibid., p. 260)

Now consider Alexander Hamilton's soubriquet for the people, a great beast. His pithy point does not resonate well. But Madison shows, in *The Federalist*, that liberty requires that sub-groups be put into creative tension that defangs the great beast. Individual liberty is promoted by stringent bounds on freedom of action of groups of any size.

Madison's theory is embodied in the 1787 Constitution: the agencies of government operate in parallel; powers are shared, not separated (see the obscure treaty process). [6] Nor is the American Constitution based on Montesquieu's misreading of the British one.

Tocqueville next addresses the particulars of democratic despotism after 1789.

o This radical revolution ineluctably led to a ruin in which the Ancien Régime's worst features were preserved and its best ones discarded: a people so ill prepared to govern itself could not hope to institute total reform without producing chaos; an absolute prince would be a less-dangerous reformer. If the revolution had been directed by a despot, and not in the name of the people, France would have better prospects for becoming a free country.

o By the time the French became committed to liberty, they were also committed to notions precluding liberty.

o Thus they arrived at an ideal of society whose virtual aristocracy was comprised of civil servants, an all-powerful directorate. The French wanted to be a free people, but they had the quality of good servants.

o Finally, fatigued by their futile efforts to gain liberty, the French chose equality: many decided that being equal under a master, that living under a master had a certain *douceur* after all.

o "We have become much more like the economists of 1750 than the liberals of 1789." (Ibid., pp. 265–266)

Tocqueville places the onus unfairly borne by Descartes on the economists! And an exhausted nation finally ceded absolute power to Bonaparte.

Democratic Despotism in America. In America the people's judges run wild. Tumbrels drag disgraced evangelists, inside traders, wives of defeated dictators, famous tax evaders, libertine legislators et al. to celebrity trials, attended by *tricoteuses* and vicariously scanned by millions of *voyeurs*. The people's tribunes, media virtually immune from a law of libel, lynch defendants of various sorts. And politically correct "scholars" stifle anti-democratic sedition. Criteria based on how governments are selected, rather than on what they do, impel democratic despotism.

Variations on Democratic Despotism. Jefferson seems ambivalent towards democratic despotism. At Paris, in 1789, he was a preternatural Whig liberal. But, at other times, he prattles about liberty trees fertilized by revolutionaries' blood. And sometimes he seems more concerned about majority-suffrage than with individuals' privileges and immunities.

o Liberty and equality may not intersect. Unfranchised people, ineligible to participate in government, may be exempt from public duty. If protected from private exercises of power not requiring their ratification, they would have liberty: Edwardian England, in which a few thousand people seem to have virtually ruled the British empire, is an apotheosis of liberty.

What is Liberty? How It is Still Misunderstood (see A-1)

Tocqueville limns the tussle between liberty and equality. "Equality" leads to democratic despotism; and it will always exercise sway over the mass-mind, incapable of comprehending the subtleties of liberty. Thus Whig liberty does not grant entitlements (cf. rights); it is an absence of duty, together with immunity from exercises of power that change the jural map in ways that do not require confirmation by affected persons. [7] The welfare state confers massive entitlements on members of the society, dual to duties to fund transfers, so that the welfare state often comprises a "money spin". Working at the margin, if "gross national liberty" increases, "gross national entitlements" fall *pari passu*. Duties are dual to rights; a "no-right" is dual to absence of duty. Roman citizens were entitled to bread and oil rations, the services of the magnificent public baths, free entrée to bloody spectacles in splendid amphitheatres and to superb public libraries (e.g. the Basilica Ulpia), etc. But their duties, including tax obligations, were often onerous; and their immunities from exercise of imperial (and, in principle, paternal) power slight. (True, their houses were sacredly immune from physical intrusion). Or see the late Soviet Union.

Ozouf on Liberty. Dissatisfaction with "negative" liberty led to disaster — Ozouf's (1989) précis is chilling for knowledgable liberals. "There was general agreement on the distinction between aristocratic *[Whig?]* liberty, the 'English' form of liberty that could be defined without reference to equality, and 'French' liberty [based on the idea that reasonable people will reach consensus]." (Ibid., p. 718) Proper liberty seemed disorderly; just as does the market economy to naïve observers seeking a Utopia, coordinated from the centre.

"Philosophers tirelessly denounced its consequences: selfishness, weakness, apathy toward public life. The ancient ideal of liberty — the image of man as a political animal whose nature can be fully realized only through public activity — rivalled the image of liberty as independence." (Ozouf, 1989, p. 718)

Individualism does not inhere in the ideal of liberty; nor does possessiveness. Rather it pivots on non-coercive cooperation accomplished in markets in which exercises of powers enlarge spheres of action open to offerees. Madame de Staël picked up this point in 1799. (See Ozouf, 1989, p. 725.)

Ozouf also reports, at p. 725, that the Jacobins wanted "the social bond" to take precedence over individual freedom. But liberty does not exclude sympathy. The key word is *coercion*: liberty pivots on voluntarism, not selfishness. And, following Tocqueville, coerced cohesion is more apt to provoke selfish attitudes among citizens no longer able to "will" virtuous actions than love of one's fellow inmates. (In the Pauline-Kantian canon, coerced actions cannot be virtuous; Pauline virtue hinges on free choice.)

§4 EDMUND BURKE AND THE REVOLUTION IN FRANCE

I think Edmund Burke's *Reflections on the Revolution in France* (1790) a bad book — prolix, unsound and often malicious. I shall gloss it, after surveying its banal remarks on religion.

Burke and Religion. Burke supports Christianity as an adjoint to the state's stability; the emperor Julian the Apostate persecuted its communicants because of its putatively debilitating effects on his realm. He and the emperor share the same theory. Julian did not claim that the ancient myths were true (did Burke believe the Whig ones?), but thought the state religion a useful binding force; and lamented the fissaparous effects of Christian doctrine, concerned as it is with individual salvation under an eschatology in which the state is irrelevant. [8] He extols Christianity's utility to the state; and bewails the fissaparous effects of the Enlightenment.

A Gloss of Burke's Reflections. Burke is in a muddle about the theory of liberty: "the effect of liberty to individuals is that they may do what they please." (*Reflections*, p. 91)

□ To be fair, eighteenth-century common law often deployed Burke's intension of "liberty." (Craig Penney makes this point.)

○ Burke shares Montesquieu's improper conception of the British constitution, espied by Tracy and Jefferson. He recommends that the French invent a history conformable to this addled myth. Then aristocratic privilege and power would be embedded in French polity, so that aristocrats' intellectual footlings, like Burke, would enjoy corresponding ancillary benefits.

"You will observe, that from Magna Carta to the Declaration of Right, it has been the uniform policy of our constitution to claim and assert our liberties, as an entailed inheritance derived to us from our forefathers, and to be transmitted to our posterity; as an estate especially belonging to the people of this kingdom. ... We have an inheritable crown; an inheritable peerage; and a house of commons and a people inheriting privileges, franchises and liberties from a long line of ancestors." (*Reflections*, p. 119)

This is a nice précis of boilerplate Whig history. And the passage explains Burke's sympathy for the American revolution: the American Whigs' theory was based on the one he extols — but Hume's *History* expunges mythic visions of German wildernesses transmogrified into Gardens of Eden. As time passed, Jefferson and Burke chose different dinners from the Whig menu. The British system mutated into supremacy of the House of Commons, and then of the Cabinet, and, sometimes, of the Prime Minister, so that Burke's version of the British constitution sinks without trace; as does Hamilton's romantic reconstruction of Walpole's system.

His measured Whig view promptly, hyperbolically, vaporizes; soothing fumes rise from the Irish *émigré's verre de fine* as he contemplates his freshly-minted past.

"Our political system is placed in just correspondence ... with the order of the world ... wherein, by the disposition of a stupendous wisdom, moulding together the great mysterious incorporation of the human race, the whole ... in a condition of unchangeable constancy, moves on through the varied tenour of perpetual decay, fall, renovation, and progression. [9] ... We have given our frame of policy the image of a relation in blood; ... binding up the constitution of our family affections; keeping inseparable, and cherishing with the warmth of all their combined and mutually reflected charities, our state, our hearths, our sepulchres and our altars." (Ibid., p. 120)

Compare this fustian with Hume's quiet scepticism!

o Burke asks, "why cannot you French envelop yourselves in this sort of salubrious fog?"

"You might, if you pleased, have profited of our example, and have given to your recovered freedom a correspondent dignity. Your privileges, though discontinued, were not lost to memory. [10] Your constitution, it is true ... suffered waste and dilapidation; but you possessed in some parts the walls, and in all the foundations of a noble and venerable [reparable] castle. ... You had all these advantages in your antient states; but you chose to act as if you had never been moulded into civil society, and had everything to begin anew." (Ibid., pp. 121–122)

These lines are a travesty of the (British!) empiricist Patriots. But monstrous iniquities did follow.

o At p. 227, Burke expounds Montesquieu's theory, so repellant to Jefferson.

"Have they *[a group, including Lafayette, which anxiously solicited Jefferson's advice]* never heard of a monarchy directed by laws, controlled by a judicious check from the reason and feeling of the people at large acting by a suitable and permanent organ?"

He then claims to be amazed that the French rejected his concoction; and even claims that in some sense they possessed it, and discarded it in 1789 in favour of a pure democracy: "Aristotle observes that a democracy has many striking points of resemblance with a tyranny." (Ibid., p. 228)

Burke's view of "1789" is false; but it illuminates the mind-set of Alexander Hamilton and the New England Federalists; and helps explain Jefferson's fears of counter-revolution by American "monocrats." Abolition of a constitutionally privileged class discombobulated them.

o At the end of his book, Burke predictably urges the British not to risk contamination by the French example. He sets the stage for the British war on the French revolution: *Delenda est Carthago.*

"In what I did, I should follow the example of our ancestors. I would make the reparation *[repairs]* as nearly as possible in the style of the building. ... Not being illuminated with the light *[!]* of which the gentlemen in France tell us they have got so abundant a share, our ancestors acted under a strong impression of the ignorance and fallibility of mankind." (*Reflections*, pp. 375–376)

Tocqueville Criticizes Burke's Reflections

I first supply the raison d'être of the disappointing upshot of the French upheaval, and then limn Fr Copleston's assessment of Montesquieu: what was the English constitution really about? (He kills Montesquieu with kindness.)

In the Ancien Régime, the state became a Gulliver among Lilliputians; it destroyed the ethical integrity of the aristocratic order, which became a polygot, privileged caste. The upshot was a passion for equality — or, better, pervasive envy — outdistancing love of liberty. Nor was "liberty" properly perceived. As for Montesquieu, he adored liberty but did not know what it was.

Jefferson perceived the French situation much as Tocqueville did (later); and Tocqueville seems to me to supply the key to understanding the French revolution. Jefferson has been smeared: Tocqueville's critique of Burke clarifies American as well as French history.

COPLESTON (*HP*: 6:I) ON "MONTESQUIEU AND LIBERTY"

"In his analysis Montesquieu [1689–1755] had one eye on the English constitution, which he admired and the other on the French political system which he disliked. ... Montesquieu ... insists that political liberty involves the separation of powers. [11] ... There is one nation, England, which has political liberty for the direct end of its constitution. ... It has been said by some writers that Montesquieu saw the English constitution through the eyes of political theorists such as Harrington and Locke and that when he talked about the separation of powers as the signal mark of the English constitution he failed to understand that the Revolution of 1688 had finally settled the supremacy of Parliament *[see Ch. 3]*. ... But even if Montesquieu saw and interpreted the English constitution in the light of [a deficient theory] and even if the phrase 'separation of powers' was not an adequate description of the concrete situation, it seems clear that the phrase drew attention to real features of the situation." (Copleston, 1960/1964, pp. 26–28)

Tocqueville's Critique. Burke said to the French, "if you wish to correct your government, all you need do is consult your ancient traditions. Or, if you cannot retrieve your ancestors' constitution, look to England, where the ancient common law is preserved."

○ Burke did not see that the Revolution's principal target was "the ancient common law of Europe." (Op. cit., p. 81)

□ A phrase like "the haphazard clutter of ancient user" would be more telling than "the ancient common law of Europe."

○ Tocqueville analyses "evolution" differently from Burke. He argues that the evolution of the Ancien Régime led to an impasse that could be resolved only by a mighty act of will. Indeed a new American order was proclaimed in 1776, under cover of Whiggish history; and the Constitution reformed the United States. What is more, he shows that the Ancien Régime eradicated what may have been trace quantities of French liberty.

○ Once it is understood how the French aristocracy evolved into a caste, Burke's analysis crumbles: as the nobles' power to command waned, their exclusive prerogatives as primary servants of the king waxed: an aristocracy became a caste. (Ibid., p. 165)

Tocqueville continues:

○ Burke was misled by the ease with which many French bourgeois obtained patents of nobility and office; he drew an analogy to England's "open aristocracy." Consider the French facts.

○ Louis XI created many nobles in order to reduce the nobility's power; and his necessitous successors sold titles.

□ Necker increased to 4,000 the number of offices entailing titles of nobility.

○ Burke focused on ease of entry into the nobility. But the upshot really pivoted on the degree of discrimination in favour of the nobility — much greater in France than in England. [12]

○ The English bourgeoisie readily made common cause with the aristocracy. The dim criteria for class-distinctions had little practical effect; and did not provoke material resentment and envy. The French and English situations were quite different.

○ The fact that the barrier separating the French nobility from other classes was so permeable made discriminations in favour of the nobility more arbitrary and so the more onerous and humiliating.

▫ Never in French history was "nobleness" so easily acquired as in 1789; and never were the classes so separated from each other.

○ Massive material discriminations were made against bourgeois who quite properly found no significant geneological differences between themselves and many members of the privileged caste.

Burke's powers of prophecy were formidable. He divined the fall of the monarchy and anticipated the sordid scenes that were to unfold — many readers forget that the author of *Reflections* has not seen the things he foretells. But Burke's prescience flowed from a bad theory. Turning again to Tocqueville,

○ Burke did not understand that the new masters of France were spawned by the Ancien Régime he so regretted.

○ The Ancien Régime deprived the French of even the possibility of sympathy with each other, leading to active cooperation. By 1789, there was no "collective memory" of people freely acting together politically.

○ In the Revolution's upshot, massive centralized powers passed from the quite mild royal institutions to a brutal, irresponsible sovereign assembly. The very factors that led to the monarchy's fall made its successor so dreadful.

○ Ironically, never had religious tolerance, mild government and general benevolence been so prominent as in the eighteenth century. The most inhumane of revolutions was spawned by circumstances that had also softened manners.

▫ The contrast between the benignity of the Revolution's theories and the violence of its acts cannot surprise one who understands that it was prepared by the most civilized and executed by the most uncultured and uncouth of the nation's classes. (Ibid., pp. 315–316) Marx's subsequent influence put an unjustifiable "economic" spin on this remark that continues to exercise malevolent sway.

○ Why did the Revolution lose its way? The passion for equality overwhelmed that for liberty, fulfilling a destiny prepared by the evolution of the Ancien Régime.

□ Towards the end of the Ancien Régime, the passion for liberty and that for equality seemed on a par with each other. Nor did the French understand why they could not be both equal and free. (Nor do most people understand this point in 1992.)

□ The tragedy is heightened by the fact that the enthusiasm, generosity and "virility" of the "men of 1789" will preserve "1789" in immortal memory. (Ibid., pp. 317–318)

The Patriots of 1789 brought France close to a régime of Whig liberty. But liberty was crushed by democratic despotism: the masses succumbed to envy of the intellectual as well as the material refinement of the élite; and thrashed about in escalating episodes of wild play.

Interpolation. The ancient European order, finally led by Britain, made war against revolutionary France. And the intellectual Patriots of 1789 were incapable of commanding mass levées or disseminating simplistic radical propaganda, motivating conscripts to fight for the New Order — if not for the ancient Motherland (see Stalin's Great Patriotic War). The charismatic young General Bonaparte was a more likely object of emotional transfer than the admirable philosophers, mathematicians et al. of 1789. The engine of the destruction of prospects for Whig liberty was the military ardour, and its correlative passions, that saved France from quite prompt restoration of the Ancien Régime. Whether or not Napoleon was *au fond* a soldier of the Revolution, Bonapartism was in the cards.

○ Tocqueville brings his argument to a cadenced close: the institutions of the Ancien Régime had inculcated divisive feelings and habits of obedience. The unfolding events of the Revolution intensified these and other principal properties of the Ancien Régime so that centralization became greater than ever.

"On s'est borné à placer le tête de la liberté sur un corps servile." (Ibid., p. 319)

§5 THOMAS JEFFERSON AND THE REVOLUTION IN FRANCE

Jefferson's *Autobiography* (1821) centres on the French revolution; and he explains that he relied on current notes and copies of correspondence. This vibrant material anticipates Tocqueville's book and further demolishes Burke's theses. What is more, it displays a master politician in action.

In a letter to John Adams, dated 30 August 1787, he comments on the opening scenes of the revolution: "the revolt of the nobles." He is quite thrilled; and offers a rubicund prognosis.

"From the separation of the Notables to the present moment has been perhaps the most interesting interval ever known in this country. Above all the establishment of the Provincial assemblies ... bid fair to be the instrument for circumscribing the power of the crown and raising the people into consideration. ... I think that in the course of three months the royal authority has lost, and the rights of the nation gained, as much ground by a revolution of public opinion only, as England gained in all her civil wars under the Stuarts." (*Writings,* pp. 906–908)

He celebrates a Whig miracle. But the Demos has not yet showed up.

Further Preliminaries

1787–1788: Jefferson Returns to Paris in 1788. Three letters — to George Washington, the unanimously elected President, 4 December 1788; Richard Price, 8 January 1789; and John Adams, 9 May 1789 — build an interesting counterpoint to the *Autobiography* (1821).

He adroitly discusses vents for agricultural surpluses and commercial policy in a letter to Washington, labelled "Commerce, War and Revolution." (*Writings,* pp. 929–935). Then he reports that, "as soon as the convocation of the States-general was announced, a tranquillity took place thro' the entire kingdom." But the entrance of the bourgeoisie made the Notables uneasy; the revolution entered its second phase. He frets that the still-influential king may override the Notables. His glass is clouded: the state of play is murky.

His letter to Richard Price (*Writings*, pp. 935–939: "Convening the Estates General") concerns the influence of the American on the French revolution — a contention scouted by Phillipe Raynaud, in the *Critical Dictionary of the French Revolution* (1989). M. de Calonne had to appeal to the nation: "the dissipations of the court had exhausted the money and credit of the state." A subtle complexity occupies Jefferson's mind: *au fin* the Crown will coalesce with the commons against the privileged orders, a familiar theme in French and English history.

"The court was well disposed towards the people, not from principles of justice or love to them; but they want money. No more can be had from them. They are squeezed to the last drop. The clergy and nobles, by their privileges and influence, have kept their property untaxed hitherto. They then remain to be squeezed, and no agent is powerful enough for this but the people. The court therefore must ally itself with the people. ... The people will probably send their deputies expressly instructed to consent to no tax ... unless the unprivileged part of the nation has a voice equal to that of the privileged; that is to say, unless the voice of the Tiers Etat be equal to that of the clergy and nobles." (*Writings*, p. 938)

The American v. the French Revolution. Raynaud's analysis is badly flawed: he confuses the Revolution's Rousseauian turn with its *raison d'être*. But the Whig "Patriots" of 1789, including Jefferson and Talleyrand (!), deplored holistic concoctions like the General Will (revived in contemporary welfare economics).

Democracy provoked the turn for the worse: Whig subtleties perplexed the masses and bored the demagogues who rose to the top of the boiling cauldron. American Whigs kept incipient demagogues out of play; and America's immense land reserves finessed urban mobs, a trick taken by Jefferson.

Raynaud accurately describes what went wrong; but does not properly distinguish French from American thought.

"The two revolutions grew out of very different experiences, which led to the formation of two institutional logics at odds on many points. Where the French held that factions could be neutralized only through submission to the General Will, the Americans sought to tame factions by assigning them a limited but explicitly recognized place in the institutional framework. Separation of powers, which led to the Americans to stress the importance of the judiciary, seemed to the French *[and surely to the British]* to require absolute primacy of the legislature." (Raynaud, 1989, pp. 597–598) [13]

Raynaud's comment on "the importance of the judiciary" is ill founded. The Jeffersonians strove to keep the judiciary in its cage. And the Constitutional power of the Supreme Court to review acts of Congress is problematical — Crosskey would say non-existent. The grotesque enlargement of the rôle of the courts and the legal profession in the United States reflects recent usurpations; and in Canada an eccentric constitutional sea-change. (See Ch. 3.)

Jefferson's Letter to John Jay. See *Writings*, p. 949ff.: "A Report from Versailles," anticipating the *Autobiography*.

o The Patriotic Party, including Talleyrand, was impatient with Necker (the father of Madame de Staël with whom Talleyrand was unstably linked for some time).

o Jefferson worries that the nobles will agree to equal taxation in exchange for restoration of the principal features of the Ancien Régime. (Writings., p. 952)

The Autobiography's Narrative

Jefferson thinks pressure "for a fixed constitution, not subject to changes at the will of the king," very proper. (*Writings*, p. 78)

"Nor should we wonder at this pressure when we consider the monstrous abuses of power under which [the French] were ground to powder, when we pass in review the weight of their taxes, and inequality of their distribution; the oppressions of the tithes, of the tailles, the corvées, the gabelles, ... the shackles on commerce by monopolies; on industry by gilds *[sic]* and corporations; on the freedom of conscience, of thought, and of speech ... and of the person by lettres de cachet; the cruelty of the criminal code, the atrocities of the rack, the venality of judges partial to the rich, [14] ... the enormous expenses of the queen, the princes & the Court; the prodigalities of pensions & the riches, luxury, indolence and immorality of the clergy. Under such a mass of misrule and oppression, a people might justly press for a thoro' reformation." (Ibid., p. 78)

After much pulling and hauling, the king, deploying shrewd defensive tactics, but lacking a strategic plan, called Necker to the Treasury in September 1788. And a States General was promised for May 1789.

"The effect of this change of ministers, and the promise of the States General at an early day, tranquillized the nation. But two great questions now occurred. 1. What proportion shall the number of deputies of the [third estate] bear to those of the Nobles and Clergy? And 2. shall they sit in the same, or in distinct apartments?" (Ibid., p. 79)

The first and second estates sought to throttle the third. Public opinion fiercely resisted these efforts. And there was extracted from the always reluctant king a declaration (27 December 1788) that the orders should sit in a single chamber; and that the number of third-estate delegates should be equal to one-half of the lot. And:

"A Report of M. Necker to the king of about the same date contained other very important concessions [:] ... that the king could neither lay a new tax nor prolong an old one ... [;] [that the king will study] how far the Press may be made free. ... [The king] had not but a wish for the good of the nation, and for that object no personal sacrifice would have ever cost him a moment's regret. But his mind was weakness itself, his constitution timid, his judgement null, and without sufficient firmness even to stand by the faith of his word. His queen too, [15] haughty and bearing no contradiction, had an absolute ascendancy over him. ... The resolutions of the morning formed under [the advice of Necker and other moderates] would be reversed in the evening by the influence of the queen and the Court." (Ibid., p. 80)

The frightful winter of 1788–1789 caused widespread misery, contributing to tension in the May assemblage of the States General. His description of that session displays detailed knowledge, shrewdly synthesized by a master politician. The "Noblesse" cut up rough.

"[Their] greater intercourse with enlightened society had liberalized [the minds of the metropolitan aristocracy] and prepared them to advance up to the measures of the times. But the Noblesse of the country, which constituted two thirds of that body, went far in their rear." (Ibid., pp. 82–83)

He "went ... daily from Paris to Versailles, and attended [the] debates, generally till ... adjournment." ... "Shall the States sit in one, or in distinct, apartments?" [16] Shall they vote by "heads or by houses?" Led by abbé Sièyes, "the most logical head of the nation," the Commons, joined by some clergy, formed a National Assembly; and, on 20 May, they were locked out of their chamber. The stage is set for the Tennis-Court Oath.

"[The commons] repaired to ... the Jeu de paume and there [swore] never to separate of their own accord, till they had settled a constitution for the nation ... and if separated by force, they would reassemble in some other place. The next day ... they were joined by a majority of the clergy. The heads of the Aristocracy saw that all was lost without some bold exertion. ... The court party were now all rage and desperate." (Ibid., p. 84)

What the army will do? Is it loyal to the crown?

Jefferson Soliloquizes. The soliloquy reveals the resolute revolutionary's perception of the French crisis, and much more. *(Writings,* p. 85)

o "A successful reformation of the government in France" would lead to "general reformation" all through Europe. This was just what the traditional powers feared. (In the eighteenth century, "revolution" meant "reformation.")

o The Patriot leaders had confidence in Jefferson, the author of the Declaration and a preeminent revolutionary.

○ Jefferson urged an "immediate compromise" with the sitting government. Indeed the king offered a virtual bill of rights; and the preconditions for parliamentary integrity, including:

    □ A representative legislature;

    □ Annual legislative sessions;

    □ Laws were to originate in the Parliament (implying an end to rule by decree);

    □ Parliament was to have exclusive powers of taxation and appropriation;

    □ The responsibility of ministers to Parliament.

○ The Patriot leaders rejected his counsel. "Events proved their lamentable error." [17]

The Narrative Resumes. Political tumult followed. The king backtracked. The commons soon got back the upper hand.

"On [25 May 1789], forty-eight joined the Tiers *[third estate]*. ... There were then with them 164 members of the Clergy, although the minority of that body still sat apart. ... On the 26th, the Archbishop of Paris *[and earlier the Duc d'Orléans]* joined the Tiers." (*Writings*, pp. 86–87)

The soldiery now firmly allied itself with the commons. And the Assembly, dominated by the third estate, went into vigorous action. An agenda for drastic constitutional reform was agreed; and "a declaration of the rights of man, as the preliminary of their work, was accordingly proposed by the Marquis de Lafayette." (Ibid., p. 87)

Again the court backtracked: it connived in an advance of foreign troops on Paris. There were popular risings in support of the Tiers. Groups of Parisians clashed with German and Swiss troops, minions of the king. Disorder grew. The king, unable to cope with the breadth and intensity of popular support for the (mostly high-born) Patriot leaders of the Tiers, gave way. The upshot was a famously pathetic scene.

"The king landed at the Hôtel de Ville. There M. Bailly presented and put into his hat the popular cockade, and addressed him. The king being unprepared, and unable to answer, Bailly went to him, gathered from him some scraps of sentences, and made out an answer, which he delivered to the audience as from the king. *[The crowd shouted 'vive le roi et la nation.']* The king was conducted by a garde bourgeoise to ... Versailles ... " (*Writings*, pp. 91–92)

The author of the Declaration of Independence was thrilled — as were many Englishmen, including Wordsworth, Coleridge and Fox — by the glittering triumph of Whig liberty.

ANOTHER SOLILOQUY. The splendid vista was to disintegrate. The king, momentarily "a passive machine in the hands of the national assembly," was prepared to participate in the new order: "a wise constitution would have been formed, hereditary in his line, himself placed at his head." (Ibid., p. 92)

THE QUEEN THROWS A SPANNER INTO THE WORKS. The wicked witch of the west, Marie Antoinette, exercised "absolute sway over [the king's] weak mind, and timid virtue." Jefferson throws a swingeing blow at Burke in the course of the following, rather comical, jeremiad — which shows how fire blended with ice in the character of a consummate politician.

"This angel [Marie Antoinette], as gaudily painted in the rhapsodies of the Rhetor Burke, with some smartness of fancy, but no sound sense, was proud, disdainful of restraint, indignant at all obstacles to her will, eager in the pursuit of pressure, and firm enough to hold to her desires or perish in their wreck. ... Her opposition to [Reform], her inflexible perverseness, and dauntless spirit, led herself to the guillotine, and drew the king on with her, and plunged the world into crimes and calamities [forever staining] the pages of modern history. I have ever believed that had there been no queen, there would have been no revolution. *[I.e. there would have been non-violent root-and-branch reform.]* The king would have gone hand in hand with the wisdom of his sounder counselors, who, guided by the increased lights of his age, wished only ... to advance the principles of their social institutions." (Ibid., pp. 92–93)

NECKER IS RECALLED. The king's virtual capitulation to the "Patriots" included the recall of Necker. And, on 4 August 1789, tremendous work was done.

"The assembly abolished all titles of rank, all the abusive privileges of feudalism, the tythes and casuals of the clergy ... and, in fine, the feudal regimen generally. ... Many days were employed in putting into form of laws the numerous demolitions of ancient abuses, which done they proceeded to a declaration of rights." (*Writings*, p. 94)

The "Patriots" asked Jefferson to join their deliberations. He declined, and then swallowed his scruples, joining a six-hour soirée to which he says he was "a silent witness." (His *volte face* reflected anxiety about aristocrats' efforts to exploit Patriotic dissension: the aristocrats "moved in phalanx.")

○ There was a consensus that the crown should continue. But such issues as the royal veto power, unicameral *v.* bicameral chambers and life tenure for members of an upper house were moot.

○ The debate was impressive. Cf. "coolness and candour," together with "a logical reasoning, and chaste eloquence, disfigured by no gaudy tinsel of rhetoric or declamation, and truly worthy of being parallel with the finest dialogues of antiquity."

○ The result was an agreement that the king should have a veto and that there should be a popularly elected, unicameral legislature.

○ "The aristocracy [were] reduced to insignificance and impotence" — Jefferson tacitly registers his dissent from Montesquieu's principles. (Ibid., p. 96)

○ He promptly told the Court of the soirée. No umbrage was taken. Indeed his intervention was encouraged: he might counter Hotspurs and promote "a wholesome and practicable reformation only."

The narrative breaks off. He is about to return to America; his privileged access to the stupendous scene is to end.

TJ on the French Revolution from a Near Shore. This fiery extract verges on the bourgeois *Weltanschauung* that created a burst of liberty in the nineteenth century, up to 1914.

"There are three epochs in history signalized by the total extinction of national morality. [18] The first was of the successors of Alexander, not omitting himself. The next the successors of the first Caesar, [19] the third our own age. This was begun by the partition of Poland, followed by that of the treaty of Pilnitz; next the conflagration of Copenhagen; [20] then the enormities of Bonaparte partitioning the earth at his will, and devastating it with fire and sword; now the conspiracy of kings, the successors of Bonaparte, blasphemously calling themselves the Holy Alliance. ... " (*Writings*, p. 93)

○ What was Jefferson's "global" view of the French revolution? See *Writings*, pp. 97–98.

□ Despite the revolution's immense consequences, up to 1821, "we are but in the first chapter of its history."

□ The "tyrants of the North" have ranged themselves against the French revolution. But "it is irresistable." Why? Because the appeal to the rights of man, begun in America, and immortalized by his Declaration, cannot be stopped.

□ The ineluctable tide of liberty "is a wonderful instance of great events from small causes. [21] So inscrutable is the arrangement of causes and effects in this world that a two-penny duty on tea, unjustly imposed in a sequestered part of it, changes the condition of all its inhabitants."

□ His deep insight into "1789" owes much to his intimate relations with "the leading Patriots, and more than all of the Marquis Lafayette, their head and Atlas, who had no secrets from me." Furthermore, he was well acquainted with the "Court party" and diplomats (all working against the Revolution) accredited to the Court.

□ True, he was 78 in 1821, but "my information was always and immediately committed in writing to Mr Jay [*the foreign minister so to speak*] and often to my friends [*Mr Jay was not a friend*], and a recurrence to these letters now insures me against errors of memory."

Some Loose Ends. Like most French Whigs, Jefferson was quite euphoric in October 1789, when he crossed the Channel for Cowes and thence to America. "My wish had been to return to Paris ... to see the end of the revolution, which I then thought would be certainly and happily closed in less than a year." Jefferson was unable to foresee the destructive latency of democratic despotism — not at such a moment: joy reflects delusion.

○ How far did his feelings for France go? It is inconceivable that he would subordinate American to French geopolitical interests; he would never have conducted with Frenchmen the sorts of interviews Hamilton had with the British envoys, Beckwith and Hammond, when Jefferson was Secretary of State. What is more, he helped design American neutrality in subsequent European wars against France, perhaps violating America's treaty with France. But he was a *lumière*: his culture, like France's, descends directly from antiquity. His deep commitment to French values, accompanying fidelity to American interests, is often distorted by mundane writers, apt to transmute classical ideals into political expediency.

"I cannot leave this great and good country without expressing my sense of its preeminence of character among the nations of the earth. A more benevolent people I have never known. ... Their eminence too in science, the communicative dispositions of their scientific men, the politeness of the general manners, the ease and vivacity of their conversation, give a charm to their society which is found nowhere else. ... So ask the travelled inhabitant of any nation, in what country ... would you rather live? — Certainly in my own, where are all my friends, my relations and the earliest and sweetest affections and recollections of my life. [22] Which would be your second choice? France." (*Writings*, p. 198)

Jefferson and the Revolution from a Far Shore: 1791–1796

Jefferson worried that American Anglophiles and "monocrats" would exploit deterioration of French conditions in order to put the United States into orbit around Britain; he sometimes equivocated, but the danger was real. See his letter of 4 February 1791 to George Mason. He is the more anxious for a good result in France so that American Anglomaniacs, especially a "heretical sect" of Hamiltonians, will not profit. (See *Writings*, p. 971)

The Terror posed knotty problems for him (cf. infra). Its sanguinary consequences weighed less for him than global prospects for Whig liberty. But its excesses outraged eighteenth-century sensibility: many high-minded friends of liberty turned against the Revolution; some wanted to pull it up root and branch. President Washington's cool reaction to the dehabilitation of the Revolution is the more interesting. Dumas Malone (1962, pp. 41–42) shows that the President supported Secretary Jefferson's policies towards the First Republic, following the execution of Louis XVI. He was strongly committed to *Realpolitik*; and he was *engagé* in the tactical implementation of his foreign policy [23]

See Jefferson's letter of 3 January 1793 to William Short, American *chargé d'affaires* in Paris — soon to be studied in another, rather bloody-minded, connection:

"The tone of your letters had for some time given me pain, on account of the extreme warmth with which they censured the proceedings of the Jacobins in France. ... The Jacobins ... yielded to the Feuillants and tried the experiment of retaining their hereditary executive. The experiment failed completely, and would have brought about the re-establishment of despotism had it been pursued. The Jacobins saw this, and the expunging [of] that officer was of absolute necessity. And the Nation was with them in opinion. ... The reserve of the President of the United States had never permitted me to discover the light in which he viewed [recent upheavals in France]. ... But your [recent letter induced him to break silence and to notice the extreme acrimony of your expressions. ... He desires me therefore to write to you on this subject. He added that he considered France as the sheet anchor of this country and its friendship as a first object. There are in the U. S. some characters of opposite principles, some of whom are high in office, others possessing great wealth, and all of them hostile to France and fondly looking to England as the staff of their hope. ... Excepting them, this country is entirely republican. ... The successes of republicanism in France have given the coup de grâce to their prospects and I hope to their projects." (*Writings*, pp. 1003–1006) [24]

The Genet Affair. Jefferson was irrefragably committed to American neutrality in the European wars of the French revolution, which began in 1793. The fragile nation's interest called for neutrality. And the neutrality policy seems to have been well designed and executed. George Canning (1770–1827), no friend of the New Republic, agreed. See Malone (1962, p. 80): "If I wished for a guide in a system of neutrality, I should take that laid down by America in the days of the presidency of Washington and the secretaryship of Jefferson in 1793." (See Malone, 1962, p. 80 — Canning wrote in April 1823.)

Jefferson doubtless abided Genet too long — but not very long; and he had to look over his shoulder towards the "Anglicans," delighted by the contretemps and anxious to exploit it in order to restore the power of the French monarchy.

"Varennes" is part of the story. He agitatedly informed the President, at a levée, of the flight of Louis XVI and his interception at Varennes, in June 1791. It was clear that the Revolution could not preserve legitimacy — which was not regained until 1958, when the Fifth Republic was established by virtual coup d'état.

The Genet affair ran its course between May and August 1793 — especially in view of wretched American communications, the scales fell from his eyes quite promptly; and he had to travel some conceptual distance.

o On 19 May 1793, Jefferson wrote to Madison that M. Genet had presented his credentials. "It is impossible for anything to be more affectionate, more magnaminious, than the purport of his mission. ... He offers everything and asks nothing." (*Writings*, pp. 1008–1009)

o By August 1793, it was obvious "that this incorrigible man [Genet] had to go; and Jefferson's best hope lay in distinguishing between the agent and the country." (Malone, 1962, p. 123)

"I Would See Half the Earth Desolated." Sometimes, the fiery revolutionary triumphed over the learned Whig. During his reprimand of 3 January 1793 to William Short (for his intemperance),

the outgoing Secretary of State launched into a diatribe that President Washington surely did not see. This segment of the letter begins quite moderately — keeping in mind that the first French republic was under relentless assault by the powers of the old order, ineptly assisted by *émigré* French nobles.

o Jefferson readily concedes that, in the First Republic's struggle to repel invasion, many niceties were violated. Inevitably, guilty persons were convicted without trial; and so were some innocents. Nor did President Lincoln solve the equation sixty-seven years later.

o He deplores the fall of the innocent, as he would if they had been war casualties. He becomes quite shrill, sounding like Rousseau:

"It was necessary to use the arm of the people, a machine ... blind to a certain degree. A few of *["the people's"]* cordial friends met at their hands the fate of enemies. But time and truth will rescue and embalm their memories, while their posterity will be enjoying that very liberty for which they would never have hesitated to offer up their lives. The liberty of the whole earth was depending on the issue of the contest, and was ever such a prize won with so little innocent blood?" (*Writings*, p. 1004)

There is more!

"My own affections have been deeply wounded by some of the martyrs to this cause, but rather it should have failed, I would have seen half the earth desolated. Were there but an Adam and an Eve left in every country, and left free, it would be better than it now is." (Ibid., p. 1004)

What are we to make of this silly screed? There are extenuations. He had reason to be chagrined at reactionary invasions of America's "sheet anchor." And he remained committed to American neutrality — the unsentimental upshot of his and Washington's *Realpolitik*. Still his friends must be discomfited: his self-control was imperfect; but he mostly confined his outbursts to quite private letters and talk with friends. I reckon he relied on Madison (and, later on, Gallatin too) to rein himself in. [25]

The Terror. François Furet's (1989a) penetrating article on the Terror (*Critical Dictionary,* pp. 137–150) properly emphasizes its devastating consequences for the Revolution's reputation. What actually happened? Some statistics, gleaned from Furet's article, follow.

From March to September 1793, there were 70–85 executions.(So far the substance of Jefferson's *démarche* to Short looks supported.) Two-hundred more fell from October 1793 to early January 1794. [26] There may have been 1,575 more executions as the Terror accelerated up to the fall of Robespierre on 27 July 1794, ending the Terror. Fewer than 1,900 fell in Paris; but there were 13,975 victims outside of Paris; the national toll was thus about 16,600. My desultory reading had suggested a much larger total; Jefferson's toleration of the Terror becomes quite plausible.

And,

o Anxiety and uncertainty aroused by the Terror must be taken into account.

o The Terror virtually ended with Robespierre's liquidation in July 1794 (9 Thermidor) — after it had run sixteen months; claiming most of its victims over its last seven months. "Though later reorganized, it had permanently lost the quasi-legitimacy and frightful utility it had derived for sixteen months." (Ibid., pp. 141–142)

The Mazzei Letter. By 24 April 1796, Jefferson was leader of the opposition to General Washington's second, quite-purely-Federalist, administration, which was viciously attacked. And Dumas Malone owns that he did things in opposition that he had earlier scrupled not to do. (After March 1801, he was never again in opposition.) After all, Washington's monumental persona and the purity of his motivation in public affairs may be *sui generis.*

In his letter to Mazzei, not meant for publication, he alleged that Washington was a victim of an "Anglican" conspiracy. And that sufficed to shiver the political timbers. This is the actionable part of an otherwise banal missive.

"In place of that noble love of liberty and republican government which carried us triumphantly through the war, an Anglican monarchial and aristocratical party has sprung up, whose avowed object is to draw over us the substance, as they have already done the forms, of the British government. ... Against us *[described as 'the main body of our citizens']* are the Executive, the Judiciary ... [and] all timid men who prefer the calm of despotism to the boisterous sea of liberty. ... It would give you a fever were I to name to you the apostates who have gone over to these heresies, men who were Sampsons in the field and Solomons in the council, but who have had their heads shorn by the harlot England." (*Writings*, pp. 1036–1037)

But the rot can be stopped, and then repaired, "[if we] awake and snap [our] Lilliputian cords with which they have been entangling us during the first sleep which succeeded our labours." (A vivid prophecy that he will win the Presidency and begin "the second American revolution.")

General Washington resented the Mazzei letter. He viewed his second administration differently from Jefferson and was entitled to feel smeared by him. But, by April 1796, Washington was a spent force; he was already in the shadows. What counted was control of the levers of power from March 1797 onward. And Jefferson's characterization of the Federalists is plausible — John Adams's virtues counted for little: he lacked a power-base. The Mazzei letter foretells the strident tone of the political conflict about to erupt in earnest. Jefferson was a fierce combatant, uninterested in polishing up totems.

§6 ALEXANDER HAMILTON ON THE REVOLUTION IN FRANCE

I think that Hamilton's biographer, and editor of his papers, J. E. Cooke (1982), reads the French revolution incorrectly, but he has much company. These are his principal points:

○ Hamilton, unlike Jefferson, did not think the French revolution akin to the American one.

○ The American revolution was a Whig revolution; "the French revolution ... was a social upheaval that sought to uproot not so much royal tyranny, as all tradition." Cooke adds Marxian spice, probably supplied by Georges Lefebvre, to Burke's dish, and is amply refuted in this chapter.

○ Hamilton wrote, on 18 May 1793, that "there is no real resemblance between what was the cause of America and what is no less great than that between liberty and licentiousness." (*Papers*: xiv, p. 476) For Cooke "licentiousness" means "atheism, anarchy and the eventual emergence of demagoguery."

○ Now for Marx!

"Neither Jefferson nor Hamilton understood [that] the French revolution really was ... a struggle by the bourgeoisie to remove the shackles of feudalism and to secure control of the state for its own benefit. Hamilton confused the bourgeoisie with the sans-cullotes; Jefferson equated the French aristocracy and the American bourgeoisie." (Cooke, 1982, pp. 126–127)

Cooke avidly distills the frenzies of a defunct economist.

Hamilton seemed more tolerant of the Revolution in February than in May 1793. See his letter to William Short (!), quoted by Malone (1962, p. 47) — he discerns a different crowd of American opportunists.

"The popular tide in this country is strong in favour of the last revolution in France *[referring to the expunging of Louis XVI]*; and there are many who go, of course, with that tide, and endeavour always to turn it to account. For my own part, I content myself with praying most sincerely that it may issue in real happiness and advantage of the nation."

I suspect Hamilton abided the Terror's excesses as readily as Jefferson did. His financial policy filled his mind. When Britain set its face hard against the French republic, he was inevitably sucked into its orbit.

NOTES

1. Furet misstates Enlightenment philosophy, which doted on British empiricism. Nor is hostility to supersitition "Cartesian." True, the *lumières* reluctantly concluded that some "design" was necessary for things to come right; just as the Whiggish lawyers in the Constitutional Convention of 1787 supplied a massive dose of "design," radically reforming American politics, in response to much-less-exigent circumstances than the French ones circa 1789–1794 et seq.

2. Benthamism nests in this "general truth." And "choice" in economic theory concerns points in commodity space; it lacks ethical content.

3. François Furet and Mona Ozouf reluctantly conclude that General de Gaulle's contrivance of election of the President of the French Republic by universal suffrage resolved dissonances in French politics going back to the execution of Louis XVI. ... "[General de Gaulle] apparently hit on the key to creating a monarchial republic that after two hundred years had reconciled Ancien Régime and Revolution." (*Critical Dictionary*, p. xxi)

4. The *Concise Columbia Encylopedia* (1983, p. 157) states that, after 1392, when Charles VI became intermittently insane, France was ruled de facto, and plundered, by his uncle, Philip the Bold, and his brother, Louis d'Orleans. Their rivalry led to a civil war that laid France open to an invasion by Henry V of England.

5. Madison's "*Federalist* Number 10" plumbs democratic despotism. He grasps that liberty is an absence of duty, together with immunity from others' exercises of powers constricting one's "jural space." The context is "dualistic": *A*'s freedom is antithetical to *B*'s liberty. But a degree of

coercion is ineluctable: privileges (absences of duty) and immunities are insubstantial if not protected; liberty requires the government's aegis.

Jefferson on democratic despotism makes up a mixed bag. He writes that the members of an uninhibited legislature may become a set of *n* tyrants, worse than merely one. But he also celebrates the wisdom of an ill-defined entity, "the people," who can be trusted to exert daunting power; he is sometimes under the sway of Rousseau. His fears of counter-revolution, of a "monocrat" resurgence, partially resolve the contradiction: he may rhetorically exaggerate the merits of a "classless" republican system in order to combat reactionary federalism.

6. Crosskey (1953) cogently argues that the 1787 Constitution established a powerful national government; and reduced state-powers to "police." (In the eighteenth century, "police" concerned local regulation of every-day life, including public safety; "polity" encompassed commerce [broadly construed], diplomacy, military affairs, etc.) The states were dealt out of the power game.

The "states rights" model offered by Jefferson and the sinuous Madison contradicts Crosskey and John Marshall (?). Crosskey hypothesizes that Marshall — under the glowering gaze of the Jeffersonians, eager to impeach nationalist judges — sometimes suppressed his true views.

7. *Exchange*, central in the economic sphere, confers rights (of acceptance) on offerees that change the jural map substantively. Your offer to buy my house is an exercise of power. If I accept, I acquire the right to put my house to you on the terms you state. The private-ownership, free-market economy is intrinsically liberal; substantive changes in the jural map are then accomplished only through mutual exercise of free will. (See "Hohfeld's *Fundamental Legal Conceptions* and Liberty" infra.)

8. Norman Cantor (1969) pitches Julian's motivation into a different, but related, key.

"Julian the Apostate has aroused the interest of many scholars and students of literature, especially those who have a higher regard for classical culture than for Christianity. ... [He] had a grand vision of restoring pagan religion and classical culture to a new, high level. ... He soon began to persecute the Christian clergy and finally prohibted them from engaging in education. But the non-Christian peoples of the empire were more interested in various kinds of mystery religions than in Julian's highly sophisticated and intellectual brand of Roman paganism. ... Before he could really do any damage to the Christian church, he was killed in 363 while fighting the Persians, and henceforth the rulers of the Roman empire in both east and west were always Christian." (Ibid., pp. 50–51)

Edward Gibbon predictably esteems the Apostate. See *Decline and Fall*, vol. ii, chs. xxii–xxiv, pp. 419–558 (the Bury edition, 7 vols.). The following brief excerpts convey the tenor of Gibbon's gripping discussion, an epitome of Enlightenment thought.

o "The vehement zeal of the Christians, who despised the worship, and overturned the altars, of those fabulous deities, engaged their votary in a state of irrenconciliable hostility with a very numerous party of his subjects." (Ibid., p. 457)

o "But the genius and power of Julian were unequal to the enterprise of restoring a religion which was destitute of theological principles, of moral precepts, and of ecclesiastical discipline ...." (Ibid., p. 472)

o "A just and severe censure has been inflicted on the law which prohibited the Christians from teaching the arts of grammar and rhetoric." (Ibid., p. 487)

o "The Christians who had now possessed about forty years the civil and ecclesiastical government of the empire, had contracted the insolent vices of prosperity, and the habit of believing that the saints alone were entitled to reign over the earth. ... [If] we seriously reflect on the strength and spirit of the church, we shall be convinced that, before the emperor could have extinguished the religion of Christ, he must have involved his country in the horrors of a civil war." (Ibid, pp. 502–504)

9. This is a good statement of the Marshall-Pigou conception of the economic stationary state. See ch. 2 of my 1988 book.

10. Tocqueville explains that antique French liberties were exiguous and were in any case irretrievably lost. (See the text.)

In an interesting discussion of "The Hierarchic Conception of Society," Huizinga (1924/1984, ch. 3, p. 46ff.), relying on Pollard, shows how far back the cleavage between the English and French social systems went. The distinction is critically important: it is at the bottom of both Tocqueville's analysis of the Ancien Régime and Burke's misconception of it.

"Mediaeval political speculation is imbued to the marrow with the idea of a structure of society based upon distinct orders. ... The idea of an 'estate' is not at all limited to that of a class; it extends to every social function, to every profession, to every group. ... [The] French system of the three estates of the realm [was] in England, according to Pollard, ... only secondarily and theoretically adopted after the French model." (Ibid., p. 47)

11. Montesquieu and Burke both say that a hereditary aristocracy preserves liberty. Alexander Hamilton may have sought to create such a class by granting privileged access to government-stock operations — a horrid concept execrated by Thomas Jefferson.

12. Marc Bloch's *Feudal Society* (1940/1961/1966) shows how Tocqueville's signal distinction of characteristics of British from French nobility was embedded by the thirteenth century.

"Yet England had an aristocracy as powerful as any in Europe. ... At the top was the narrow circles of earls and barons. During the thirteenth century this highest group had begun to be endowed with fairly definite privileges, but these were of an almost exclusively political and honorific nature; and above all, being attached to the *fief de dignité*, to the 'honour,' they were transmissable only to the eldest son. In short the class of noblemen in England remained, as a whole, more a 'social' than a 'legal' class. ... In the thirteenth century, the possession of landed wealth had been sufficient to authorize the assumption of knighthood, in fact to make it obliigatory. And although in theory [knights of the shire] were required to furnish proof of hereditary armorial bearings, it does not appear that, in practice, any family of solid wealth and social distinction ever encountered much difficulty in obtaining permission to use such emblems. ... It was mainly by keeping close to the practical things which give real power over men and avoiding the paralysis that overtakes social classes which are too sharply defined and too dependent on birth that the English aristocracy acquired the dominant position it retained for centuries." (Ibid., vol. 2, p. 331)

This may be the pith of Bloch's remarks: noble status in Britain was highly correlated with social and economic weight for a very long time. And Tocqueville shows that, in France, noble status was ill correlated with function: many French nobles were socially and economically otiose; many weighty commoners resented their inferiority.

13. The general tenor of Jefferson's letter of 3 August 1789 to Diodati (*Writings*, pp. 956–959) is much like that of his 9 May 1789 letter to John Jay. It compares the English with the proposed (mid-1789) Whig constitution for France in a way that contradicts Raynaud (1989).

"The constitution [for France] will resemble that of England in its outlines, but not in its defects. They will certainly leave the king possessed completely of the executive powers. ... Their legislature will consist of one order only ... : the representation will be equal and not abominably partial as that of England: it will be guarded against corruption, instead of having a majority sold to the king and rendering his will absolute. ... They will meet at certain epochs and sit as long as they please, instead of meeting [at the king's pleasure]. ...

"I will agree to be stoned as a false prophet if all does not end well in this country. Nor will it end [here]. Hers is but the first chapter of the history of European liberty.

"In drawing the parallel between what England is, and what France is to be, I forgot to observe that the latter will have a real constitution, which cannot be changed by the ordinary legislature; whereas England has no constitution at all: that is to say there is [no] principle of their government which the parliament does not alter at pleasure. The omnipotence of Parliament is an established principle with them." (*Writings*, pp. 957–958)

□ Jefferson refers contemptuously to the British corruption-principle admired by Hamilton. (see Ch. 2)

□ He again dissents from Montesquieu's claim that a privileged order is necessary for a liberal republican equilibrium.

14. Could the writer of these lines have ever believed that the American Bill of Rights did not apply to the states? See Ch. 3.

15. See Jacques Revel (*Critical Dictionary*, pp. 252–264) on *Marie Antoinette* (1755–1793). His assessment is more measured than Jefferson's: we are inured to Jefferson's impetuosity, expressed by a rubicund prose that grew more ardent (and more fluent) as he aged; he is a quilled Hotspur.

"Like all rumours, the legend of Marie Antoinette was based on a few facts along with many details that were merely plausible. Facts and details were freely reworked to fit the legend's own logic. Of the many lovers the queen was supposed to have had there is not the least shred of evidence apart from her long, discreet and complicated relationship with Fersen. But her imprudent [early] behaviour ... and the fact that she and the king made an odd couple rendered all the reports credible." (Ibid., pp. 257–258)

"Marie Antoinette favoured a hard line from the beginning. ... All witnesses agree that she repeatedly attempted to influence the king to take a more-intransigent course. ... [Her] hostility to the Revolution never wavered, nor did she ever signal a readiness to compromise. ... The queen, in her correspondence with Mercy-Argentau in April 1791, called for ... graduated political pressure, counting more on rising discontent within France than on armed intervention by outside forces ... " (Ibid, pp. 260–261)

Jefferson may exaggerate the queen's influence on the king. (There are inescapable parallels to titillating speculation about "First Ladies.") But he seems to rate her politics accurately.

16. In the eighteenth century, "states" often meant groups of people; "the several states" could mean "the people of *A, B,* ... *Z*" rather than "the geographical entities *A, B,* ... *Z*." (See Ch. 3.)

17. Writing to Lafayette, on 14 February 1815, Jefferson's gloss of the upheaval surrounding the *Jeu de paume* fixes the time of the fatal error in 1791 — but the letter's tenor matches that of the *Autobiography*.

"Possibly you may remember, at the date of the Jeu de paume, how earnestly I urged you *[et al.]* to enter, then into a compact with the king, securing *[a virtual bill of rights]* and a national legislature, all of which it was known he would then yield. ... You thought otherwise, and that the dose might still be larger. ... And I found you were right; for subsequent events proved they were equal to the constitution of 1791. ... Unfortunately, some of the most honest and enlightened of our patriotic friends (but closet politicians merely, unpractised in the knowledge of man) thought more could still be obtained. ... You differed from them. You were for stopping there. ... Here too you were right; and from this fatal error of the republicans ... flowed all the subsequent sufferings and crimes [against] the French nation." (*Writings*, pp. 1360–1361)

Dumas Malone explains how Jefferson's upbringing and taste impelled him to please or flatter his confrère: his letter of 14 February 1815 seems disengenuous; he is no closet politician. This trait irked the dour Yankees — the Adamses found his (any?) *souplesse* immoral. Malone also describes

Jefferson's insistence that personal (especially social) encounters be unfailingly amiable, again provoking charges of duplicity.

18. Jefferson was lucky not to have divined the horrors that were to come, beginning in 1914. Interestingly, persisting global instability, provoking the ghastly catastrophes of the twentieth century, owes much to protracted after-shocks of the French revolution, which destroyed stabilizing imperial institutions (e.g. the Habsburg and British empires).

Bertrand Russell's indictment of Rousseau's General Will as a cover for despotism was was studied in Ch. 5: nor is Jefferson guiltless on this count.

19. Jefferson cannot mean the Antonines.

"In the second century of the Christian Aera, the empire of Rome comprehended the fairest part of the earth, and the most civilized portion of mankind ... If a man were called to fix the period in the history of the world during which the condition of the human race was most happy and prosperous, he would, without hesitation, name that which elapsed from the death of Domitian to the accession of Commodus." (Edward Gibbon, *Decline and Fall*, vol. 1.)

20. Jefferson's inclusion of this lamentable incident reflects the lasting impress on his mind of the mercantile controversies of the wars of the French revolution — leading to his embargo (1807–1809) — so traumatic for him — and the War of 1812. The city was not severely damaged; true, the British ignored international law.

21. Was Jefferson a *deist*? The *OED* defines a deist as little more than a logic chopper: "one who acknowledges the existence of God upon the testimony of reason, but rejects revealed religion." I think that he believed in Einstein's *Alte*, the god of physics, imposing awesome mathematical regularities on nature; for some, man has contrived this construction, which, for others, possesses Platonic self-subsistence.

The workings of nature inspired Jefferson, like Bertrand Russell, with feelings of awe and wonder; and, again like Russell, he had an acute (if somewhat disembodied) sympathy, tinged with *tristesse*, for his fellow humans.

22. Dumas Malone explains Jefferson's devotion to family, and to *his* family (see especially *The Sage of Monticello*).

Like Washington, Adams and Madison, Jefferson was wholly commmitted to the New Republic — and was in on its creation. (Franklin's case is murky, but he had crossed the Rubicon by 1776.) This may explain his condescension towards Hamilton. It was not so much that Hamilton was an upstart: he thought the new world naïve; and was titillated by the sophistication of such old-world machinators as his friend Talleyrand. He was contumelious towards "the country that received him."

When John Adams called Hamilton "the bastard brat of a Scotch pedlar," he was doubtless more exasperated by Hamilton's rejection of the New Republic's values (and his insolence) than contemptuous of his base birth.

23. See Chateaubriand's account of his interview with President Washington in the notes to Ch. 1.

24. An interesting letter to John Adams (28 February 1796) shows that Jefferson's recollection, reported in the *Anas*, was not impaired by the passage of time and old age (aet. 75 in 1818). See Ch. 2.

"Both [the French and American] experiments are ... now fairly committed, and the result will be seen. Never was a finer canvas presented to work on than our countrymen. All of them engaged in agriculture or the pursuits of honest industry, independent in their circumstances, enlightened as to their rights, and firm in their habits of order and obedience to the laws. ... We have seen no instance of this since the days of the Roman republic, nor do we read of any before that." (*Writings*, p. 1034)

This is a plangent expression of the Horatian-Virgilian (*Georgics*) ideal. In the same letter, Jefferson may seek common ground with his once and future friend and Presidential rival; or he may be teasing Adams by reciting verse from the republican psalter that will serve Jefferson's party so well. But he was not a tease; and Adams loathed Hamilton, a loathing richly embellished and highly burnished during his Presidency, 1797-1801. And he was at the dinner Jefferson probably alludes to infra.

"If ever the morals of a people could be made the basis of their own government, it is our case; and he who could propose to govern such a people by the corruption of their legislature ... must convince himself that the human soul as well as body is mortal *[a proposition Jefferson would endorse some years later! — see Ch. 7]*. ... I am sure, from the honesty of your heart, you join me in detestation of the corruption of the English government. ... I have been among those who have feared the design to introduce it here, and it has been a strong reason with me for wishing there were an ocean of fire between that island and us." (Ibid., pp. 1034–1035)

25. Were Americans as fierce as Jefferson suggests in the letter to Short?

"I have expressed to you my sentiments, because they are really those of ninety-nine in an hundred of our citizens. The universal feasts, and rejoicings which have lately been had on account of the successes of the French showed the genuine effusion of their hearts."

Jefferson softens the blow to Short — an esteemed patriot who became one of his favourite correspondents. "You have been wounded by the sufferings of your friends." (*Writings*, p. 1004)

26. The *éclat* of many of the victims evokes Stalin's purges of high-ranking Russians.

"[Victims included] not only Marie Antoinette ... and the former duc d'Orléans (who in vain had taken up the new name, Phillipe-Egalité), but also [many] Girondins, ... followed by the remains of what had been the Feuillant group along with Bailly and Barnave. The guillotine exorcised the revolution's past at the same time as it felled the Ancien Régime." (Furet, 1989a, p. 142)

ANNEX

Two Studies in Liberty and Virtue

(A-1)

Hohfeld's *Fundamental Legal Conceptions* and Liberty

(A-2)

Frank Knight and the Ethics of Competition

Hohfeld's *Fundamental Legal Conceptions* and Liberty

[Yale] President Hadley's son ... mastered Hohfeld's analysis and explained it to his father. ... The President ... said: 'That enables us to define liberty.' [1]

Hohfeld's masterly analysis establishes a jural conservation principle. Representing a jural property or quantity by the vector $\vec{x}$, the dual conjugate of $\vec{x}$, $\vec{x}*$, is equal in length and opposite in direction to $\vec{x}$ so that the vectors sum to zero. So liberty, a composite of jural properties, is "bounded." Such "boundedness" makes freedom antithetical to liberty. And trade-offs between liberty and other values pertaining to the good life — such as peace of mind, good health and access to beauty — are stringently bounded. Cardinal paradigms of economic theory remorselessly control the moves of the pieces on the social chessboard. The feasible action-space is harshly pent; the promised land proves a wasteland.

A précis of Hohfeld's system is supplied — with help from Arthur Corbin and, especially, Walter Wheeler Cook. Then, after more comment, some problems in the theory of liberty are assessed.

§1 HOHFELD'S SYSTEM

"In the second of the articles on *Fundamental Legal Conceptions* (1919), [Hohfeld brought] out clearly the fact that legal relations *in rem* ('multital' ones) differ from those *in personam* ('paucital') merely in the fact that in the case of the former there exists an indefinite number of legal relations, all similar, whereas in the case of the latter the number of similar relations is always definitively limited. For this reason he suggested the

295

name 'multital' for those which are *in rem* and 'paucital' for those *in personam* ... It is frequently said that an owner of property has '*a right in rem*' as distinguished from '*a right in personam.*' ... What the owner of property has is a very complex aggregate of rights, privileges, powers and immunities. These legal relations prove ... to be ... 'multital.' ... Note the plural form, 'rights.' ... Instead of having a single right *in rem*, the 'owner' of property has an indefinite number of such rights — as many, that is, as there are persons [2] under correlative duties to him. ... The usual analysis to which we have been accustomed has treated a very complex aggregate of legal relations as though it were a single thing, a unit." (W. W. Cook, 1919/1964, pp. 13–15)

Some of Hohfeld's System's Implications. The most important implication of Cook's analysis is for *duality*: jural quantities are couples, e.g. (*a, b*). *A*'s ownership of Blackacre, or a car, comprises paired relations with *B, C,* ... See the theory of descriptions: *A*'s ownership of Blackacre finds all other persons values of *x* in "x has duties to *A* in connection with Blackacre." We catch a hint of the principal consequence of Hohfeld's system for the theory of liberty: if *B* is to be relieved of a duty to *C* and/or become less exposed to *D*'s exercises of powers, then the positions of *C* and *D* deteriorate: *C*'s rights diminish, as do *D*'s powers. (Cf. infra.)

Now turn to implications for liberty and freedom, focussing on *B*'s exposure, or not, to exercises of power by *D*. The dual to *B*'s diminished exposure to *D*'s actions (say that *D* is no longer able freely to redraw Blackacre's property line with *D*'s adjacent Greenacre) is loss of *D*'s freedom. There is more. The social value of freedom is problematical: insofar as *D*'s action exposes *B* to unavoidable consequences, *D*'s freedom impinges on *B*'s liberty. More emphatically, freedom, as ordinarily defined (putting aside Nietzsche!), encompasses ability to exert power against others. Outside a sealed room, freedom impinges on others' liberty.

Some Theory of Liberty

The private-ownership market economy features benign exercises of power, creating options that may be declined.

Liberty, Equality and Freedom: Economics and Politics. Liberty is consistent with virtually any degree of economic inequality. Nor are the ideas of liberty and freedom congruent. Nor is liberty a sufficient condition for the good life; indeed the good life mandates trade-offs against liberty. (See Bertrand Russell's remarks on the good life, cited in the Preface.)

A society may — and sometimes should — create entitlements for impoverished people. The new measures will reduce liberty: new duties (to finance the entitlements) are created. There may indeed be a golden rule for liberty-accumulation: a society may accumulate excessive stocks of liberty relative to some objective function.

Turning to freedom, Franklin Roosevelt's *four freedoms* (freedom from want, fear, etc.) illustrate how the correct analysis has been twisted out of shape. Stipulate that proposals conjugate to the "four freedoms" promote the good life. Now scan the position of a beneficiary of resulting transfers. She may be more free *from* want. But the word "free" then has no jural connotation. Jurally, entitlements and duties have been created, so that liberty is diminished; type X liberty has not been substituted for type Y liberty; liberty has simply contracted.

Should intrinsically political rights, privileges, etc. be distinguished from economic ones? I do not see how such a distinction can properly be made. Why should there be an intrinsic right to curse speakers at university seminars; and not to dispose of one's income as one pleases? The actions of speaking and consuming are on the same physiological, if not moral, plane. What is more, as Craig Penney points out in an unpublished manuscript, ch. 9 of Magna Carta uses "nor disseized of his liberties (libertatibus)" in the sense of economic quantities (including rights and privileges). And he also points out that the *Oxford English Dictionary* cites numerous uses of liberty, or liberties, in statutes from the twelfth to the seventeenth century as

297

meaning a grant of an economic quantity. *Inter alia*, he cites *Pipe Roll* 11 Henry II (1189) 107, vol. 11 of the Pipe Roll society.

The correct analysis boils down to this. Trade-offs control virtually all deliberate human action: contraction of *A*'s "economic liberty" may promote "social welfare"; while contraction of *A*'s "political liberty" may not be perceived to promote any proper objective. But policy action then has a merely pragmatic foundation; no valid jural distinction can be made between economic and political quantities.

Knight and Hohfeld's Liberty. (See A–2) More than 65 years ago, Prof. Knight pointed out that "agents" (or, better, elementary particles) of the economy are organized into authoritatively disciplined teams: most people operate under commands; and choices between teams (groups) one might join are restricted. Workers function in totalitarian environments. They have many rights and many, sometimes onerous, duties. But their privileges and immunities, their liberties, are heavily restricted. The currency of the individualist paradigm, sometimes coined by life-tenured savants, has limited circulation.

The Government and the Individual. Government, exercising vastly more authority than any citizen, towers over masses of Lilliputians. No citizen can deeply penetrate the government's action-space. Nor do election episodes disturb "Gulliver's" drill; the citizen is under disability and is acutely exposed to coercive government action.

Rhetoric (cf. the Democratic Dogma) about the General Will blinds people to loss of liberty: historically-unacceptable intrusions into private lives are readily accepted, so long as crusading legislators are elected on a broad franchise and civil servants are under the nominal control of elected "leaders." The Democratic Dogma is much more comprehensible to the mass mind than the subtleties of Whig liberty.

Christian Liberty; Democratic Despotism. The Grand Inquisitor may invigilate actions that do not directly penetrate others' spaces. This evokes Christian liberty: a slave or prisoner can attain Grace, infinitely more important in patristic Christianity than material well being or physical freedom. Hence the ineluctable conflict between the City of God and secular institutions, including liberty.

Liberty concerns what can happen to one, not what one can do: disenfranchised people may have liberty; and democracy may eradicate liberty — see Tocqueville on Democratic Despotism supra. Think of a mild monarchy or of an idealized Edwardian England, ruled de facto by a few thousand enlightened quasi-optimates [3] — free from democratic despotism and immune to charisma; indeed that Other Eden of Whig liberty, eighteenth-century England, had a highly restricted franchise. Citizens were free from onerous duties and were showered with immunities.

States of Nature. The zero-sum property of a correct analysis vitiates rhetoric about maximizing liberty, let alone freedom.

It will be shown that appropriate codes of law are necessary conditions for liberty. Liberty is a property of a matrix of privileges and immunities, so that its "quantity" measures the degree to which others' actions on (against) one are blocked; it measures counterfreedom!

In a state of nature (cf. Hobbesian Horror) freedom is complete. In a sort of reverse-entropy process, the state of nature may transist into feudalism in which a few especially fierce warlords are at upper reaches of a tidy pyramid, tapering to the king. In feudal equilibrium, rights (entitlements) and duties are abundant; and the privileges and immunities of the masses are sparse indeed. Thus a villain, entitled to military protection and owing many duties, is exposed to (is not immune from) his master's hunt trampling his personal plot and may be compelled to perform services he is not under duty to perform (see the affair of the shrimp salad infra).

In a state of nature X has no duties and is subject to any exercise of power he cannot block, perhaps through threat of massive physical physical retaliation — international relations, especially in the military-diplomatic sphere, are similarly ordered. In a state of nature, action, or potential for action, predominates. One is not jurally incompetent to do anything. Still the hideous freedom of a state of nature has bewitched theorists (like Rousseau and Nietzsche).

Closing out the preliminary discussion, study of transitions from states of nature, including feudalism, suggests a conservation principle, entailing a (nil) quantity invariant against choice of coordinates, or whatever. If new rights are created, so are correlative duties. If one is less exposed to others' actions, their disabilities are increased, etc. The Hohfeldian matrices display a controlling zero-sum property. The theory of liberty becomes fiendishly difficult: stringent trade-offs govern all possible transmutations. This may be the only clear guidepost: liberty concerns the extent to which one is subject to others' wills; freedom concerns the range over which one can exercise one's will. The most stringent trade-off is between liberty and freedom.

§2 HOHFELD'S PARADIGM

The Paradigm

	Statics	
Jural Opposites	RIGHT	PRIVILEGE (NO DUTY)
	NO-RIGHT	DUTY
Jural Correlatives	RIGHT	PRIVILEGE (NO DUTY)
	DUTY	NO-RIGHT
	Dyanmics	
Jural Opposites	POWER	IMMUNITY
	DISABILITY	LIABILITY (EXPOSURE)
Jural Correlatives	POWER	IMMUNITY
	LIABILITY	DISABILITY

Some notes on the paradigm follow.

o The monads or atoms possessing rights (e.g.) or under disability (e.g.) are ill-defined. The situation is quite amorphous. Hohfeld and

Cook seem to contemplate Messrs Green, Brown et al., not Toyota, IBM, IRI or British Airways. Jural relations are even more complex than Hohfeld suggests. But no harm is done: Hohfeld's purpose is to show how complex they are.

○ What is *equality* in Hohfeld space? In "Hohfeldian statics," Green may be Brown's virtual lord: Green has many duties towards Brown: Green supplies most of Brown's sustenance. In this caricature of feudalism, Brown may have no duties towards Green; and Brown may have to submit to Green in many ways. Brown need not assist Green, but perhaps Lord Green's hunt often rides roughshod over Brown's crops; Lord Green's steward may press Mrs Brown into service in the manor-house kitchen when the Comte de Vaucluse visits Greenacres in pomp. These exercises of power, reflecting Lord Green's freedom, are in spite of absence of duty towards Lord Green by *famille* Brown.

It is hard to see what jural equality may mean. Cf. the importance of the passive voice: liberty does not so much concern what I can do to you as what you cannot do to me, and vice versa. If our powers are jurally unimpeded, our exposures are functions of things like physical strength. If we have no duties towards each other, we also lack rights. So the "optimal quantity of liberty" is far less than its maximized potential.

○ Feudal paradigms deepen the analysis. Entrants into feudal service transform no-duties into duties and acquire entitlements; the lord's privileges (no-duties), his liberties, are correspondingly reduced.

○ Pitching up development, prior to a more systematic glossing of Hohfeld's theory, Being (statics) contrasts with Becoming (dynamics). The controlling logic emerges from certain contrasts of formal properties of action in a voluntarist private-ownership/free-market régime with that in a feudal system.

Black's exposure to Pink's power to create a right which, if exercised, puts Pink under a duty to sell his house to Black for $X is very different from exposure to Pink's power to subject Black to military service (see knight's tenure in feudal law). Libertarians cherish the former instance: Black can put the state of Being (the "static" matrix) back into status quo ante by rejecting Pink's offer.

Mutations of Hohfeld's "static" matrix, describing "Being," are accomplished by actions described by Hohfeldian dynamics, leading, in a voluntarist régime, to exercises of power creating rights in other parties to activate value-enhancing exchange. In the dynamics of a feudal, or welfare-state, process, rights (entitlements) are acquired in exchange for assumptions of duty so that aggregate privilege decays. Entrants into feudal service renounce no-duties and are assigned duties (accompanied by fresh entitlements); while lords' privileges (no-duties) are correspondingly reduced. If entitlements abate, liberty waxes; if entitlements wax, liberty wanes. And a more-opaque property is revealed: exchanges in the private-ownership economy noncoercively mutate the "static" Hohfeld matrix so that exposures are benign and "mutations" welcome. The economic sphere finesses the cruel algebra of the political one. [4]

Analysis of the Hohfeldian Matrices

The statical matrices display state-values. The dynamical matrices display potentials for changing the quantities of the statical matrices. "Opposition" is in the sense of A and *Not-A*. Correlatives are obtained from opposites by transposing the elements of the second row of the former matrix. Correlatives display duality; and the model's juice is extracted from it by exploitation of its correlative features.

The statical matrices display states of play at points in time; they are balance sheets — arrays of cumulants, residues of action. The dynamical matrices, displaying potentials for action, depict the system's motor force; cumulative consequences of motor force are enregistered in the statical matrices.

Liberty in the Private Ownership Economy. The markets of a private-ownership economy make one happily iiable (exposed) to exercises of powers to offer contracts, e.g. to propose purchases and sales. Such exertion confers powers to accept offers; the liabilities of creators of such powers are assumed voluntarily. Acceptance imposes duties on the acceptor and the offeror to perform. But exercise of one's potential to alter the state variables of the jural matrices imposes no duties on others unless they choose to assume duties. If such offers are barred by frictions, like those imposed by transactions costs or by jural obstruction, one is immunized against the opportunity of having rights conferred on one!

The free market generates rights correlative to duties assumed by offerors; but it does not impose involuntary duties. In liberal orderings, powers to create rights, or privileges, are welcome; just as powers to create involuntarily imposed duties are deplored. Liberals want to be immune from exercises of power not leaving one free to choose whether proposed changes in jural state values should occur.

Contract Law. Contract law centres on innovating powers. Thus X invests Y with the right to buy Blackacre by making an offer to sell. Members of liberal societies are typically in mutual relations *ab initio* — subject to some rather-chilling qualifications about minors, and indeed family life. (See "Frank Knight and the Ethics of Competition.") And what is now *ab initio* has been generated by earlier exercises of powers making possible changes in rights, duties, etc. Structures are continuously, and quite spontaneously, being creatively destroyed and reconstituted. [5]

REVERSIBLE SLAVERY: LIBERTY IN THE COASEAN VOID. What if Z contracts to be A's slave? The jural balance sheet may look frozen — liberals will abhor such a transaction for this reason alone. But a more complete analysis is surprisingly problematical, partly because of the Coase theorem (1960), which intersects so many things that it may be empty.

Spontaneous emancipation cannot be rejected on the planes of theory or history.

"It is at least conceivable that, in the long term, slavery was unviable in the sense that a fundamental change in the formal master-slave relationship might have left both parties better off. Under slavery, owners profited by confiscating the difference between what a slave produced and what a slave consumed; [6] Yasuba (1971) and others leave little doubt that this surplus was substantial. But it is also possible that the surplus could have been larger if slaves had had incentives to work [to their potential] ... If the traditional forced labour relationship was very wasteful ... the [manumission] arrangement might have dominated traditional slavery and eventually have led to voluntary emancipation." (Lee & Passell, 1979, pp. 169–170)

Slavery in the ancient world was much more complex than in America. (See Finley, 1985, ch. 3 and my 1991 book, ch. 10. Also Nicholas, 1962/1969.) Finley and Nicholas interestingly discuss the Roman *peculium* (a slave's virtual personal estate) — pivotal here, since a slave could thus "buy his way out." [7]

The analysis exposes an otherwise obscure dimension of economic exploitation of slaves: [8] if a slave cannot accumulate a *peculium*, he obviously cannot hope to buy his way out: loans against slaves' future earnings were surely unobtainable in the Roman empire, just as comparable transactions are infeasible now. Indentured service, common in British North America, generated virtual *peculia*: servants bought their ways out programatically, while masters were assured of adequate returns on investments in servants in substantially competitive markets.

§3 SELECTIVE ANNOTATIONS OF THE HOHFELDIAN APPOSITIONS

Rights

RIGHT/NO-RIGHT; RIGHT/DUTY. Justice Cave, in *Allen v. Flood*, explains what is a right? "The violation or disturbance of [a right] can be remedied or prevented by legal process." And the correlative of "right" is "duty."

A right limits the ambit of others actions. It is an affirmative claim against another. So J. S. Mill's famous definition of liberty boils down to the vacuous statement, "there should not be a law unless there should be a law." Viz.,

"The only purpose for which power can rightfully be exercised over any member of a civilized community, against his will, is to prevent harm to others."

Say that the owner of Whiteacre is compelled by law to grant an easement to esteemed scholars interested in the properties of its quite unique soil. Is the law improper under Mill's criterion? No! Harm resulting from refusal of an easement is registered by some social objective function. But Mill almost surely would have opposed such legislation: he did not contemplate harm incident to *inaction*. His criterion is at best incomplete and may be meaningless.

No-Rights

If I have "no-right," I cannot jurally compel others, singly or *en masse*, to do something. The correlative of "no-right" is "no-duty"; no-right maps into privilege (absence of duty). And liberty is a complex bundle of privileges and immunities (non-exposures) barring coercion.

CREATION OF RIGHTS; ANNIHALATION OF LIBERTY. If *A* acquires a right, which may be an entitlement to a pension, another (or others) must discharge a duty. A right generates a field of force inhibiting others' behaviour. Right-creation annihalates liberty; Mill's precept is more invalid still. This is not to say that rights should not be created; but it conclusively demonstrates that liberty is not a product of right-creation.

REMARKS ON THE WELFARE STATE; AND ON THE FAMILY. Envisage a transformation of the ("static") matrix of state-values. Privilege is to be elided: the right/duty correlative pair is to dominate. The upshot may be an egalitarian society without liberty: households in an idealized Scandanavian society, may have no disposable income. The mass of rights (entitlements) of members of an ultra welfare state is accompanied "1:1" by an anti-mass of duties. (Some duties are collective: no particular person is charged with one's medical care.) Members of a polar-opposite laisser-faire society have no rights (no entitlements); if a mass of rights is annihalated, so is a mass of duties. A member of such a society has no duties — and her stock of liberty is maximized.

"Inferior" members of a family — surely children — are showered with entitlements; while their privilieges (no-duties) are sparse. Indeed the family is the supreme embodiment of the welfare-state principle: a welfare régime is in *loco parentis* to its members.

It perplexes me that the family — often an epitome of authority and a hive of turmoil — is a darling of libertarian writers. Surely its Roman sources are not auspicious for liberty: under Roman law, a family member was helpless against the will of the *paterfamilias*; Roman liberty was an increasing function of constriction of the *paterfamilias* by the state. [9]

"In the early law, and to a considerable extent throughout Roman history, the family is the legal unit. Its head, the *paterfamilias*, is the only full person known to the law. His children, of whatever age, though they are citizens and have rights in public law, are subject to his unfettered power of life and death. Again, only he can own property, and anything his children acquire belongs to him alone. This *patria potestas* was thought by the Romans to be peculiar to themselves. The powers of a Greek father served only a protective purpose, like those of a guardian and ended when the child came of age. ... If a father could kill his child he could also sell him. ... If the sale was made within Roman territory, the child did not become a slave, but had a quasi-servile status (*in mancipio*), which differed from slavery ... mainly in that his rights as a free man were only in suspense and therefore revived if he were manumitted." (Nicholas, 1962/1969, pp. 65–67)

WHAT IS THE STATE? Karl Popper innoculates his readers against *holism* (see his *Poverty of Historicism*). Useful analogies do not run from biological entities (people) to abstractions like the state or the people. The people are neither free nor unfree; persons are. Hofeld's notation makes it easy to sweep away the General Will. The government, an administrative structure, is a simpler idea than the state. The state is but a set of "pautical" relations.

J. R. Commons's (1924/1974, p. 149) discussion of the state is excellent — and his strangled prose reflects the problem's intransigence:

"The state itself is but one of many going concerns, whose sovereign working rules are but a larger collective will. ... The state is not 'the people,' nor 'the public,' it is the working rules of the discretionary officials of the past and present who have had and now have the legal power to put their will into effect within the limits set by other officials."

Privileges

PRIVILEGE/DUTY; PRIVILEGE/NO-RIGHT. Hohfeld (1919, p. 47, based on Hohfeld, 1913) quotes from an "unusually discriminating and instructive passage in Mr Justice Cave's opinion in *Allen v. Flood*." This is what Cave, J. said (as quoted by Hohfeld, 1919, p. 48):

"Thus it was said that a man has a perfect legal right to fire off a gun, when all that was meant was that a man has a freedom *[sic]* or liberty to do so, so long as he does not violate or infringe anyone's rights in doing so, which is a very different thing from a right, the violation or disturbance of which can be remedied or prevented by legal process."

Mere absence of duty (privilege) does not confer a right: *B*'s absence of duty to weed *C*'s garden does not impose a duty on C not to impress *B* into service as *C*'s gardener (cf. the *corvée* of the Ancien Régime). If *B*'s privilege is reinforced by creation of a right, against *C* and others, that his privilege be respected, then the quantity of *C*'s freedom is diminished. To repeat, except in hermetically isolated contexts, freedom is antithetical to liberty: rhetoric about liberty and freedom crumbles under the pressure of the controlling jural "conservation theorems." [10]

What is worse, strict "hermetic isolation" is a non-starter in jural-philosophical analysis. Thus it may seem that J. S. Mill's hostility to sumptuary legislation, imposing duties correlative to the state's right to assure the "propriety" of one's life, is unassailable. [11] But that is not true. Reflecting on Bertrand Russell's puzzling point, Professor Hayek owns that, if the community believes Yahveh will wreak dire vengeance on all if homosexual practices are condoned — or if Simenon's Maigret stories continue to be published — Mill's criterion justifies repression. Farewell, "hermetic enclosure."

Hohfeld (1919, pp. 48–49) continues:

"While there are numerous other instances of the apt use of the term 'liberty,' both in judicial opinions and in conveyencing documents, it is by no means so common or definite a word as privilege. The former is far more likely to be used in the sense of physical or personal freedom (i.e. absence of physical restraint) as distinguished from a legal relation; and very frequently there is the relation between two definite individuals. Besides all this, the term 'privilege' has the advantage of giving us, as a variable, the adjective 'privileged'."

Even Hohfeld misprizes liberty. And his sophistic protection of liberty's semantical integrity drains it of its substance: if privileges against self-incrimination are not buttressed by duties, imposed upon the state, inter alia, to respect such privileges (duties accompanied by correlative rights), then we shall be little more than Niobes, all full of tears, as liberty is habitually violated. Nor can the redoubtable Walter Wheeler Cook redeem liberty's substantive purport; his very lucidity pitches up unease about liberty's nakedness.

"We are not asserting that the person having the privilege has an affirmative claim against another, i.e. that the other is under a duty to refrain from publishing the defamatory matter, as we are when we use 'right' in the strict sense, but just the opposite. The assertion is merely that ... there is an absence of duty on the part of one publishing the defamatory matter to refrain from doing so. ... So in reference to the duty of a witness to testify: upon some occasions we say that the witness is privileged, i.e. there is an absence of duty to testify, as in the case of the privilege against self incrimination." (Introduction to Hohfeld, 1919)

Now turn to *the affair of the shrimp salad*. Hohfeld (1913/1919) points out that even Professor Grey's "able and entertaining work," *Nature and Sources of Law* (1909), seems to hold that "all legal relations can be comprehended under the conceptions right and duty," with regrettable consequences. Thus, Grey writes that,

"The eating of shrimp salad is an interest of mine, and, if I can pay for it, the law will protect that interest, and it is therefore a right of mine to eat shrimp salad which I have paid for." (Grey , 1909, sec. 48)

Hohfeld (ibid., p. 41) distinguishes a privilege (correlative to a no-right) of eating shrimp salad from a right to eat a shrimp salad (correlative to others' duties).

"These two groups of relations seem perfectly distinct; and the privileges could ... exist even though the rights ... did not. *A, B, C* and *D*, being the owners of the salad, might say to *X*, 'eat the salad if you can; you have our licence to do so, but we don't agree not to interfere with you.' In such a case the privileges exist, so that if *X* succeeds in eating the salad, he has violated no rights of any of the parties. But it is equally clear that if *A* had succeeded in holding so fast to the dish that *X* couldn't eat the contents, no right of *X* would have been violated." (Ibid., p. 42)

"A 'liberty,' considered as a legal relation ... must mean, if it has any content at all, precisely the same thing as privilege." And Hofeld supplies rather compelling evidence that "the dominant technical meaning of privilege is ... negation of legal duty." (Ibid., p. 45) *X*'s liberty *sans* accompanying immunities and, in some cases rights, is empty.

Hohfeld and Cook might gag at my controlling criterion: liberty is secure only if conjugate freedoms are blocked. More proof is in order. Take another of Hohfeld's examples: absence of duty to testify against oneself is substantively empty if others are free to compel one's testimony. What is more, it is hard to see how such exertions of power can be blocked without creating duties (rights). (Agents must be protected against coercion even in Coase's consensual domain.) Or consider religious freedom: the privilege of not having to attend officially sanctioned rites is of paltry value if others are not under a duty not to molest one's sect's meetings.

Mill on Liberty. It has just been shown that considerable coercion must be exerted by the state to block out actions of agents against each other, reinforcing no-right-to-interfere proscriptions. Mill properly emphasizes coercion: non-coercion is a liberal value that must be supressed in order to constrain action (freedom) intruding on others' actions, keeping in mind that the optimal "stock of liberty" is much smaller than the maximized one. And, according to the same wobbly criterion, action that does not have intrusive effects should be protected. But most action has appreciable intrusive effects.

Any civilized society imposes numerous duties, including tax-obligations, on its members — correlative to direct and indirect entitlements (including those of the unborn). Some coercion is ineluctable. Mill tries to define its optimal quantity; his book could have been called *On Coercion*. And he sees that freedom, so far as it leads to exposure, is antithetical to liberty, except to the extent that one is merely exposed to opportunities to choose — liberty runs unimpededly within the private-ownership, free-market economy.

A Précis of the Controlling Analysis. Shoring up of liberties, so that powers cannot be exercised to eradicate them, reduces the total "stock of liberty"; new duties, correlative to new rights, are created. (In order to make surviving liberties effective, their stock must be reduced.) Thus, if C is vested with an "unprotected" privilege, others have no right to enter C-acre (so that C has no duty to permit entry); but C remains exposed to entry. And if C's privilege is transmuted into a right of immunity, imposing duties not to trespass on C-acre, others' liberties are curtailed (by new duties). Shoring up of a liberty entails extinguishment of other liberties through creation of a right of immunity against exercise of power extinguishing the privilege.

It follows that freedom and liberty are antithetical. Analysis reduces liberty to immunity from coercion; and shows that liberty concerns what may (not) happen to one, not what one may do. For example I may be privileged to publish: I am under no duty not to publish. That does not prevent you from smashing my press: for liberty to be meaningful, freedom must be curtailed.

Whig liberty, often unhappily called negative liberty, stringently constrains freedom. Mill saw this. But he did not accommodate to the fact that almost everything one does affects others in even a quite-simple society. Save for myriad rules and regulations, reducing liberty as well as freedom, we would raucously jostle against against each other. *Au fin* the law is the *sine qua non* for liberty; the law doles out our liberties.

Powers

POWER/DISABILITY; POWER/LIABILITY (EXPOSURE). We turn to potentials for change (dynamics) *v.* state-variable quantities (statics). W. W. Cook picks up the argument:

"In Hohfeld's terminology any human being who can by his acts produce changes in legal relations has a legal power or powers. Whenever a power exists, there is at least one other human being whose legal relations will be altered if the power is exercised."

Cook continues along lines full of meaning for political economy:

"In Hohfeld's system a liability [exposure] may be a desirable thing. One who owns a chattel may abandon it. By doing so he confers upon [all] a legal power to acquire ownership by taking possession. ... Before a chattel is abandoned, every person other than the owner is under a legal liability to have suddenly conferred upon him a new legal power. ... So also any person can by offering to enter into a contract with another person confer upon the latter — without his consent — a power of accepting the offer to bring into existence new relations. It follows that every person in the community who is legally capable of contracting is under a liability to have such a power conferred upon him at any moment."

Desirable (pro-liberty) exercises of initiating powers create new legal quantities without abating existing rights and privileges. Acceptance further changes the jural map; and initially passive persons, recipients of proposals, can annihalate the fresh jural quantities by rejecting the proposals.

The state merely enforces contract and helps resolve disputes. Economic efficiency is promoted, and coercion vanishes, in this subspace.

Immunities

IMMUNITY/LIABILITY (EXPOSURE); IMMUNITY/DISABILITY. See W. W. Cook (1919, p. 9):

"When we speak of the right of a person not to be deprived of his liberty or property without due process of law, the idea sought to be conveyed is of exemption ... from a legal power on the part of persons composing the government *[an admirable usage]* to alter his legal relations in a certain way. ... The real concept is one of exemption from legal power, i.e. immunity, ... the generic term to describe any legal situation in which a legal relation vested in one person cannot be changed by the acts of another person. Correlatively, the one who lacks the power is said to be under a disability. ... A power therefore bears the same general contrast to an immunity that a right does to a privilege. A right is one's affirmative claim against another; whereas an immunity is one's freedom from the legal power or control of another as regards some legal relation."

Cook makes another penetrating remark:

"The greatest merit of [Hohfeld (1917)] consists in bringing out clearly the fact that legal relations in rem (*multital* legal relations) differ from those in personam (*paucital* legal relations) merely in the fact that in the case of the former there exists an indefinite number of legal relations, all similar, whereas in the case of the latter the number of similar relations is always definitely limited."

In a feudal order, jural relationships are frozen; in the private-ownership, free-market economy, non-imperative exercises of "initiatory" legal powers are, so to speak, maximized. Transparent jural membranes seal off infusions from one sector to another; but valves can be voluntarily opened in response to offers; opportunity is maximized, but undesired "input" is blocked. Or think of glass partitions permitting one-way viewing: privacy is preserved, but proposals can be received. Liberty is imbedded in a complex ordering; and, since it hinges on immunity, it is antithetical to freedom over a wide range of potential action. And liberty may be antithetical to the good life, requiring creation of entitlements and correlative duties in order to enhance (say) public amenities, so that the culture is preserved. [12]

§4 APPLICATIONS OF HOHFELD'S ANALYSIS

When Orangeacre Common is carved into fees simple in Redacre and Yellowacre, privileges (no-duties) are liquidated and rights (*cum* duties) are created. And latent powers to reverse Orangeacre's fissure, persist: the "static" jural matrix is transmutable; and it is reversible. Market actions enhancing economic value realize the potentials described by the "dynamic" Hohfeld matrix.

What is so important here is that markets shun coercion. The private-ownership, free-market economy promotes liberty. Let us review the particulars.

A transaction creating, or liquidating, rights and duties does not enhance liberty. Indeed it may reduce liberty: property rights in Orangeacre Common were doubtless quite sparse; Redacre and Yellowacre are subject to a dense mass of property rights (and correlative lative, or conjugate, duties). But jural constellations are reversible in the free-market economy: plasticity falls short of Coase's parable, but it is substantial.

Let non-coercion replace liberty as our shibboleth. That done, the invisible hand of competition becomes pivotal: value-enhancing exchanges promote economic efficiency and eschew coercion (except for police functions like contract enforcement). But they do not assure the good life: the society's evolution may appall cultured persons.

Markets in Voting Rights. Why should there not be markets in political voting rights, as there are in company shares? (And stockholders may sell their votes or give proxies.)

The economic theory of government concerns rent-seeking trafficking. That is what *log rolling* is all about; e.g. protection of the steel industry is obtained in exchange for votes in Congress for protection of the aircraft industry.

In many instances, if voters could sell their votes on individual issues (if they could unbundle their franchises), participatory democracy would share desirable properties of market economies. Consider a grain-subsidy proposal. It is almost surely (Pareto) suboptimal: the demand price of the measure's opponents (forming a bloc) will exceed that of its proponents. Or a highway linking Alpha and Beta may be proposed. Again Pareto efficiency seems to be promoted by markets in unbundled voting rights. One reason is that a general-equilibrium perspective is preserved. But isolated transactions among blocs lead to inefficiency: New York Congressmen, comitted to Long Island defence contractors, then coalesce with California Congressmen, committed to California ones: boondoggles are mutually supported, coast to coast.

Alas, practical limitations mandate bundled voting-rights transactions in which X sells her general franchise to Y. And as concentration increases, so fewer entities controlled more "bundles," a relative handful of agents will break open the bundles antisocially: special interests will predominate. [13]

The theory of exchange plainly has currency outside economics. But the economic theory of government does not pivot on selfish "rent-seeking"; it applies to Congresses of angels, let alone domains of "imperfect benevolence."

Non-Economic Domains of Preference. Say that a subset of the society are angels, not seeking economic rent, but concerned about national defence, acid rain, the greenhouse effect, etc. Assume that the angels form a company which makes a political takeover bid, offering to buy voting rights. [14] The analysis pivots on the supremacy of the idea of exchange; and outcomes are reversible. Patriotic descendants of dissolutes may buy back voting rights from loutish descendants of virtuous vote-buyers. So a beneficent stationary state [15] may evolve: voting rights on issues without direct economic purport (cf. public support of the arts, construction of inspiring public buildings, etc.) will be perpetually held by a shifting cast of "optimates."

The feasibility of reversibility hinges on prices commanded by voting rights in markets. But a beneficent calculus muffles the caveat: "high" prices may reflect intense concern for the good life: an optimate's inability to buy voting rights may reflect the degree to which voting rights are being exercised in ways she favours.

General Equilibrium. The analysis has prescinded from general equilibrium. Ideally the full set of choices is contemplated by all agents at all times; as are all the consequences for all issue-resolutions of the decision taken on the ith issue. I may support a $10m grant for the production of Schubert's banal symphonies because of anticipated indirect consequences: the even more banal music of Bruckner may then be suppressed. Choices cannot properly be studied in isolation.

Concluding Remarks on Evolution and on Coercion. A correct appraisal of evolution in human affairs — e.g. culture and views on the nature of the good life — stands that of Professor Hayek on its head. Why should the culture spontaneously evolve towards the good life envisaged by the High Renaissance? Indeed I think it more likely to collapse under the weight, if not the assault, of democratic despotism. [16] This much seems certain: evolution of ethical or cultural structures is sharply distinct from that of physical processes. The reason is simple: the Good lies outside "the world of necessity."

In the upshot, liberals must be prepared to accept abhorrent consequences of régimes of non-coercion in the hope, if not the faith, that the Good will finally win out, perhaps because of well-aimed persuasion. President Hadley was right: Hohfeld defines liberty. Would he be pleased?

NOTES

1. A. L. Corbin (1964), Foreword to Hohfeld (1919/1964).

2. *Persons* are often artificial entities, like corporations. This complexity, rather neglected by Hohfeld and Cook, but not by Knight, buttresses Hohfeld's arguments.

3. John Adams and other American founders envisaged training optimates to take up leading positions in the New Republic. They may have been inspired by imperial Rome's "civil-service-mandarin" academy on the Palatine.

4. The Coase Theorem describes how, in frictionless situations, unattainable in the real world, the "cruel algebra" of the political sphere may be transformed into the text's benign economic calculus.

5. Reversibility becomes important. Thomas Jefferson fails to take the "reversibility" trick in his interesting proposal to limit contract-maturity. (See Ch. 5.)

   In ch. 2 of my 1988 book and in "Joan Robinson" (1991b), I discuss reversibility in connection with entropy in economic theory. Social processes are irrevocable as well as irreversible. Some economic theorists try to preserve reversibility through the extraordinary device of the immortal eunuch.

6. The master may have paid for the present value of the implicit stream of rents when he acquired the slave. In a purely competitive slave holding, slave-capturing economy, the exploitative gap precisely compensates slave capturers and shippers in the long run: slavery will not yield supernormal profit.

7. Slaves, in the Roman empire, were not racially or ethnically distinctive. Nor did freed slaves comprise a visible bloc.

8. Exploitation concerns withholding of portions of values of marginal products — a definition owing to Joan Robinson's orthodox phase.

9. The text infra shows that the Greek father was but a protector of his children.

316

10. Commons (1924/1974) makes rather the same point: "liberty, as such, is only the negative of duty, the absence of restraint or compulsion. But 'freedom' is positive. ... Freedom is power." (Ibid., pp. 118–119) (He elides liberty's immunity-component.) He continues:

"If we start with Herbert Spencer's *[improper]* concept of the individual as a free man existing prior to law, then man's liberty has gradually been taken away from him by the common law ... But if we start with individuals as subjects of conquest, slavery, serfdom, then liberty has gradually been taken away from masters and bestowed on subjects." (Ibid., p. 126)

The text shows that liberty is nil in a state of nature.

11. See compulsory use of seat belts, perhaps to be followed by intrusive kitchen inspectors, seeking to promote lower insurance premia. Puritans like John Adams are prone to support sumptuary measures. So citizens become exposed to governmental powers to create duties to use seat belts and/or to eschew fatty foods.

12. What about "Coase" and what about "evolution"? The Coase parable concerns social optimization through voluntary exchange. And it is virtually irrelevant for a sophisticated society.

Evolution may lead to destruction of classical civilization; and may have already done so. The good life can be sustained only by exercises of will: indeed the "aggregate quantity of liberty" is itself a product of public choice.

13. Premia are paid in share markets for blocs of shares affording control. The controlling logic spans voting markets too: middlemen will strive to assemble vote-bundles giving control of various zones in issue-space.

14. Or consider purchases of votes by groups for or against abortion (choice) or sodomy. How much do you really care about abortion? Let there be a market test!

Sales of bundled voting rights leave purchasers (say proponents of "choice") with massive residues — allowing them to create monopolies, or seek other rents in the wake of their success on "choice." They might obtain charters of monopoly to purvey iced tea.

The complexities are daunting, but no more so than in the purely economic sphere.

15. The component human particles are in ceaseless transition; the state-variables are stationary only in a macro sense. See ch. 2 of my 1988 book.

16. The antinomy of freedom and liberty may entail the study's deepest meaning. This is the circle to be squared: liberty may be quashed by democratic despotism; "one man, one vote" may erode liberty. And the public interest may be ignored by factions operating in flawed parliaments.

Recall earlier remarks on Edwardian British government, especially the great Campbell-Bannerman and Asquith cabinets. The sophisticated controlling group was immune to charisma; and large enough to block concentration of power. Enlightened (if imperfect) benevolence promoted the public interest. The Edwardian system seems to me to realize the aims of Mill's *Representative Government*.

Frank Knight
and the Ethics of Competition

This study seeks to explain Knight's moral philosophy and to link it to the book's. Easily done: Knight has fascinated me for many years. [1]

§1 ON UNDERSTANDING FRANK KNIGHT

Economic Philosophy. Along lines Knight sometimes obscures, the idealized model of competition does not entail rivalry and is compatible with ceaseless search for the Good, an activity that is intrinsic to civilized intellectual action.

○ The tastes and preferences of economic particles are at best unstable, a point I emphasize more than Knight chooses to do.

○ The competitive paradigm is based on uncoerced acceptance, or rejection, of proposals driven by value-enhancing motivation: competitive systems are liberal.

○ The "values" of the competitive paradigm are but price-weighted sums, instrumentally important for achievement of Pareto optima, themselves ephemera, shadows cast by transient mutations of ethical values that cannot be measured, or even conceived, by scientific (positive) economics.

○ The real economic world pivots on rivalry and greed; its agents are invidiously motivated. And its action will almost surely violate the criteria of higher cultures. The liberal must bite her lip and plod on, committed to non-coercion as an ethical value, but aware of ghastly potentials of evolutions of human actions. One thing is sure: "scientific" economics cannot discern the properties of the good life; welfare economics can at most suggest action relative to criteria it is incompetent to evaluate.

Remarks on Rationality. Frank Knight thought civilized human action to be ultimately concerned with attainment of a supra-rational Summum Bonum. [2] But Reason is necessary for attainment of the Summum Bonum (e.g. the Aristotelian Mean). Thus one must study the score to enter Mozart's Paradiso; e.g. the emotion provoked by the fourth movement of his Jupiter Symphony pivots on the intricacies of its four-part fugue. At its summit, art is the Summum Bonum, an end in itself. It is absurd to say that the D-Minor Quartet (K.421) or Leonardo's *Annunciation* gives pleasure: sublime works are not titillating toys. [3]

All this said, it is quite legitimate for econometricians to report that, at the margin, the representative consumer is willing to trade off one minute of viewing time of Raphael's *School of Athens* for two bowls of minestrone per period. [4] Econometric calculations pertain to a different domain of discourse than ethical criticism. Economics is not competent to comment on the inner life of elementary economic particles (blobs).

§2 KNIGHT ON THE ETHICS OF COMPETITION

Consider these summary remarks:

"The striking fact in modern life is the virtually complete separation between the spiritual ethics which constitute its accepted theory of conduct and the unethical, uncriticized notion of efficiency which forms its substitute for a practical working ideal. ...

"It was pointed out that the competitive *[i.e. rivalrous]* economic life has value-implications on the production side, the most notable of which is its appeal as a competitive game. An examination from this point of view reveals notable shortcomings of business considered purely as a game. There is also a certain ethical repugnance attached to having the livelihood of the masses of the people made a pawn in such a sport, however fascinating the sport may be to its leaders. [5]

"Finally we have called in question from the standpoint of ideal ethics the predominance of the institution of sport, or action motivated by rivalry, and — in particular — have contrasted it with the Pagan ethics of beauty or perfection and the Christian ideal of sprituality." (Knight, 1922, 1923/1935, pp. 73–75)

I propose to develop these themes, supplying context for Knight's moral and economic philosophy, going back to the ancients and to Hume, Kant, William James et al.

Human Wants as Data (?). There follows a synopsis of portions of "Ethics and the Economic Interpretation," Part I of Knight (1922, 1923/1935 — see pp. 19–31).

Human wants cannot properly be treated as data. Indeed "[wants] are from a more-critical point of view the most obstinately unknown of all the unknowns in the whole system of variables with which economic science deals." What is more, if human wants were merely data, economics would not make contact with ethical theory. Knight, being trained in philosophy, turned to David Hume for help in resolving the quandary: might not wants be "values" or "oughts" rather than facts? Yes! Nor are these values or "oughts" merely hedonistic: the idea of the Good, cherished by Knight, requires discrimination between higher and lower wants; the search for criteria for such discrimination has dominated cultured minds for millennia. Indeed his "common sense individual" seeks more and better wants, not satisfaction of those he has. [6] "This feeling about what one should want, in contrast with actual desire, is stronger in the unthinking than in those sophisticated by education." (How did he discover this curious result?)

The stage is set for a critique of "wants." At the core of Knight's theory is an apposition of science and ethics: it is not surprising that Immanuel Kant will be painted into the picture.

Wants and the Idea of "Self." The "evolution" of the wants of an elementary economic particle poses knotty difficulties for correct economic science, leading to a "macro" approach to microeconomics. Knight's theory rests comfortably in a schematization in which the elementary economic particles (biological agents) are unstable blobs whose tastes or wants are in ceaseless flux and perhaps not identifiable.

I have called the upshot "I today am not I tomorrow"; and augmented the theme in 1988 with Marcel Proust's description of a person's biography as a *"suite de moi."* This seems the ineluctable consequence of the fact that the "agents" of economic theory are biological entities — notwithstanding such bizarre contrivances as infinitely-lived eunuchs, whose perfectly well-defined and stable preferences extend out to the time at which the sun will burn out.

Knight writes, in his "Ethics of Competition," about criticisms of "mainstream economics" by J. M. Clark, Walton Hamilton and Thorstein Veblen. They emphasize "the factual instability of wants and their liability to be changed as well as satisfied by business activity." But "wants are not only changeable in response to all sorts of influences, it is their essential nature to change and grow." He finally resolves the dissonance created by this point: the critique by Clark, Hamilton, Veblen et al. leads to a more-careful formulation of scientific, or positive, economics; scientific economics lacks moral-philosophical content; and Hume's definitive ethical critique lies outside pure deduction (*pace* Kant's monumental labours). He continues,

"A sounder culture ... leads to a form of tolerance very different from the notion that one taste or judgment is as good as another. ... The consideration of wants ... inevitably gravitates into a criticism of standards, ... very different ... from the comparison of given magnitudes. ... Wants and the activity they motivate constantly look forward to new and 'higher,' more evolved and enlightened wants. ... Life is not fundamentally a striving for satisfactions, but rather for bases for further striving." (This remark has Bergsonian overtones; Knight esteemed Bergson.)

Knight is surprisingly loath to attack either utility theory or utilitarianism head-on. Yet his remarks, just above, are devastating for both; they establish the incompatability of utility theory, let alone utilitarianism, with the moral philosophy of western civilization. What is more,

"The authors of great imaginative literature ... have never fallen into such palpable delusion as the belief that men neither strive for happiness or expect to be made happy by their striving. The same has been true of philosophers and religious thinkers of all time, and even economists have recognized the futility of attempting to satisfy wants. ... Nor do we know what they want." (Ibid., p. 51)

(But Epicurus and the English utilitarians seek happiness.)

Summarizing, wants — if they can be defined — evolve endogenously and are not teleologically directed. There is no discernable accumulation point for the transition, or, better, flux, of tastes and preferences, importantly because the process is not mechanical. It may be a road to nowhere.

What is Economics? Knight anticipates economists' imperial ambitions:

"In so far as ends are ... data, then all activity is economic. ... The assumption that wants or ends are data reduces life to economics, and raises again the question ... is life all economics or does this view require supplementing by an ethical view of value? ... What is to be said of ethics? If we are to establish a distinct place for ethics ... it must be done by finding ends or standards which are something more than than scientific data. ... For those to whom ethics is only a more or less 'glorified' economics, *virtue* is correspondingly reduced to an enlarged prudence." [7] (Ibid., pp. 36–37)

"Discussion of a criticism of values will, like literary and artistic criticism, run in terms of suggestion rather than logical statement, in figurative rather than literal language, and its principles will be available though sympathetic interpretation rather than intellectual cognition." (Ibid., pp. 40–41)

Frank Knight was not a utilitarian. (Nor am I.) But he is unwontedly leery of any but oblique attacks on marginal-utility theory. Indeed he calls marginal utility theory "the culmination ... of the rationalistic and individualistic intellectual movement of which the competitive economic system ... is one aspect and modern science and technology are others." [8] He identifies two streams of criticism of marginal utility economics.

The first calls marginal-utility unduly "rational." If radically redesigned, it imitates portions of Knight's criticism. Marginal utility theory is otiose in scientific economics. And, what is worse, one cannot hope to track closely the action of individual economic particles: the actions of these flickering blobs is virtually impossible to observe, let alone explain.

The second stream of criticism — claiming that marginal utility economics is unscientific — seems more robust: surely a theory relying on invisible occurances that does not enhance explanation of what can be observed is invalid. But Knight transposes the argument into a different key.

"The advocates of a purely statistical science do not seem to realize that [if economics is to relate to] human problems of means and ends, it must be concerned with goods and services, not in themselves, but as representing values or sacrifices. These cannot be treated as physical things but must be defined in the same vague and shifting terms as the human impulses, successes and failures which the scientific mind finds such unsatisfactory material." (Knight, 1935, p. 160)

This passage describes a domain barred to economics. The fact that scientific economics — based on macroeconomic foundations of the action of "unstable" elementary economic particles (quantum physics is "macro" in the same sense) — recognizes this truth should not be held against it. Knight's proper enemies are the modern "scientific" welfare economists, seeking to conquer the domain properly abandoned by positive economics. True, positive economics is ethically significant in at least two ways.

o Economic inefficiency is arguably immoral: a state of play in which *A* can reach a more-preferred position, without any other agent having to accept a less preferred one, relative to (ill-defined) preferences is at the least ethically problematical.

o Furthermore, the good life, whatever else it may be, entails the fruits of a successful economy to *some* extent.

Knight's Critique of the Ethics of Capitalist Régimes. The critique does not concern the model of competition projected by pure economic theory. The ideal competitive model is ethically empty, except for its promotion of voluntarism and rejection of coercion. It may promote abhorrent values, but its rôle is instrumental: the economic model of competition is a soldier of fortune, ready to promote any value-system conformable to the properties of distributed computing and decentralized decision making (so that no agent has more than a thimble-full of information) — so long as offers and acceptances are not coerced. Knight's critique concerns private-ownership economies *en vigeur* — and so the emulation, rivalry and highly disciplined (and authoritative) economic organizations of the real world. Nor is this distinction always clear in his writing.

Turn to the second part of "The Ethics of Competition." (1923/1935) The paper "inquire[s] into the standards of value implicit in the laisser-faire or individualist social philosophy." (Knight, 1935, p. 42) Relying on Hayek, I should pitch this passage differently. A society of selfless, altruistic agents will deploy a version of the competitive economic model for the sake of economic efficiency. It is the only known feasible way to generate and efficiently process information. The competitive model is a powerful technical instrument, but a quite empty ethical vessel.

"There can be no question ... that the valid criticisms of the existing economic order relate chiefly to its value standards, and relatively much less to its efficiency in the creation of such values as it recognizes." (Ibid., p. 43)

Again, if "the existing economic order" is to be the economic model of pure competition, this passage is highly problematical: the only salient value standard of such a system is non-coercion. But the system *en vigeur* supplies Knight with abundant material — cf. emulation and rivalry; the extent to which leaders of business teams are engaged in "play"; etc. In the upshot the quality of life of many people is the product of outcomes of games played by high company officers. And, less sententiously, many wants satisfied by the system are surely created by it, as J. M. Clark, Walton Hamilton and Thorstein Veblen said.

Knight continues along lines excessively concerned with "individualism" and insufficiently focussed on "distributed computing."

"The argument for individualism ... from Adam Smith down may be summarized in a sentence as follows: a freely competitive organization of society tends to place every productive resource in that position ... where it can make the greatest possible addition to the total social dividend as measured in price terms ... In the writer's [FHK's] opinion, such a proposition is entirely sound, but it is not the statement of a sound ethical social ideal, the specification for a Utopia." (Ibid., p. 48)

He next claims that "in the conditions of real life no possible social order based on a laisser-faire policy can justify the familiar ethical conclusions of apologetic economics." I have already dissented from his indictment: it would be better to put the onus on oligopoly, disciplined "team play," suppression of individual creativeness, the philistinism of mass media, all prominent in contemporary "advanced" societies.

"In the first place, an individualistic competitive system must be made up of freely contracting persons. ... Our 'individualism' is really 'familism': all minors, the aged [et al.] have their status-determining bargains made for them by other persons." (Ibid., p. 49)

His theory of agency is coarse, but he makes a good point, which may be understated. Shareholders nominate boards of directors to watch over their interests; most individual shareholders are smothered; and pliant boards are often cowed by glib managers.

His point about "familial individualism" demands close attention:

"Moreover, the most free individual, the unencumbered male in the prime of life, is in no sense an ultimate unit or social datum. He is in large measure a product of the economic system. ... In fact, human activity is largely impulsive, a relatively unthinking and undetermined response to stimulus and suggestion." (Ibid., pp. 49–50)

D'accord! But his gloss is awkward. He seems to make the case (already proved) for macro-foundations of micro-economics obliquely, if not accidentally. Nor does he deal subtly (here) with consequences of necessary imperfection of agents' knowledge: he compares an ideal system, based on omniscient agents, with feasible systems. What is more, the genius of the private-ownership economy lies in its coordination of the bytes of information available to individual agents. The upshot hinges on coordinative power, not on the quality of wants being served. This is the core of the remarkable work of Adam Smith and F. A. Hayek.

On "Self." (See Ch. 7.) A successful analysis of individualism pivots on a clear perception of self, an evanescent idea. What is more, preference structures cannot be observed; only consumption action is visible.

If "self" vanishes, freedom of the will becomes problematical. Knight discusses the underlying philosophical quandries especially subtly.

"What is 'really' perceived, and what is 'only' inferred or seen because it is wished? ... No clear separation can be made. ... Hume agreed ... with Berkeley that the primary as well as the secondary qualities of objects all resolve themselves into mental states of the experiencing subject. Hume added that the subject himself also disappears in the same mental states. *[What is left to be said about human will?]*

"No logical answer has ever been given to the reasoning of Hume. ... There is no such thing as the perception of reality, and all that exists is the flow of conscious experience of which 'I' am immediately aware. ('I' is to be understood to be not a self in any real sense, but just a stream of consciousness ... The stream of consciousness, sensations, and the like are artificial constructions.)

"The answer at the end of every line of inquiry is instrumentalism. Reality is not what is logical, but what it suits our purposes to treat as real. This was the upshot of the thought of Kant, the next great name in the history of philosophy after Hume. It was the great German thinker who made the transition from scepticism to pragmatism. *[I cannot accept that Kant's philosophy is the source of pragmatism!]* It is impossible to perceive or imagine the real world without recognizing the equally real character both of purposes and of intellectual concepts. Thought is impossible without these non-factual data.

"There is no such thing as either immediate or positive knowledge; it is all a matter of the relative cogency of reasons, or usefulness of believing one thing as compared with another. [9]   Scientific truth is a critical rather than a logical category." (F. H. Knight, 1925/1935, pp. 86–97)

Knight says (at p. 97) that his argument is developed with ultimate proficiency by Henri Bergson and William James. [10]

BERTRAND RUSSELL AND MARCEL PROUST ON "SELF."   Russell makes Knight's point with more punch.

"... When we say, 'I think first this and then that,' we ought not to mean that there is a single entity 'I' which 'has' two successive thoughts. We ought to mean only that there are two successive thoughts. We ought to mean that there are two successive thoughts which have causal relations of the kind that makes us call them parts of one biography ... and that these thoughts are connected with the body which is speaking in the way ... in which thoughts and bodies are connected."   (Bertrand Russell, 1927/1979)

I have often referred to Marcel Proust's *"suite de moi,"* related to "I today am not I tomorrow," especially in connection with the "flickering blob." (Russell's *Analysis of Mind*, 1921, is a treasure trove on "self.")

IMPLICATIONS FOR WELFARE ECONOMICS AND PUBLIC CHOICE. Much work in these fields is philosophically baseless. Thus "issue space" in public-choice theory has myriad dimensions: preferences of "elementary particle" voters are hopelessly unstable. Hume's remorseless regress to the passions mandates this upshot, a point Knight takes. (See W. S. Kern, 1987)

The Real Rivalrous World. An economy comprised of angels would emulate the paradigms of the competitive model. Nor does a farmer have any selfish reason not to help extinguish a fire in his neighbour's barn. But the oligopolistic economy *en vigeur* surely does entail rivalry. Indeed the violent game of American football (vicious beanbag) feeds the fantasies of businessmen. This, not the Smith-Hayek paradigm, is the proper object of Knight's critique. "There is truth in the allegation that unregulated competition puts a premium on deceit and corruption." (Ibid., p. 50) What is more:

"As to the human qualities developed by business activity and requisite to enjoyment of and successful participation in it ... we shall dismiss the subject by quoting Ruskin. ... 'In a community regulated by laws of demand and supply ... the persons who become rich are ... industrious ...; the persons who remain poor are the entirely foolish ... and ... the entirely merciful, just, godly persons.' " (Knight, 1935, pp. 65–66) [11]

I disagree with Ruskin. The personal expenditures of the winners of the business game and, indeed, the "rich" as a class, are not very important in advanced western economies. Their rôle is to manage productive wealth; and their management-principle keys on maximizing value-weighted sums — conformably with the "fundamental theorems" of welfare economics.

REMARK. Scholars, clambering to sustain an *haut-bourgeois* life-style, may envy capitalists who can do so, in bad taste. The dénouement is open to ethical criticism. Compare the pay of philosophers with that of football players. The upshot may conform to Pareto optimality, so that the plumbing services of a mechanically competent professor of philosophy will be more valued than his antinomies.

Alternatives to Acquisitive Rivalry as an Ethical Ideal. [12] A stimulating critique starts uncertainly. "The competitive system, viewed simply as a want-satisfying mechanism, falls far short of our highest ideals." (Ibid., p. 57) No! The competitive system is but a mechanism. It is ethically neutral, subject to a monumentally important exception: it abjures coercion.

GRECIAN IDEALS

"Surely no justification of competition *[acquisitive rivalry]* as a motive *[cf. motives such as winning business games, conspicuous consumption and invidious pleasure]* is to be found in the Aristotelian conception of the Good as that which is intrinsically worthy of man as man, or the Platonic idea of archetypical goodness." (Ibid., p. 72)

I suspect the following passage contains the key to Knight's most penetrating ethical critique.

"Very wise and penetrating remarks on the character of various wants will be found in Wicksteed's *Common Sense of Political Economy*. Patrick Geddes's essay on John Ruskin in the [University of Chicago] *Round Table* [radio broadcasting] series is a brilliant argument for the reduction of all economic values to aesthetic standards." (Ibid., p. 51, n.)

CHRISTIAN IDEALS. Now consider Knight's interesting, emotionally taut, discussion of Christian ideals: Pauline virtue is not rooted in aesthetics!

"If there is anything on which divergent interpretations [of Christian thought agree on it is] the admission that the Christian conception of goodness is the antithesis of the competitive *[rivalrous]* one. ... The Christian ethical ideal contrasts as sharply with the Greek as either does with modern *[?]* ideas. ... Any *ethical* judgment of activity must be based not upon its efficiency ... but upon the character of the result or the character of the motive. ... The Greek view [pivots on] the character of the result, and gives an ... aesthetic conception of ethical value; [13] Christianity centres [on] the motive ... [Pauline] Christianity makes virtue consist in conscientiousness, in doing what one believes to be right, rather than in the correct perception of objective goodness. ... It is from Christianity (and from Kant, who merely systematized Christian, or Pauline, principles) that modern common sense derives its conceptions of what is ethical." [14]

Further Discussion of Liberty and Virtue

Immanuel Kant sought to reconcile the world of necessity, the world of science, with the noumenal world of the human spirit, a world of freedom. And he saw that Pauline virtue nests in a world of freedom: for an action to be virtuous, it must be *chosen*: virtue pivots on choice. Moreover, in the Judeo-Christian ethic, acts are approved mostly for their motives — objective consequences are irrelevant for critical judgment. (So Christian liberty is a sort of inner freedom: see Eliot's "the inner freedom from the practical desire.")

Dorothy L. Sayers's introduction to her translation of Dante's *Divine Comedy* expands the study's scope.

"We must also be prepared, while we are reading Dante, to accept the Christian and Catholic view of ourselves as responsible rational beings. We must abandon any idea that we are slaves of chance, or environment, or our subconscious; any vague notion that good and evil are merely relative terms or that conduct and opinion do not really matter; any comfortable persuasion that, however shiftlessly we muddle through life, it will somehow or other come out all right. ... We must try to believe that man's will is free, that he can consciously exercise choice, and that his choice can be decisive to all eternity. For the *Divine Comedy* is precisely the drama of the soul's choice. *[She tacitly distinguishes mind from matter.]* It is not a fairy story, but a great Christian allegory, deriving its power from the terror and splendour of Christian revelation." (Introduction to her translation of the *Divine Comedy*, 1949, pp. 10–11)

The Preface probed *Axel's Castle*, Edmund Wilson's fine critique of a number of writers very different from Dante, including Yeats, Joyce, Valéry, Rimbaud, Gertrude Stein, et al.

The individual responsibility discussed by Dorothy Sayers is wholly different from the "idealistic philosophical" individualism discussed by Edmund Wilson: the latter is a skewed descendant of the philosophical development associated with Berkeley and Hume (noted by Knight); "the point of insanity" concerns the German "idealist" proposition that one's self comprises "reality," a bizarre distortion of Berkeley's and Hume's sceptical philosophies.

It is easy to defend Wilson's stark contrast of twentieth-century with mediaeval thought. But another theme, "twentieth century introspection inducing inaction," looks chimerical. Indeed the early Christians believed that the world was about to come to an end: they tended to be indifferent to terrestrial events, as Edward Gibbon vividly explains. And Stoicism, perhaps the most elevated classical moral philosophy, leads to "acceptance of the universe," to withdrawal of the ego from worldly affairs. Nor is it plausible that the good life should be an action-cult: Aristotle thought God must be a philosopher, surely not an athlete or grain speculator.

§3 KNIGHT ON FREEDOM AND REFORM

Knight's "Ethics and Economic Reform" (1939/1947) is a mixed bag. Thus his treatment of distributive justice is flawed: he confounds the value of liberty with that of equality; and he confuses the managerial rôle of the rich (as custodians of much of the society's capital stock) with their consumption. But he analyses other issues with panache.

"Social ethics must look to the distant future and take into account the unborn and the whole character of culture and not merely relations between given individuals." (Knight, 1939/1947, p. 72)

This position is reinforced by the more-sophisticated, sceptical view of self imposed by modern philosophy: the blob (the elementary economic particle) cannot underpin micro-economics, let alone social ethics: the foundations of micro-economics are "macro," roughly like those of quantum physics.

His reference to the unborn is telling: economists often chimerically bundle the "utility" of living persons and their potential descendants into a well-defined, time-invariant utility function.

Democratic Despotism? "Mere competitive persuasion of the masses [is not] a good test of the truth ... of a question. The saving face of liberalism [is] in [its] ... commitment to minimizing the functions of government and the sphere of its activity ... and the use of coercion, negative for the most part, to prevent coercion by individuals and private groups. This means using it to enforce the ideal of mutual free consent as the basis of social relations. ... Apart from this ideal ... the notion of majority rule would probably never have been seriously defended by competent thinkers as essentially better than other forms of tyranny." (Knight, 1939/1947, p. 79)

This is an ideal statement of the credo of Whig liberty, pivoting on faith in the ultimate outcome of uncoerced "dialogue." [15]

"The Rights of Man and Natural Law" (Knight, 1944/1947, pp. 262ff.) Knight manages something Thomas Jefferson never did. He expels natural law from the theory of the rights of man. His argument leads to a proper perception of liberalism as a way of striving

332

for "better wants" and deeper insight; not as a revelation of an intrinsic (perhaps divinely-inspired) ordering.

"It will be evident that 'natural law,' properly defined, is the opposite of 'natural.' To the extent that men are aware of it, it is a highly artificial product of social mental life, exceeded in artificiality only by the creative products, or mere abberations, of individual minds. ... A true moral law rests on a recognized conflict between what is not resolved by established customs and norms. ... It reflects a threefold cleavage, in varying degree, within the individual (self-criticism), and between different individuals in a culture group (mutual criticism), and within the group as a whole (group self-criticism). A moral law, with any content whatever, about which there is no disagreement or even no serious disagreement is essentially a contradiction; if not self-contradictory in the abstract logical sense, it is at least contrary to all historical reality."

Scepticism about Economism. The following excerpt from *Freedom and Reform* (1947, p. 379ff.), vividly entitled "The Sickness of Liberal Society," is marred by Knight's endemic confusion of the competitive paradigm with properties of oligopolistic rivalry, and by his failure to compare the system *en vigeur* with a specific alternative rather than a vague ideal.

"[The analyst] must be struck by the limitations of the economic view of conduct. ... Reflection will show that in 'economic life' itself motives are highly mixed and in large part not distinctively 'economic.' That is, the 'value' to individuals and groups of the goods and services they want and strive to get is not mainly intrinsic; they are symbols of success. [16] Economic activity has [much of] the character of a competitive game or sport; [17] ... Economic 'success' is largely competitive; and the symbols are in large part culturally determined, and their concrete form more or less a historical accident." (Knight, 1947, pp. 385–386) [18]

§4 SUMMARY AND CONCLUSIONS

The following précis depicts Knight's core ideas, scraping off glosses reflecting his volatile (and endearing) temperament and eliding his masterly contributions to "technical" economic theory.

○ Values are not facts.

○ Man is an aspiring, not a desiring, being or, more cautiously, man is an aspiring as well as a desiring being.

○ Human wants are not objective and measurable magnitudes: "any such view ... reduces the 'higher' wants to a secondary position as compared with 'lower' and interprets human life in biological terms." (This is precisely what "economism" does.)

○ A system is to be judged relative to the wants it creates, not just in terms of how well it satisfies the wants that exist.

□ Such judgments cannot be objective and, if made, in some sense, by a society, will be enforced coercively to some degree. Liberals seek the optimal feasible minimum of coercion: they abide outcomes (like rock music and the decline of *haute cuisine*) they deplore.

○ The game-aspect of rivalrous economic life is troubling: should one's material well-being, indeed one's happiness or sense of fulfillment of one's human potential, depend on the outcome of a game? Is success in any sort of contest a noble objective?

○ The agents of the competitive economy of pure theory could just as well be computers programmed to play chess. The schematization is merely instrumental: it can serve Dr Fu Manchu as well as Liberty; many sets of preferences will do.

□ Many are prone to criticize "capitalism" for efficiently translating base desires into action.

○ Frustration over inability to persuade people to want something else does not lure the (perhaps tempted) liberal into the toils of coercion.

○ All of the study's sometimes-serpentine paths lead back to David Hume. In ethical criticism, *is* gives way to *ought*.

1. Unfortunately, Professor Knight deploys competition in the sense of rivalry, so that the idealized competitive model — formally indifferent to régimes of resource-ownership — is easily misperceived.

2. "Rationality" is hard to discern. A rational person groping in a fog may be indistinguishable from a simply irrational one. Badly informed major premises may lead to behaviour that looks quite mad to those able to form accurate ones.

3. See the Preface's "Excursus into Aesthetics." J. S. Mill (1806–1873) predictably surpasses Jeremy Bentham's wretched aesthetic canon — but not by enough.

"The art of music is good, for the reason, among others, that it produces pleasure; but what proof is possible to give that pleasure is good?" (*Utilitarianism*, 1863/1939, p. 898ff.)

4. Similarly, psychologists quantitatively compare the "pleasure" a monkey gets from consuming three bananas with that from two heads of Romaine lettuce. The text's strictures are not in play so long as ethical value is not attributed to such measurements.

5. This remark exposes a perplexing fault that has a number of ramifications: the schematization alternative to the private-ownership economy is not specified. Knight points out elsewhere that to say an arrangement is unalterable is to say it is optimal.

6. Elizabeth Longford's biography of the Duke of Wellington (cf. *Pillar of State*) cites Ernest Bevin's observation that the tragedy of the British working classes lies in the poverty of their wants rather than in their (undoubted) poverty.

7. Ethical assessments cannot ignore prudence: consequences matter. Still "we do not offer praise and affection on the basis of conduct alone or mainly, but quite irrationally on the motives themselves." (Ibid., p. 38)

8. This panegyric seems misplaced to me. What does Knight mean by individualism? The vast empty spaces of utility theory accomodate benevolence. What is more, his system seems to me to annihilate utility theory.

9. Knight does not retreat from his position that systems are to be judged relative to the wants they create, not just in terms of how well they satisfy existing ones; and that man is an aspiring, not a desiring, being. The context is epistemological, not ethical or teleological. The truth of instrumental constructions lies in their usefulness.

10. Subrato Roy (1989) barely refers to Knight; and fruitlessly seeks to undermine Hume.

11. The quotation from Ruskin is in Upton Sinclair's *The Cry of Justice: An Anthology of Social Protest*, p. 752.

12. Knight points out that "evolution" cannot bottom a critique of a system's virtue.

13. I should say that the Stoics sought a sense of harmony with the cosmos. For that matter, the listener's or viewer's artistic experience does not solely concern objective sound values or colour-properties. It is not the picture that is beautiful; the set of sensations induced by the viewer's experience is called "beautiful." In principle, the upshot may be metricized. Certain values of electro-mechanical-chemical readings may correspond with the exclamation, "this is *beautiful!*" But a complete criticism of a work of art must be subjective. It may be possible to forecast the particulars of a value judgment; but aesthetic value cannot be assessed scientifically.

14. Knight is not a Jansenist: free will drives his theory of virtue. But, like his friend, T. S. Eliot, and the Jansenists, he does not accomodate to "works."

15. The competitive paradigm is tenable for a number of ideologies: it simply entails distributed computing and decentralized programming; operators at each node maximize value-weighted sums — solving a collective problem. But its eschewal of coercion is ethically significant.

16. Thorstein Veblen often intensifies Knight's themes; Veblen was a great colourist, but a poor harmonist.

17. Analogies to sporting competition are still more pointed in 1992 than in Knight's time. Grotesquely compensated gladiators are rôle models for great industrialists. Successful athletic coaches are paid huge fees to motivate squads of corporate officers.

18. Knight clashes with utilitarianism in "Freedom as Fact and Criterion," reprinted in *Freedom and Reform* (1947). Utilitarianism pivots on well-defined stationary preferences. It neglects the character of wants; it concerns satisfaction of existing ones.

Bibliography

A

Abro, A. d' (1939/1951) *The Rise of the New Physics* (New York: Dover; 1951) — originally published in New York by D. van Nostrand (1939) as *Decline of Mechanism*

Acton, Lord (J. E. E. Dalberg-Acton) (1877 et seq./1985) *Essays in the History of Liberty* (Indianapolis, Indiana: Liberty Classics), J. R. Fears, ed.

Adair, D. (1944) "Alexander Hamilton on the Constitution (*sic*)," *William & Mary Quarterly Historical Magazine* (Apr)

Adams, D. R., Jr. (1980) "American Neutrality and Prosperity, 1793–1808: A Reconsideration," 40 *Journal of Economic History* 713–738 (Dec., no. 4)

Adams, Henry
(1879/1943) *The Life of Albert Gallatin* (New York: Lippincott), reprint-
    ed in New York by Peter Smith (1943)
(1889–1890/1986) *History of the United States during the Administrations
    of Thomas Jefferson* (New York: Viking Press, Library of Amer-
    ica), vols. 1 & 2 of his four-volume *History of the United States
    during the Administrations of Thomas Jefferson and James Madi-
    Madison*
(1904/1912/1983) *Mont Saint Michel and Chartres* — the 1983 ed. is in-
    cluded in *Henry Adams* (New York: Library of America
    [Viking]), E. & J. N. Samuels, eds.
(1904/1983) "A Dynamic Theory of History," in *Henry Adams* (1983)
(1904/1983) "A Law of Acceleration," in *Henry Adams* (1983)
(1906/1983) *The Education of Henry Adams*, in *Henry Adams* (1983)
(1909/1983) "The Rule of Phase Applied to History," in *Henry Adams*
    (1983)

Appleby, J. (1984) *Capitalism and a New Social Order: The Republican Vision of the 1790s* (New York: New York University Press)

Archer-Hind, L. (1925) "Introduction," *Samuel Johnson* (1777/1925)

Aristotle, *The Nicomachean Ethics* (H. Rackham, trans.), J. A. K. Thomson, ed. *The Ethics of Aristotle: The Nicomachean Ethics Translated* (London: Allen & Unwin)

Ayer, A. J. (1972/1986) *Bertrand Russell* (Chicago: University of Chicago Press) — originally published in New York by Viking (1972)

Ayer, A. J. (1980) *Hume* (New York: Hill & Wang, Farrar, Straus & Giroux)

B

Bagehot, W. (1873/1927) *Lombard Street* (London: John Murray), 14th ed., posthumous — originally pub. in London by Henry S. King

Beard, C. A. (1913) *An Economic Interpretation of the Constitution of the United States* (New York: Macmillan)

Beard, C. A. (1934/1966) *The Idea of National Interest* (Chicago: Quadrangle Books; 1966) — originally published in New York by Macmillan (1934)

Bergson, Henri (1907/1911/1944) *Creative Evolution* (New York: Random House, Modern Library), a reissue of A. Mitchell's trans. (1911) of *L'évolution créatrice* (Paris: 1907)

Berkeley, G. (1709 *et seq.*/1950) *A New Theory of Vision and Other Writings* (London: Dent, Everyman's Library), A. D. Lindsay, ed.

Blackstone, Sir William (1723–1780) *Commentaries on the Laws of England*, 4 vols.

Bloch, M. (1940/1961/1966) *Feudal Society* (Chicago: University of Chicago Press), 2 vols., L. A. Manyon, trans. — cf. *La Société féodale* (Paris: 1940)

Brant, I. (1948) *James Madison the Nationalist* (New York & Indianapolis: Bobbs Merrill)

Brant, I. (1970) *The Fourth President: A Life of James Madison* (London: Eyre & Spottiswoode) — a one-volume condensation of his six vol. work

Brill, A. A. (1938) *Introduction* to A. A. Brill, ed. (1938) *The Basic Writings of Sigmund Freud* (New York: Modern Library)

Burke, Edmund (1790/1986) *Reflections on the Revolution in France* (London: Penguin)

Burke, Edmund (1992) *Further Reflections on the Revolution in France* (Indianapolis, Indiana: Liberty Classics), D. E. Ritchie, ed. — a miscellaneous collection

Burney, Dr Charles (1776–1789/1935/1957) *A General History of Music From the Earliest Ages to the Present Period* (New York: Dover), 2 vols. — the original ed. was in four vols. The 1957 ed. reprints Frank Mercer's "modern 2nd ed.," the source for this book.

Burstein, M. L.

(1949) "Note on *Erie v. Tompkins*," 17 *University of Chicago Law Review*

(1986) *Modern Monetary Theory* (London & New York: Macmillan & St. Martin's Press)

(1966/1988a) "Colonial Currency and Contemporary Monetary Theory" — in (1988a) (1967/1988a) "Homer on Interest Rates" — in (1988a)

(1988a) *Studies in Banking Theory, Financial History and Vertical Control* (London & New York: Macmillan and St. Martin's Press)

(1988b) "The Macro-Foundations of Micro-Economics" — in (1988a)

(1988c) "The Political Economy of Alexander Hamilton" — in (1988a)

(1988d) "Beyond the Banking Principle" — in (1988a)

(1988e) "Knut Wicksell and the Closure of His System," in (1988a)

(1989) *Open Economy Monetary Economics* (London & New York: Macmillan & New York University Press)

(1991a) *The New Art of Central Banking* (London & New York: Macmillan and New York University Press)

(1991b) "History versus Equilibrium: Joan Robinson and Time in Economics," in I. H. Rima, ed. (1991, pp. 49–61)

Burtt, E. A., ed. (1939) *The English Philosophers from Bacon to Mill* (New York: Modern Library)

C

Cambridge Historical Encyclopaedia of Great Britain and Ireland (Cambridge: Cambridge University Press; 1985), C. Haigh, ed.

Cantor, N. F. (1969) *Medieval History : The Life and Death of a Civilization* (New York: Macmillan Pub. Co.), 2nd ed.

Carlyle, A. J. (1941/1963) *Political Liberty: A History of the Conception in its Middle Ages and Modern Times* (London: Oxford University Press) — reprinted in London by Frank Cass (1963)

Chandler, L. V. (1959) *The Economics of Money and Banking* (New York: Harper), rev. ed.

Chateaubriand, Vicomte François-René de (1850/1951) *Mémoires d'outre-tombe* (Paris: Gallimard), 2 vols.

Chinard, G. (1925) *Jefferson et les Idéologues* (Baltimore)

Churchill, Winston S. (1933/1967) *Marlborough: His Life and Times* (London: Harrap; 1933) — reissued in London by Sphere Books (1967), 4 vols.

Coase, R. (1960) "The Problem of Social Cost," 3 *Journal of Law and Economics* 1

Cohen, M. R. (1926) "The Myth about Bacon and the Inductive Method," 23 *Scientific Monthly* 505

Cohen, M. R. & E. Nagel (1934) *An Introduction to Logic and Scientific Method* (New York: Harcourt, Brace)

The Concise Columbia Encyclopedia (New York: Columbia University Press; 1983)

Commons, J. R. (1924/1974) *Legal Foundations of Capitalism* (Clifton, N. J.: Augustus M. Kelley; 1974) — a reissue of the 1924 ed., published in New York by Macmillan

Cook, W. W. (1919/1964) "Introduction: Hohfeld's Contributions to the Science of Law," in Hohfeld (1919/1964, pp. 3–21) — reprinted from 28 *Yale Law Journal* 721 (1919)

Cooke, J. E. (1982) *Alexander Hamilton* (N.Y.: Charles Scribner's Sons)

Copleston, Frederick, SJ
History of Philosophy [HP] (Garden City, N. Y.: Doubleday, Image Books)
(1946/1962) vol. 1, *Greece and Rome,* in two parts
(1950/1962) vol. 2, part i: *Mediaeval Philosophy: Augustine to Bonaventure*
(1959/1964) vol. 5, *Modern Philosophy: The British Philosophers*, part i, *Hobbes to Paley*
(1959/1964) vol. 5, *Modern Philosophy: The British Philosophers*, part ii, *Berkeley to Hume*

(1960/1964) vol. 6, *Modern Philosophy*, part i, *The French Enlightenment to Kant*

(1959/1960) vol. 6, *Modern Philosophy*, part ii, *Kant*

(1966/1967) vol. 8, *Modern Philosophy: Bentham to Russell*, part ii, *Idealism in America; The Pragmatist Movement; The Revolt Against Idealism*

(1974/1977) vol. 9, *Maine de Biran to Sartre*, part i, *The Revolution to Henri Bergson*

Corbin, A. L. (1964) "Foreward " to Hohfeld (1919/1964)

A Critical Dictionary of the French Revolution (1988/1989) (Cambridge, Ma.: Harvard University Press, Belknap) — A. Goldhammer, trans.; F. Furet & M. Ozouf, eds.

Crosskey, W. W. (1953) *Politics and the Constitution in the History of the United States* (Chicago: University of Chicago Press), 2 vols.

Crosskey, W. W. (1954) "Charles Fairman, 'Legislative History,' and the Constitutional Limitations on State Authority," 22 *University of Chicago Law Review* 1–143 (no. 1, Autumn)

D

Dante (Dante Alieghiere) [1265–1321] (Harmondsworth: Penguin) *The Divine Comedy*

Cantica I, *The Inferno (L'Inferno)*, 1949, D. L. Sayers, trans.

Cantica II, *Purgatory (Il Purgatorio)*, 1955, D. L. Sayers, trans.

Cantica III, *Paradise (Il Paradiso)*, 1962, D. L. Sayers & B. Reynolds, trans.

David, P. A. (1967) "The Growth of Real Product in the United States Before 1840: New Evidence, Controlled Conjectures," 27 *Journal of Economic History* 151–197 (June, no. 2)

Dawson, C. (19–) A Monument to St. Augustine

Descartes, René (1637 *et seq.*/1912) *A Discourse on Method, etc.* (London: Dent, Everyman's Library), A. D. Lindsay, ed. — many times reprinted

Destutt de Tracy, A. C. L. (1817/1970) *A Treatise on Political Economy* (Augustus M. Kelley; 1970) — Thomas Jefferson supervised the 1817 trans. (published by Joseph Mulligan: Georgetown, D. C.) of Tracy's *Traité de la volonté* (1815), which was republished in Paris in 1823 as *Traité d'économie politique.*

Destutt de Tracy, A. C. L. (1828) *Commentaire sur l'esprit des lois de Montesquieu* (Paris: Madame Lévi, Librarie, Quai des Augustins, n° 25)

Dicey, A. V., *Introduction to the Study of the Law of the Constitution* (London: Macmillan), 9th ed.

E

Einstein, Alfred (1945/1962) *Mozart: His Character, His Work* (New York: Oxford University Press)

Eliot, T. S.
(1932) *Selected Essays, 1917-1932* (London & New York: Faber & Harcourt, Brace)
(1936) *Collected Poems, 1909-1935* (London & New York: Faber & Harcourt Brace)

Ellison, T. (1968) *The Cotton Trade of Great Britain* (New York: Augustus Kelley)

Engerman, S. (1970) "A Note on the Consequences of the Second Bank of the United States," 78 *Journal of Political Economy* (July/August)

F

Fairman, C. (1953) "The Supreme Court and the Constitutional Limitations on State Governmental Authority: Review of Crosskey (1953)," 21 *University of Chicago Law Review* 40 — other reviews are in 54 *Columbia Law Review* 450 (1954) and 67 *Harvard Law Review* 1456 (1954)
The Federalist (1788/1961, Middletown, Conn.: Wesleyan U. Press), J. E. Cooke, ed.

Ferris, T., ed. (1991) *Physics, Astronomy and Mathematics* (Boston: Little, Brown)

Filmer, R. (1680) *Patriarchia: A Defence of the Natural Power of Kings against the Unnatural Liberty of the People*

Finley, M. I. (1985) *The Ancient Economy* (London: Hogarth Press), 2nd ed.

Flexner, J. T.
(1965-1972) *George Washington [GW]* (Boston: Little, Brown), 4 vols.
(1965) *The Forge of Experience, 1732-1775*, vol. 1
(1968) *George Washington in the American Revolution, 1775-1783*, vol. 2

(1970) *George Washington and the New Nation, 1783–1793*, vol. 3

(1972) *Anguish and Farewell, 1793–1799*, vol. 4

(1978) *The Young Hamilton: A Biography* (Boston: Little, Brown)

Fogel, R. W. & S. L. Engerman, eds. (1971) *The Reinterpretation of American Economic History* (New York: Harper & Row)

Fogel, R. W. & S. J. Engerman (1974/1989) *Time on the Cross* (Boston: Little, Brown)

Frankel, J. A. (1982) "The 1807–1809 Embargo Against Great Britain," 42 *Journal of Economic History* 291–308 (No. 2, June)

Freedberg, S. J. (1971/1986) *Painting in Italy: 1500–1600* (London: Penguin), 2nd ed. — reprinted with revisions and additional notes, 1990

Freud, Sigmund (1923/1927/1950) *The Ego and the Id* (London: Hogarth Press), Joan Riviere, trans. — originally published in 1923 as *Das Ich und das Es*

Furet, F. (1988/1989a) "The Terror," *Critical Dictionary* (1988/1989, pp. 137–150)

Furet, F (1988/1989b) "Tocqueville," *Critical Dictionary* (1988/1989, p. 1021ff.)

Furet, F. & M. Ozouf. eds. (1988/1989) *A Critical Dictionary of the French Revolution* (Cambridge, Ma.: Harvard University Press) — A. Goldhammer, trans.; first published as *Dictionnaire critique de la révolution française* (Paris: Flammarion)

G

Gauchet, M. (1988/1989) "Necker," in Furet & Ozouf (1988/1989, p. 287ff.)

Gibbon, Edward (1776–1787/1909/1974) *The Decline and Fall of the Roman Empire*, Bury edition, 7 vols. (London: Methuen; 1909) — AMS Press, New York (1974)

Gilson, E. (1943) *Introduction à l'étude de saint Augustin* (Paris), 2nd ed.

Girton, L. & D. Roper (1978) "J. Laurence Laughlin and the Quantity Theory of Money," 86 *Journal of Political Economy* 599

Goodhart, C. (1985/1989) *The Evolution of Central Banks* (Cambridge, Ma.: MIT Press; 1989)

Gray, J. (1984/1986) *Hayek on Liberty* (Oxford: Blackwell), 2nd ed.

Grey, (1909) *Nature and Sources of Law*

Gunter, F. (1990) "Thomas Jefferson on the Repudiation of Public Debt," Unpublished, Bethlehem, Pa.: Lehigh University

H

Haines, C. G. (1959) *The American Doctrine of Judicial Supremecy* (New York: Russell & Russell)

Halévy, E. (1928/1955) *The Growth of Philosophical Radicalism* (Boston: The Beacon Press) — a republication of the 1928 issue by Faber & Faber in London, M. Morris, trans.

Hallam, H., *The Constitutional History of England from the Accession of Henry VII to the Death of George II* (London: John Murray), 9th ed., 1857 — see esp. vol. iii

Halmos, P. R. (1991) "The Legend of John von Neumann," in Ferris, ed. (1991, pp. 614–628)

Hamilton, Alexander

Papers of Alexander Hamilton, Syrett, H. C. et al., eds. (New York: Columbia University Press; 1961–1978), 26 vols.

(1962) vol. vi, Syerett, H. & J. Cooke, eds.

(1963) vol. vii, Syrett, H. & J. Cooke, eds.

(1966) vol. x, Syrett, H. C. & J. E. Cooke, eds.

(19-) vol. xiv

(1790) *Report on Public Credit* — see *Papers*, vol. vi

(1791a) *Report on the Bank* — see *Papers*, vol. vii

(1791b) *Report on the Subject of Manufactures* — see *Papers*, vol. x, pp. 1–340, the final version is at pp. 230–340

Hamilton, E. J. (1968) "John Law," *International Encyclopaedia of the Social Sciences* (New York: The Free Press), vol. 9, p. 73ff.

Hamilton, E. J. (1969) "The Political Economy of France at the Time of John Law," 1 *History of Political Economy* 123

Hamilton, Edith (1961) *Introduction* to *The Collected Dialogues of Plato* (in Hamilton and Cairns, eds., 1961: *The Collected Dialogues of Plato*)

Hammond, B. (1947) "Jackson, Biddle & the Bank of the United States," 7 *Journal of Economic History* 1 (no. 1, May)

Hammond, B. (1957) *Banks and Politics in the United States — from the Revolution to the Civil War* (Princeton: Princeton University Press)

Hammond, J. L. & B. (1911) *The Village Labourer, 1760–1832*

Hammond, J. L. & B. (1917) *The Town Labourer, 1760–1832*

Hammond, J. L. & B. (1919) *The Skilled Labourer, 1760–1832*

Harris, S. E. (1930) *The Assignats* (Cambridge, Ma.: Harvard University Press)

Hart, A. G. (1935) "The 'Chicago Plan' for Monetary Reform," 2 *Review of Economic Studies* 104

Hart, H. L. A. (1982) *Essays on Bentham* (Oxford: OUP)

Hayek, F. A.
(1948) *Individualism and Economic Order* (Chicago: University of Chicago Press)
(1952/1979) *The Counter-Revolution in Science: Studies on the Abuse of Reason* (Indianapolis, Indiana: Liberty Press; 1979), 2nd ed. — first ed. publ. by the Free Press in Glencoe, Ill. (1952)
(1960) *The Constitution of Liberty* (Chicago: University of Chicago Press)
(1976) *Denationalization of Money* (London: Institute of Economic Affairs)

Head, B. W. (1985) *Ideology and Social Science: Destutt de Tracy and French Liberalism* (Dordrecht: Martinus Nijhoff)

Historical Statistics of the United States (U. S. Govt. Printing Office)

Hobbes, Thomas (see Copleston, *HP,* 5:i, p. 213ff., for Hobbes's works)
(1928) *The Elements of Law, Natural and Politic* (Cambridge: Cambridge University Press), 2nd ed. — F. Tönnies
(1938) *Of Liberty and Necessity* (Kiel), C. von Brockdorff, ed.
(1946) *Leviathan* (Oxford: Oxford University Press), M. Oakeshott, ed.

Hohfeld, W. N. (1919/1964) *Fundamental Legal Conceptions as Applied in Judicial Reasoning* (New Haven: Yale University Press — forward by A. L. Corbin (1964); introduction by W. W. Cook

Holdsworth, W. S. (1924) *A History of English Law* (London: Methuen), vol. v

Hughes, J. (1987) *American Economic History* (Glenview, Ill.: Scott, Foresman), 2nd ed.

Huizanga, J. (1924/1984) *The Waning of the Middle Ages* (New York: St. Martin's Press) — first pub. in London by Edward Arnold (1924)

Hume, David

(1739–1740/1817/1911) *A Treatise of Human Nature* (London: Dent, Everyman's Library), 2 vols., A. D. Lindsay, ed. — many times reprinted. The work was reissued in 1817; and the reissue was republished by Dent in 1911.

(1777/1987) *Essays, Moral, Political, and Literary* (Indianapolis, Indiana: Liberty Classics), E. F. Miller, ed. — including his *Essays and Treatises on Several Subjects and Ten Unpublished Essays* (1777 op. post.)

(1778/1983) *The History of England from the Invasion of Julius Caesar to the Revolution in 1688* (Indianapolis, Indiana: Liberty Classics), 6 vols.

¶ See especially vol. v of the Liberty Classics ed.: ch. xlv ("James I"); chs. l–lix (on Charles I)

(1778/1983) "My Own Life," reprinted in vol. i of *History of England*

Hutcheson, F.

(1772) *Works* (Glasgow), 5 vols.

(A citation schema based on G. Wills, 1978, pp. 372–373)

[1] *A Inquiry into the Original of our ideas of Beauty and Virtue* (1725)

[2] *An Essay on the Nature and Conduct of the Passions and Affections* (1728)

[3] *Philosphiae Moralis Institutio Compendiaria* (1745)

[4] *A Short Introduction to Moral Philosophy* (1747)

[5] *A System of Moral Philosophy*, vol. i (1755)

[6] *A System of Moral Philosophy*, vol. ii (1755)

[7] *Opera Minora*, 1735–1756 (1756)

I, J

James, J. A. & R. E. Sylla (1980) "The Changing Nature of American Public Debt, 1690–1835," Brussels, *Proceedings* of the 9th International Symposium on Public Debt in the 18th and 19th centuries

James, William (1904/1912) "Does Consciousness Exist?," reprinted in his *Essays in Radical Empiricism* (London: Longmans, Green: 1912, *op. post.*), R. B. Perry, ed.

Jay, John, Alexander Hamilton & James Madison — Publius (1788) *The Federalist*

Jefferson, Thomas (1984) *Writings* (New York: Viking, Library of America), M. D. Peterson, ed.

Jensen, N. (1958) *The New Nation: A History of the United States during the Confederation, 1781–1789* (New York: Knopf)

Johnson, Dr Samuel (1777/1925) *Lives of the English Poets* (London: Dent, Everyman's Library), 2 vols., L. Archer-Hind, ed.

K

Kant, Immanuel (1787/1934) *Critique of Pure Reason* (London: Dent, Everyman's Library), 2nd ed., J. H. D. Meiklejohn, trans.

Kant, Immanuel (1785/1964) *Groundwork of the Metaphysic Morals* (New York: Harper & Row), trans. with an introduction by H. J. Paton; see esp. pp. 80–98

Kern, W. S. (1987) "Frank Knight's Three Commandments," 19 *History of Political Economy* 639

Kerner, G. C. (1990) *Three Philosophical Moralists: Mill, Kant and Sartre* (Oxford: The Clarendon Press)

Keynes, J. M. (1936) *The General Theory of Employment, Interest and Money* (London: Macmillan)

Kindleberger, C. P. (1984) *A Financial History of Western Europe* (London: Allen & Unwin)

Klein, B. (1974) "The Competitive Supply of Money," 6 *Journal of Money, Credit and Banking*

Klein, B. (1975) "Our New Monetary Standard: The Measurement and Effect of Price Uncertainty, 1880–1973," 13 *Economic Inquiry* 461–484 (April)

Knight, F. H.

(1922) "The Ethics of Competition, i," 36 *Quarterly Journal of Eco-Economics*, reprinted in Knight (1935)

(1923) "The Ethics of Competition, ii," 37 *Quarterly Journal of Eco-Economics* 579–624 — reprinted in Knight (1935)

(1935) *The Ethics of Competition* (New York: Harper)

(1939) "Ethics and Economic Reform," 6 (N. S.) Economica 1–29, 296–321, 398–422, reprinted in Knight (1947)

(1944) "The Rights of Man and Natural Law," 44 *Ethics* 124 (1944), reprinted in Knight (1947, P. 262ff.)

(1947) *Freedom and Reform* (New York: Harper)

Koch, Adrienne (1943/1957) *The Philosophy of Thomas Jefferson [PTJ]* Gloucester, Mass.: Peter Smith; 1957) — a republication of the 1943 ed., published in New York by Columbia University Press

Koch, Adrienne (1950/1964) *Jefferson and Madison: The Great Collaboration* (New York: Knopf)

L

Lee, S. P. & P. Passell (1979) *A New Economic View of American History* (New York: Norton)

Lefebvre, G. (1962) *The French Revolution from its Origins to 1793* (New York: Columbia University Press)

Leonardo da Vinci, ed. anon. (New York: Reynal & Co.; 1956)

Levi, E., *Introduction to Legal Reasoning* (Chicago: University of Chicago Press)

Liesse, A. (1911) "Evolution of Credit and Banks in France," Senate Document 522, *Banking in France and the French Bourse*, National Monetary Comm., vol. 15 (Washington: Government Printing Office)

Lindsay, A. D. (1911) *Introduction* to Hume's *Treatise of Human Nature*

Locke, John (1698/1960/1988) *Two Treatises of Civil Government* (Cambridge: Cambridge University Press), ed. with an introduction and notes by P. Laslett

Longford, E. (1972) *Wellington: Pillar of State* (London: Weidenfeld & Nicolson)

M

Macaulay, T. B. (Lord)
(1835/1968/1979) "Review of Sir James Mackintosh, 1834," in his abridged *History*, H. Trevor-Roper, ed. (1968/1979, pp. 546–557)

(1848–1861/1968/1979) *The History of England* (Harmondsworth, Middlesex: Penguin), H. Trevor-Roper, ed. — a reissue of the 1968 ed., pub. by Washington Sq. Books, New York, in 1968

(1848–1861/1980) *The History of England* (London: Dent) 3 vols.

McCoy, D. R. (1980) *The Elusive Republic: Political Economy in Jeffersonian America* (Chapel Hill, N. C.: University of North Carolina Press)

McDonald, F.

(1958) *We the People: The Economic Origins of the Constitution* (Chicago)

(1965/1979) *E Pluribus Unum: The Formation of the American Republic* (Indianapolis, Indiana: Liberty Press), 2nd ed. — the first ed. (Boston: Houghton, Mifflin; 1965) is republished with changes

(1974) *The Presidency of George Washington* (Lawrence, Ka.: University Press of Kansas)

(1976) *The Presidency of Thomas Jefferson* (Lawrence, Ka.: University Press of Kansas)

(1979) *Alexander Hamilton* (New York: Norton)

(1985) *Novus Ordo Seclorum: The Intellectual Origins of the Constitution* (Lawrence, Ka.; University Press of Kansas)

Malone, D.

(1948–1981) *Jefferson and His Time*n, (Boston: Little, Brown), six vols.

(1948) *Jefferson the Virginian*, vol. 1

(1951) *Jefferson and the Rights of Man*, vol. 2

(1962) *Jefferson and the Ordeal of Liberty*, vol. 3

(1970) *Jefferson the President: First Term, 1801–1805*, vol. 4

(1974) *Jefferson the President: Second Term, 1805–1809*, vol. 5

(1981) *The Sage of Monticello*, vol. 6

Malthus, T. R. (1798 et seq.) *An Essay on the Principle of Population and a Summary View of the Principle of Population* (London: Dent, Everyman's Library), 2 vols.

Mandeville, B. (1714/1989) *The Fable of the Bees or Private Vices, Publick Benefits* (Indianapolis, Ind.: Liberty Press), 2 vols.

Manin, B. (1988/1989) "Montesquieu," *Critical Dictionary* (1988/1989, p. 728ff.)

Markham, F. (1963) *Napoleon* (New York: New American Library)

Marshall, Alfred (1923) *Money, Credit & Commerce* (London: Macmillan)

Matthews, R. K. (1984) *The Radical Politics of Thomas Jefferson: A Revisionist View* (Lawrence, Ka.: University Press of Kansas)

Mayer, D. (1988) "Policy and Principles in the Age of Jefferson: A review of Nelson (1987)," 5 *Humane Studies Review* 9, no. 3, GMU

Mill, J. S. (1844/1874/1968) *Essays on Some Unsettled Questions of Political Economy* (New York: Augustus Kelley; 1968), reprinting the 2nd [1874] edition, pub. in London by Longmans, Green

Mill, J. S. (1859) *On Liberty* (London) — reprinted in Burtt, ed. (1939)

Mill, J. S. (1861) *Considerations on Representative Government* (London) — reprinted by OUP and Bobbs-Merrill (New York, 1958)

Mill, J. S. (1863) *Utilitarianism* (London) — reprinted in Burtt, ed. (1939)

Montesquieu, Charles Louis de Secondat (baron de La Brède) [1689–1755] (1950–1955) *Oeuvres complètes* (Paris)

Montesquieu (1945) *De l'esprit des lois* (Paris), 2 vols. — G. Truc, ed.

Moore, G. E. (1903/1922) *Principia Ethica* (Cambridge: Cambridge University Press)

Morrill, J. (1985) "Government and Politics: England and Wales, 1625–1701," in *The Cambridge Historical Encylopaedia of Great Britain and Ireland* (1985)

N

Nelson, J. R. (1987) *Liberty and Property: Political Economy and Policy Making in the New Nation, 1789–1812* (Baltimore, Md.: Johns Hopkins University Press)

Nicholas, B. (1962/1969) *An Introduction to Roman Law* (Oxford: Oxford University Press), 3rd ed.

Nietzsche, F.(1887/1935) *The Genealogy of Morals* (New York: Random House, Modern Library), H. B. Samuel, trans.

Nock, A. J. (1926/1983) *Mr Jefferson* (Delevan, Wisconsin: Hallberg Pub. Corp.; 1983)

North, D. (1961/1966) *Growth and Welfare in the American Past, A New Economic History* (Englewood Cliffs, N. J.: Prentice-Hall), republished by Norton in New York in 1966

Nozick, R. (1974) *Anarchy, State and Utopia* (New York: Basic Books)

O

Orieux, Jean (1970) *Talleyrand ou le sphinx incompris* (Paris: Flammarion)

The Oxford History of the Classical World (1986) (New York: Oxford University Press), Boardman, J., J. Griffin & O. Murray, eds.

Ozouf, M. (1988/1989) "Liberty," *Critical Dictionary* (1988/1989, p. 716ff.)

Ozouf, M. (1988/1989) "Voltaire," *Critical Dictionary* (1988/1989, p. 869ff.)

P, Q

Pagels, E. (1988) *Adam, Eve, and the Serpent* (New York: Random House)

Paton, H. J. (1948) *The Categorical Imperative: A Study in Kant's Moral Philosophy* (Chicago: University of Chicago Press)

Penrose, R. (1989) *The Emperor's New Mind: Concerning Computers, Minds and the Laws of Physics* (New York: Oxford University Press)

Peterson, M. D. (1960) *The Jefferson Image in the American Mind* (New York: Oxford University Press)

Plato, *The Collected Dialogues of Plato* (New York: Bollingen Foundation, 1961) — distributed by Random House (Pantheon Books), Edith Hamilton & Huntington Cairns, eds. (cf. *Eudoxus, Lysis, Meno, Republic*)

Plumb, J. H. (1950/1963) *England in the Eighteenth Century* (Harmondsworth: Penguin)

Plumb, J. H. (1956/1966) *The First Four Georges* (London: Fontana/ Collins), first published in London in 1956 by B. T. Batsford

Popper, Karl R. (1957) *The Poverty of Historicism* (London: Routledge & Kegan Paul)

Popper, Karl R. (1959) *The Logic of Scientific Discovery* (London: Routledge & Kegan Paul)

Postlethwayt, M. (1776) *The Universal Dictionary of Trade and Commerce* (London)

R

Raphael, D. D. & A. L. Macfie (1976/1982) Introduction to *Theory of Moral Sentiments (TMS* — Adam Smith)

Raynaud, P. (1989) "American Revolution," *Critical Dictionary* (1988/1989, p. 593ff.)

Reeves, R. (1982) *American Journey: Travelling with Tocqueville in Search of Democracy in America* (New York: Simon & Schuster)

Revel, J. (1988/1989) "Marie Antoinette," *Critical Dictionary* (1988/1989, pp. 252–264)

Rima, I. H., ed. (1991) *The Joan Robinson Legacy* (New York: M. E. Sharpe)

Rockoff, H. (1971) "Money, Prices and Banks in the Jacksonian Era," ch. 33 of Fogel, R. W. & S. L. Engerman, eds. (1972)

Rosen, C. (1971) *The Classical Style* (London: Faber & Faber)

Rousseau, J.-J. (1762) *The Social Contract (Du contrat social)*, often reprinted, e.g. in the Everyman's Library series

Roy, S. (1989) *Philosophy of Economics: On the Scope of Reason in Economic Inquiry* (London: Routledge International Library of Philosophy)

Russell, Bertrand (1872–1970)

(1912/1946) *The Problems of Philosophy* (London: O. U. P.)

(1918, 1924/1972/1985) *The Philosophy of Logical Atomism* (London: Allen & Unwin)

(1921/1989) *The Analysis of Mind* (London: Allen & Unwin)

(1925a/1957) "What I Believe," republished in "Salvation: Individual and Social," *Why I am not a Christian* (London: Allen & Unwin)

(1925b/1985) *The ABC of Relativity* (London: Allen & Unwin)

(1927/1986) *An Outline of Philosophy* (London: Allen & Unwin)

(1929) *Our Knowledge of the External World* (New York: Norton), 2nd ed.

(1940/1980) *An Enquiry into Meaning and Truth* (London: Allen & Unwin)

(1946) *A History of Western Philosophy* (London: Allen & Unwin)

(1959/1975) *My Philosophical Development* (London: Allen & Unwin)

(1967–1969) *Autobiography* (London: Allen & Unwin)

S

Say, J.-B. (1817) *Traité d'économie politique* (Paris: Chez Deterville), 3rd ed., 2 vols.

Say, J.-B. (1834/1964) *A Treatise on Political Economy: Or the Production, Distribution and Consumption of Wealth* (New York: Augustus Kelley; 1964), a reprint of the sixth American ed. (1834), published in Philadelphia by Claxton, Remsen & Hafflefinger, trans. by C. R. Prinsep from the 4th French ed.; the 6th American ed. includes additional material trans. by C. C. Biddle

Say, J.-B. (1843/1968) *Cours complet d'économie politique* (Rome: Edzioni Bizzarri), 6th ed. — see esp. "Mélanges et Correspondance"

Sayers, Dorothy L. (1949) Introduction to Dante's *Divine Comedy,* in her translation of *The Inferno*

Sears, L. M. (1927/1966) *Jefferson and the Embargo* (Durham, N. C.: Duke University Press)

Sen, A. (1987) *On Ethics and Economics* (Oxford: Basil Blackwell)

Senior, Nassau (1830) *The Cost of Obtaining Money* reprinted as No. 5 in the Scarce Tract Series published by the London School of Economics

Sidney, Algernon (1698/1990) *Discourses Concerning Government* (Indianapolis, Indiana: Liberty Classics) — T. G. West, ed.

Smith, Adam (1759/1982) *The Theory of Moral Sentiments* [*TMS*] (Indianapolis, Ind.: Liberty Classics), reproducing the Oxford University Press edition, 1979

Smith, Adam (1776/1920) *The Wealth of Nations* (London: Dent, Everyman's Library), 2 vols.

Smith, B. D. (1985) "Some Colonial Evidence on Two Theories of Money," 93 *Journal of Political Economy* 1178 (no. 6, Dec.)

Smith, B. D. (1988) "The Relationship between Money and Prices; Some Historical Evidence Reconsidered, 12 Federal Reserve Bank of Minneapolis *Quarterly Review* 18

Smith, Véra (1936/1990) *The Rationale of Central Banking and the Free Banking Alternative* (Indianapolis, Ind.: The Liberty Press) — originally pub. in London in 1936 by P. S. King as *The Rationale of Central Banking*

Solomon, R. C. (1988) *Continental Philosophy since 1750: The Rise and Fall of the Self* (New York: Oxford University Press)

Spencer, Herbert (1897/1978) *The Principles of Ethics* (Indianapolis, Ind.: Liberty Classics), 2 vols. — a reissue of the 1897 ed. published in New York by D. Appleton.

Spengler, O. (1918/1928) *Decline of the West* (New York: Knopf), 2 vols., C. F. Atkinson, trans. See esp. vol. 1, *Form and Actuality*. (First pub. in Munich in 1918 as *Der Untergang des Abendlands*.)

Stephen, L. (1876) *History of English Thought in the Eighteenth Century* (London), 2 vols.

Stephen, L. (1900) *The English Utilitarians* (London), 3 vols. — reissued in the Scarce Tract series published by the London School of Economics

Syrett, H. and J. E. Cooke (1966) Introduction to vol. x of *The Collected Papers of Alexander Hamilton*

T

Temin, P. (1969) *The Jacksonian Economy* (New York: Norton)

Thayer, T. (1953) "The Land Bank System in the American Colonies," 13 *Journal of Economic History* 145

Thompson, E. P. (1963) *The Making of the English Working Class*

Thomsen, E. F. (1987) "Knowledge, Discovery and Prices," 5 *Humane Studies Review* 1, no. 3, George Mason University

Thornton, Henry (1802/1939/1962) *An Enquiry into the Nature and Effects of the Paper Credit of Great Britain* (London: Frank Cass; 1962) — a reissue of the 1939 ed., inc. F. A. Hayek's Introduction (London: Allen & Unwin) — originally published in London by Hatchard (1802)

Timberlake, R. H. (1978) *The Origins of Central Banking in the United States* (Cambridge, Mass.: Harvard University Press)

Timberlake, R. H. (1991) *Gold, Greenbacks and the Constitution* (Berryville, Va.: Durrell Foundation)

Tocqueville, Alexis de
(1835–1840/1945) *Democracy in America* (New York: Knopf) — the H. Reeve trans., rev. by F. Bowen and further corr. and ed. by P. Bradley, many times reprinted

(1856/1967) *L'ancien régime et la Révolution* (Paris: Gallimard) — the French ed. is used in *UTJ*

(1856/1955) *The Old Regime and the French Revolution* (New York) — S. Gilbert, trans.; an English version was published in London *circa* 1856

Tracy (See Destutt de Tracy)

Trevor-Roper, H. (1968/1979) Introduction to Macaulay's *History of England*

Tucker, R. W. & D. C. Hendrickson (1990) *Empire of Liberty: The Statecraft of Thomas Jefferson* (New York: Oxford University Press)

U, V

Vasari, G. (1550/1986) *The Great Masters* (New York: Macmillan, Hugh Lauter Levin Assoc., Inc.), M. Sonino, ed., Gaston de Vere, trans.

Vernier, R. (1987) "Interpreting the American Republic: Civic Humanism vs. Liberalism," 4 *Humane Studies Review* 1, no. 3, George Mason University

Virgil (Publius Vergilius Măro, 70–19 B.C.) *Georgics* (Cambridge, Ma.: Loeb Classical Library)

Voltaire (François-Marie Arouet, 1694–1778) (1734/1964) *Lettres philosophiques* (Paris: Flammarion)

W

Wedgwood, C. V. (1955–1964/1991) *The Great Rebellion* (New York: Book-of-the-Month Club; 1991)
· vol. 1, *The King's Peace, 1637–1641* (1955/1991)
· vol. 2, *The King's War, 1641–1647* (1958/1991)
· vol. 3, *A Coffin for King Charles: The Trial and Execution of Charles I* (1964/1991)

Wettereau, J. O. (1937) "New Light on the First Bank of the United States," 61 *Pennsylvania Magazine of History and Biography* 263 (July)

Wettereau, J. O. (1943) "The Branches of the First Bank of the United States," 3 *Journal of Economic History*

White, L. H. (1984) *Free Banking in Britain* (Cambridge: Cambridge University Press)

White, L. H. (1989) *Competition and Currency: Essays on Free Banking and Money* (New York: New York University Press)

White, L. H. & G. A. Selgin, "Laissez-Faire Monetary Thought in Jacksonian America," unpublished

Wicksell, K. (1898/1936) *Geldzins und Güterpreise* (Jena: Gustav Fischer; 1898), trans. by R. F. Kahn and published as *Interest and Prices* (London: Macmillan; 1936)

Wills, G. (1978) *Inventing America: Jefferson's Declaration of Independence* (Garden City, N. Y.: Doubleday)

Wilson, Edmund (1931) *Axel's Castle* (New York: Chas.Scribner's Sons)

Wright, G. (1974) "Cotton Competition and the Post Bellum Recovery of the American South," 34 *Journal of Economic History* 611 (Sept.)

X, Y, Z

Yasuba, Y. (1971) "The Profitability and Viability of Plantation Slavery in the United States," in Fogel & Engerman, eds. (1971)

Index of Names

- a *Constitutional nationalist*, 68, 112, 285
- on *express delegation*, 123, 131-2
- on the *general welfare* clause, 68, 132
- ·· TJ's construal of the —, 132
- on *judicial review*, 118-21 *passim*
- ·· Hamilton on —, 120
- ·· — of state legislation, 121
- on the *Judiciary Act of 1801*, 114
- on *reserved powers* (cf. the 10th Amendment), 112-13
- on *strict construction*, 111, 114
- on *substantive due process*, 117
- on the *Tenth Amendment* (See J. Madison), 131-2·

Cumberland, Duke of 64

D

Dante (Dante Alighieri) xix, xx, xxv, xxvi-xxvii *passim*, 226, 331
- on virtue (*Divine Comedy*), 331

Darby, A. 157

David, P. 156

Democritus (on "materialism") 24, 227

Descartes René 7, 24, 227-32 *passim*, 244, 249, 257
- and the Enlightenment, 236, 257
- on "self," 243, 244

Destutt de Tracy, A. 2, 6, 15, 18-19, 27, 141, 144, 187, 189, 205, 241, 255
- he is *anti-physiocratic*, 140, 191-2
- his *economic system*, 97, 191-5 *passim*
- on *exchange*, 18-19
- clasps Smith's *invisible hand*, 193

- opposes *Montequieu's system*, 193-4, 261
- ·· supported by TJ, 191
- ideas are derived from *sensations*, 239-40
- *trashes* German metaphysics, 240

Dickinson, John (*Letters from a Farmer*) 133

Domitian (Titus Flavius Domitianos) 290

Duane, W. 99

Duer, W. 143, 149
- runs bond-parking operation for AH (see the SEUM), 143
- a notorious speculator, 149

Dunne, J. 206

Du Pont de Nemours, P. S. 4, 179

E

Ebeling, Prof. 46, 52

Edward II (King of England) 101

Einstein, Albert 290

Einstein, Alfred xxvii

Eliot, T. S. xxv-xxvii *passim*, 39, 60, 330
- and Jansenism, 336

Elizabeth I (Queen of England) 104
- her difficulty in getting supplies, 105

Ellison, T. 171

Engerman, S. 44, 172

Epictetus 22, 212, 224

Epicurus 22, 219, 224, 323
- his doctrine criticized by Copleston, 212-13

I, J

M

Index of Subjects

A

Aesthetics xiv–xviii *passim*, xxiv–xxviii

Agrarianism (*v.* enterprise) 86–8
· promotes private over public banking, 86

Agriculture 140–2 *passim*, 187
· TJ's policy on and the early American economy, 156

Alienability (of land) 196–201

Alien & Sedition Acts 4, 14, 109
· reflect rising *hysteria*, 117
· and the *Kentucky Resolutions*, 116, 117
·· KR & the Bill of Rights, 115
·· KR contravene express delegation, 115
·· and federal crimes, 115

Allen v. Flood 304
· and *liberties* in Hohfeld's system, 295, 308–11 *passim*
· and *rights* in H's system, 298–300 *passim*, 304–5

American Constitution xx, 5, 13–15
· *Blackstone's* influence on the theory of, 100
· its *blocking* properties, 14–15, 22
· its *commerce clause*, 68, 115–17 *passim*
·· "commerce among the states," 115
·· *Gibbons v. Ogden*, 68, 115
·· interstate commerce, 68, 115–16
·· TJ's latently liberal view on in 1786, 133
· and the *common law* of the U. S., 109, 113–15, 132–3
· *constructed* (not a production of "evolution"), 13, 24, 244, 284
· *Eleventh Amendment* to, 126, 133
·· *Chisholm v. Georgia*, 126, 133–4
· its *enumerations*, 110–11, 195
· and *ex post facto* laws, 106, 109, 116–17
·· *Calder v. Bull*, 116–17, 126
· does it confer *general legislative authority*?, 132
· its *general welfare* clause, 67, 132
·· TJ's liberal interpretation of in 1775 & 1787, 132
·· TJ's cramped construction in 1790, 134
·· TJ's Kentucky Resolutions make the clause nugatory, 122–3
· *Hamilton* on — (Also see *Federalist Papers*), 36, 113, 115, 120
·· his disdain for the Constitution (?), 120
··· asserted by TJ, 134
···· did AH want a King and House of Lords?, 134
· *implied powers*, 110–13
·· and enumerations, 110–13, 195
· *TJ's* Constitutional system, 14–15, 110–12 *passim*
·· its *disingenuousness*, 14–15, 97, 115, 127
·· contradicted by his *embargo* policy, 164, 168, 176, 178
·· cf. *good law/bad economics*, 5, 15, 100
·· and "*states rights*," 14, 17, 97–8, 110, 285